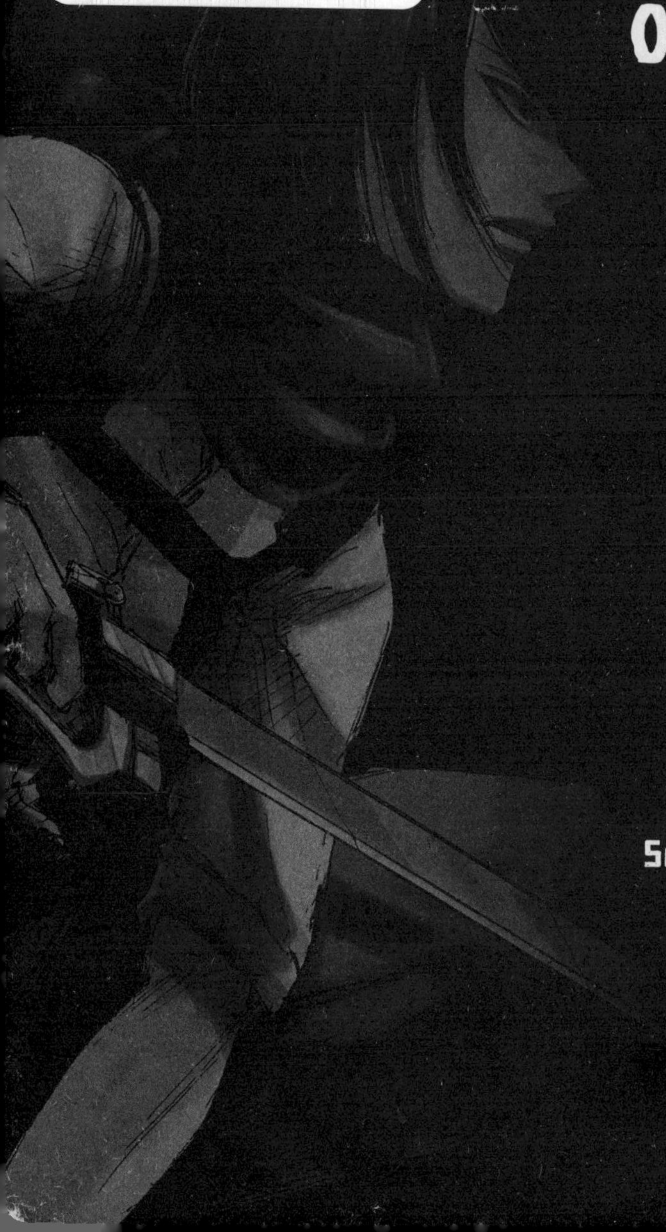

ATTACK ON TITAN
8

HAJIME ISAYAMA

"Attack on Titan" Character Introductions

Survey Corps Special Operations Squad

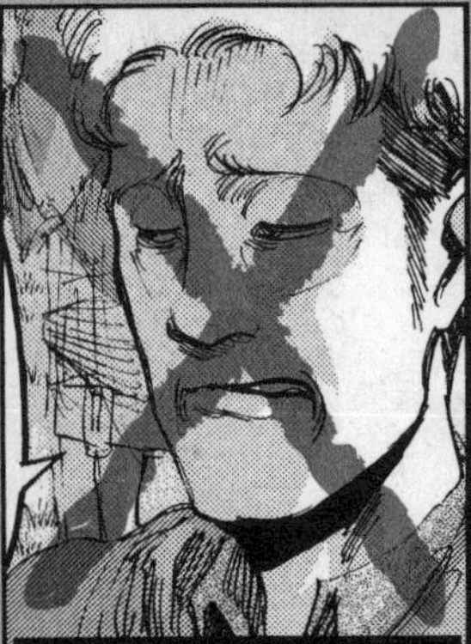

Oluo Bozado

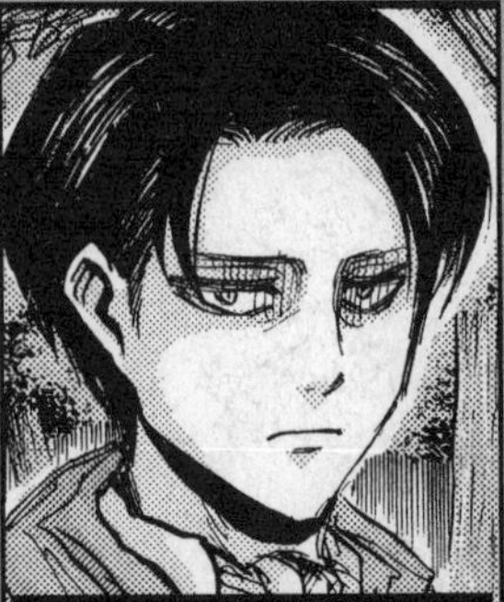

Levi: Captain of the Survey Corps. Said to be the strongest human alive.

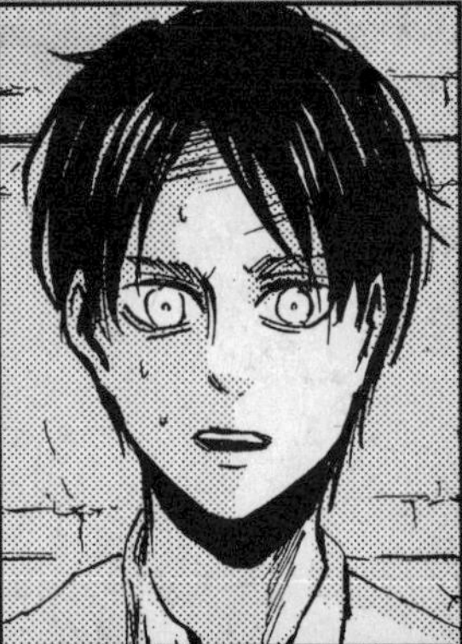

Eren Yeager: Longing for the world outside the wall, Eren joined the Survey Corps. He can turn himself into a Titan.

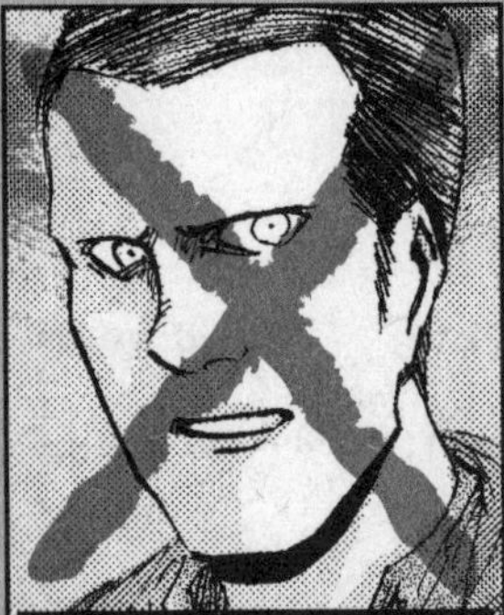

Gunther Schultz

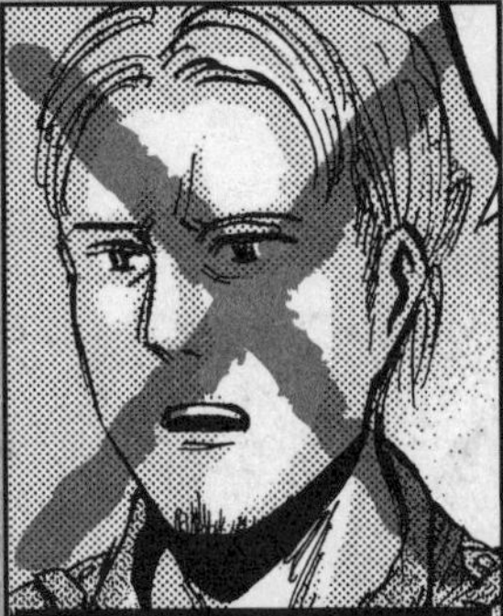

Eld Jinn

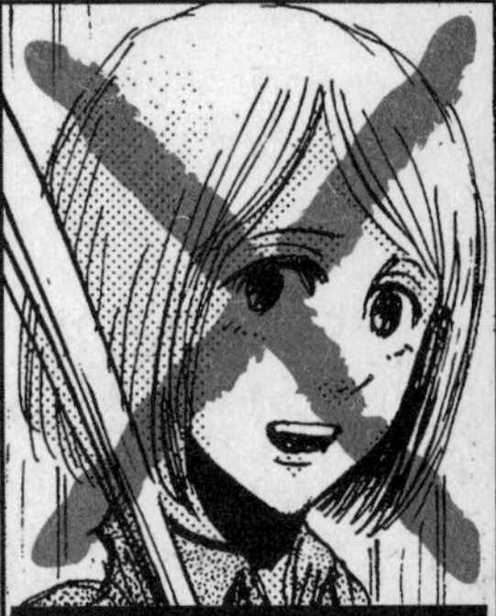

Petra Ral

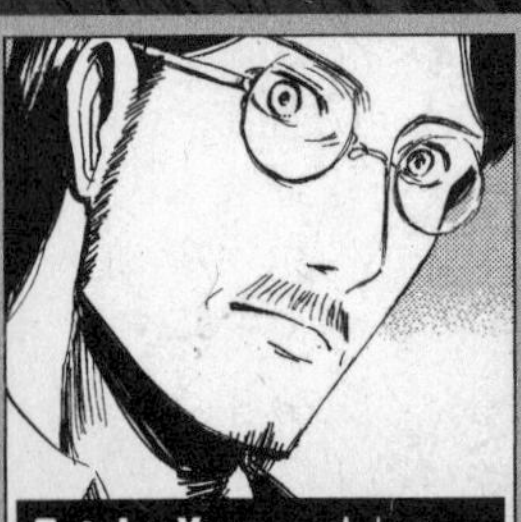

Grisha Yeager: A doctor and Eren's father. He went missing after the Titan attack five years ago.

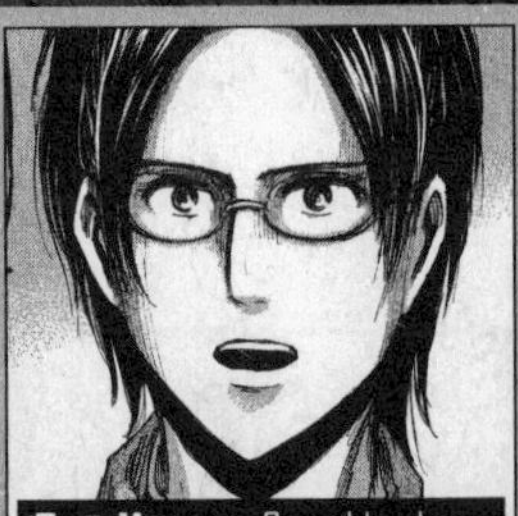

Zoë Hange: Squad leader of the Survey Corps. Responsible for the biological investigation of captured Titans.

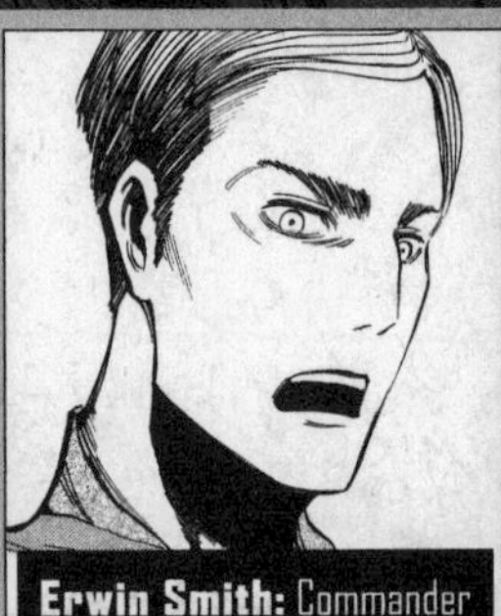

Erwin Smith: Commander of the Survey Corps.

104th Corps

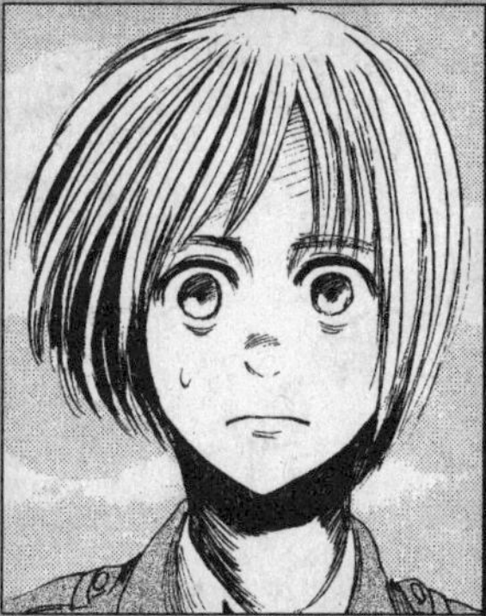

Armin Arlert:

Eren and Mikasa's childhood friend. Though Armin isn't athletic in the least, he is an excellent thinker and can produce unique ideas. A member of the Survey Corps.

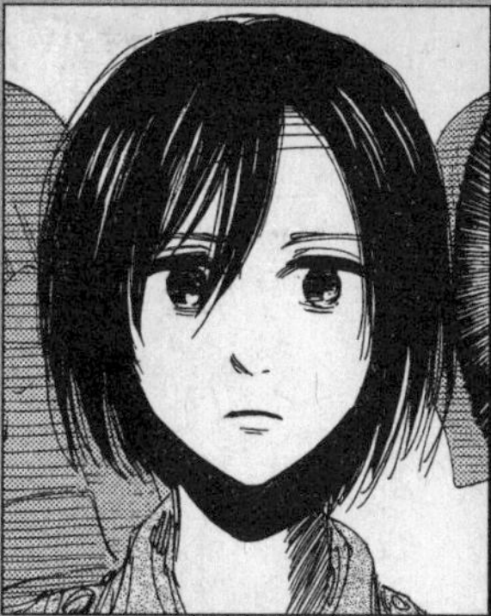

Mikasa Ackerman:

Mikasa graduated at the top of her training corps. Her parents were murdered before her eyes when she was a child. After that, she was raised alongside Eren, whom she tenaciously tries to protect. A member of the Survey Corps.

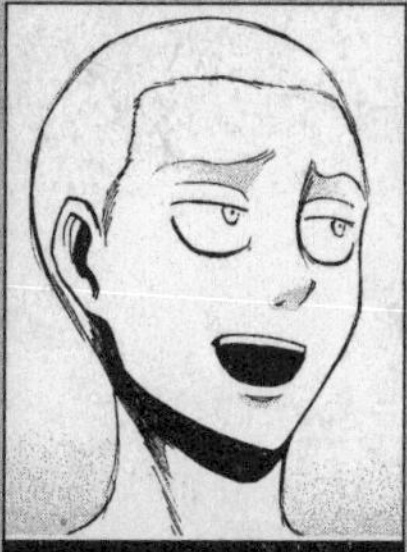

Connie Springer: Effective at vertical maneuvering, but is slow on the uptake, so his comprehension of tactics is less than stellar. A member of the Survey Corps.

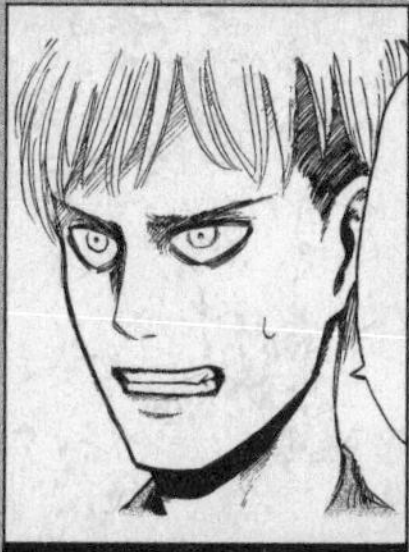

Jean Kirstein: Superior at vertical maneuvering. Jean is honest to a fault, which often puts him at odds with other people. A member of the Survey Corps.

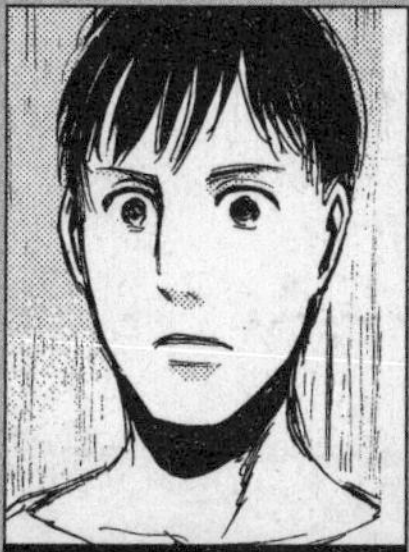

Bertolt Hoover: Has a high degree of skill in everything he's been taught, but is indecisive and lacks initiative. A member of the Survey Corps.

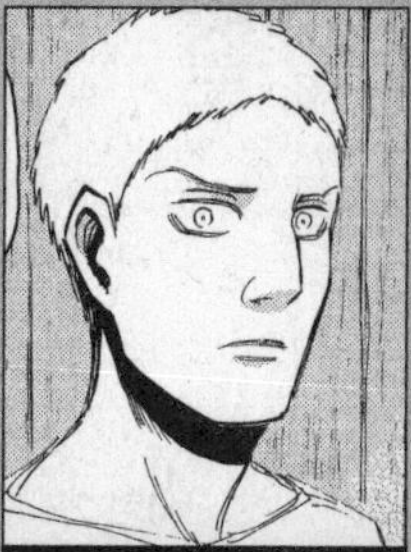

Reiner Braun: Graduated second in his training corps. Reiner is as strong as an ox and has the will to match. His comrades place a great [illegible] trust in him. A member of the Survey Corps.

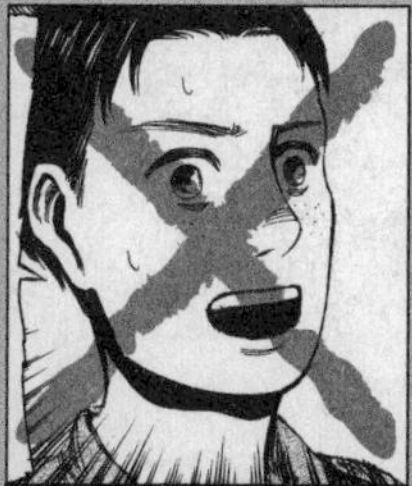

Marco Bott: Yearned to join the Military Police Brigade so he could serve the king. Marco died during the Titan mop-up operation.

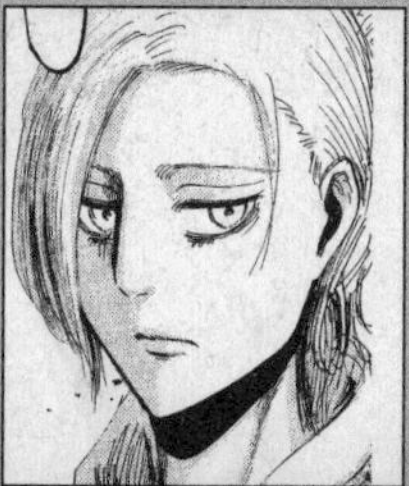

Annie Leonhart: Annie's small stature belies her great skill in the art of hand-to-hand combat. She's a realist through and through, and tends to be a loner. A member of the Military Police Brigade.

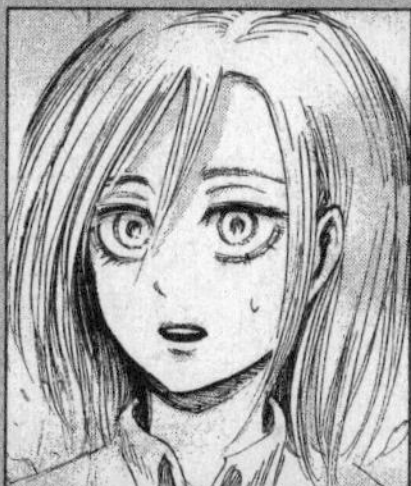

Krista Lenz: Extremely short, with a friendly, warm-hearted personality. A member of the Survey Corps.

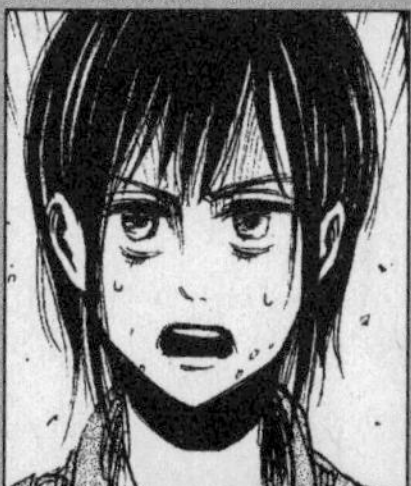

Sasha Blouse: Sasha is very agile and has remarkable instincts. Owing to her unconventionality, she isn't suited for organized activity. A member of the Survey Corps.

ATTACK on TITAN

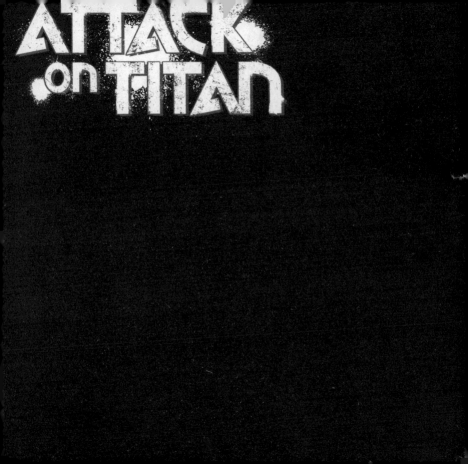

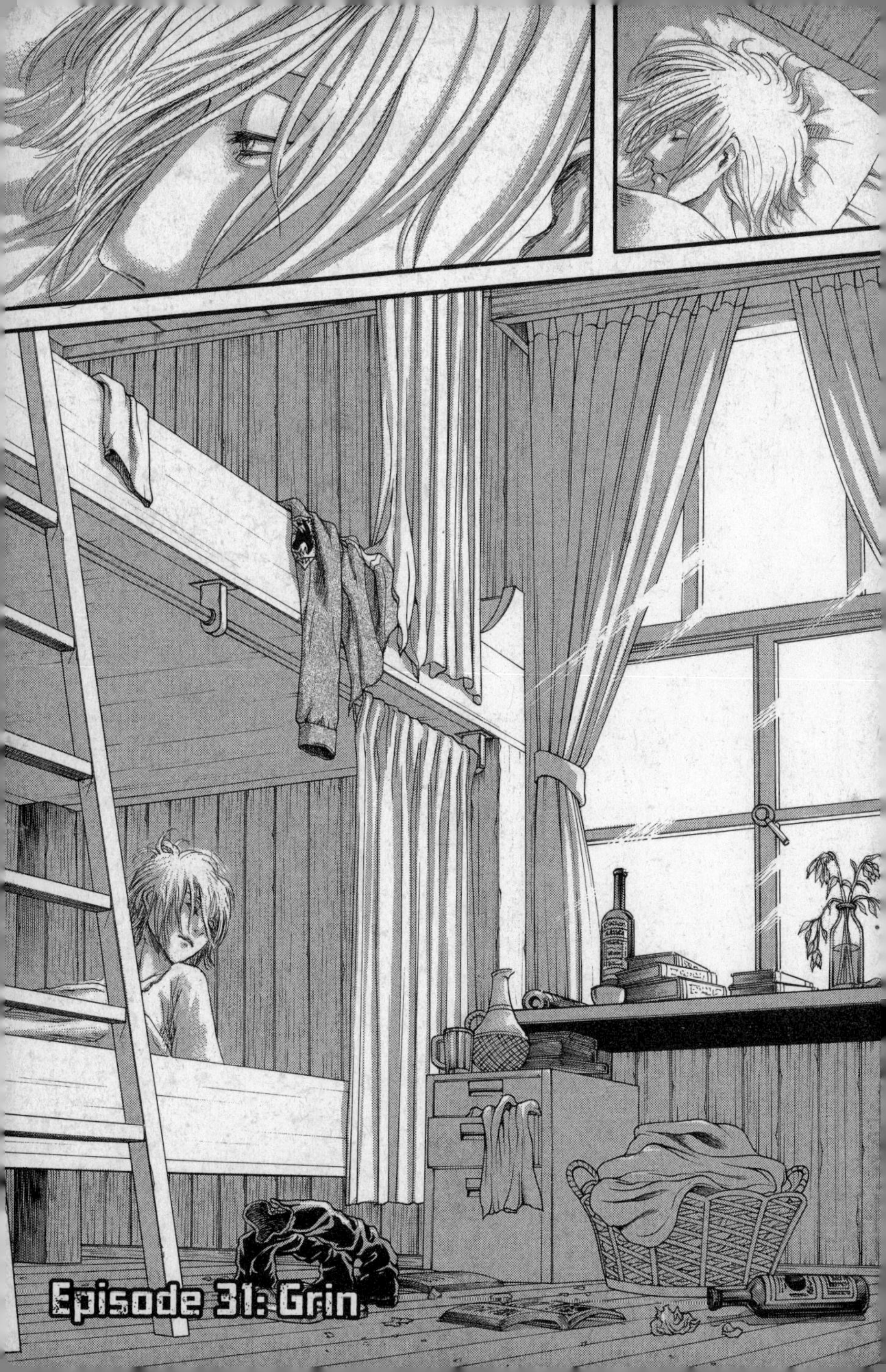
Episode 31: Grin

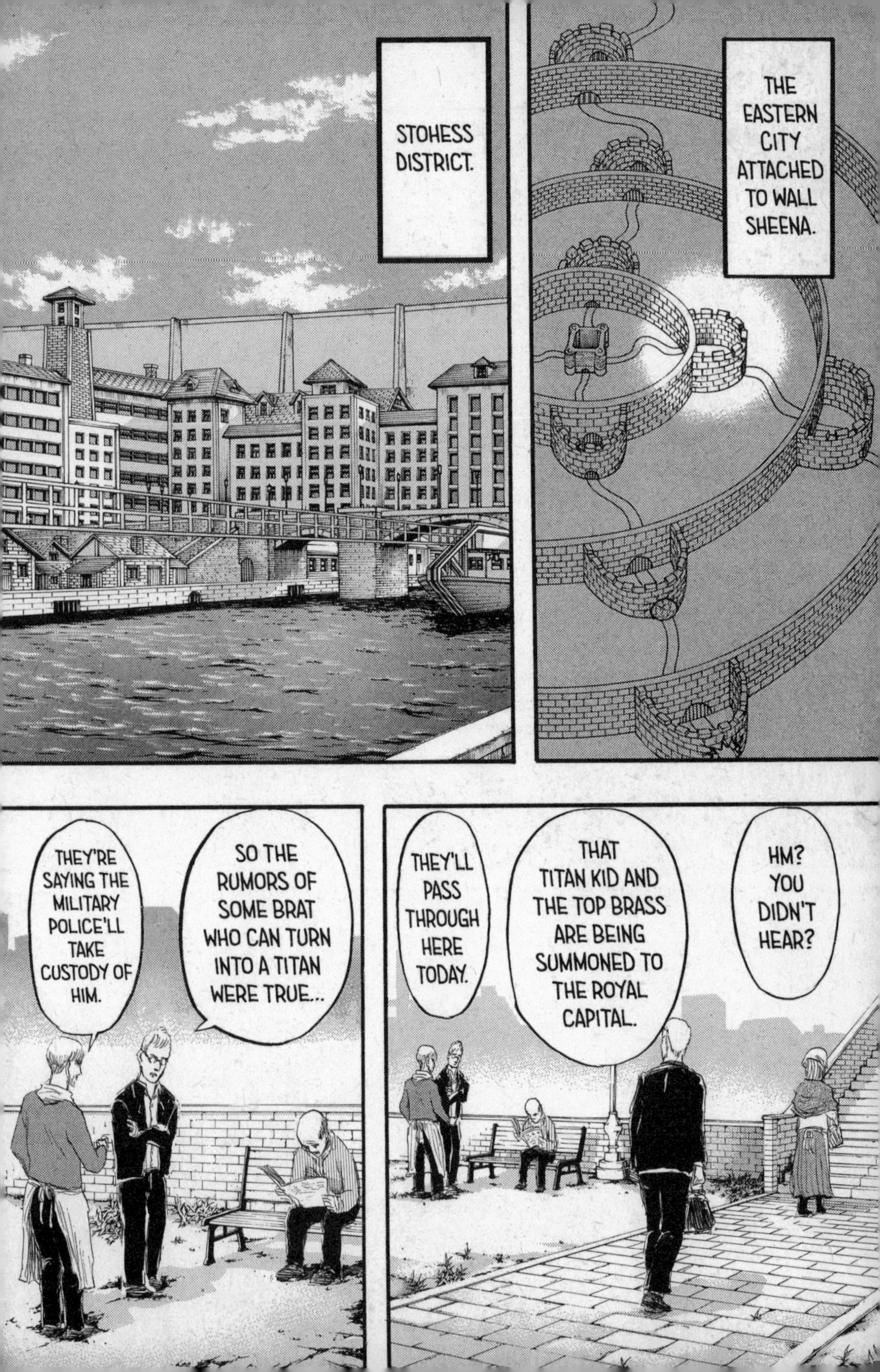
THE EASTERN CITY ATTACHED TO WALL SHEENA.
STOHESS DISTRICT.
HM? YOU DIDN'T HEAR?
THAT TITAN KID AND THE TOP BRASS ARE BEING SUMMONED TO THE ROYAL CAPITAL.
THEY'LL PASS THROUGH HERE TODAY.
SO THE RUMORS OF SOME BRAT WHO CAN TURN INTO A TITAN WERE TRUE...
THEY'RE SAYING THE MILITARY POLICE'LL TAKE CUSTODY OF HIM.

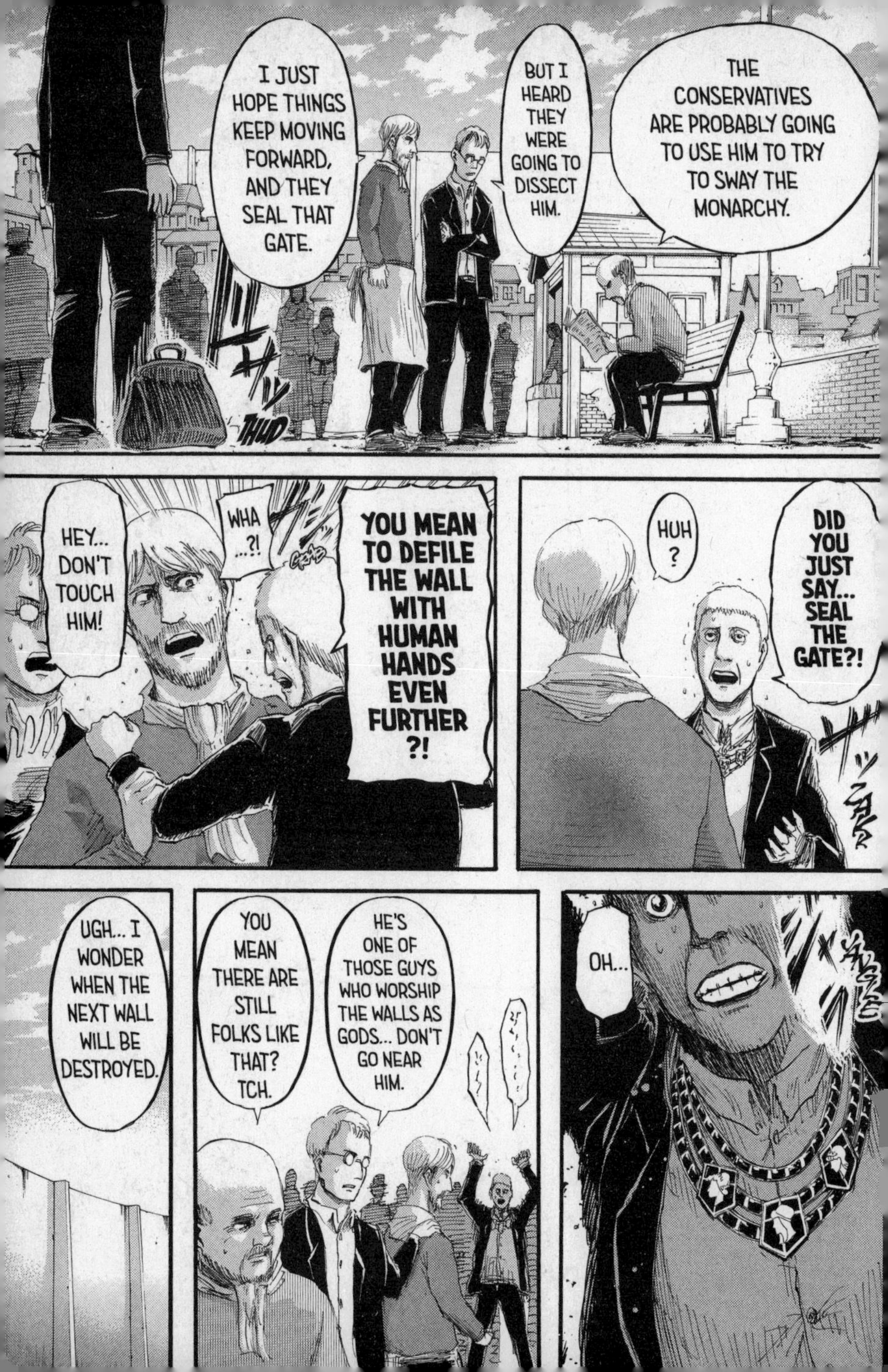
THE CONSERVATIVES ARE PROBABLY GOING TO USE HIM TO TRY TO SWAY THE MONARCHY.
BUT I HEARD THEY WERE GOING TO DISSECT HIM.
I JUST HOPE THINGS KEEP MOVING FORWARD, AND THEY SEAL THAT GATE.
THUD
DID YOU JUST SAY... SEAL THE GATE?!
HUH?
YOU MEAN TO DEFILE THE WALL WITH HUMAN HANDS EVEN FURTHER?!
WHA...?!
HEY... DON'T TOUCH HIM!
OH...
HE'S ONE OF THOSE GUYS WHO WORSHIP THE WALLS AS GODS... DON'T GO NEAR HIM.
YOU MEAN THERE ARE STILL FOLKS LIKE THAT? TCH.
UGH... I WONDER WHEN THE NEXT WALL WILL BE DESTROYED.

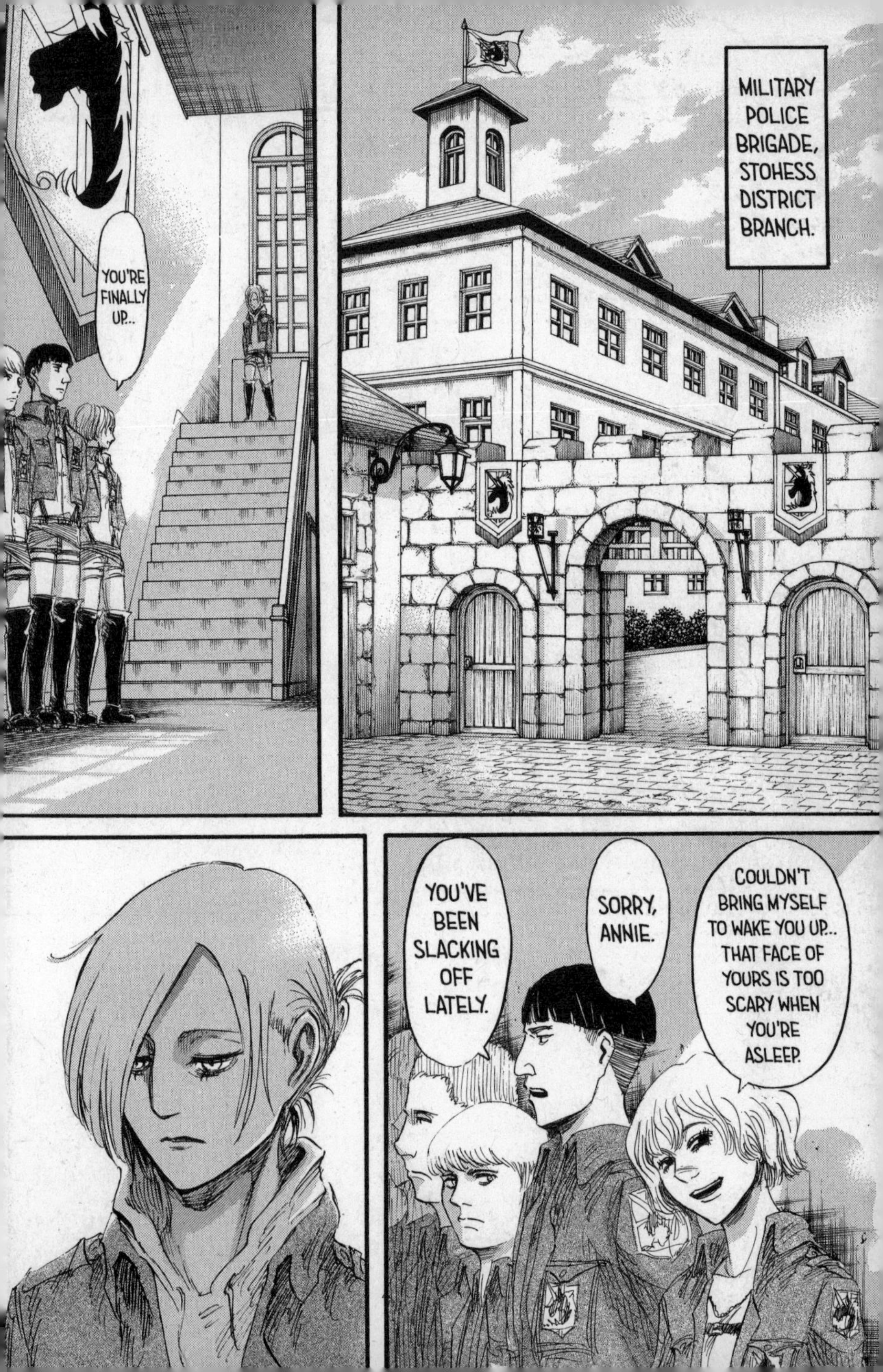
MILITARY POLICE BRIGADE, STOHESS DISTRICT BRANCH.
YOU'RE FINALLY UP...
COULDN'T BRING MYSELF TO WAKE YOU UP... THAT FACE OF YOURS IS TOO SCARY WHEN YOU'RE ASLEEP.
SORRY, ANNIE.
YOU'VE BEEN SLACKING OFF LATELY.

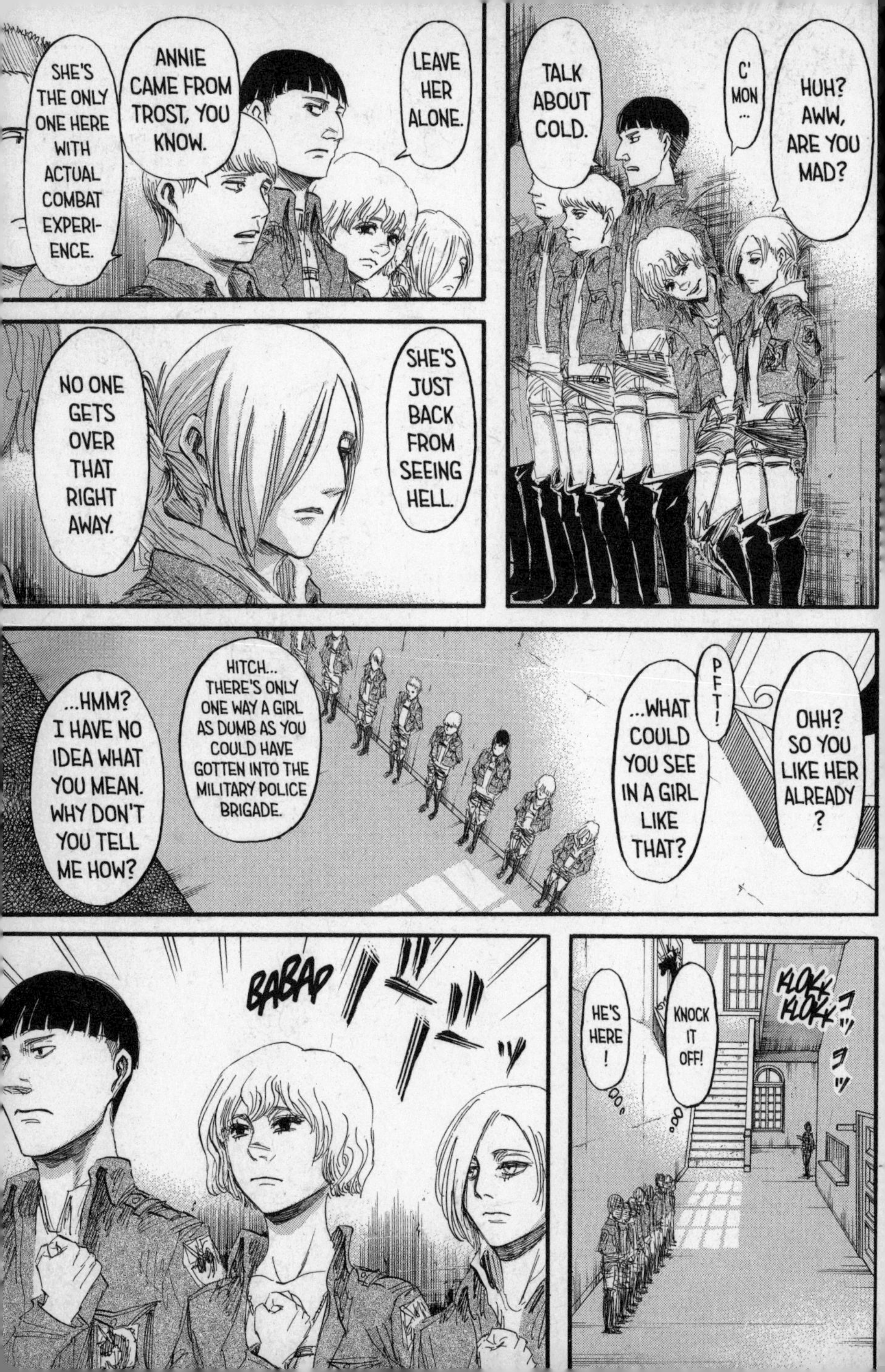
HUH? AWW, ARE YOU MAD?
C'MON ...
TALK ABOUT COLD.
LEAVE HER ALONE.
ANNIE CAME FROM TROST, YOU KNOW.
SHE'S THE ONLY ONE HERE WITH ACTUAL COMBAT EXPERIENCE.
SHE'S JUST BACK FROM SEEING HELL.
NO ONE GETS OVER THAT RIGHT AWAY.
OHH? SO YOU LIKE HER ALREADY?
PFT!
...WHAT COULD YOU SEE IN A GIRL LIKE THAT?
HITCH... THERE'S ONLY ONE WAY A GIRL AS DUMB AS YOU COULD HAVE GOTTEN INTO THE MILITARY POLICE BRIGADE.
...HMM? I HAVE NO IDEA WHAT YOU MEAN. WHY DON'T YOU TELL ME HOW?
KLOKK KLOKK
ゴッ ゴッ
KNOCK IT OFF!
HE'S HERE!
BABAP

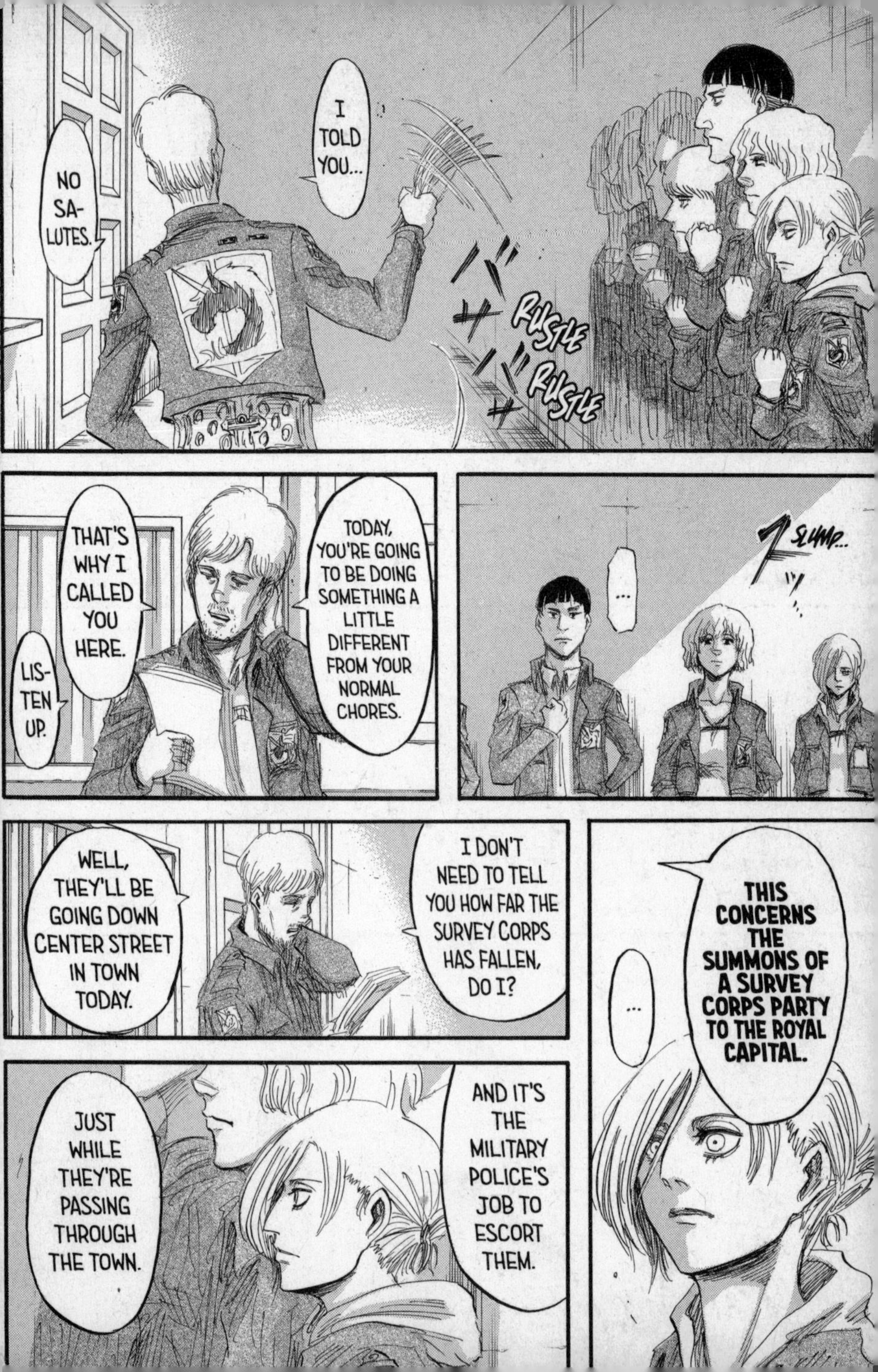

I TOLD YOU...
RUSTLE
RUSTLE
NO SA-LUTES.
SLUMP...
...
TODAY, YOU'RE GOING TO BE DOING SOMETHING A LITTLE DIFFERENT FROM YOUR NORMAL CHORES.
THAT'S WHY I CALLED YOU HERE.
LIS-TEN UP.
THIS CONCERNS THE SUMMONS OF A SURVEY CORPS PARTY TO THE ROYAL CAPITAL.
...
I DON'T NEED TO TELL YOU HOW FAR THE SURVEY CORPS HAS FALLEN, DO I?
WELL, THEY'LL BE GOING DOWN CENTER STREET IN TOWN TODAY.
AND IT'S THE MILITARY POLICE'S JOB TO ESCORT THEM.
JUST WHILE THEY'RE PASSING THROUGH THE TOWN.

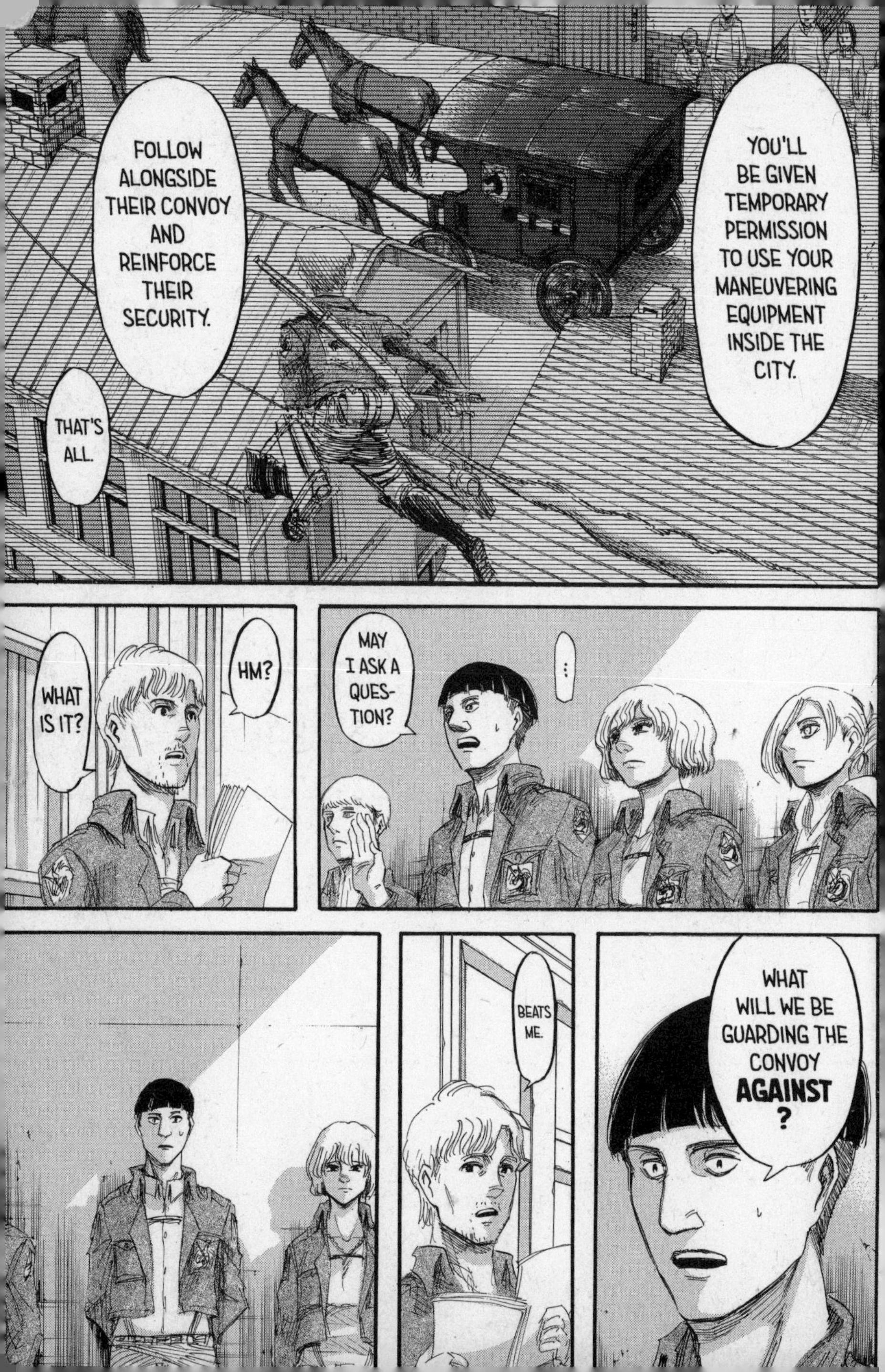
YOU'LL BE GIVEN TEMPORARY PERMISSION TO USE YOUR MANEUVERING EQUIPMENT INSIDE THE CITY.
FOLLOW ALONGSIDE THEIR CONVOY AND REINFORCE THEIR SECURITY.
THAT'S ALL.
...
MAY I ASK A QUES-TION?
HM?
WHAT IS IT?
WHAT WILL WE BE GUARDING THE CONVOY **AGAINST**?
BEATS ME.

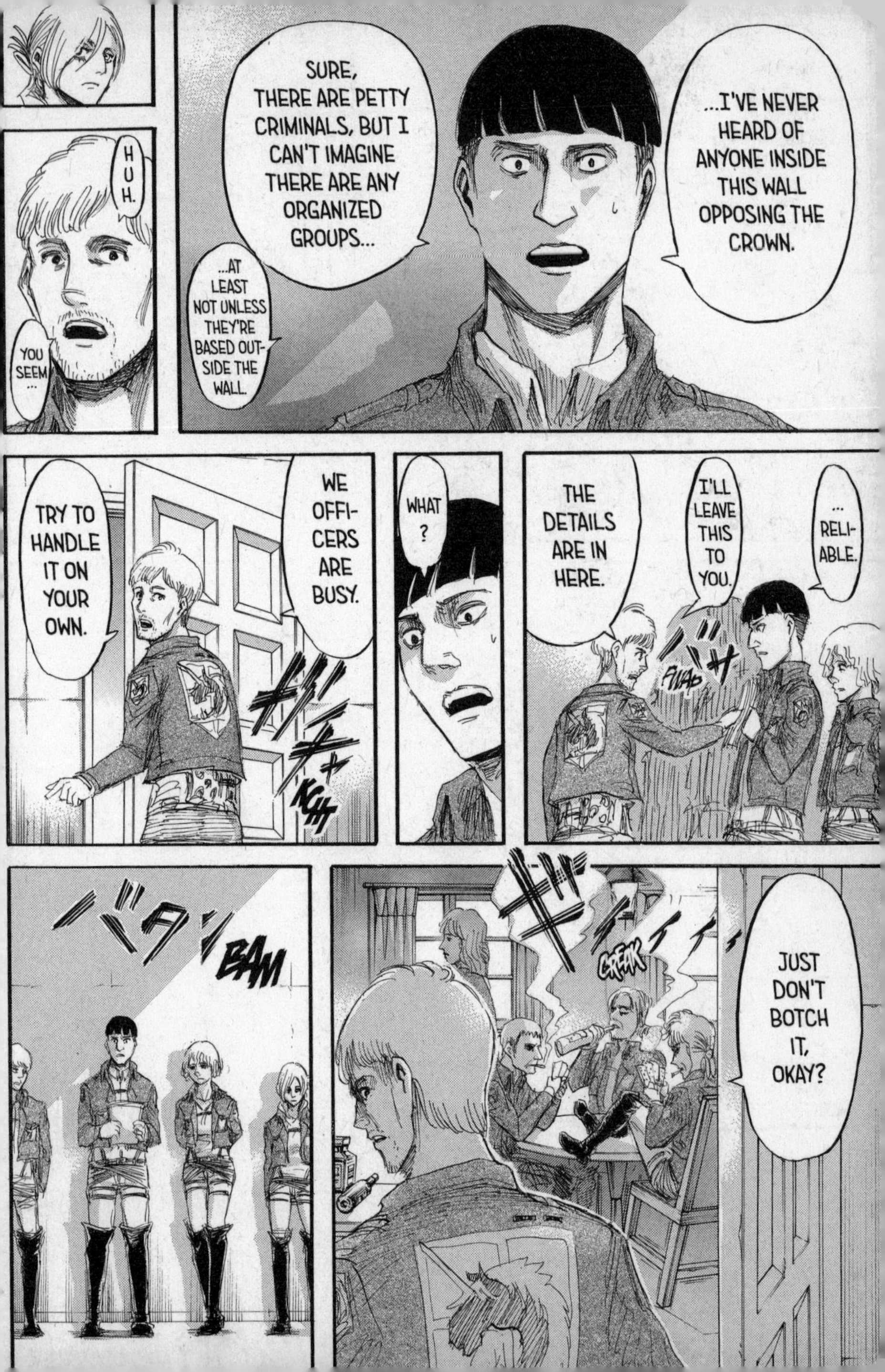
...I'VE NEVER HEARD OF ANYONE INSIDE THIS WALL OPPOSING THE CROWN.
SURE, THERE ARE PETTY CRIMINALS, BUT I CAN'T IMAGINE THERE ARE ANY ORGANIZED GROUPS...
...AT LEAST NOT UNLESS THEY'RE BASED OUTSIDE THE WALL.
HUH.
YOU SEEM...
...RELIABLE.
I'LL LEAVE THIS TO YOU.
THE DETAILS ARE IN HERE.
FWAP
WHAT?
WE OFFICERS ARE BUSY.
KCHK
TRY TO HANDLE IT ON YOUR OWN.
CREAK
JUST DON'T BOTCH IT, OKAY?
BAM

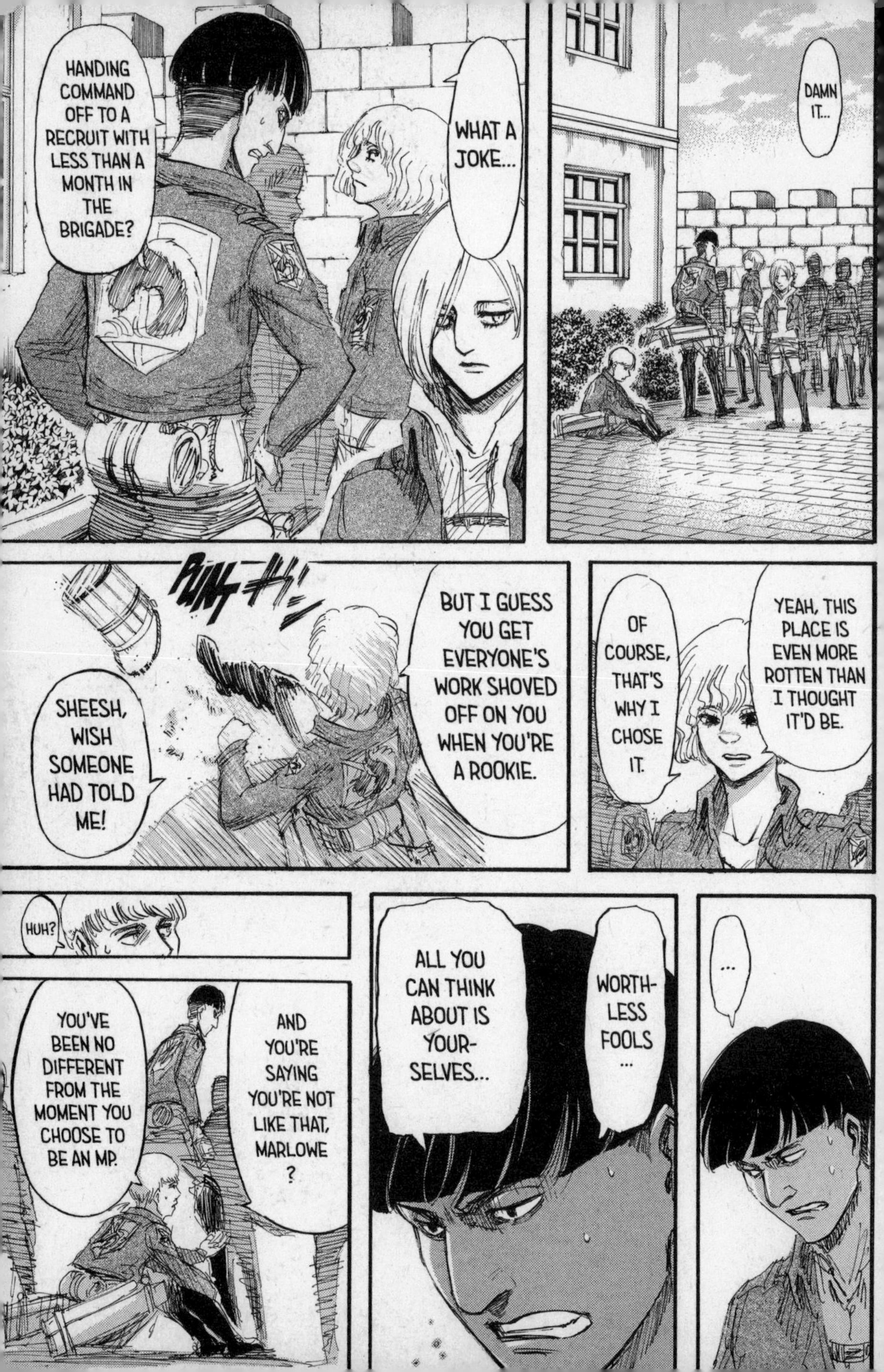
DAMN IT...
WHAT A JOKE...
HANDING COMMAND OFF TO A RECRUIT WITH LESS THAN A MONTH IN THE BRIGADE?
YEAH, THIS PLACE IS EVEN MORE ROTTEN THAN I THOUGHT IT'D BE.
OF COURSE, THAT'S WHY I CHOSE IT.
BUT I GUESS YOU GET EVERYONE'S WORK SHOVED OFF ON YOU WHEN YOU'RE A ROOKIE.
PUNT
SHEESH, WISH SOMEONE HAD TOLD ME!
...
WORTH-LESS FOOLS ...
ALL YOU CAN THINK ABOUT IS YOUR-SELVES...
HUH?
AND YOU'RE SAYING YOU'RE NOT LIKE THAT, MARLOWE ?
YOU'VE BEEN NO DIFFERENT FROM THE MOMENT YOU CHOOSE TO BE AN MP.

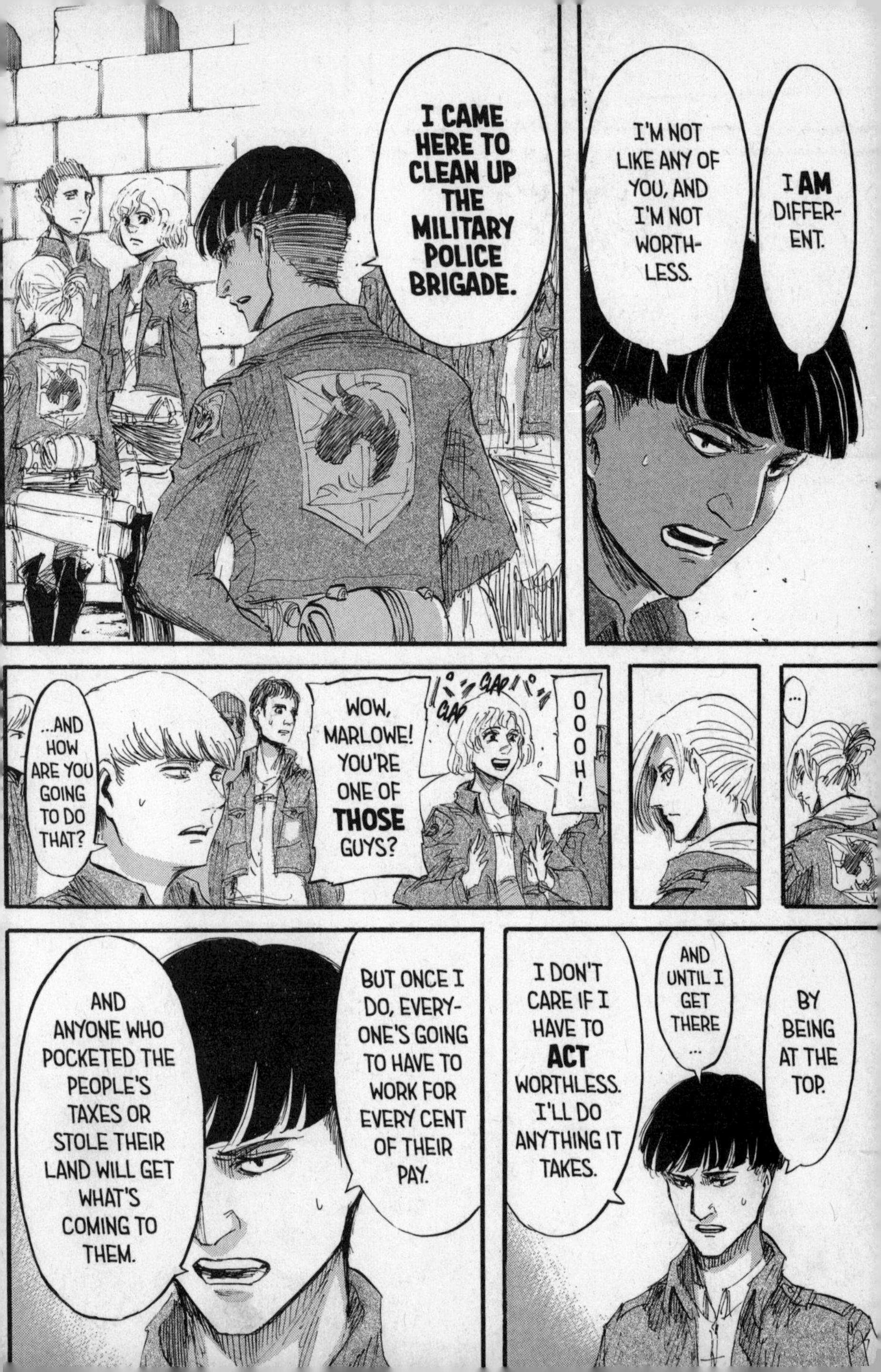
I AM DIFFER-ENT.
I'M NOT LIKE ANY OF YOU, AND I'M NOT WORTH-LESS.
I CAME HERE TO CLEAN UP THE MILITARY POLICE BRIGADE.
...
OOOOH!
CLAP
CLAP
WOW, MARLOWE! YOU'RE ONE OF THOSE GUYS?
...AND HOW ARE YOU GOING TO DO THAT?
BY BEING AT THE TOP.
AND UNTIL I GET THERE...
I DON'T CARE IF I HAVE TO ACT WORTHLESS. I'LL DO ANYTHING IT TAKES.
BUT ONCE I DO, EVERY-ONE'S GOING TO HAVE TO WORK FOR EVERY CENT OF THEIR PAY.
AND ANYONE WHO POCKETED THE PEOPLE'S TAXES OR STOLE THEIR LAND WILL GET WHAT'S COMING TO THEM.

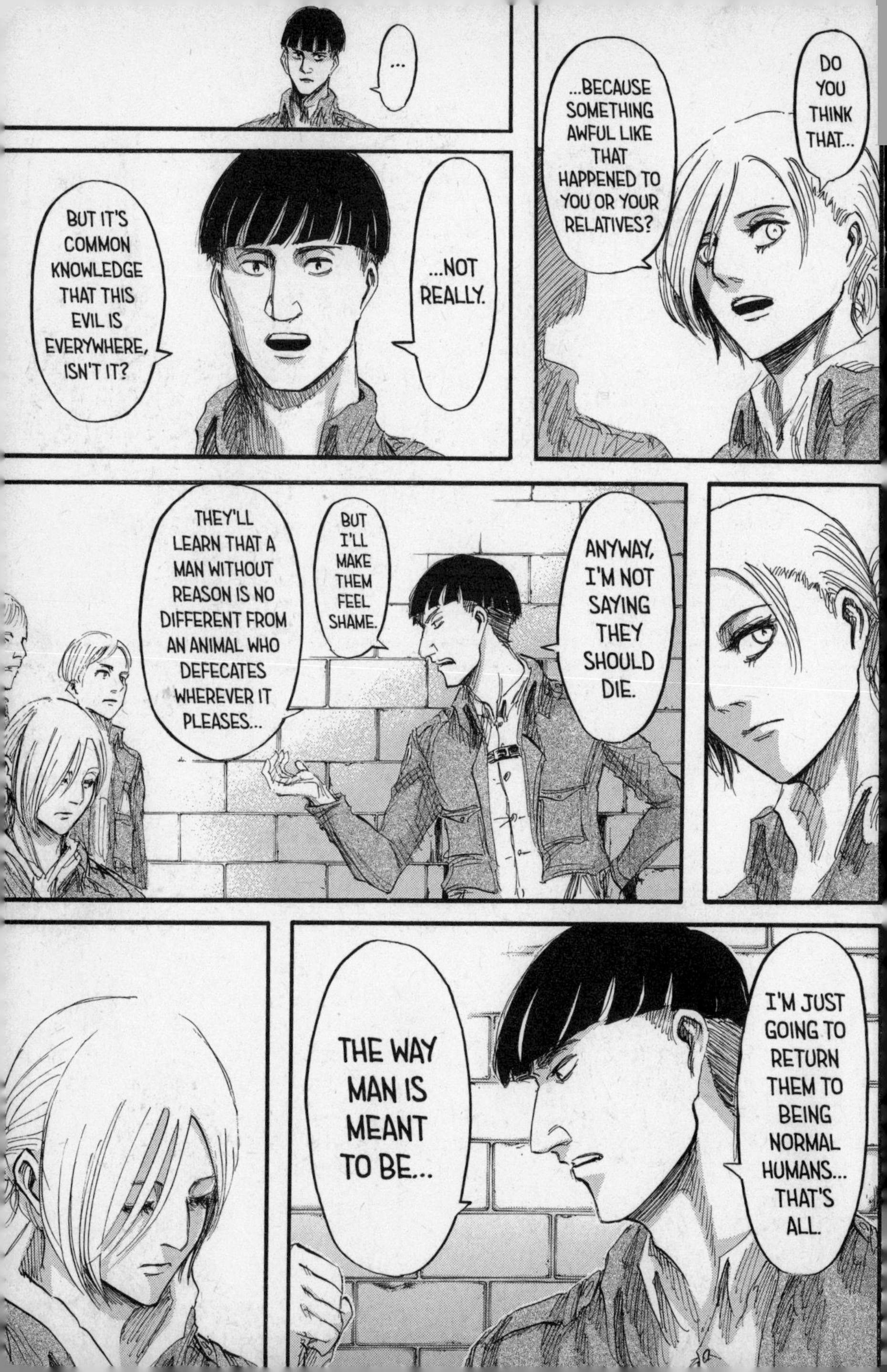
DO YOU THINK THAT...
...BECAUSE SOMETHING AWFUL LIKE THAT HAPPENED TO YOU OR YOUR RELATIVES?
...
...NOT REALLY.
BUT IT'S COMMON KNOWLEDGE THAT THIS EVIL IS EVERYWHERE, ISN'T IT?
ANYWAY, I'M NOT SAYING THEY SHOULD DIE.
BUT I'LL MAKE THEM FEEL SHAME.
THEY'LL LEARN THAT A MAN WITHOUT REASON IS NO DIFFERENT FROM AN ANIMAL WHO DEFECATES WHEREVER IT PLEASES...
I'M JUST GOING TO RETURN THEM TO BEING NORMAL HUMANS... THAT'S ALL.
THE WAY MAN IS MEANT TO BE...

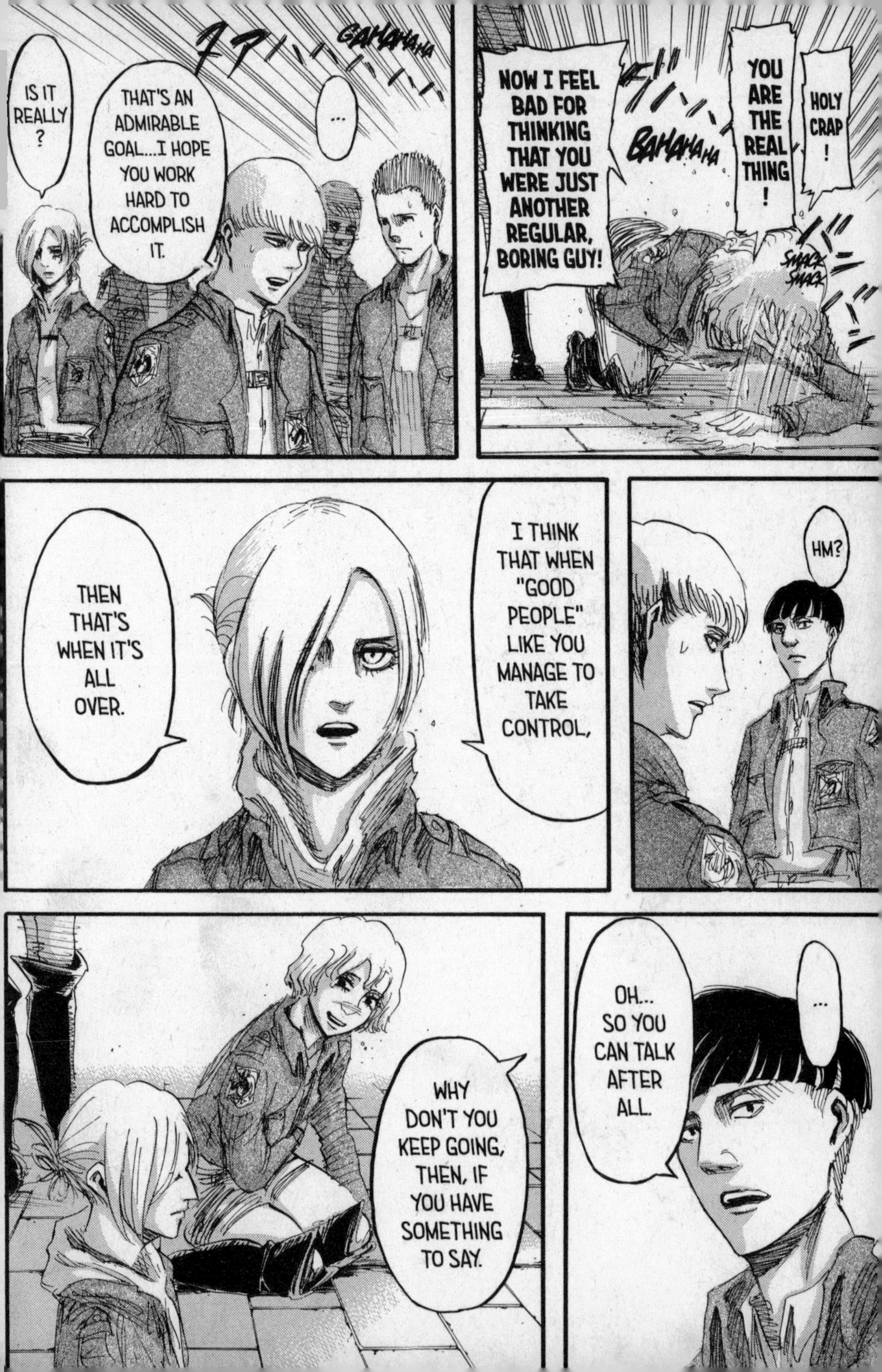
HOLY CRAP!
YOU ARE THE REAL THING!
BAHAHAHA
NOW I FEEL BAD FOR THINKING THAT YOU WERE JUST ANOTHER REGULAR, BORING GUY!
SMACK SMACK
GAHAHAHA
...
THAT'S AN ADMIRABLE GOAL...I HOPE YOU WORK HARD TO ACCOMPLISH IT.
IS IT REALLY?
HM?
I THINK THAT WHEN "GOOD PEOPLE" LIKE YOU MANAGE TO TAKE CONTROL,
THEN THAT'S WHEN IT'S ALL OVER.
...
OH... SO YOU CAN TALK AFTER ALL.
WHY DON'T YOU KEEP GOING, THEN, IF YOU HAVE SOMETHING TO SAY.

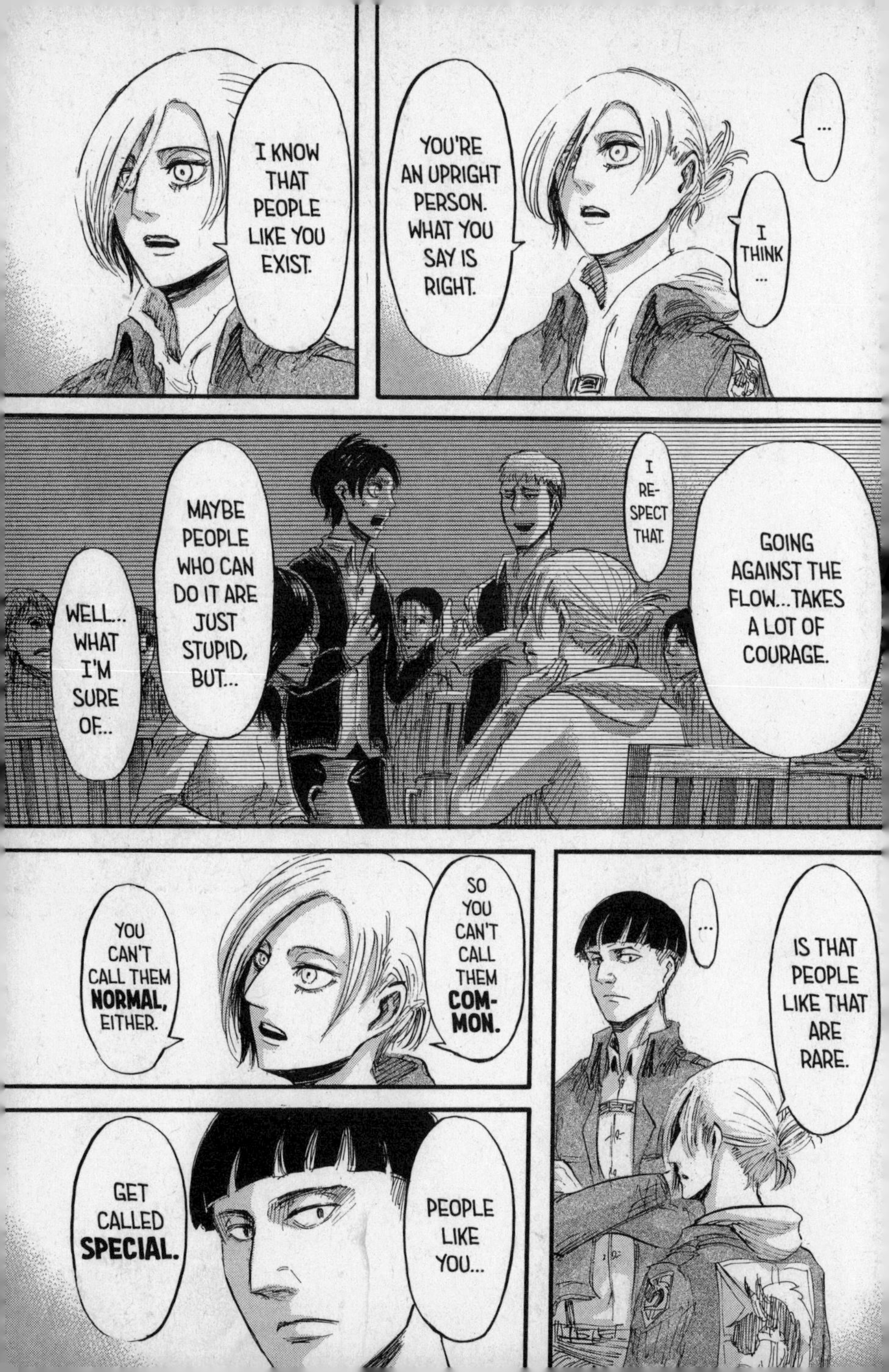
...
I THINK ...
YOU'RE AN UPRIGHT PERSON. WHAT YOU SAY IS RIGHT.
I KNOW THAT PEOPLE LIKE YOU EXIST.
GOING AGAINST THE FLOW...TAKES A LOT OF COURAGE.
I RE-SPECT THAT.
MAYBE PEOPLE WHO CAN DO IT ARE JUST STUPID, BUT...
WELL... WHAT I'M SURE OF...
...
IS THAT PEOPLE LIKE THAT ARE RARE.
SO YOU CAN'T CALL THEM **COM-MON.**
YOU CAN'T CALL THEM **NORMAL,** EITHER.
PEOPLE LIKE YOU...
GET CALLED **SPECIAL.**

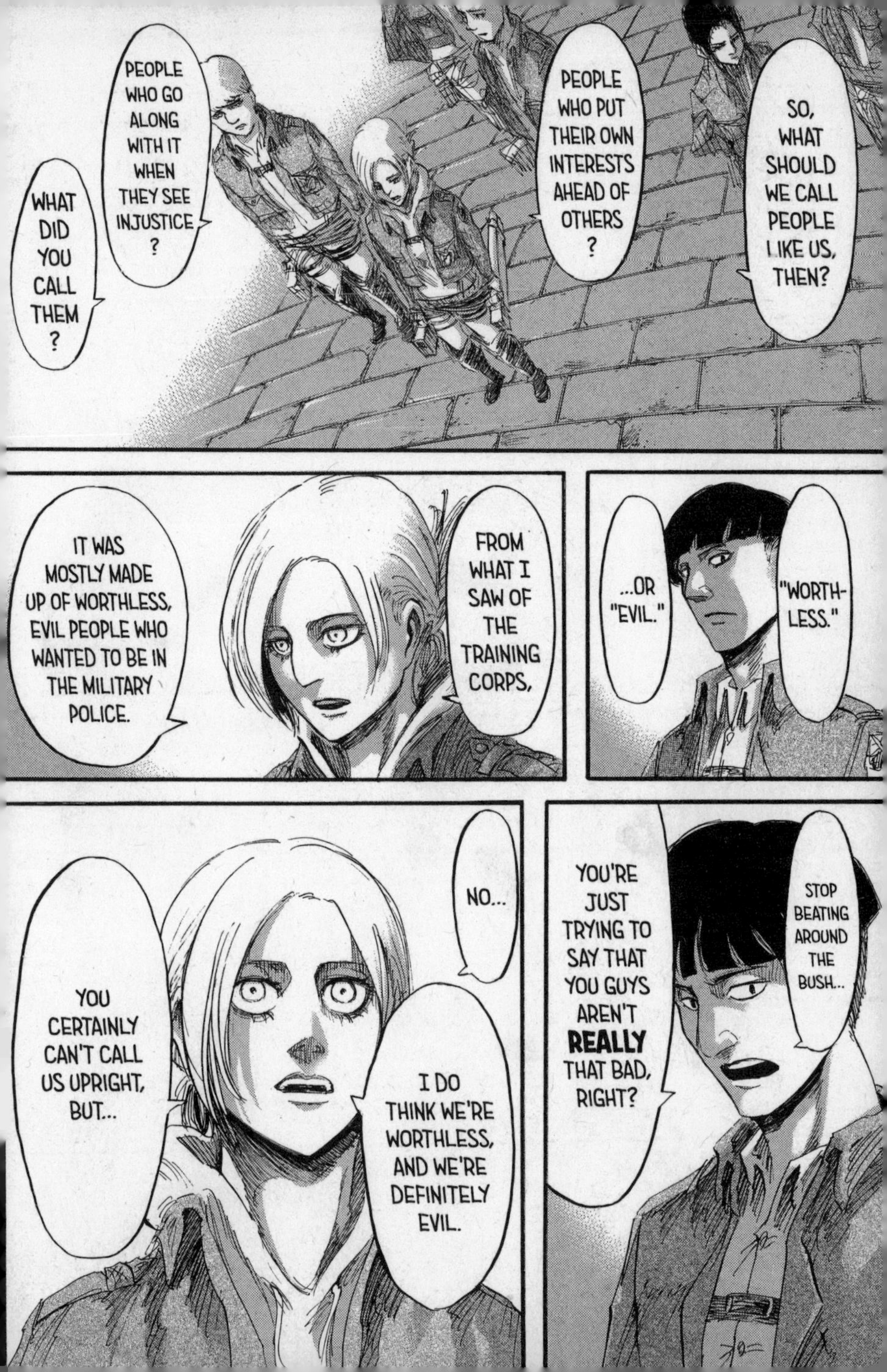
SO, WHAT SHOULD WE CALL PEOPLE LIKE US, THEN?
PEOPLE WHO PUT THEIR OWN INTERESTS AHEAD OF OTHERS?
PEOPLE WHO GO ALONG WITH IT WHEN THEY SEE INJUSTICE?
WHAT DID YOU CALL THEM?
"WORTHLESS."
...OR "EVIL."
FROM WHAT I SAW OF THE TRAINING CORPS,
IT WAS MOSTLY MADE UP OF WORTHLESS, EVIL PEOPLE WHO WANTED TO BE IN THE MILITARY POLICE.
STOP BEATING AROUND THE BUSH...
YOU'RE JUST TRYING TO SAY THAT YOU GUYS AREN'T **REALLY** THAT BAD, RIGHT?
NO...
YOU CERTAINLY CAN'T CALL US UPRIGHT, BUT...
I DO THINK WE'RE WORTHLESS, AND WE'RE DEFINITELY EVIL.

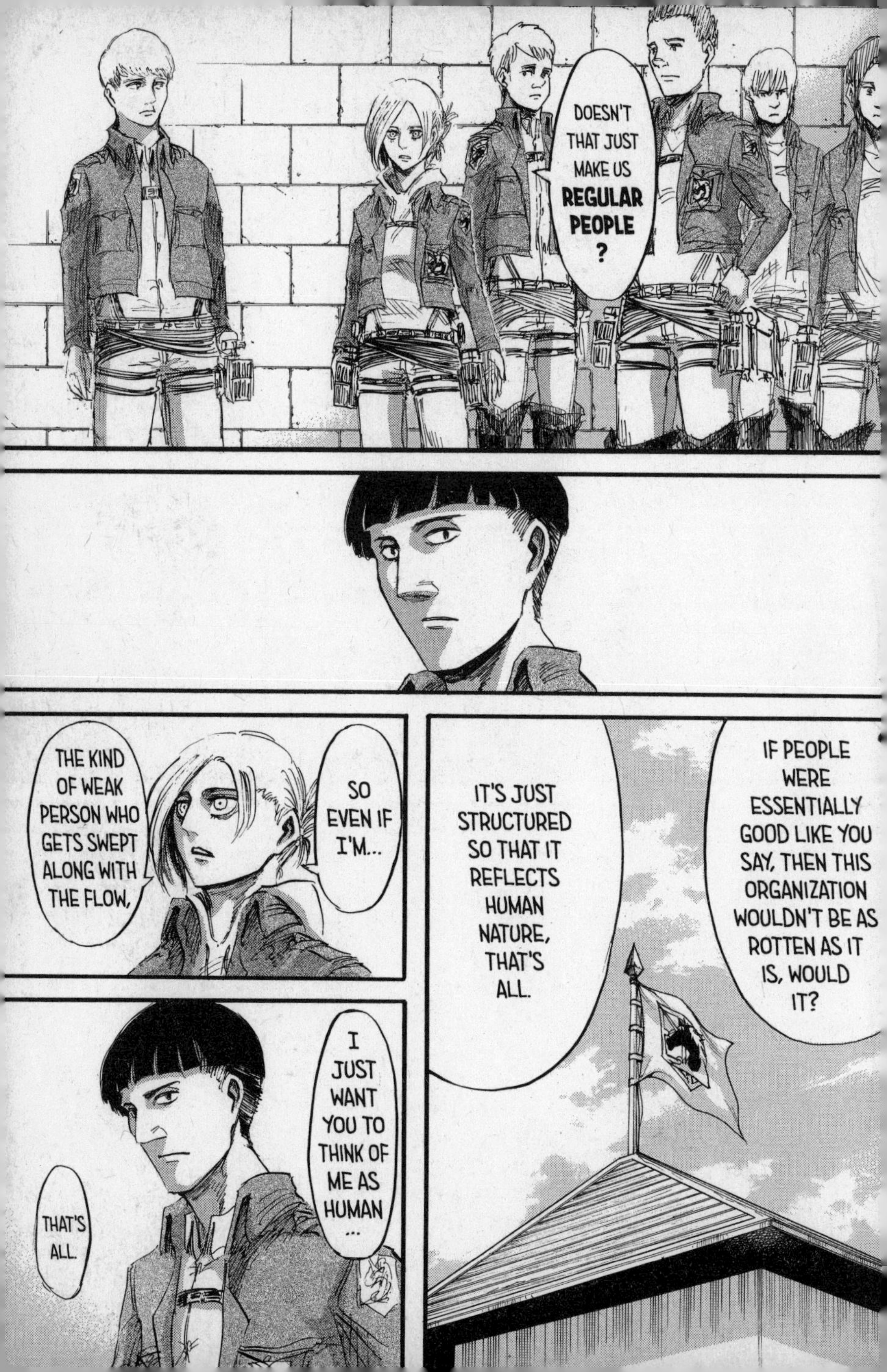
DOESN'T THAT JUST MAKE US **REGULAR PEOPLE** ?
IF PEOPLE WERE ESSENTIALLY GOOD LIKE YOU SAY, THEN THIS ORGANIZATION WOULDN'T BE AS ROTTEN AS IT IS, WOULD IT?
IT'S JUST STRUCTURED SO THAT IT REFLECTS HUMAN NATURE, THAT'S ALL.
SO EVEN IF I'M...
THE KIND OF WEAK PERSON WHO GETS SWEPT ALONG WITH THE FLOW,
I JUST WANT YOU TO THINK OF ME AS HUMAN ...
THAT'S ALL.

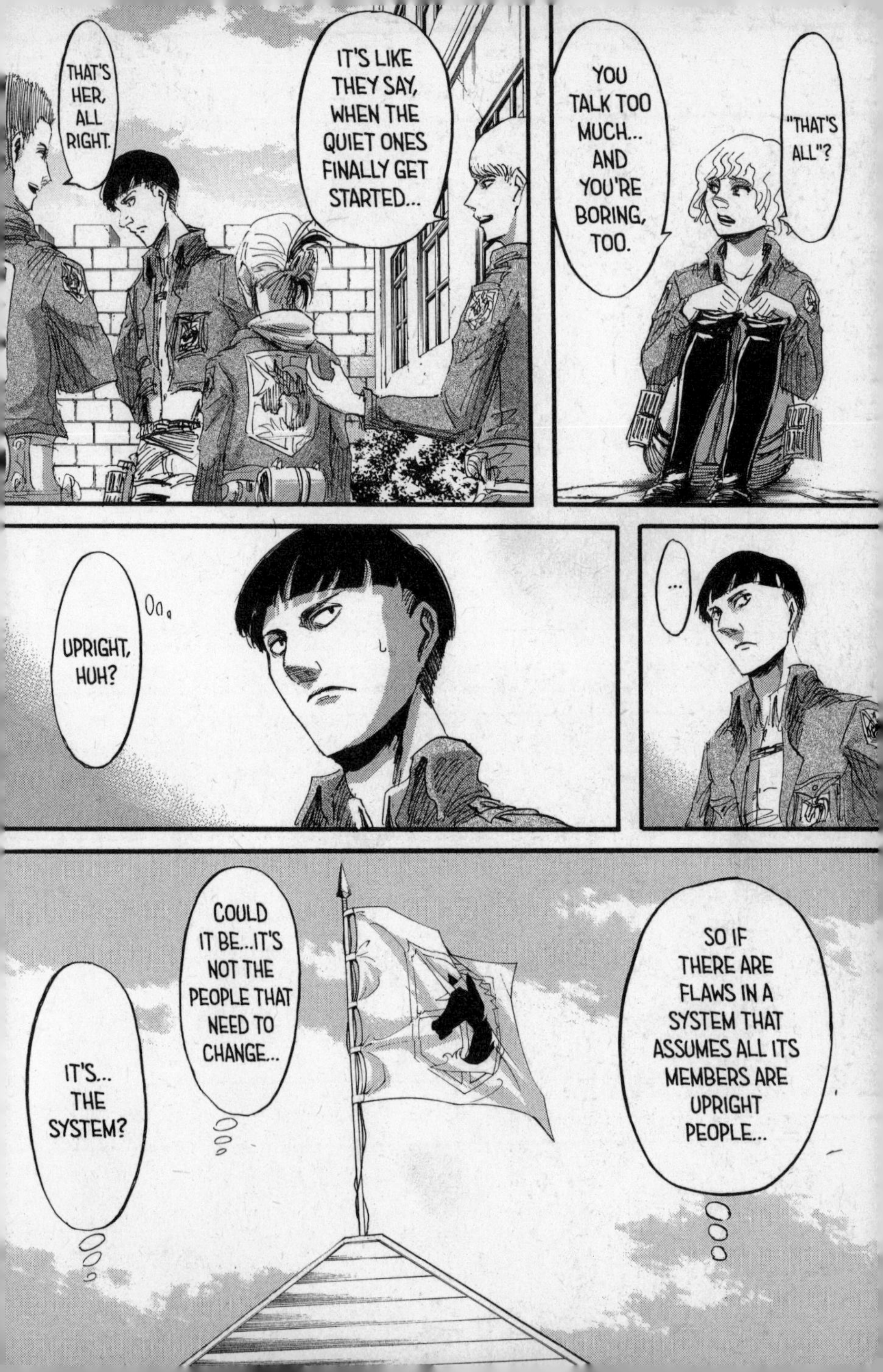
"THAT'S ALL"?
YOU TALK TOO MUCH... AND YOU'RE BORING, TOO.
IT'S LIKE THEY SAY, WHEN THE QUIET ONES FINALLY GET STARTED...
THAT'S HER, ALL RIGHT.
...
UPRIGHT, HUH?
SO IF THERE ARE FLAWS IN A SYSTEM THAT ASSUMES ALL ITS MEMBERS ARE UPRIGHT PEOPLE...
COULD IT BE...IT'S NOT THE PEOPLE THAT NEED TO CHANGE...
IT'S... THE SYSTEM?

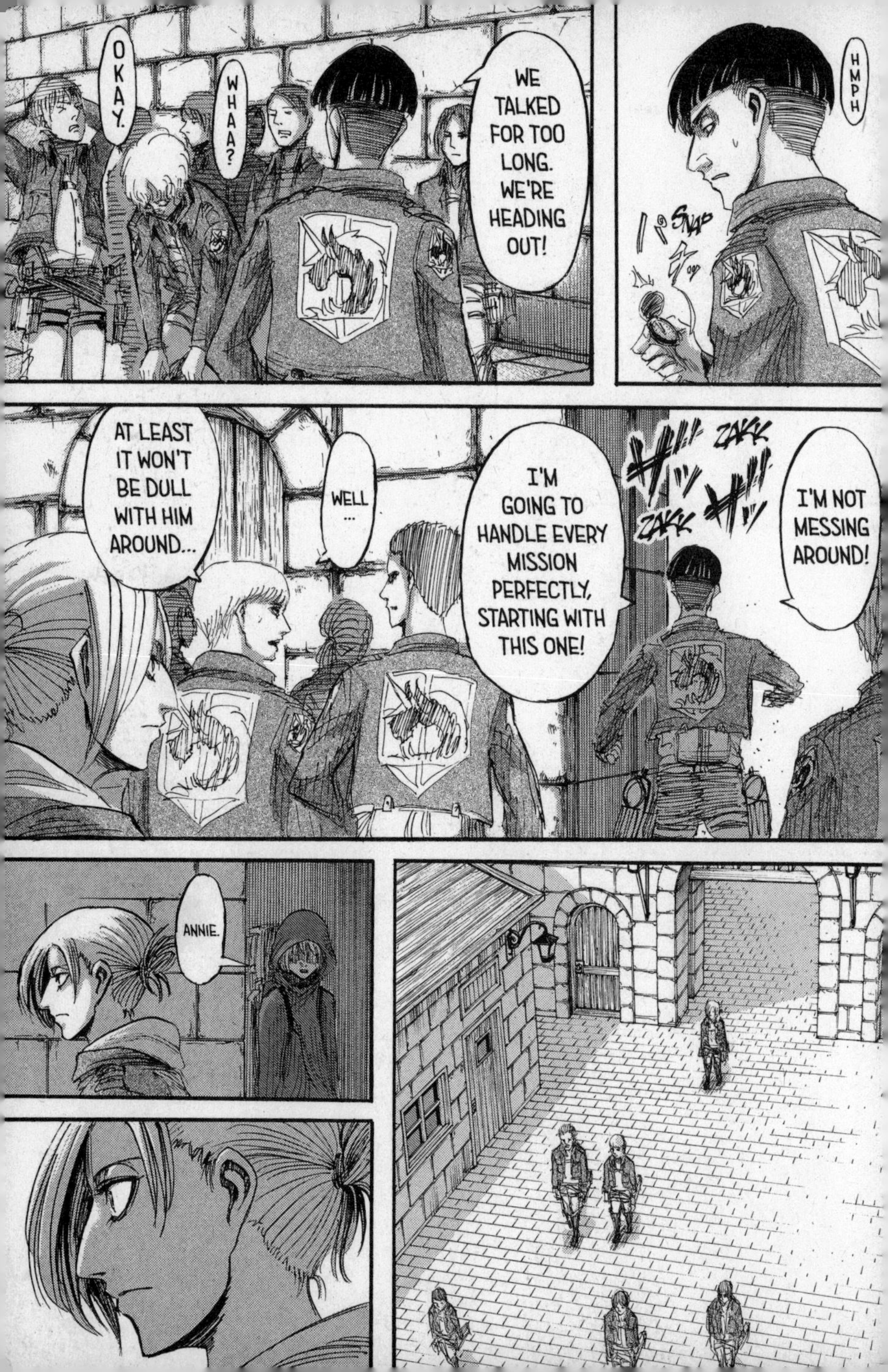
HMPH
SNAP
WE TALKED FOR TOO LONG. WE'RE HEADING OUT!
WHAA?
OKAY.
I'M NOT MESSING AROUND!
ZAKK
ZAKK
I'M GOING TO HANDLE EVERY MISSION PERFECTLY, STARTING WITH THIS ONE!
WELL...
AT LEAST IT WON'T BE DULL WITH HIM AROUND...
ANNIE.

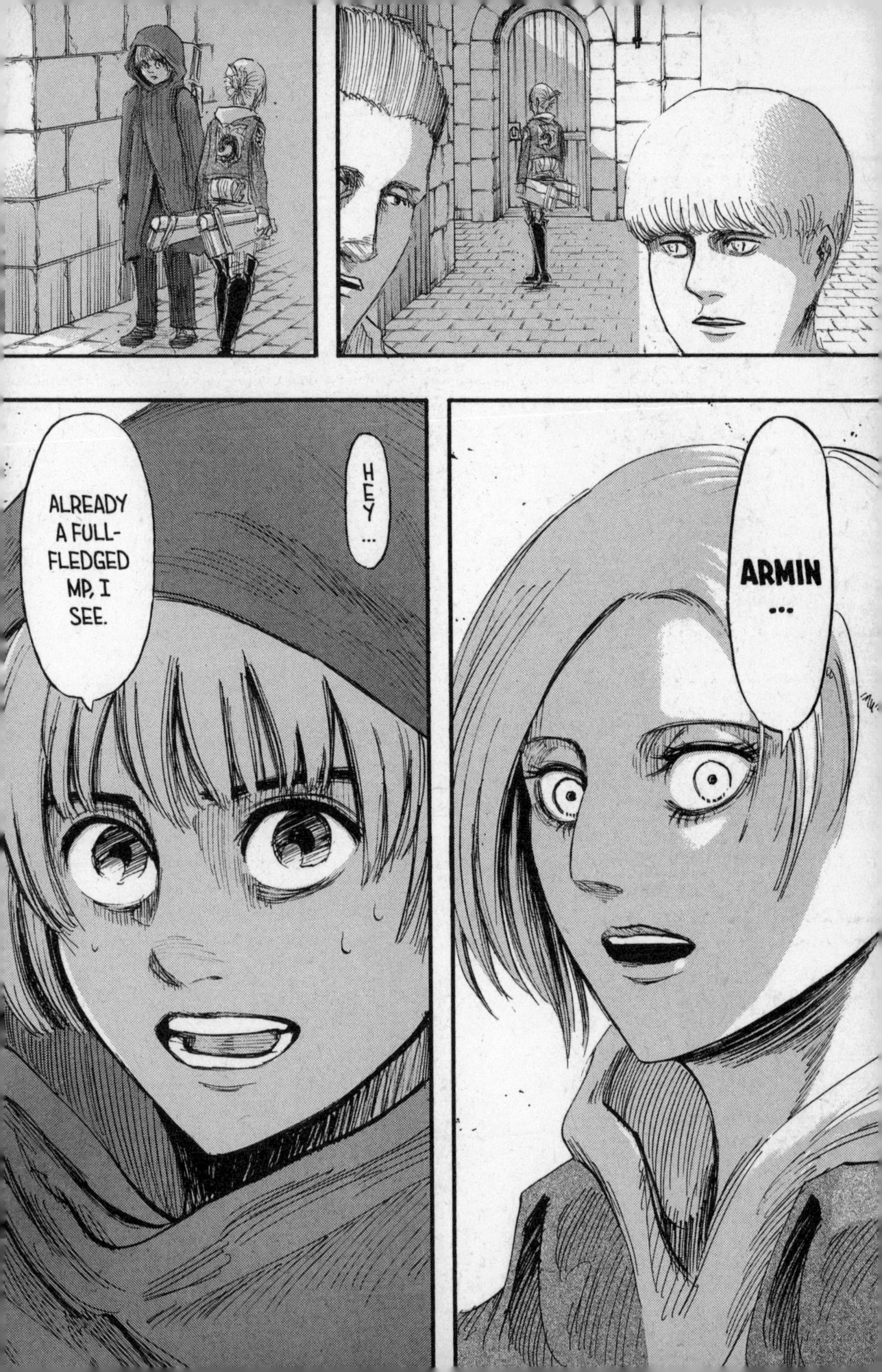
ARMIN ...
HEY ...
ALREADY A FULL-FLEDGED MP, I SEE.

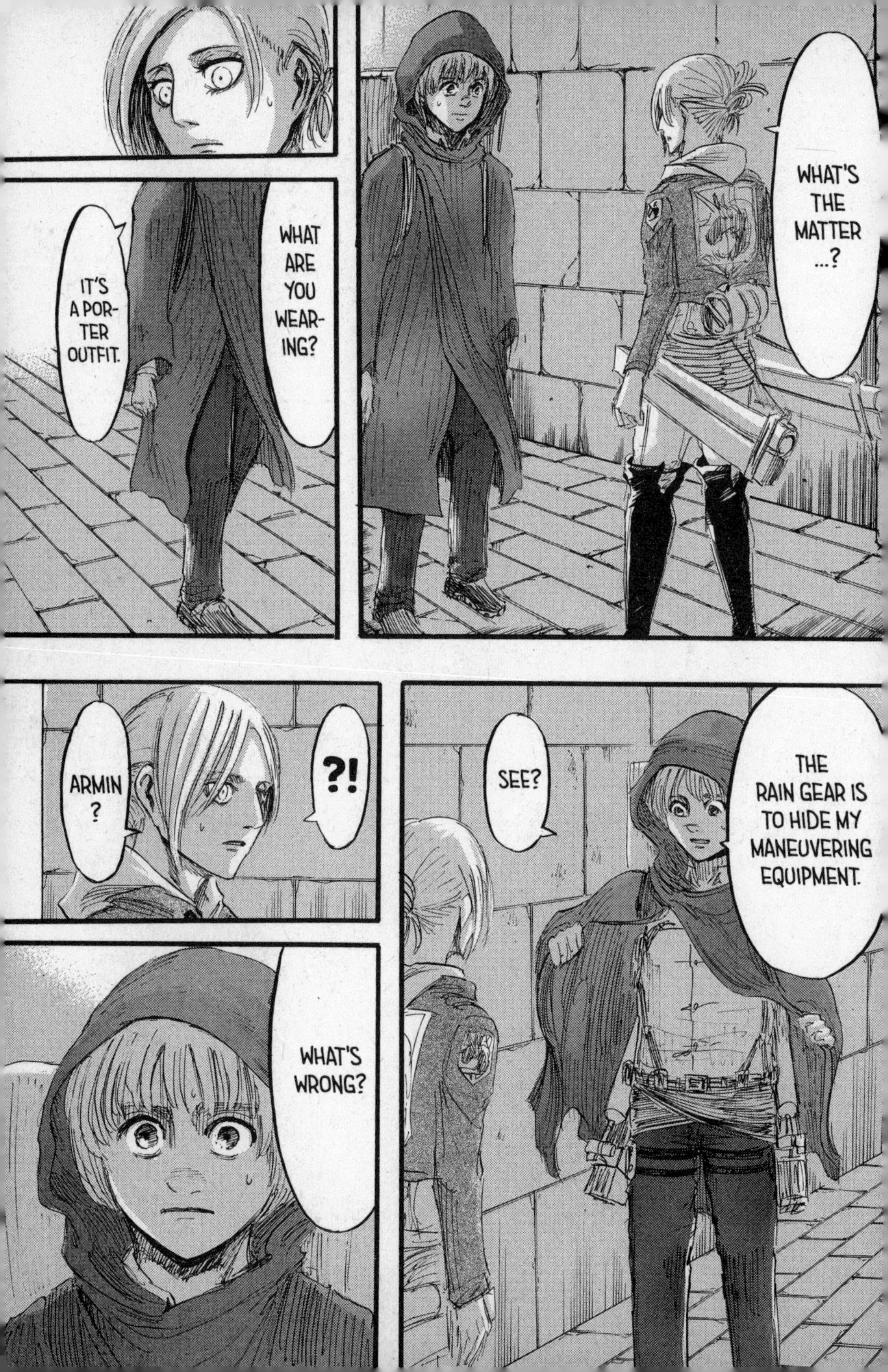
WHAT'S THE MATTER ...?
WHAT ARE YOU WEAR-ING?
IT'S A POR-TER OUTFIT.
THE RAIN GEAR IS TO HIDE MY MANEUVERING EQUIPMENT.
SEE?
?!
ARMIN ?
WHAT'S WRONG?

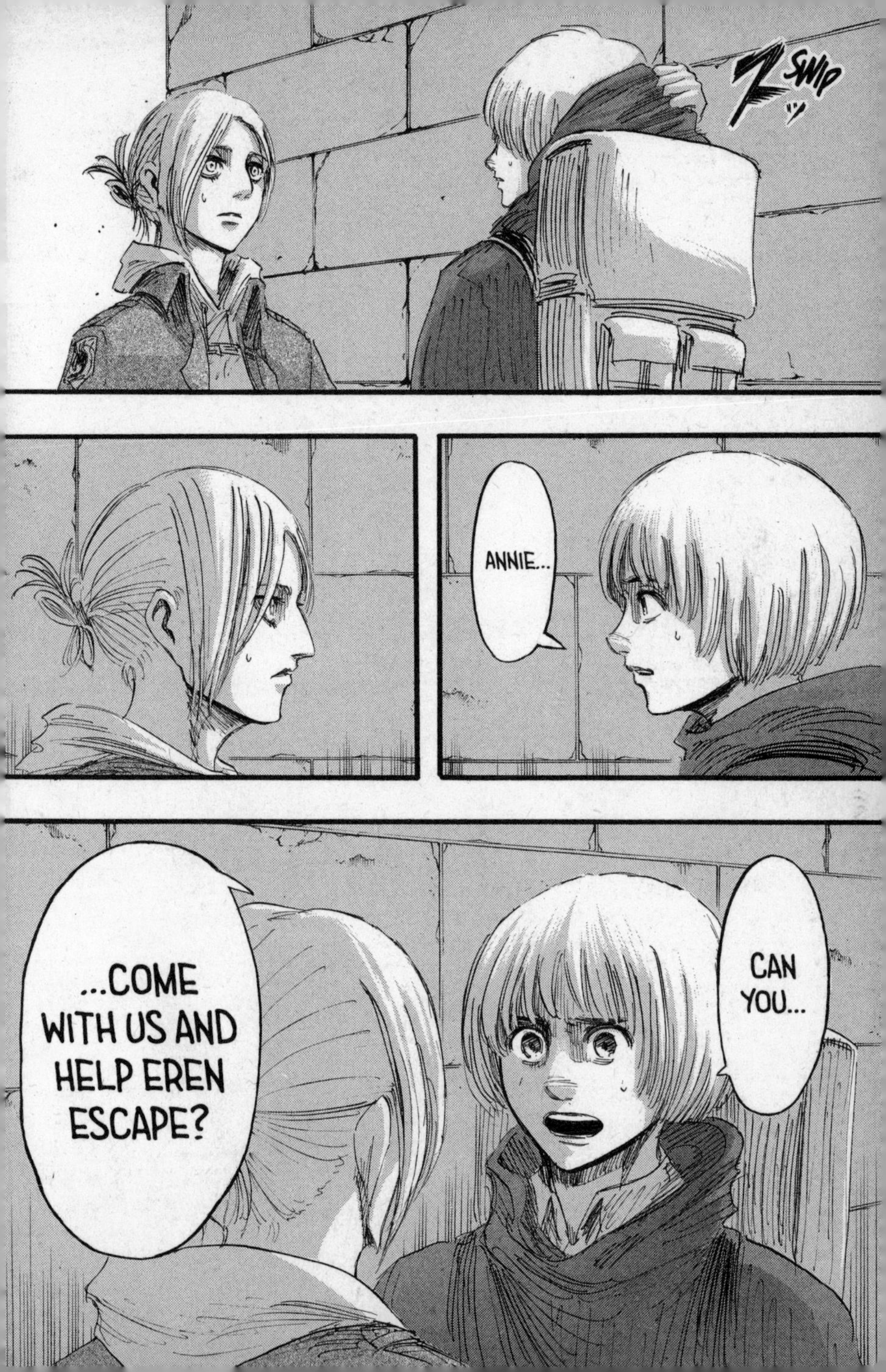
SWIP
ANNIE...
CAN YOU...
...COME WITH US AND HELP EREN ESCAPE?

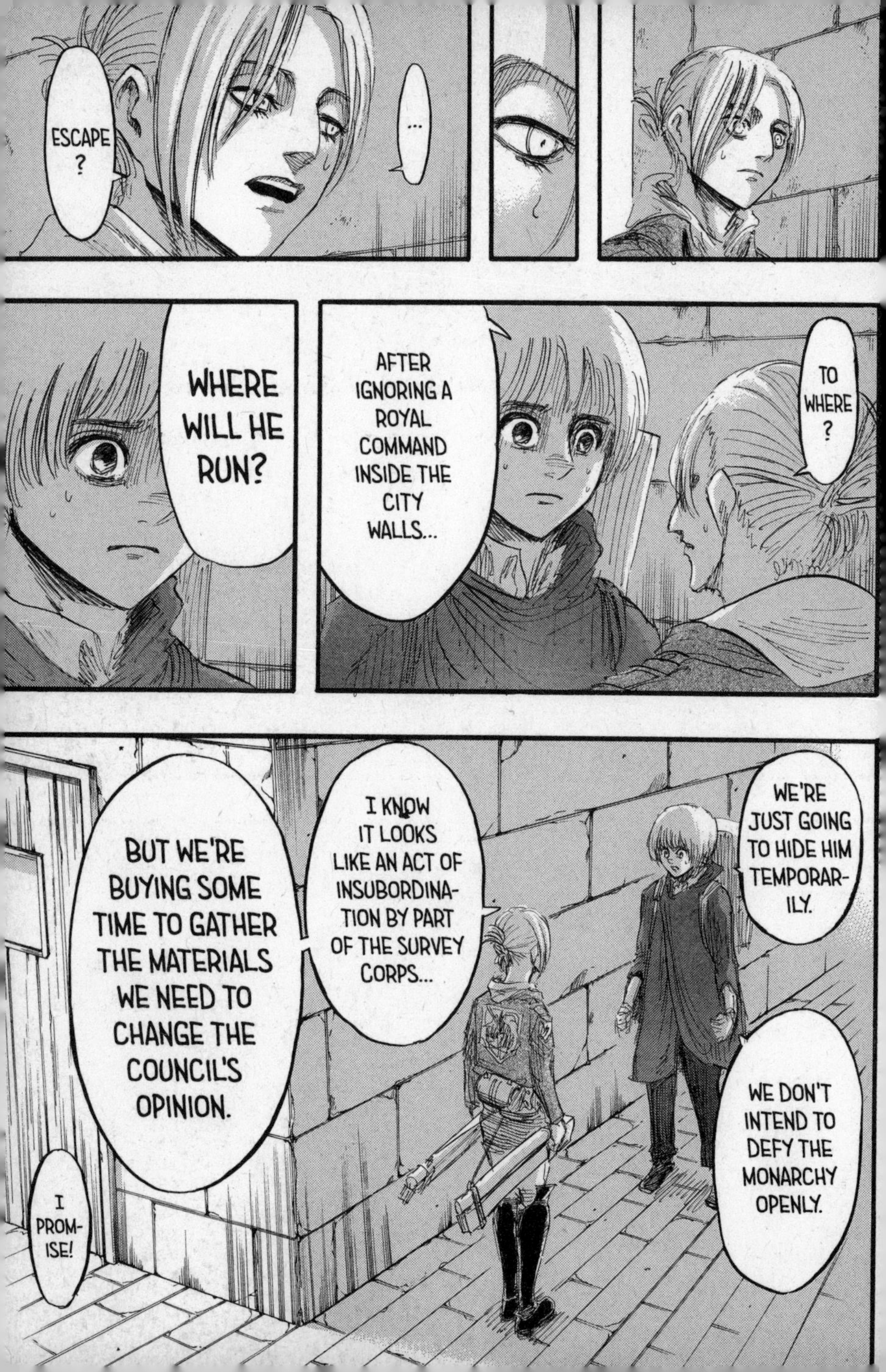
...
ESCAPE ?
TO WHERE ?
AFTER IGNORING A ROYAL COMMAND INSIDE THE CITY WALLS...
WHERE WILL HE RUN?
WE'RE JUST GOING TO HIDE HIM TEMPORAR-ILY.
WE DON'T INTEND TO DEFY THE MONARCHY OPENLY.
I KNOW IT LOOKS LIKE AN ACT OF INSUBORDINA-TION BY PART OF THE SURVEY CORPS...
BUT WE'RE BUYING SOME TIME TO GATHER THE MATERIALS WE NEED TO CHANGE THE COUNCIL'S OPINION.
I PROM-ISE!

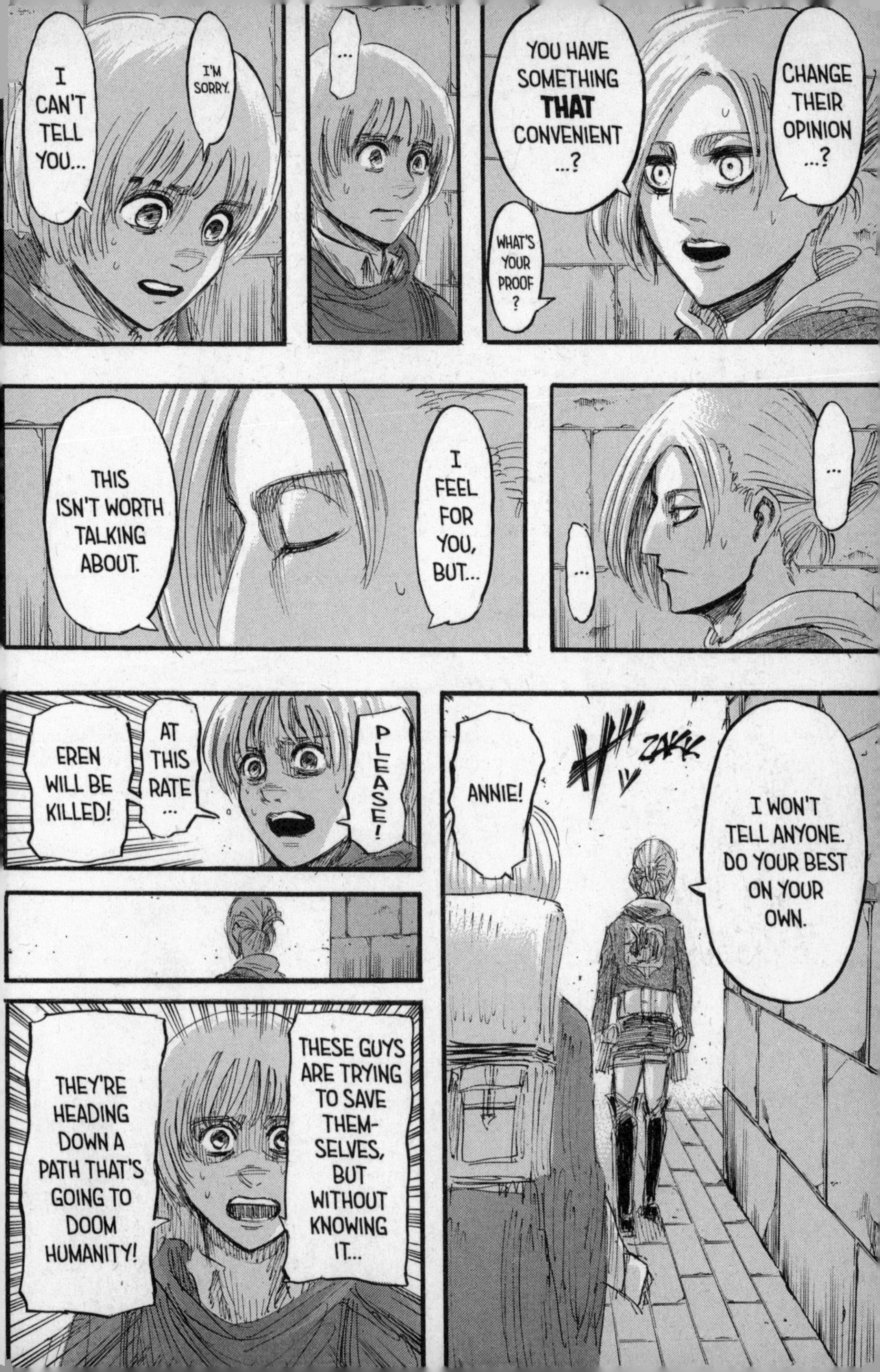
CHANGE THEIR OPINION ...?
YOU HAVE SOMETHING **THAT** CONVENIENT ...?
WHAT'S YOUR PROOF ?
...
I'M SORRY.
I CAN'T TELL YOU...
...
...
I FEEL FOR YOU, BUT...
THIS ISN'T WORTH TALKING ABOUT.
I WON'T TELL ANYONE. DO YOUR BEST ON YOUR OWN.
ZAKK
ANNIE!
PLEASE!
AT THIS RATE ...
EREN WILL BE KILLED!
THESE GUYS ARE TRYING TO SAVE THEM-SELVES, BUT WITHOUT KNOWING IT...
THEY'RE HEADING DOWN A PATH THAT'S GOING TO DOOM HUMANITY!

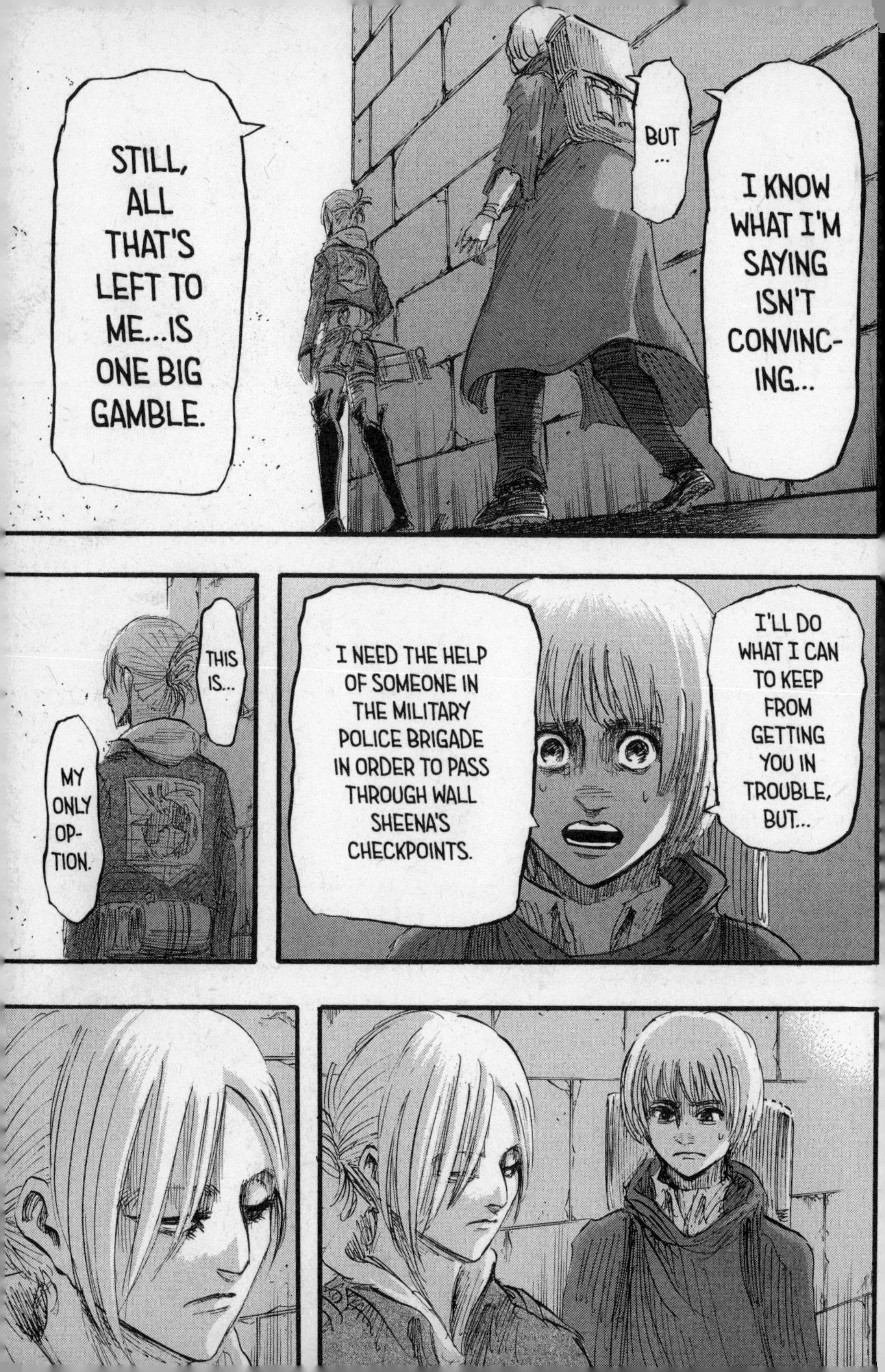
I KNOW WHAT I'M SAYING ISN'T CONVINCING...
BUT...
STILL, ALL THAT'S LEFT TO ME...IS ONE BIG GAMBLE.
I'LL DO WHAT I CAN TO KEEP FROM GETTING YOU IN TROUBLE, BUT...
I NEED THE HELP OF SOMEONE IN THE MILITARY POLICE BRIGADE IN ORDER TO PASS THROUGH WALL SHEENA'S CHECKPOINTS.
THIS IS...
MY ONLY OPTION.

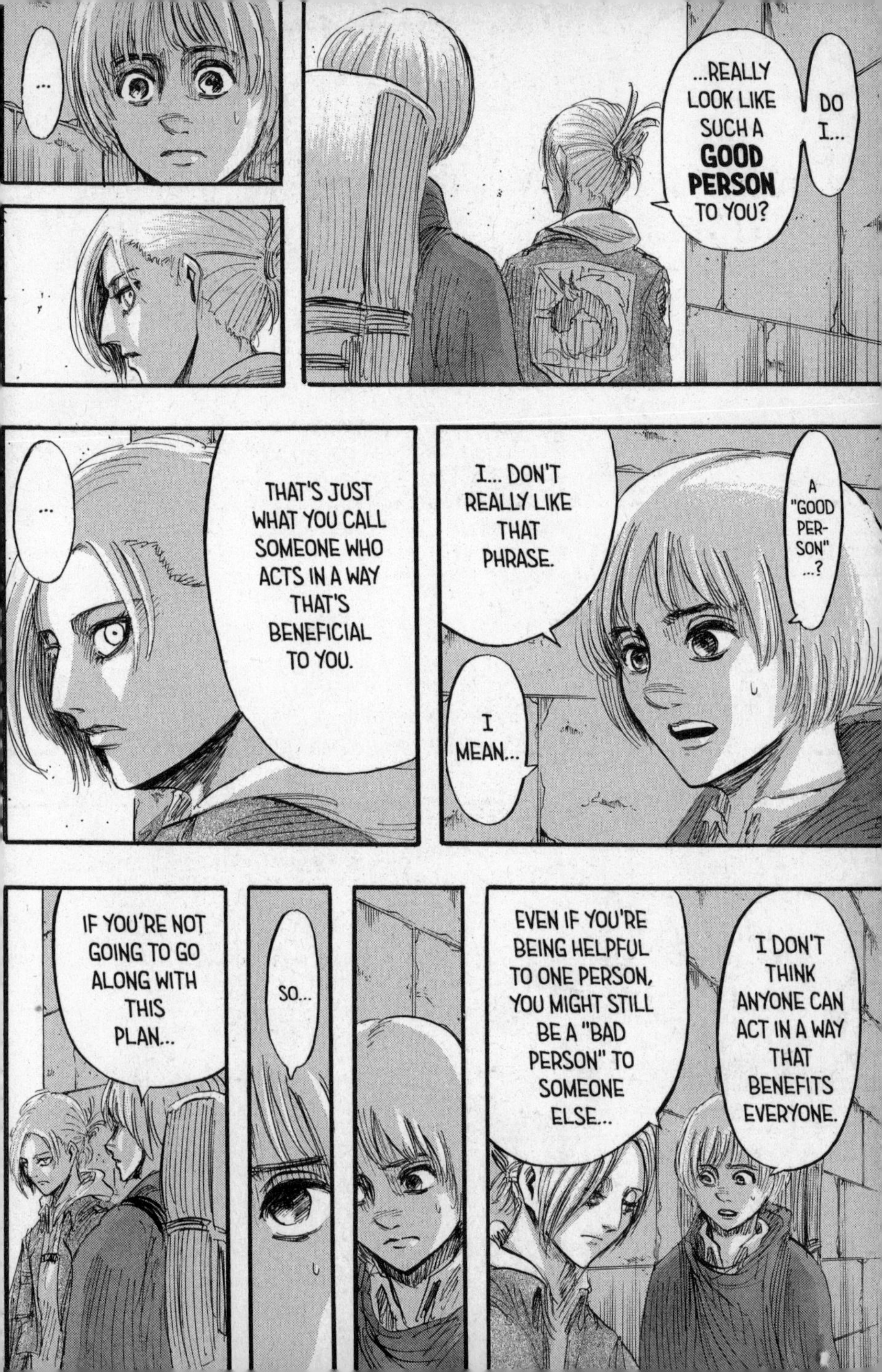

DO I...
...REALLY LOOK LIKE SUCH A **GOOD PERSON** TO YOU?
...
A "GOOD PER-SON" ...?
I... DON'T REALLY LIKE THAT PHRASE.
I MEAN...
THAT'S JUST WHAT YOU CALL SOMEONE WHO ACTS IN A WAY THAT'S BENEFICIAL TO YOU.
...
I DON'T THINK ANYONE CAN ACT IN A WAY THAT BENEFITS EVERYONE.
EVEN IF YOU'RE BEING HELPFUL TO ONE PERSON, YOU MIGHT STILL BE A "BAD PERSON" TO SOMEONE ELSE...
SO...
IF YOU'RE NOT GOING TO GO ALONG WITH THIS PLAN...

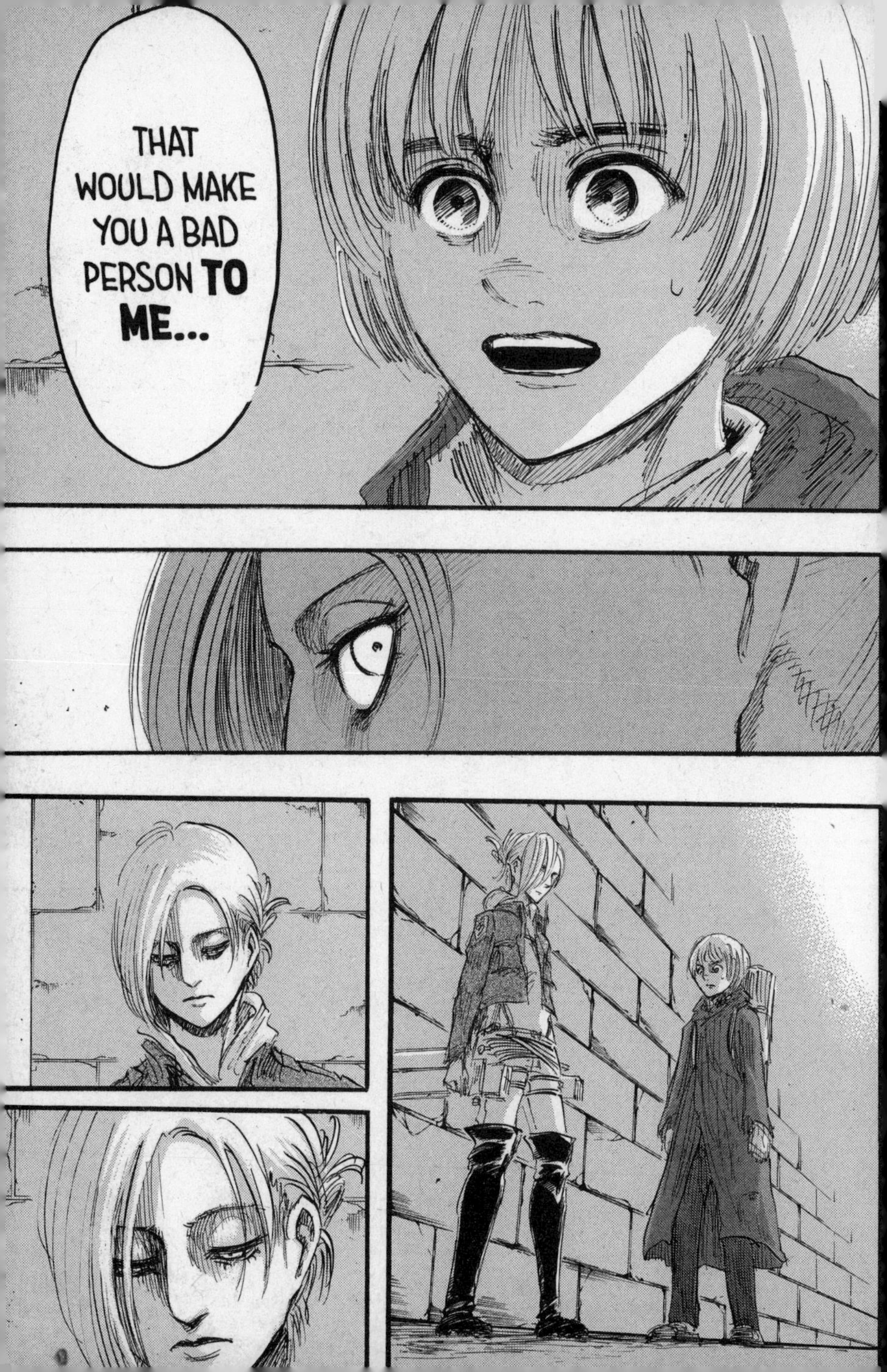
THAT WOULD MAKE YOU A BAD PERSON TO ME...

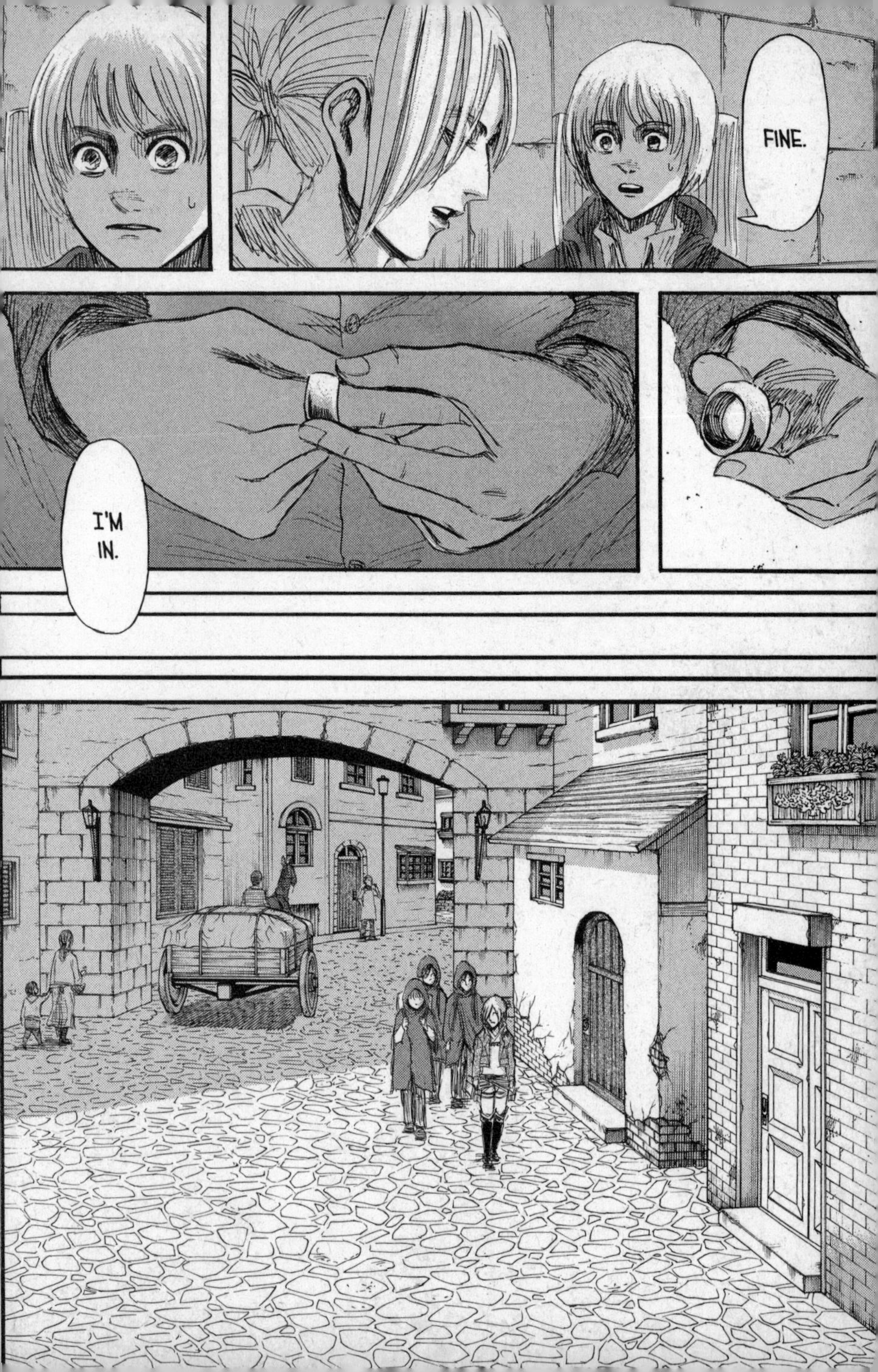
FINE.
I'M IN.

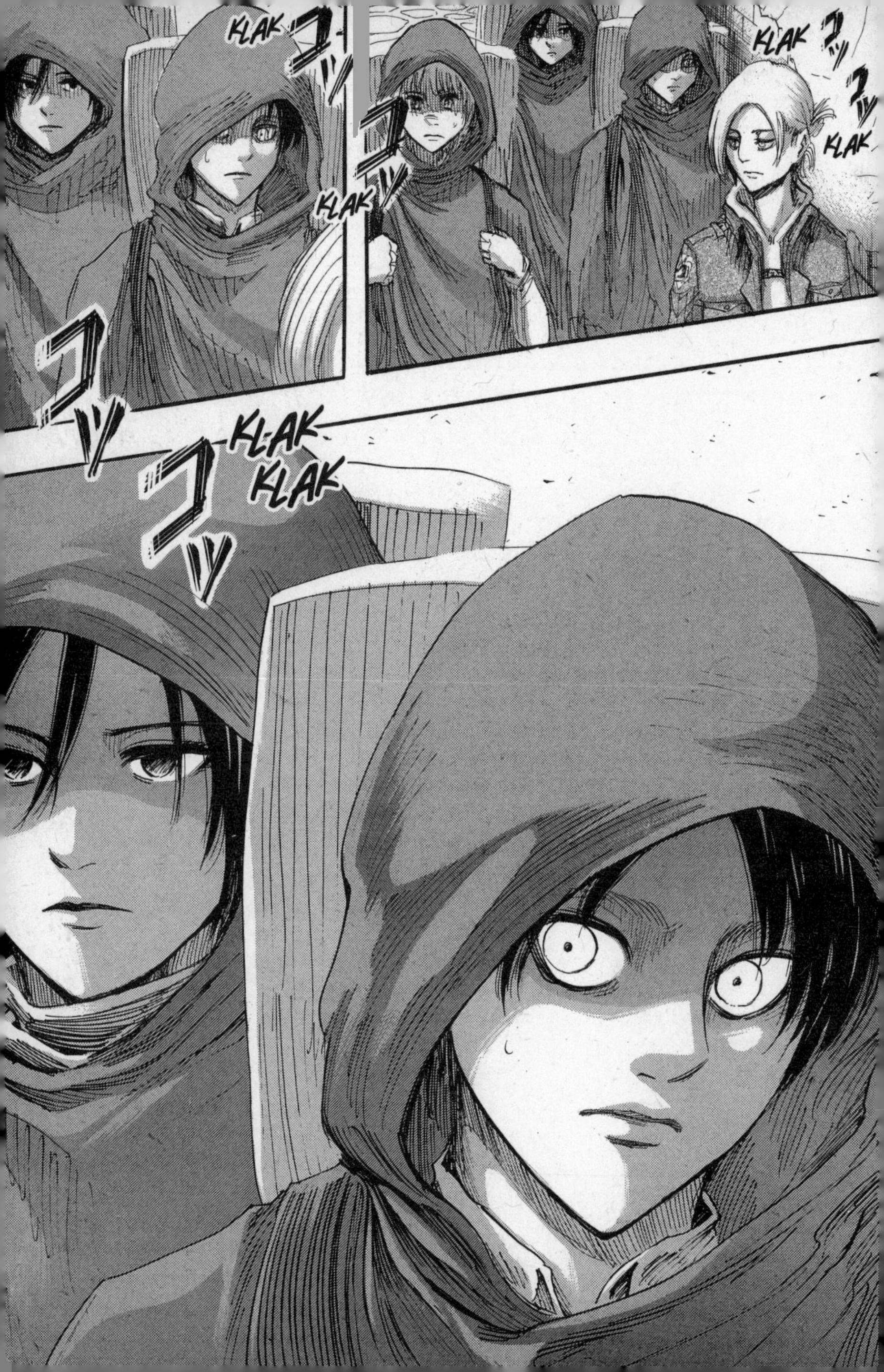
KLAK
KLAK
KLAK
KLAK
KL-AK
KLAK

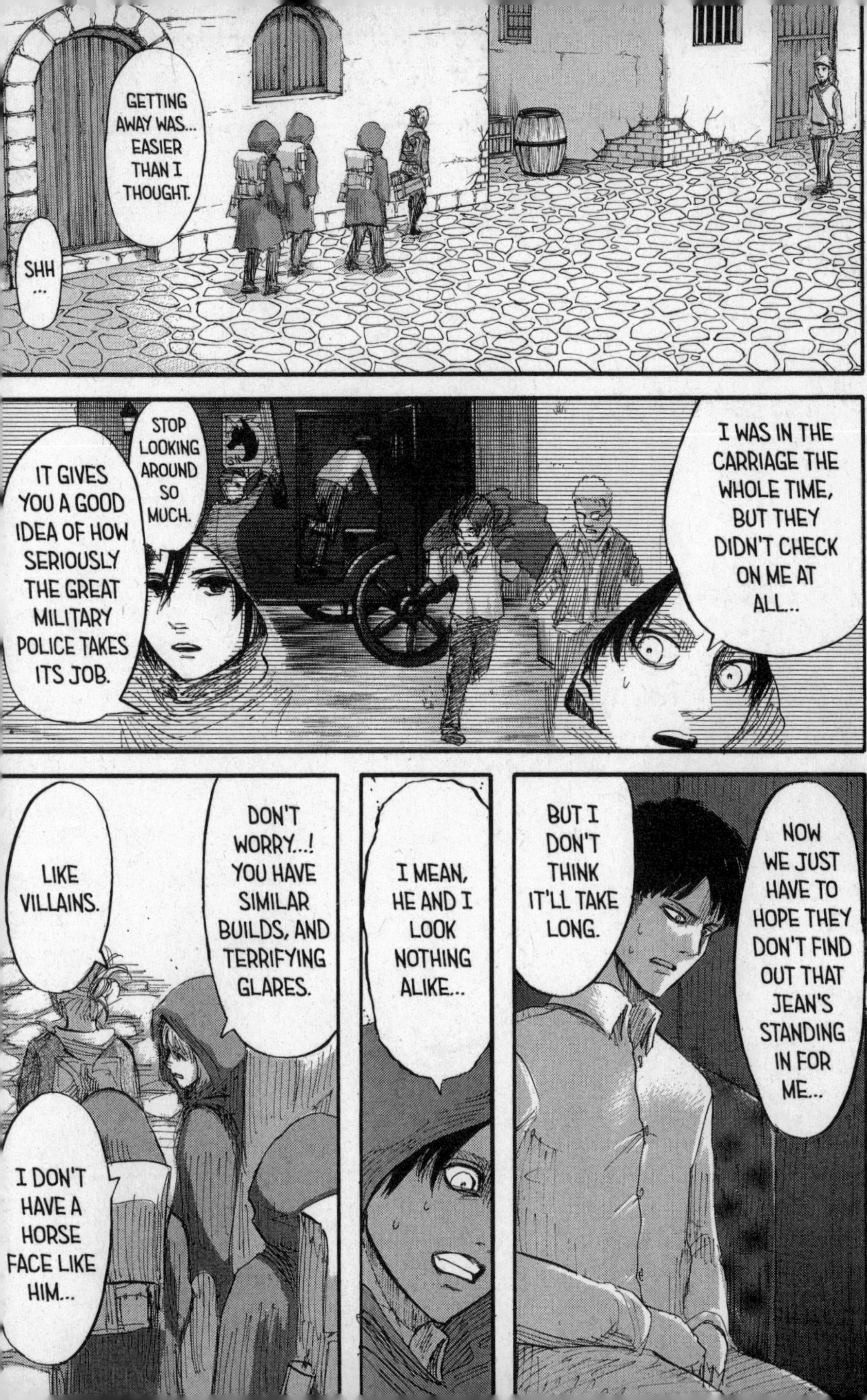
GETTING AWAY WAS... EASIER THAN I THOUGHT.
SHH ...
I WAS IN THE CARRIAGE THE WHOLE TIME, BUT THEY DIDN'T CHECK ON ME AT ALL...
STOP LOOKING AROUND SO MUCH.
IT GIVES YOU A GOOD IDEA OF HOW SERIOUSLY THE GREAT MILITARY POLICE TAKES ITS JOB.
NOW WE JUST HAVE TO HOPE THEY DON'T FIND OUT THAT JEAN'S STANDING IN FOR ME...
BUT I DON'T THINK IT'LL TAKE LONG.
I MEAN, HE AND I LOOK NOTHING ALIKE...
DON'T WORRY...! YOU HAVE SIMILAR BUILDS, AND TERRIFYING GLARES.
LIKE VILLAINS.
I DON'T HAVE A HORSE FACE LIKE HIM...

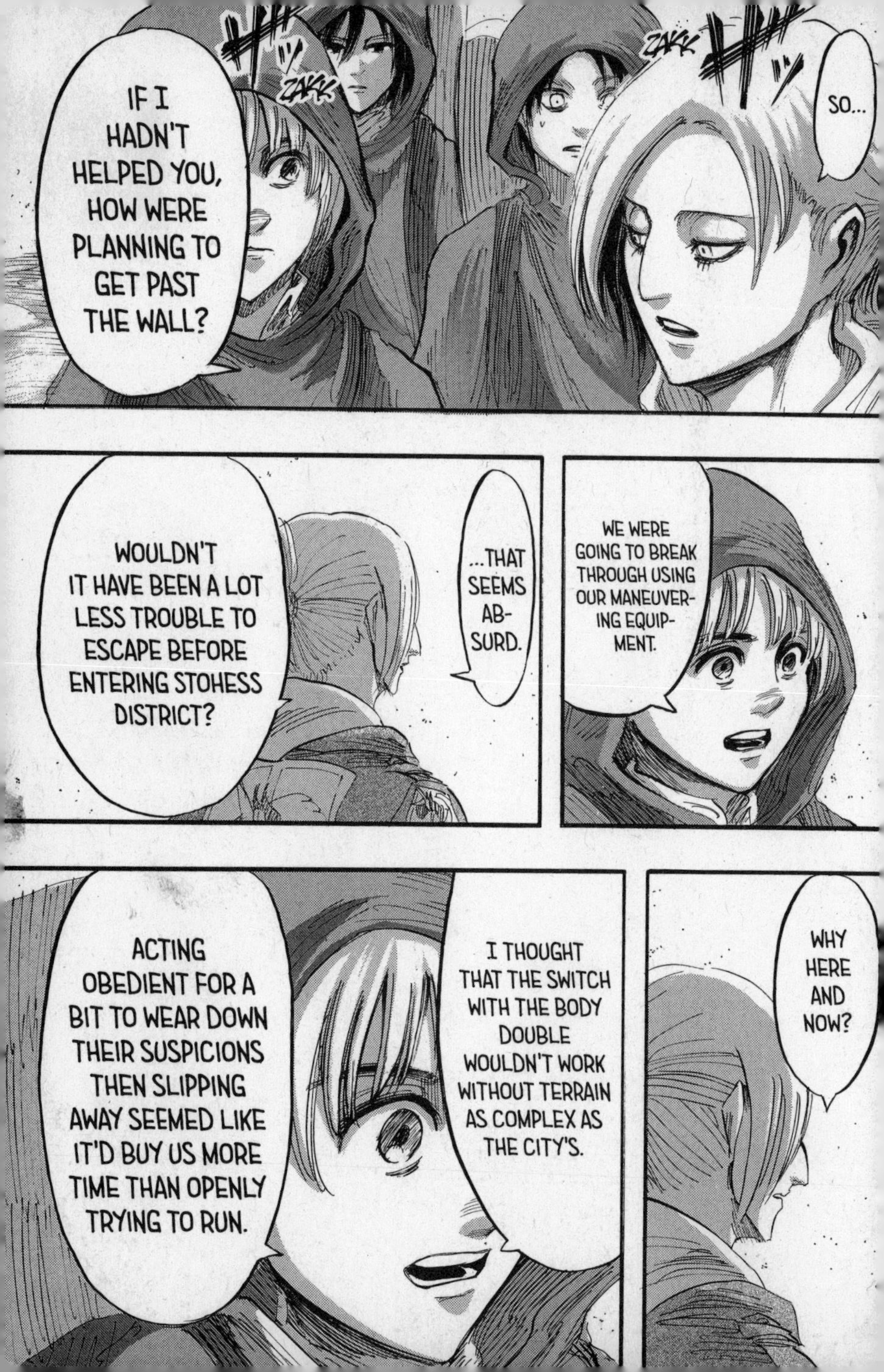
SO...
ZAKK
ZAKK
IF I HADN'T HELPED YOU, HOW WERE PLANNING TO GET PAST THE WALL?
WE WERE GOING TO BREAK THROUGH USING OUR MANEUVERING EQUIPMENT.
...THAT SEEMS ABSURD.
WOULDN'T IT HAVE BEEN A LOT LESS TROUBLE TO ESCAPE BEFORE ENTERING STOHESS DISTRICT?
WHY HERE AND NOW?
I THOUGHT THAT THE SWITCH WITH THE BODY DOUBLE WOULDN'T WORK WITHOUT TERRAIN AS COMPLEX AS THE CITY'S.
ACTING OBEDIENT FOR A BIT TO WEAR DOWN THEIR SUSPICIONS THEN SLIPPING AWAY SEEMED LIKE IT'D BUY US MORE TIME THAN OPENLY TRYING TO RUN.

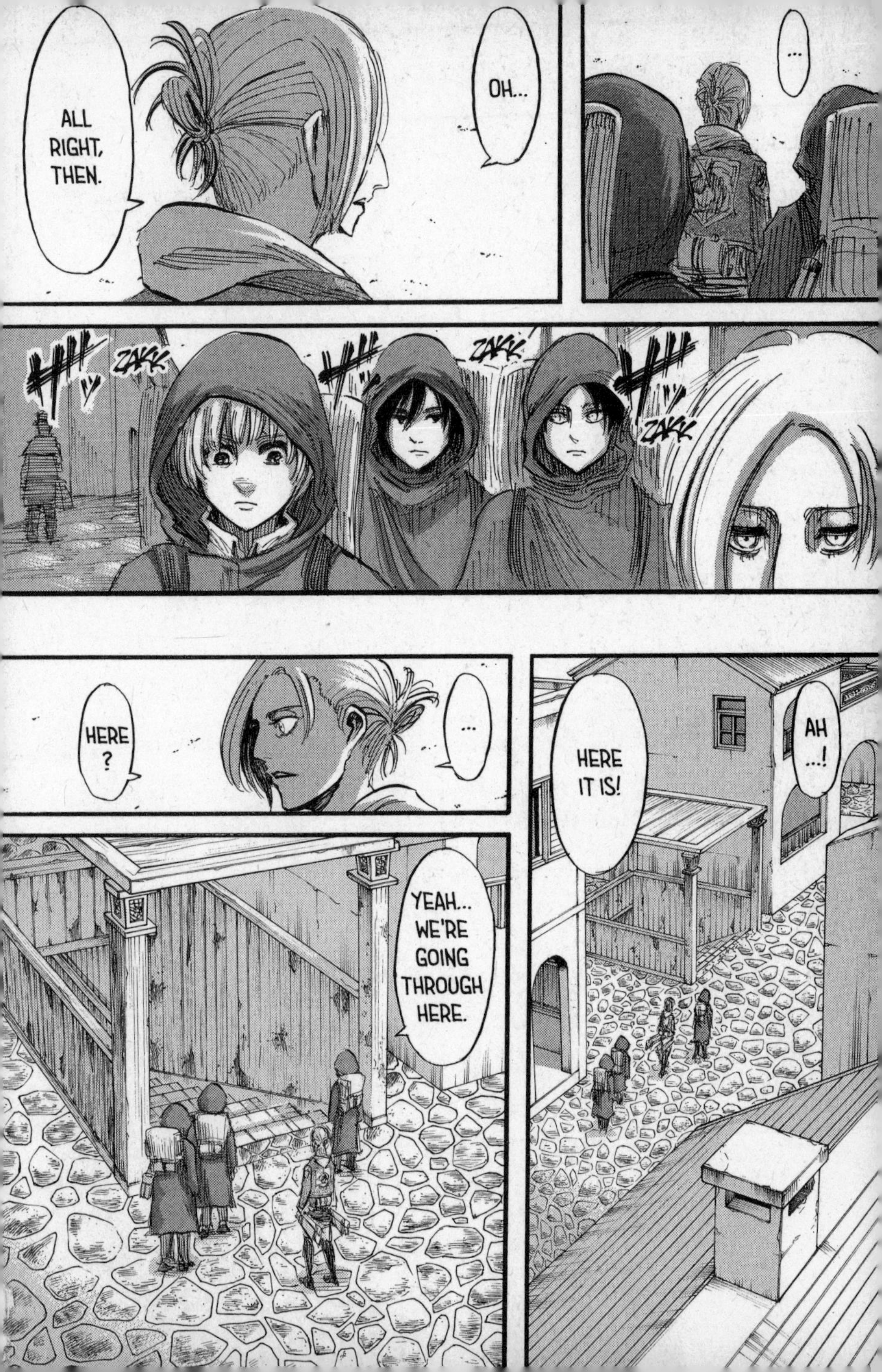
...
OH...
ALL RIGHT, THEN.
ZAKK
ZAKK
ZAKK
AH ...!
HERE IT IS!
...
HERE ?
YEAH... WE'RE GOING THROUGH HERE.

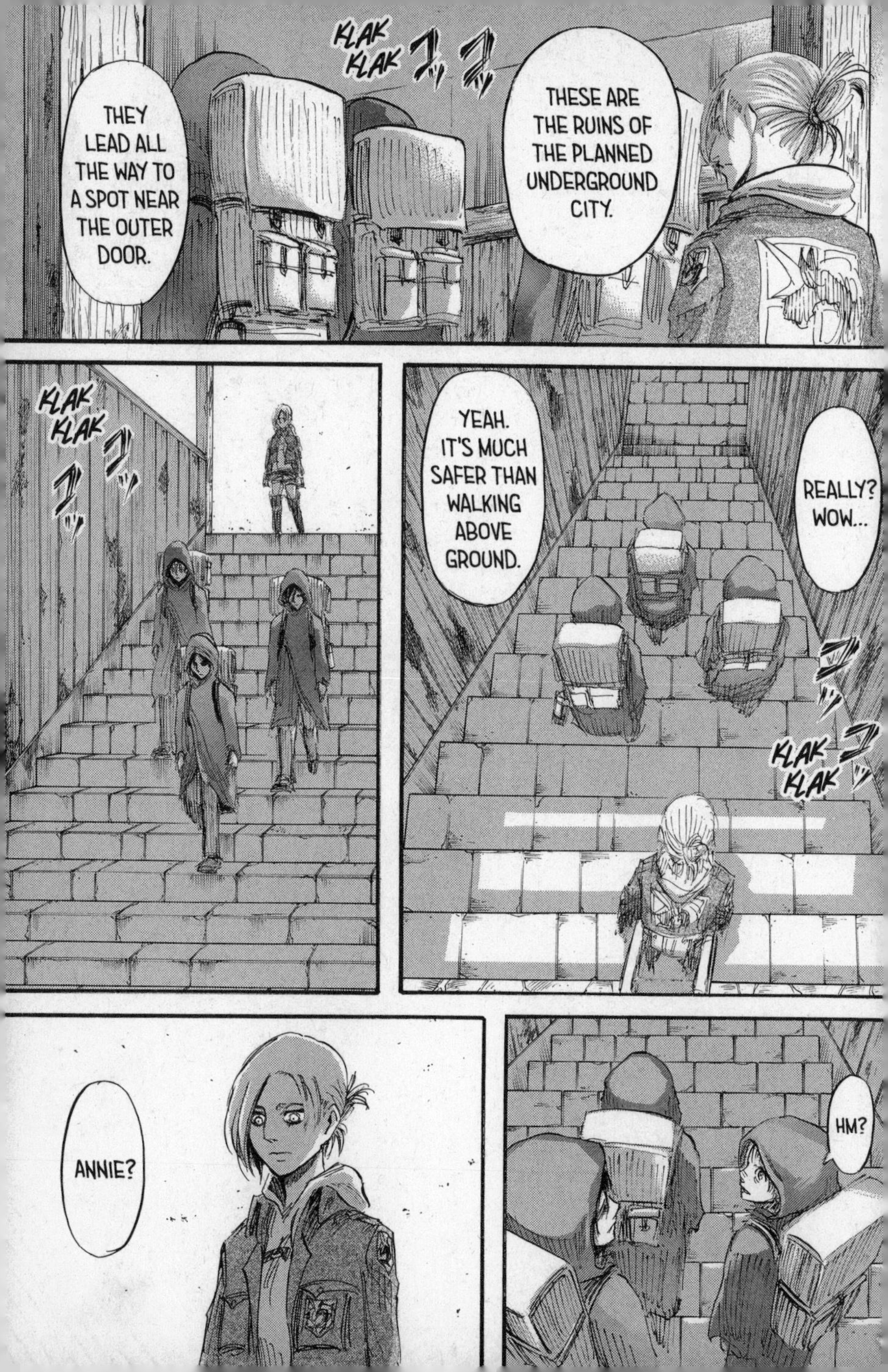
KLAK KLAK
ゴッ
THESE ARE THE RUINS OF THE PLANNED UNDERGROUND CITY.
THEY LEAD ALL THE WAY TO A SPOT NEAR THE OUTER DOOR.
REALLY? WOW...
YEAH. IT'S MUCH SAFER THAN WALKING ABOVE GROUND.
KLAK KLAK
ゴッ
KLAK KLAK
ゴッ
HM?
ANNIE?

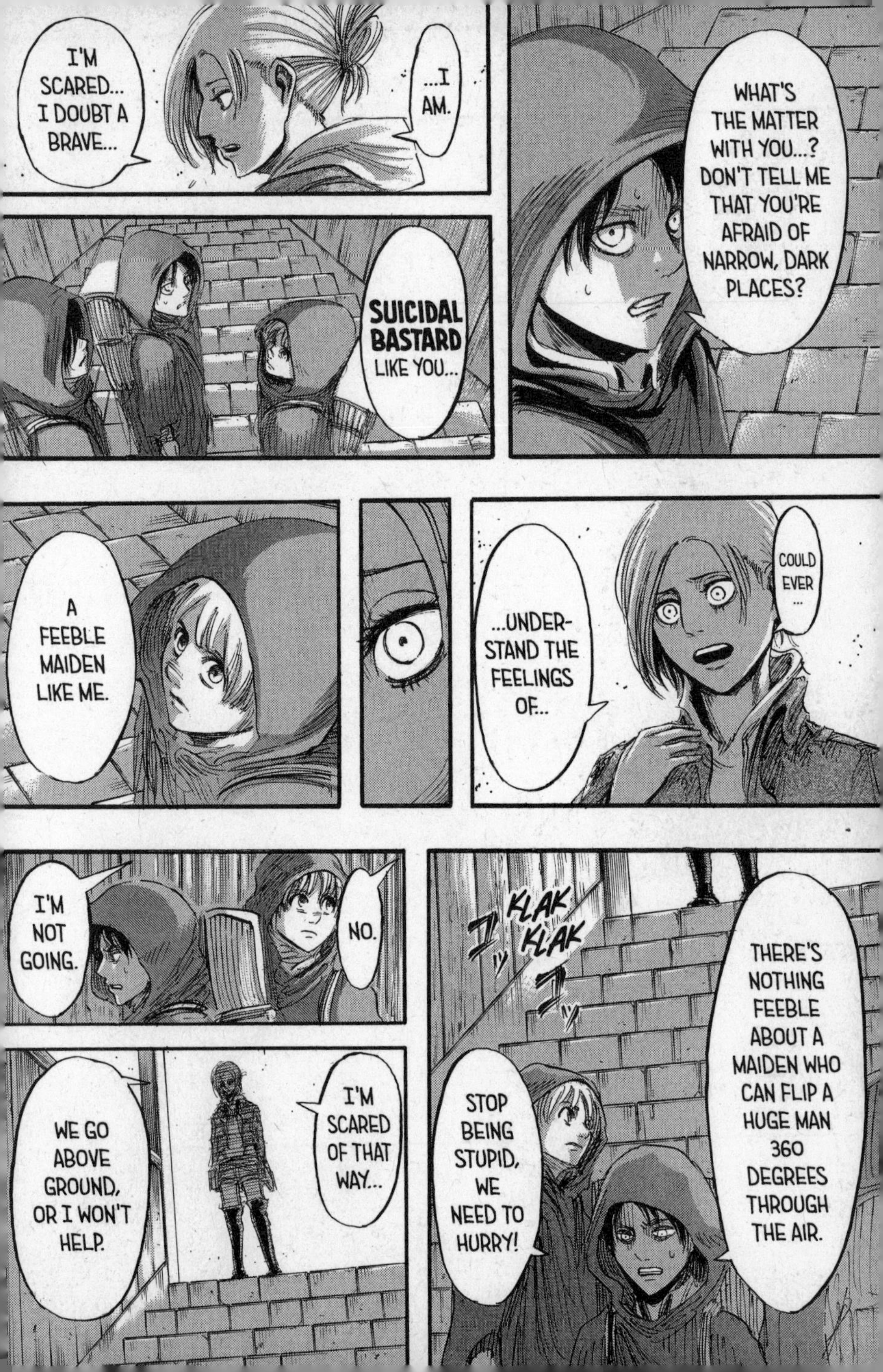
WHAT'S THE MATTER WITH YOU...? DON'T TELL ME THAT YOU'RE AFRAID OF NARROW, DARK PLACES?
...I AM.
I'M SCARED... I DOUBT A BRAVE...
SUICIDAL BASTARD LIKE YOU...
COULD EVER ...
...UNDER-STAND THE FEELINGS OF...
A FEEBLE MAIDEN LIKE ME.
THERE'S NOTHING FEEBLE ABOUT A MAIDEN WHO CAN FLIP A HUGE MAN 360 DEGREES THROUGH THE AIR.
KLAK KLAK
STOP BEING STUPID, WE NEED TO HURRY!
NO.
I'M NOT GOING.
I'M SCARED OF THAT WAY...
WE GO ABOVE GROUND, OR I WON'T HELP.

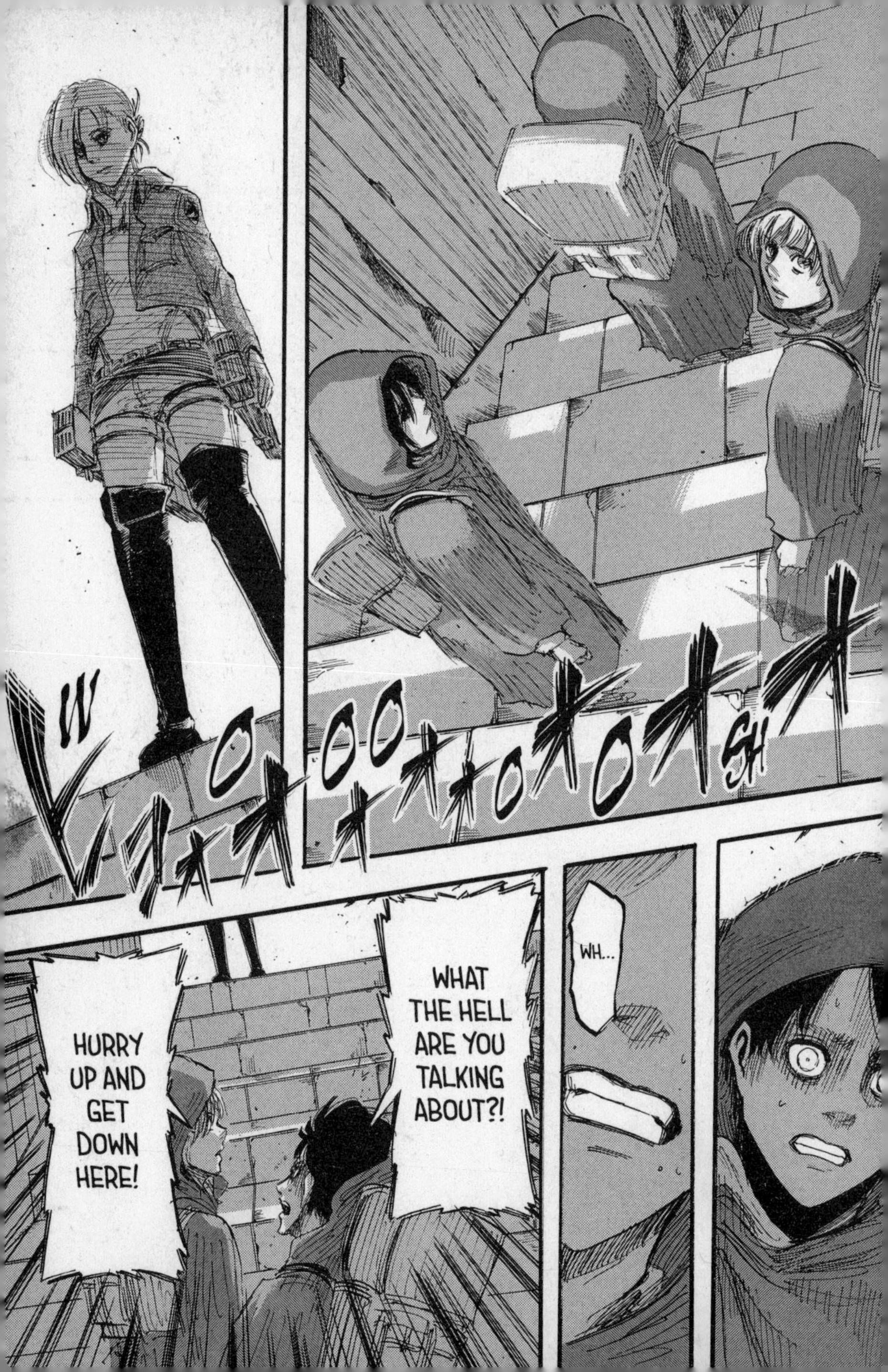
WOOOOOSH
WH...
WHAT THE HELL ARE YOU TALKING ABOUT?!
HURRY UP AND GET DOWN HERE!

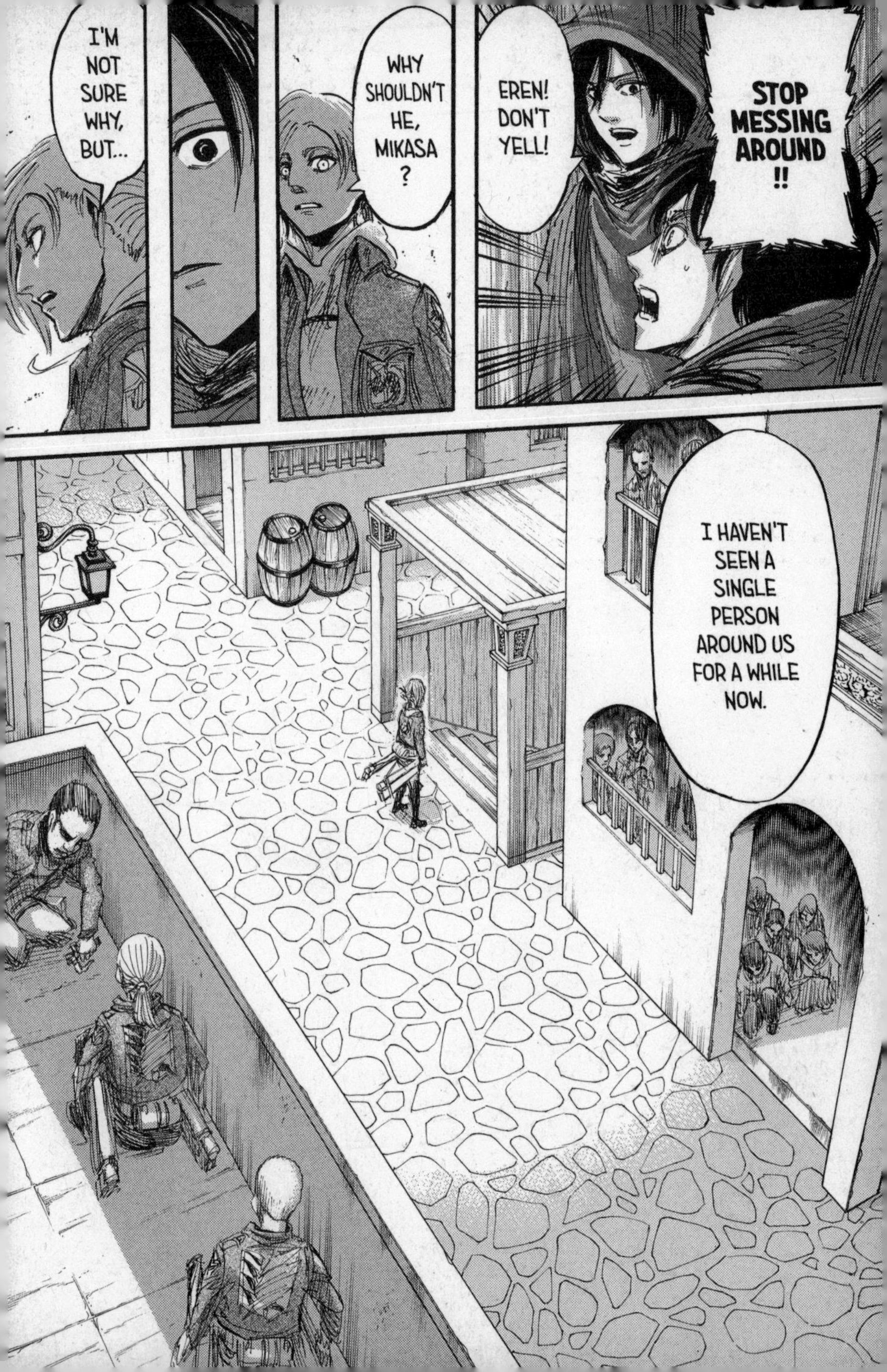
STOP MESSING AROUND !!
EREN! DON'T YELL!
WHY SHOULDN'T HE, MIKASA ?
I'M NOT SURE WHY, BUT...
I HAVEN'T SEEN A SINGLE PERSON AROUND US FOR A WHILE NOW.

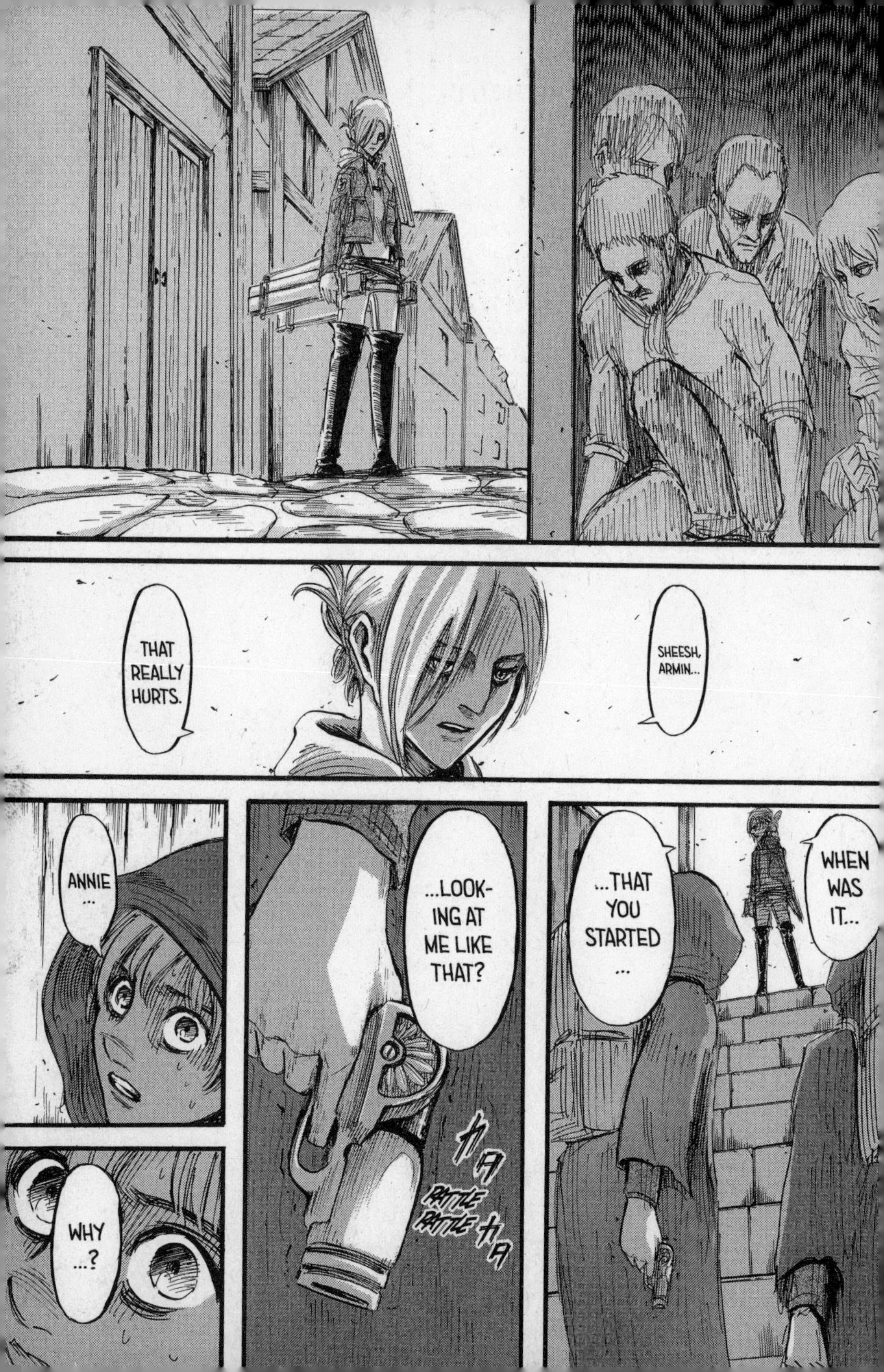
SHEESH, ARMIN...
THAT REALLY HURTS.
WHEN WAS IT...
...THAT YOU STARTED ...
...LOOK-ING AT ME LIKE THAT?
カタ カタ
RATTLE RATTLE
ANNIE ...
WHY ...?

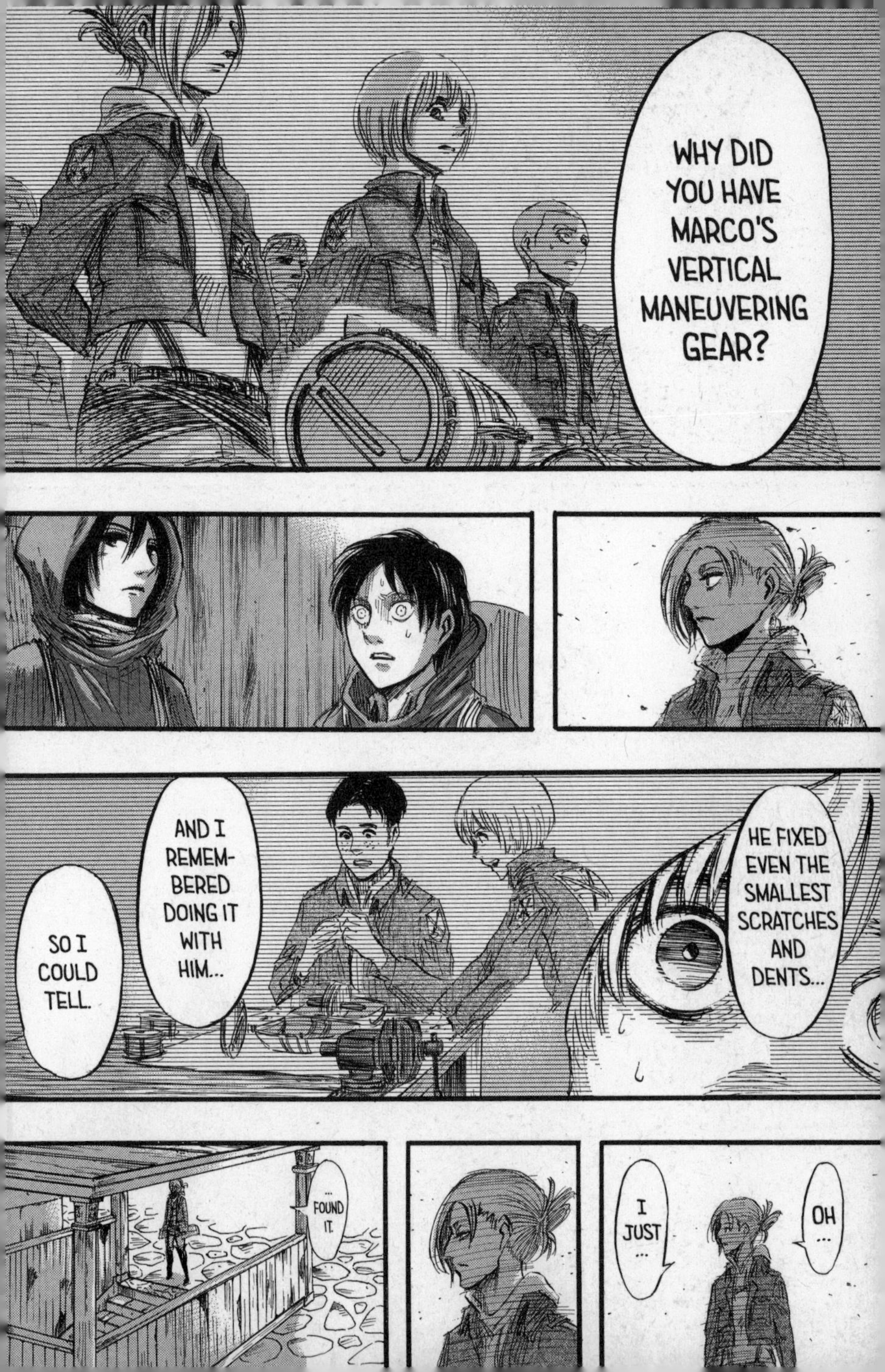
WHY DID YOU HAVE MARCO'S VERTICAL MANEUVERING GEAR?
HE FIXED EVEN THE SMALLEST SCRATCHES AND DENTS...
AND I REMEMBERED DOING IT WITH HIM...
SO I COULD TELL.
OH ...
I JUST ...
...FOUND IT.

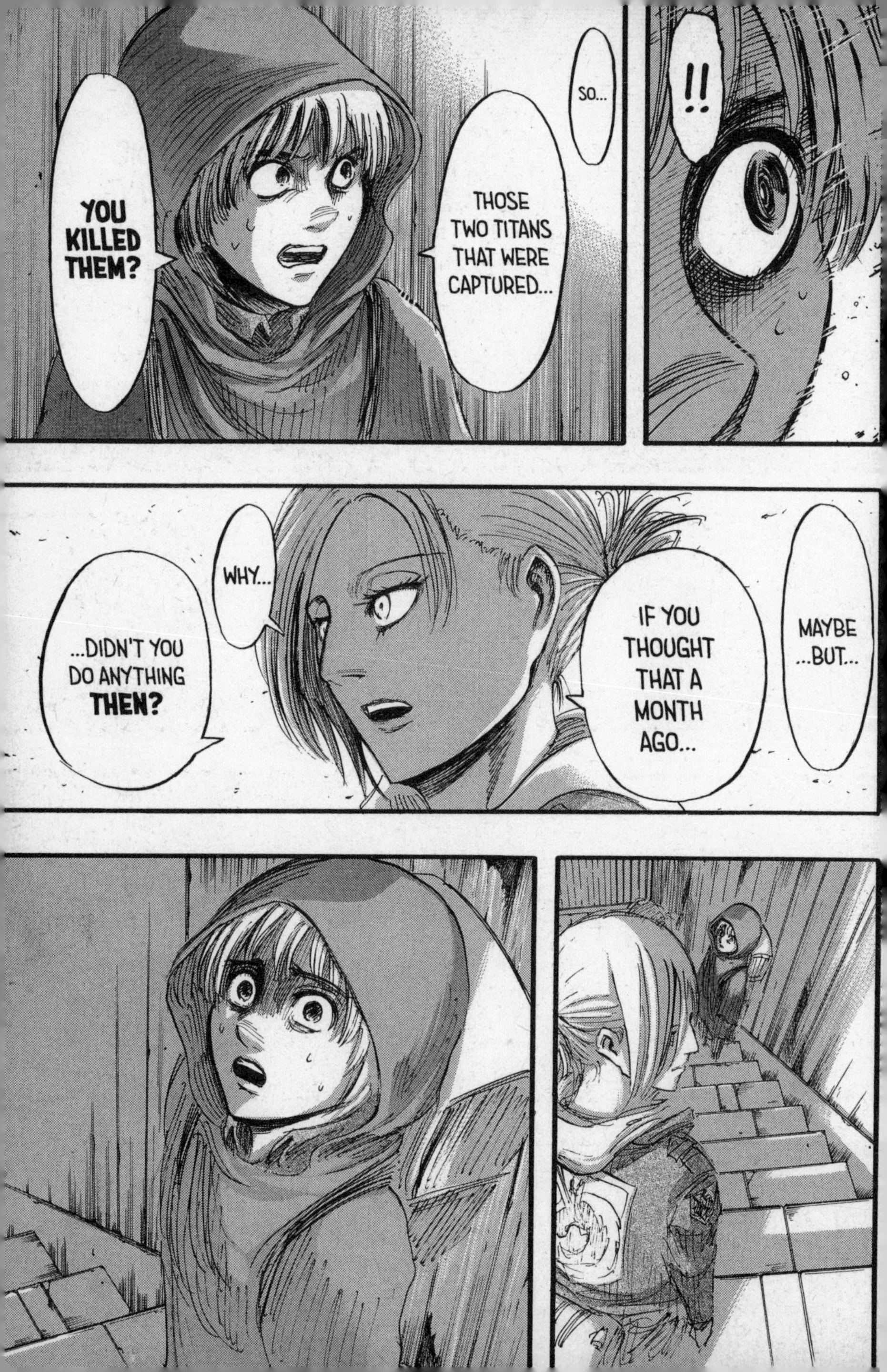
!!
SO...
THOSE TWO TITANS THAT WERE CAPTURED...
YOU KILLED THEM?
MAYBE ...BUT...
IF YOU THOUGHT THAT A MONTH AGO...
WHY...
...DIDN'T YOU DO ANYTHING THEN?

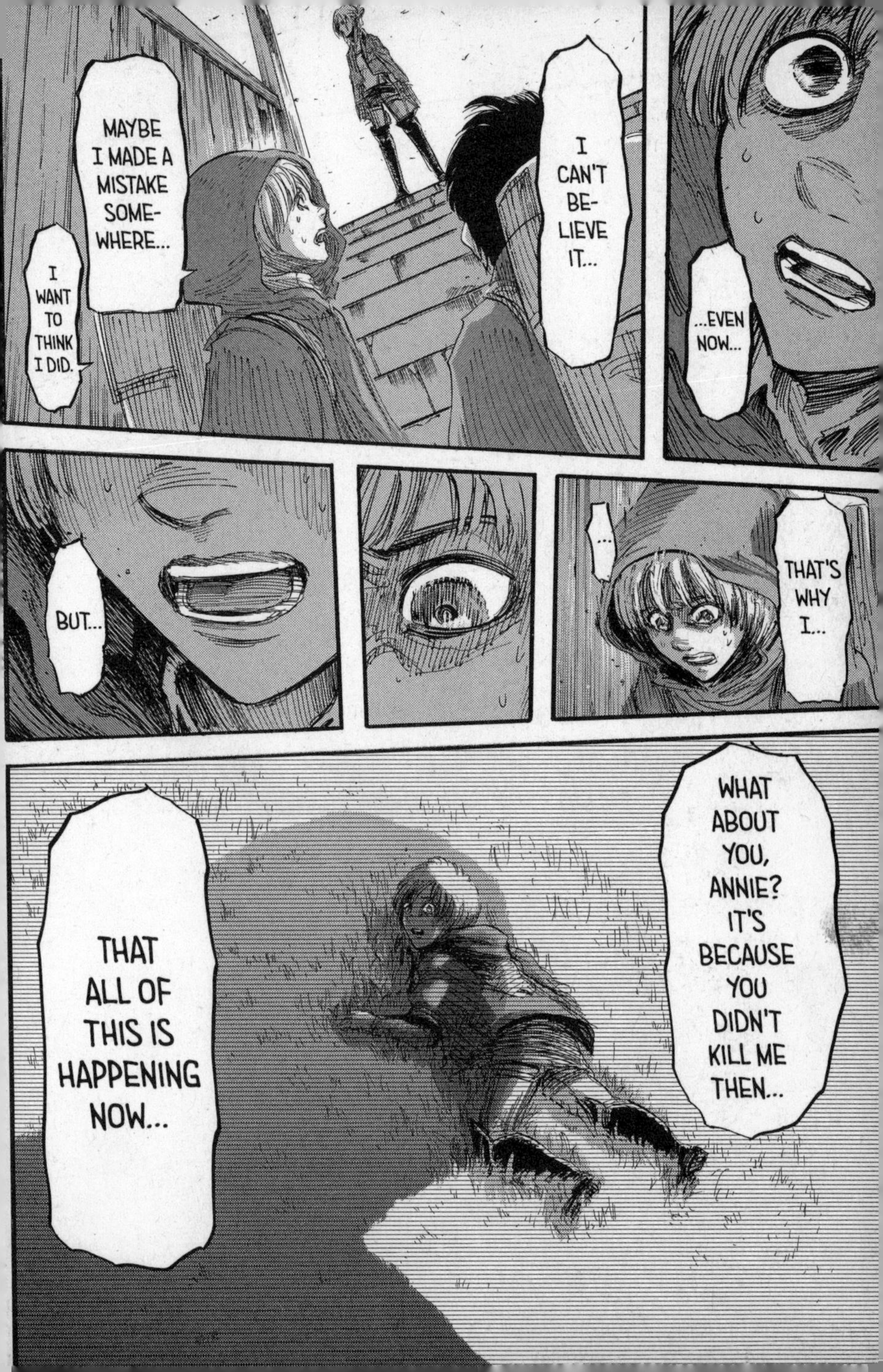
...EVEN NOW...
I CAN'T BE-LIEVE IT...
MAYBE I MADE A MISTAKE SOME-WHERE...
I WANT TO THINK I DID.
THAT'S WHY I...
...
BUT...
WHAT ABOUT YOU, ANNIE? IT'S BECAUSE YOU DIDN'T KILL ME THEN...
THAT ALL OF THIS IS HAPPENING NOW...

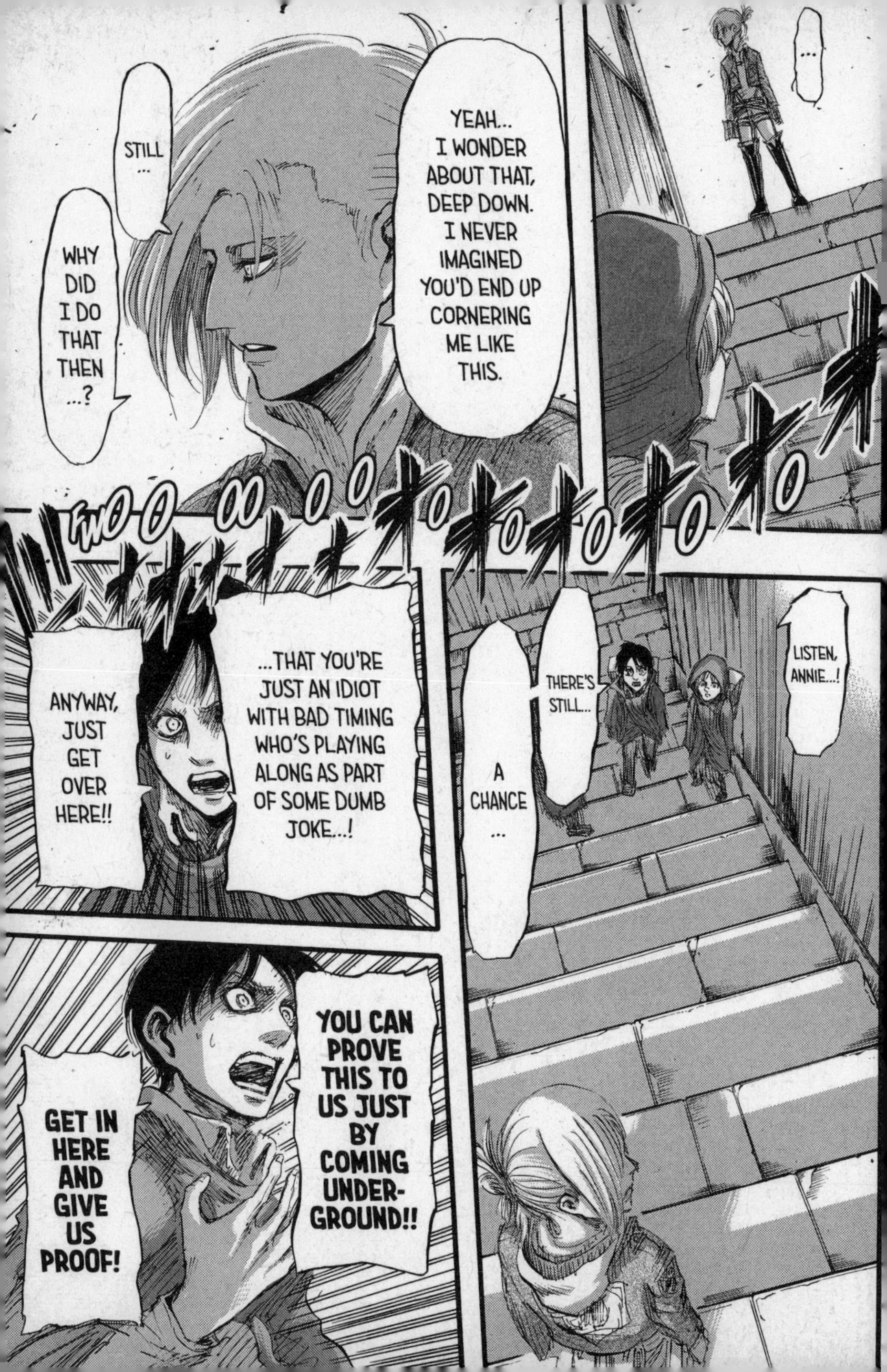
...
YEAH... I WONDER ABOUT THAT, DEEP DOWN. I NEVER IMAGINED YOU'D END UP CORNERING ME LIKE THIS.
STILL...
WHY DID I DO THAT THEN...?
FWOOOOOOOOOOOO
LISTEN, ANNIE...!
THERE'S STILL...
A CHANCE...
...THAT YOU'RE JUST AN IDIOT WITH BAD TIMING WHO'S PLAYING ALONG AS PART OF SOME DUMB JOKE...!
ANYWAY, JUST GET OVER HERE!!
YOU CAN PROVE THIS TO US JUST BY COMING UNDER-GROUND!!
GET IN HERE AND GIVE US PROOF!

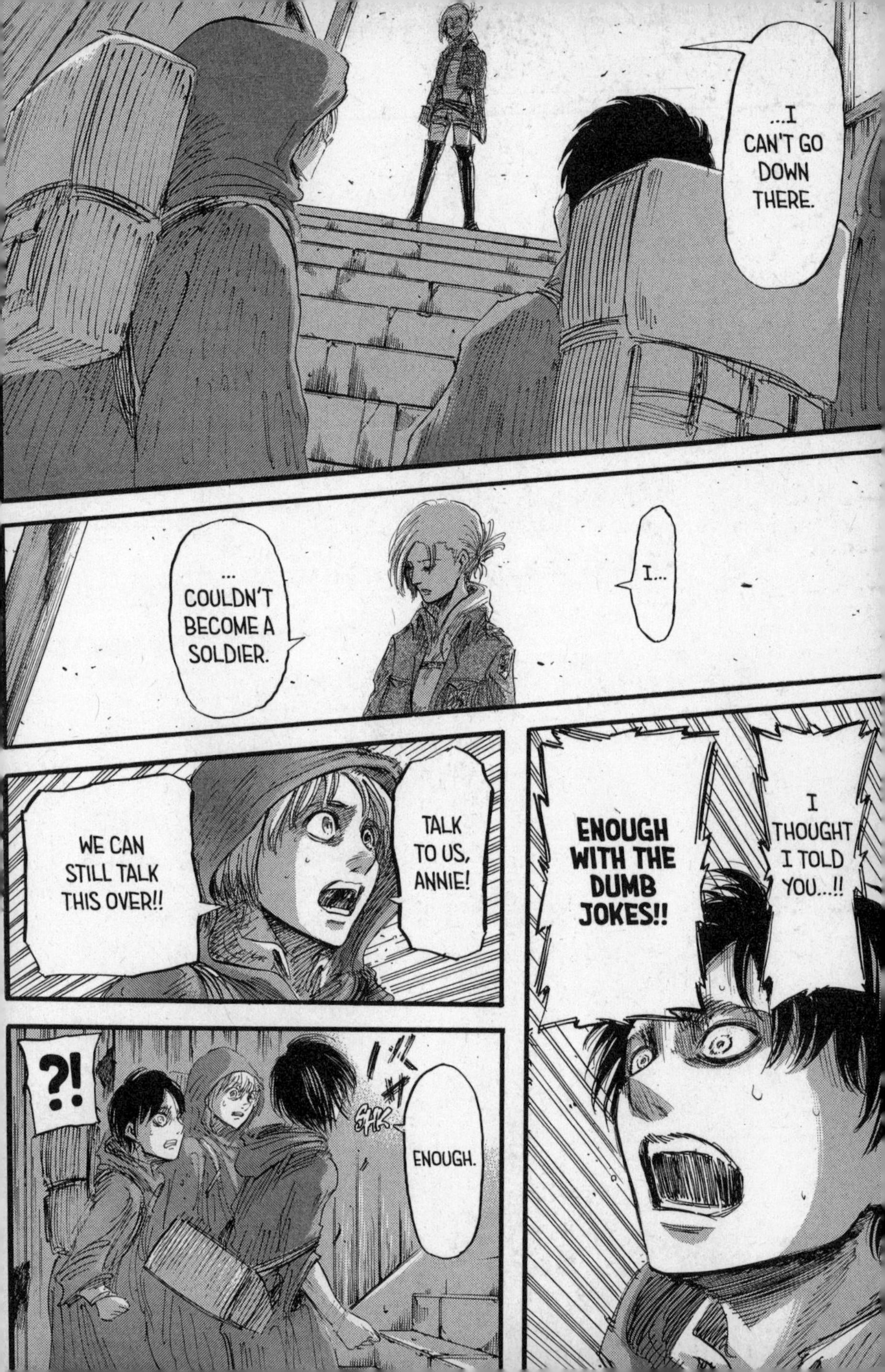
...I CAN'T GO DOWN THERE.
I...
... COULDN'T BECOME A SOLDIER.
I THOUGHT I TOLD YOU...!!
ENOUGH WITH THE DUMB JOKES!!
TALK TO US, ANNIE!
WE CAN STILL TALK THIS OVER!!
SHK
ENOUGH.
?!

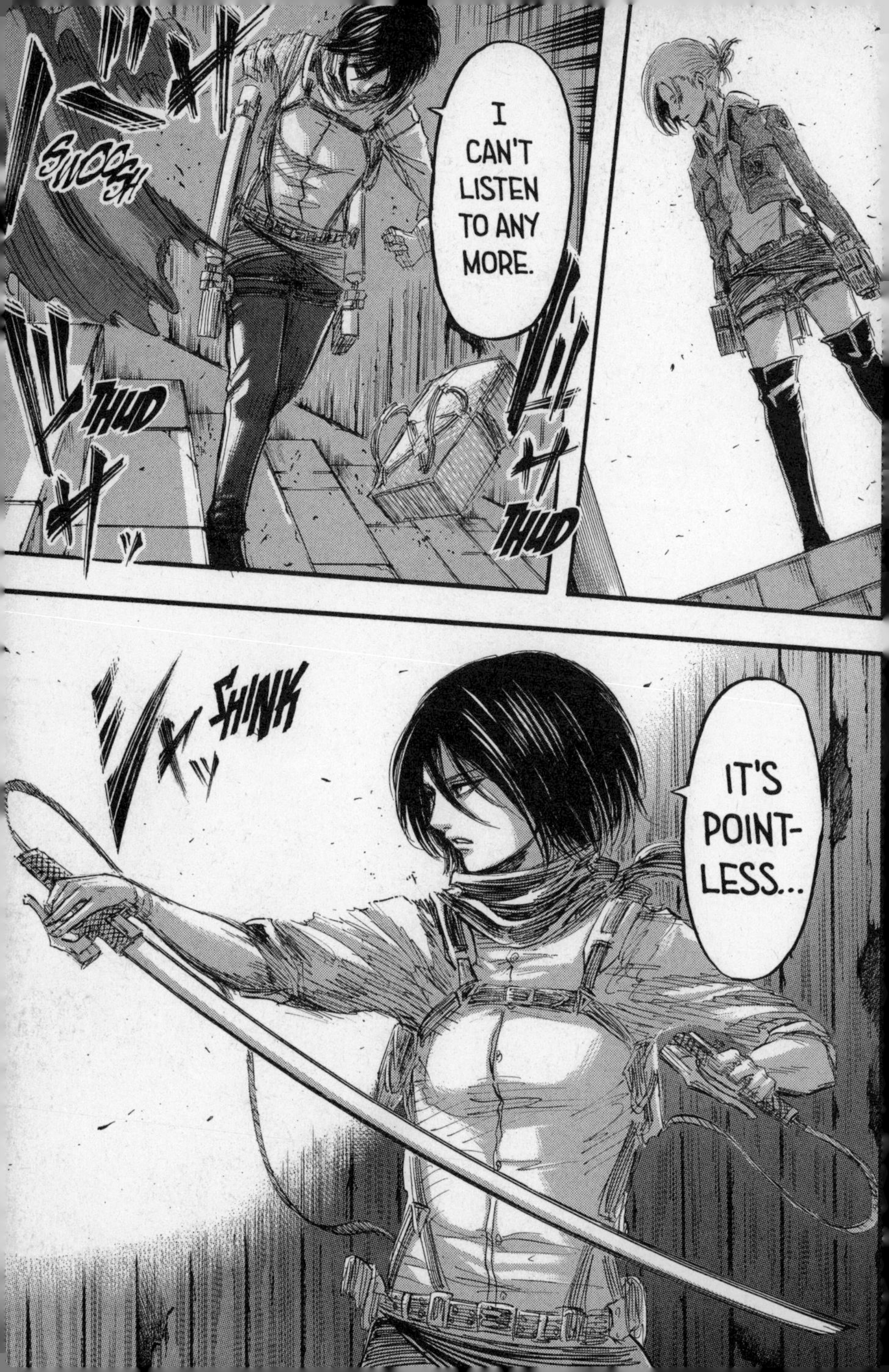
I CAN'T LISTEN TO ANY MORE.
SWOOSH
THUD
THUD
IT'S POINT-LESS...
SHINK

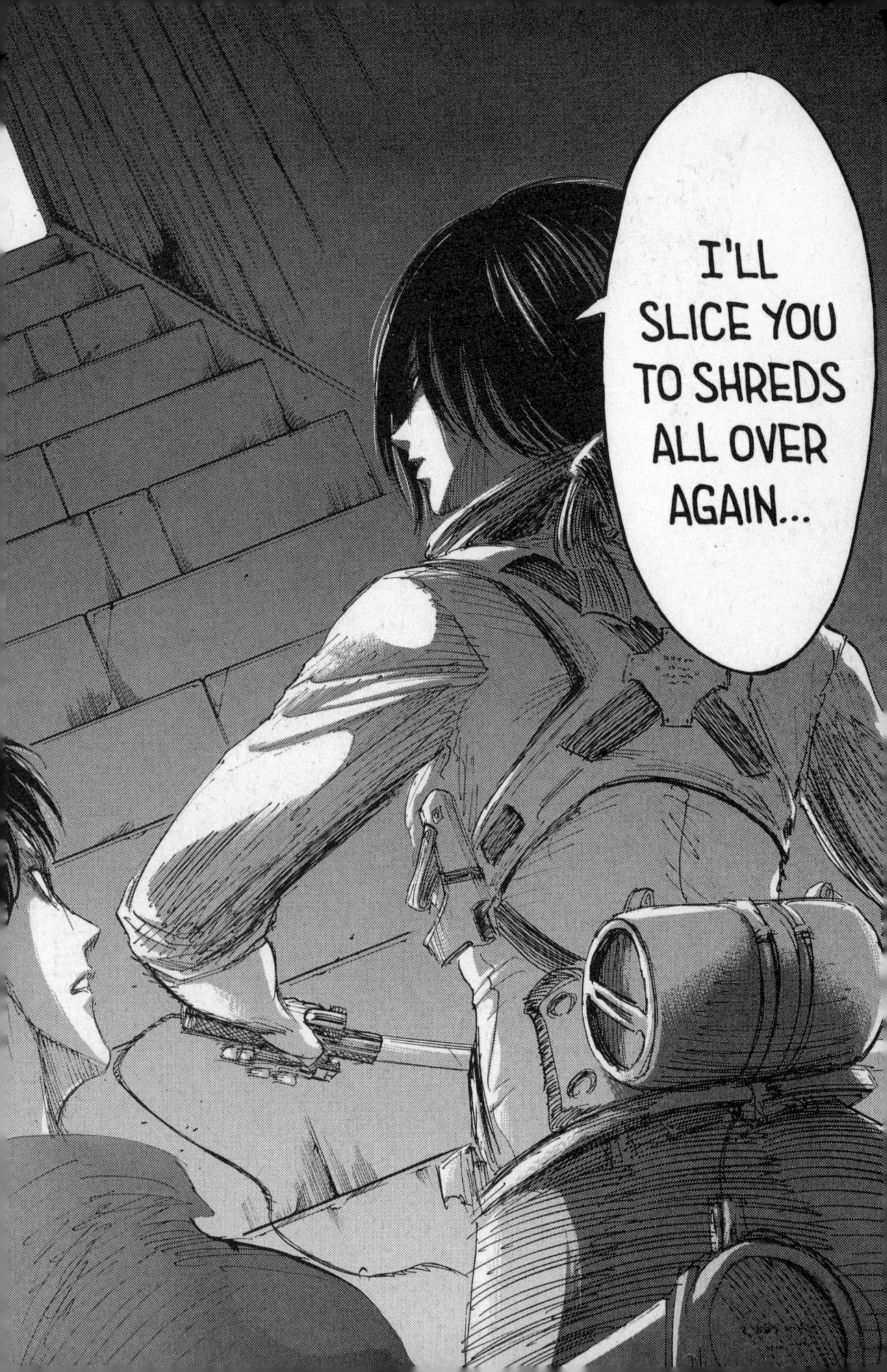
I'LL SLICE YOU TO SHREDS ALL OVER AGAIN...

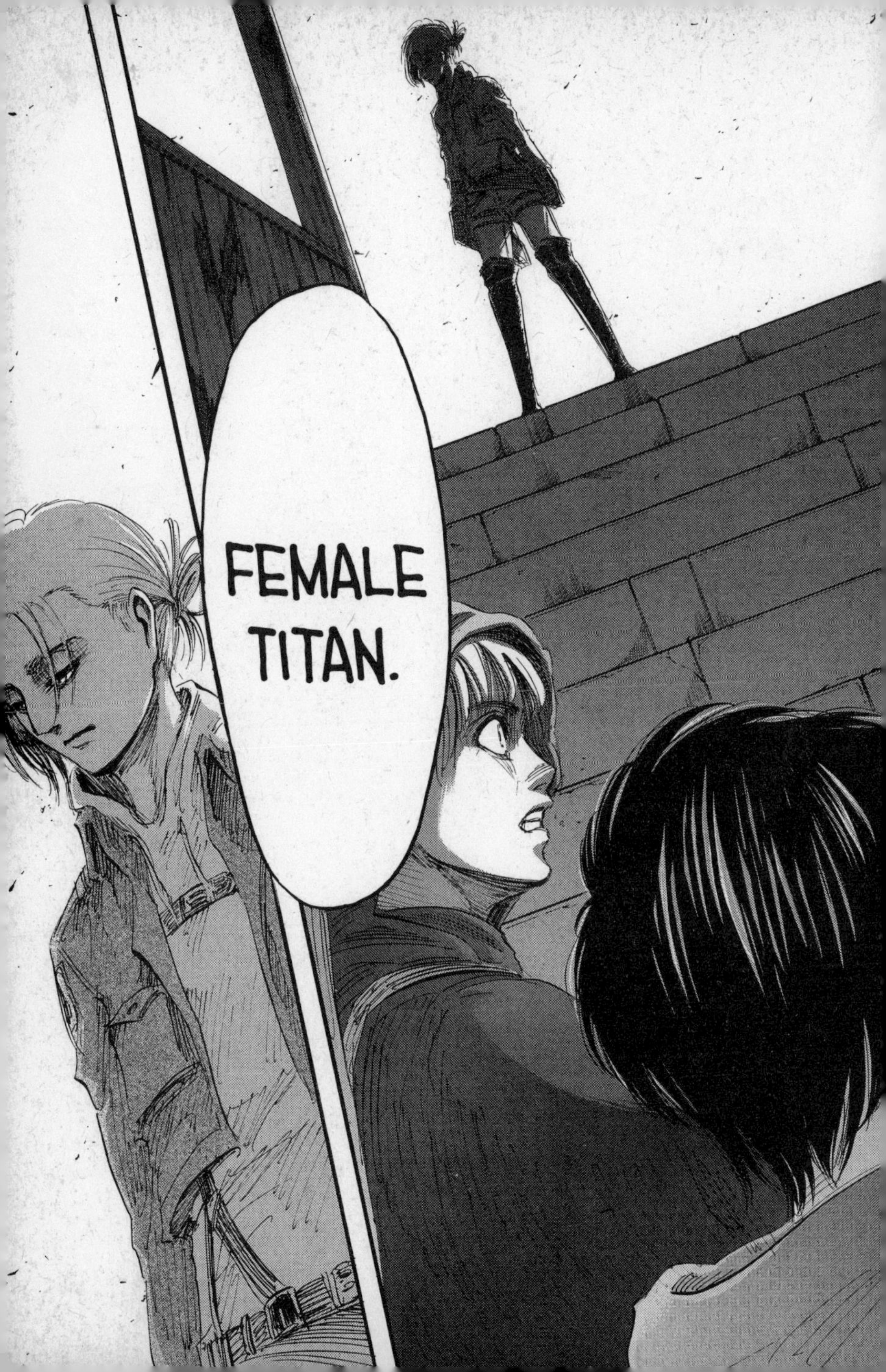
FEMALE TITAN.

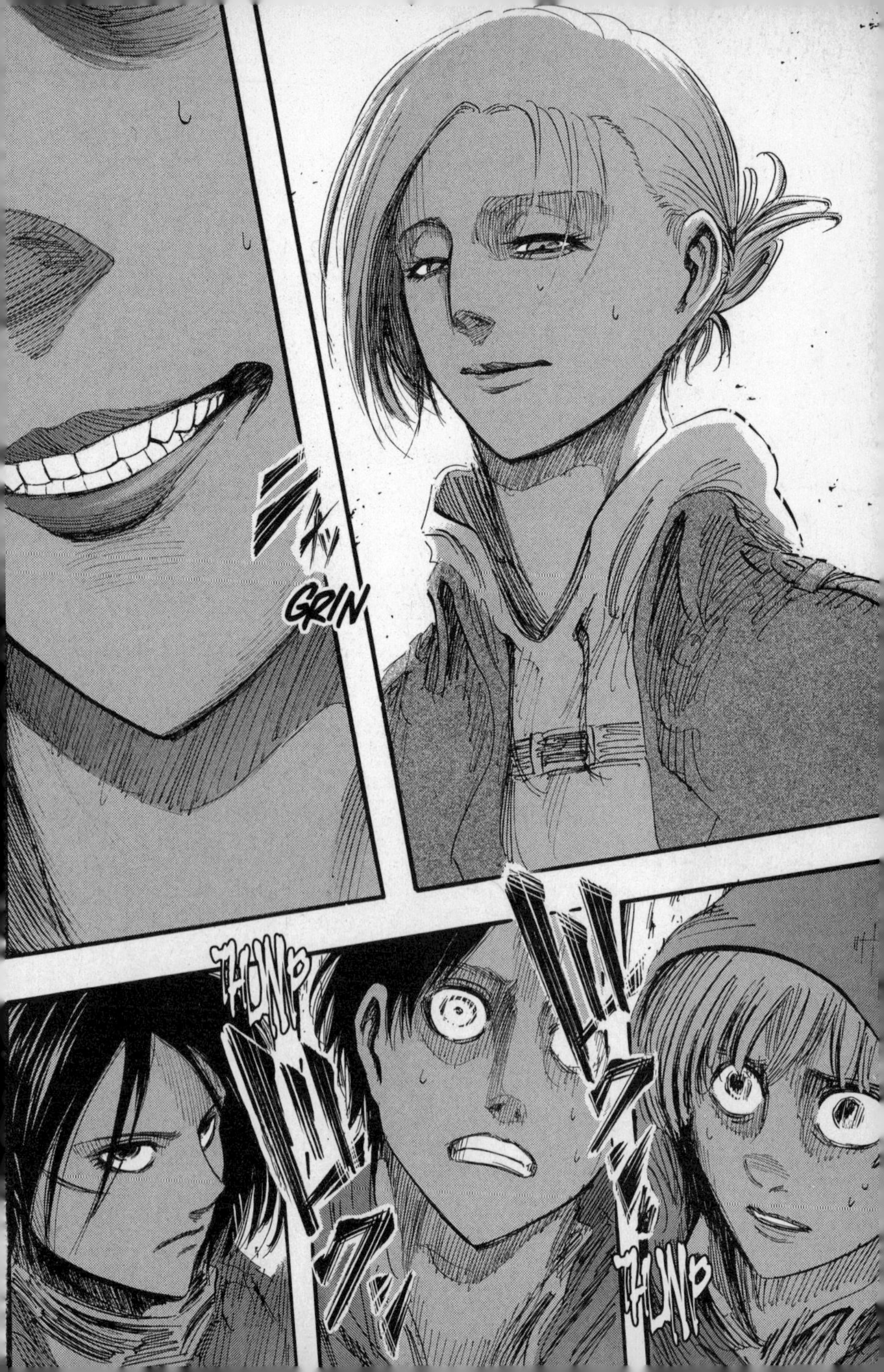
GRIN
THUMP
THUMP

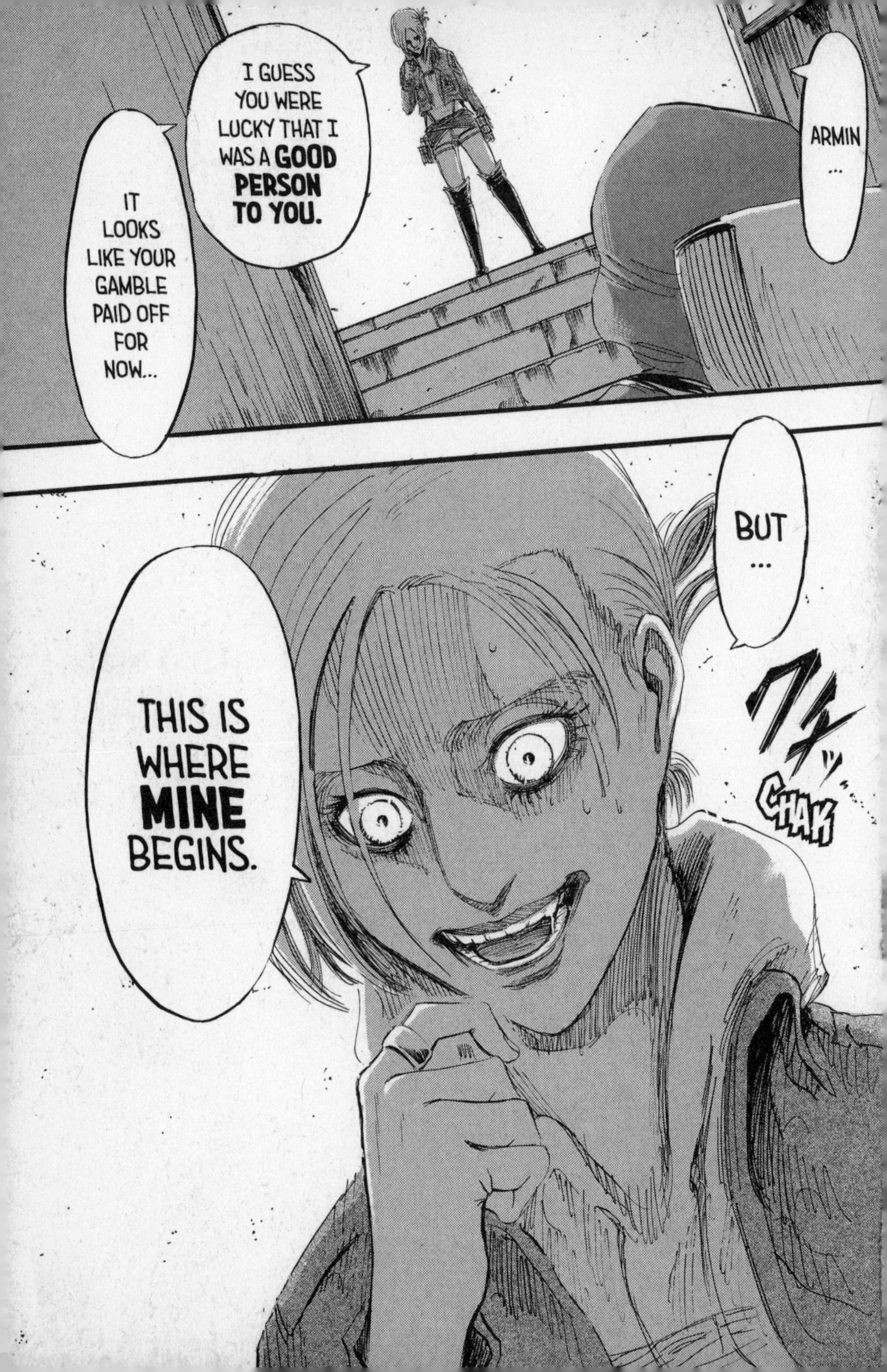
ARMIN ...
I GUESS YOU WERE LUCKY THAT I WAS A **GOOD PERSON TO YOU.**
IT LOOKS LIKE YOUR GAMBLE PAID OFF FOR NOW...
BUT ...
CHAK
THIS IS WHERE **MINE** BEGINS.

14: The Military Police Brigade

ONLY THE TEN INDIVIDUALS WITH THE HIGHEST MARKS IN THEIR YEAR'S TRAINING CORPS MAY APPLY TO THE MILITARY POLICE BRIGADE. ADDITIONAL SOLDIERS JOIN THE BRIGADE IN OTHER WAYS, SUCH AS BY TRANSFER FROM THE GARRISON AFTER GAINING EXPERIENCE THERE.

THE MILITARY POLICE BRIGADE IS ABOUT 2,000 SOLDIERS STRONG, BUT REPORTEDLY HAS AN ACTUAL FIGHTING STRENGTH OF ABOUT 5,000 SOLDIERS INCLUDING THE GARRISON, WHICH IS UNDER ITS COMMAND.

THE BRIGADE ACTS AS THOUGH IT IS ABOVE THE GARRISON, AND BEHIND THE SCENES, IT HAS THE POWER TO INFLUENCE EVERY SECTION OF THE ADMINISTRATION IN THE INTERIOR. AS IT DOES NOT COME INTO CONTACT WITH TITANS ON THE FRONT LINES, IT ALSO SUFFERS NO HUMAN LOSSES.

ABOUT 200 MPS ARE DEPLOYED IN EACH WALLED CITY. THEIR MAIN DUTIES ARE TO PRESIDE OVER THE TRAINING CORPS, SUPERVISE THE GARRISON, AND COMMAND AND CONTROL THE FIRE DEPARTMENTS. THEY ALSO ARREST AND DETAIN POLITICAL CRIMINALS AND MAJOR OFFENDERS. THE MILITARY POLICE BRIGADE IS GIVEN FIRST PRIORITY DURING INVESTIGATIONS THAT INVOLVE NOBILITY OR THE ROYAL FAMILY.

DUE TO ITS CHARACTER, THE BRIGADE OFTEN COMES INTO CONFLICT WITH THE SURVEY CORPS, WHOSE ROOTS ARE DEMOCRATIC IN NATURE.

(WITH THANKS TO UKYŌ KODACHI AND KIYOMUNE MIWA)

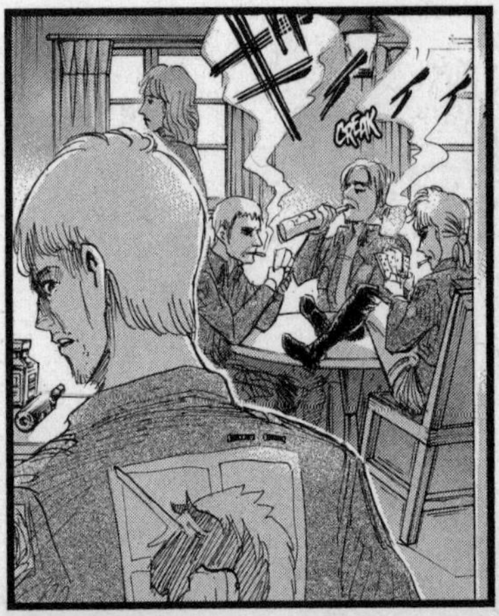
CREAK

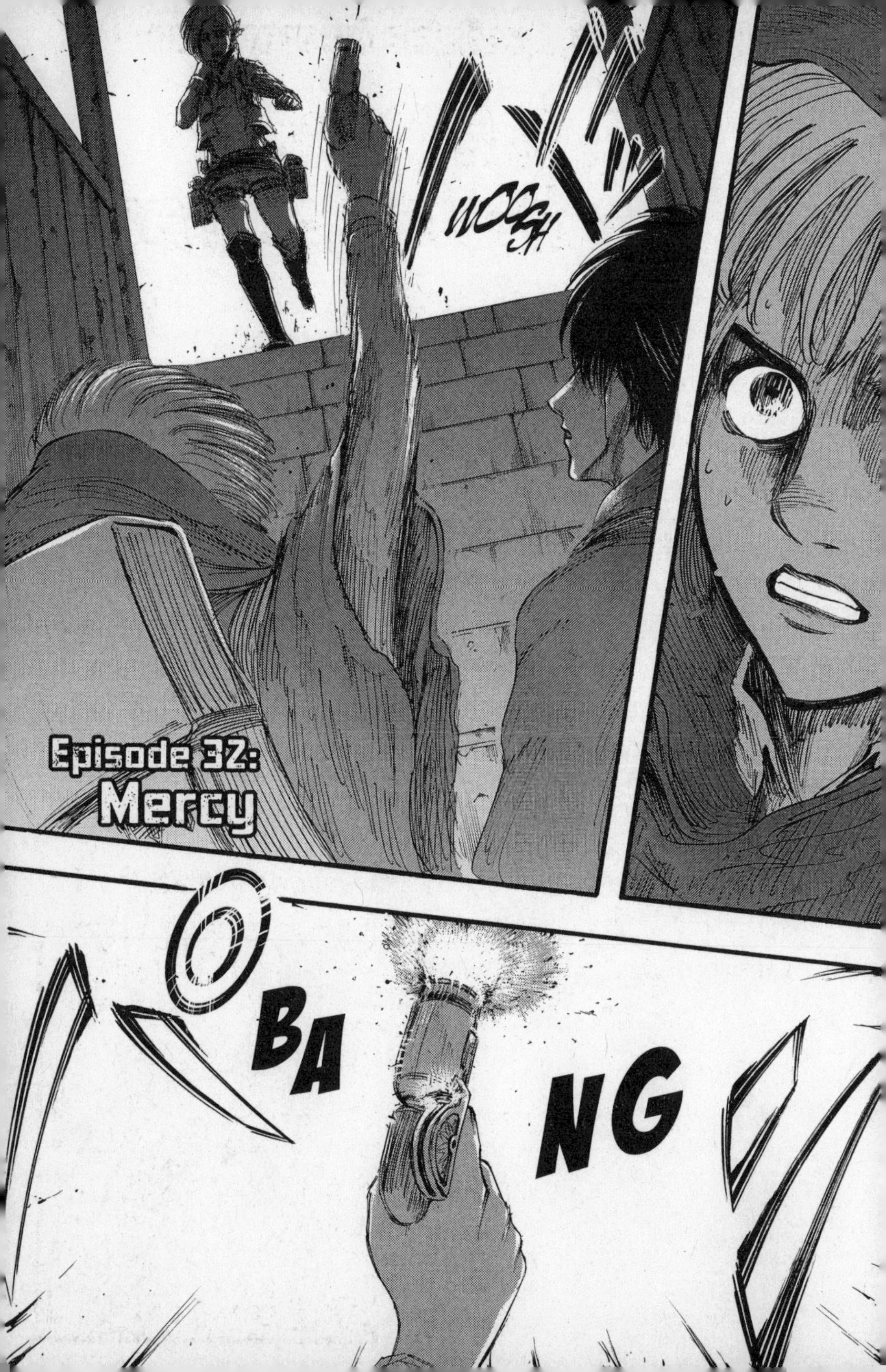
WOOSH
Episode 32:
Mercy
BANG

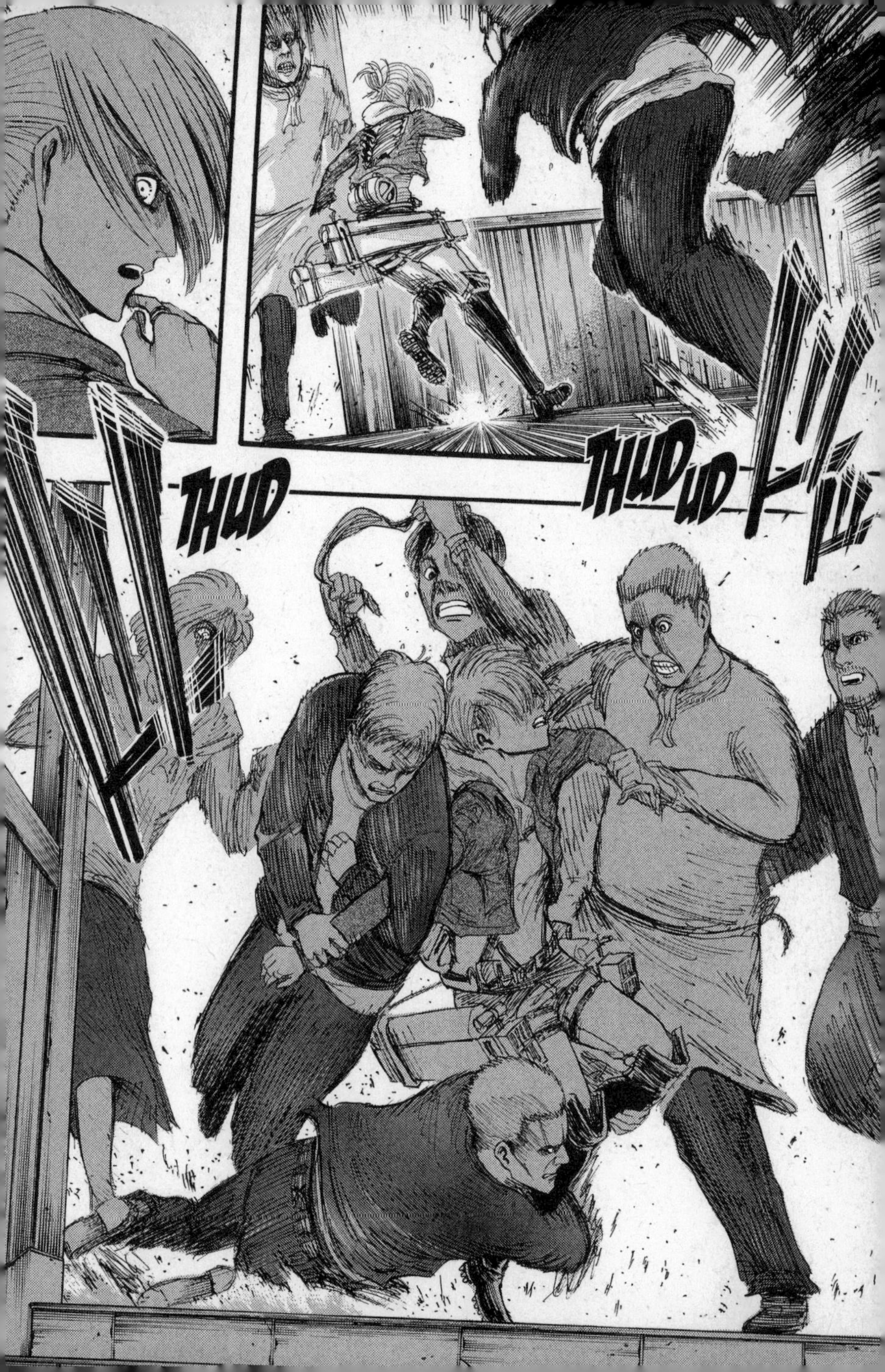
THUDUD
THUD

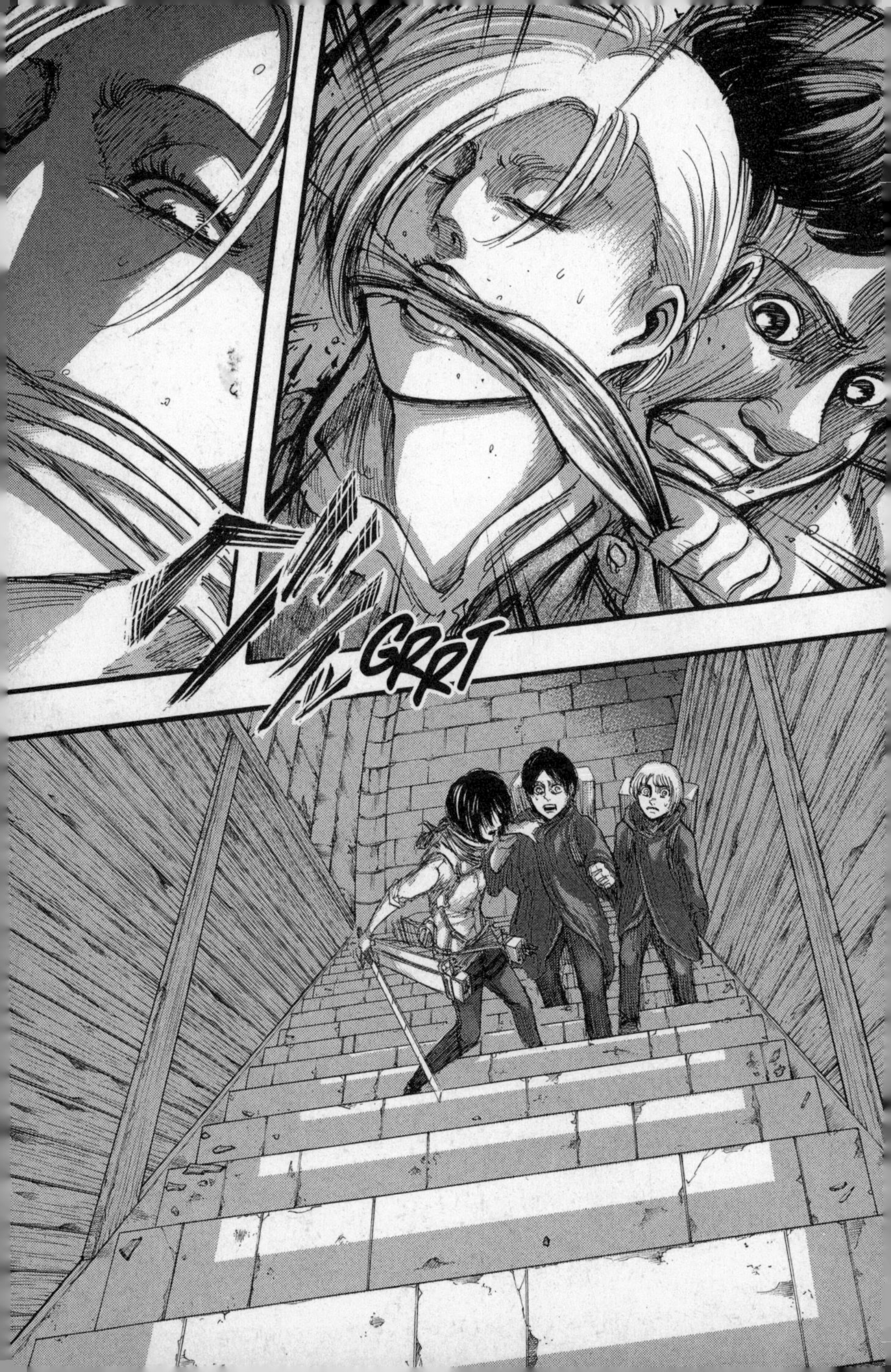
GRRT

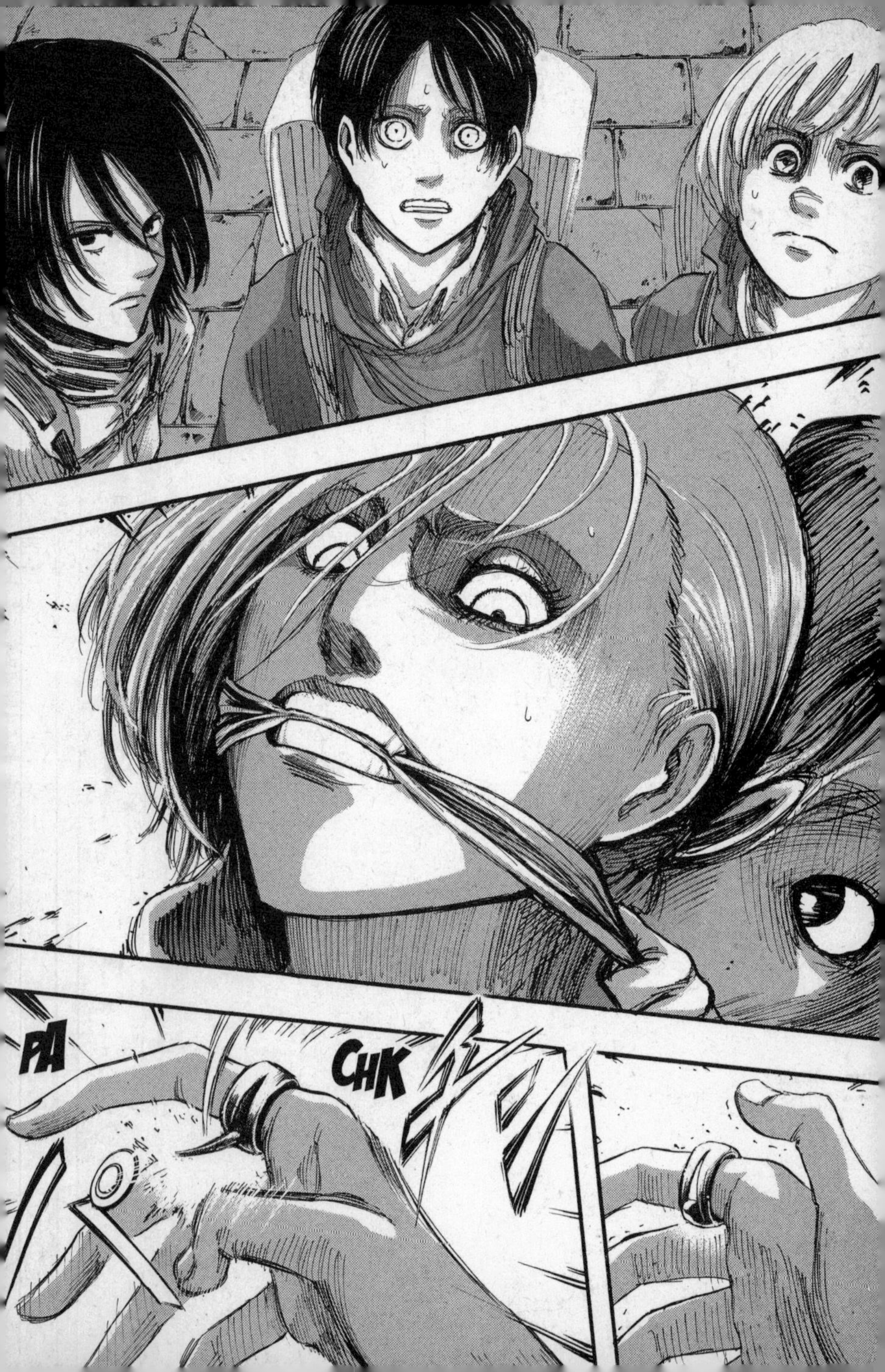
PA
CHK

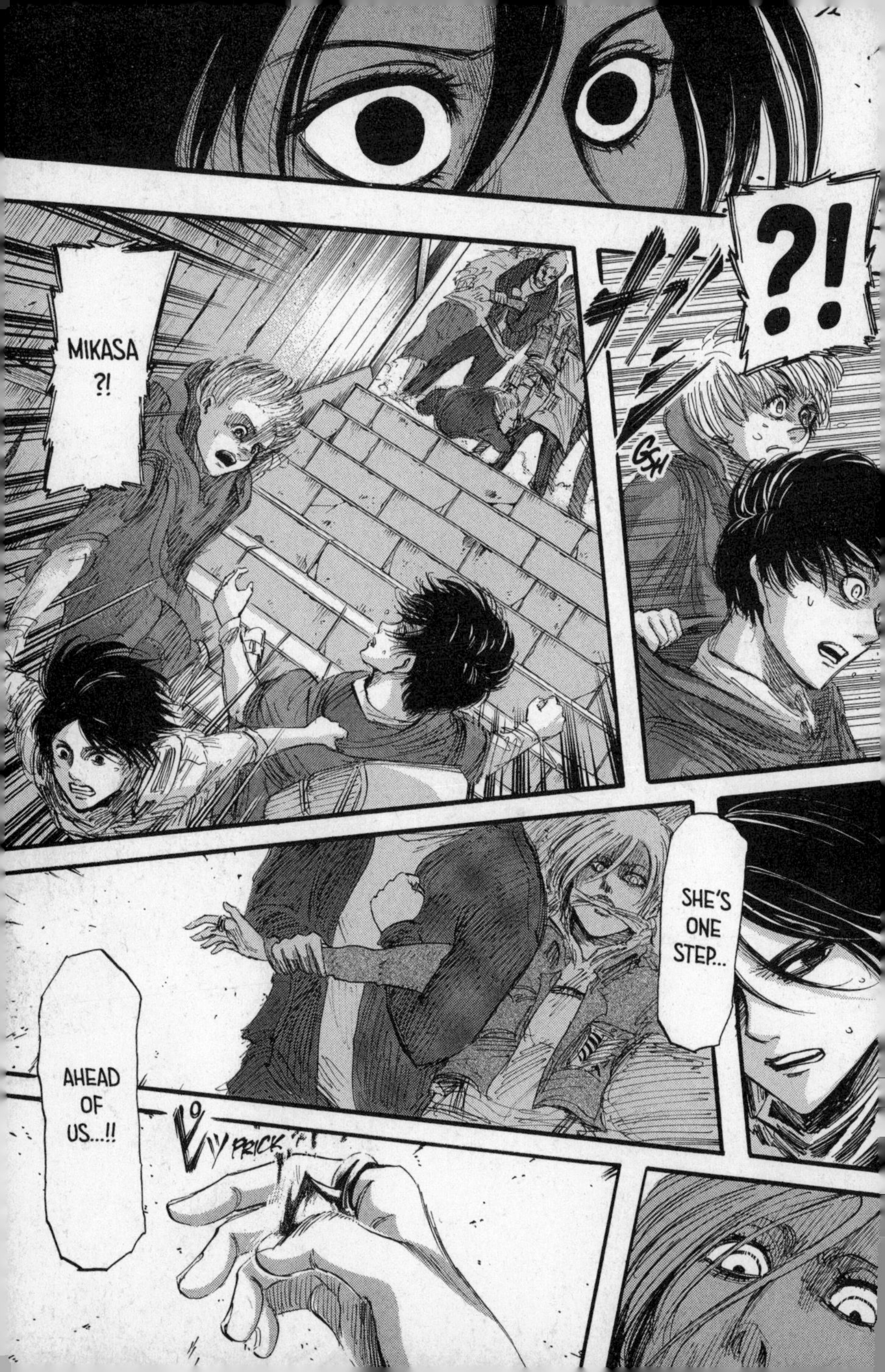
?!
GSH
MIKASA ?!
SHE'S ONE STEP...
AHEAD OF US...!!
PRICK

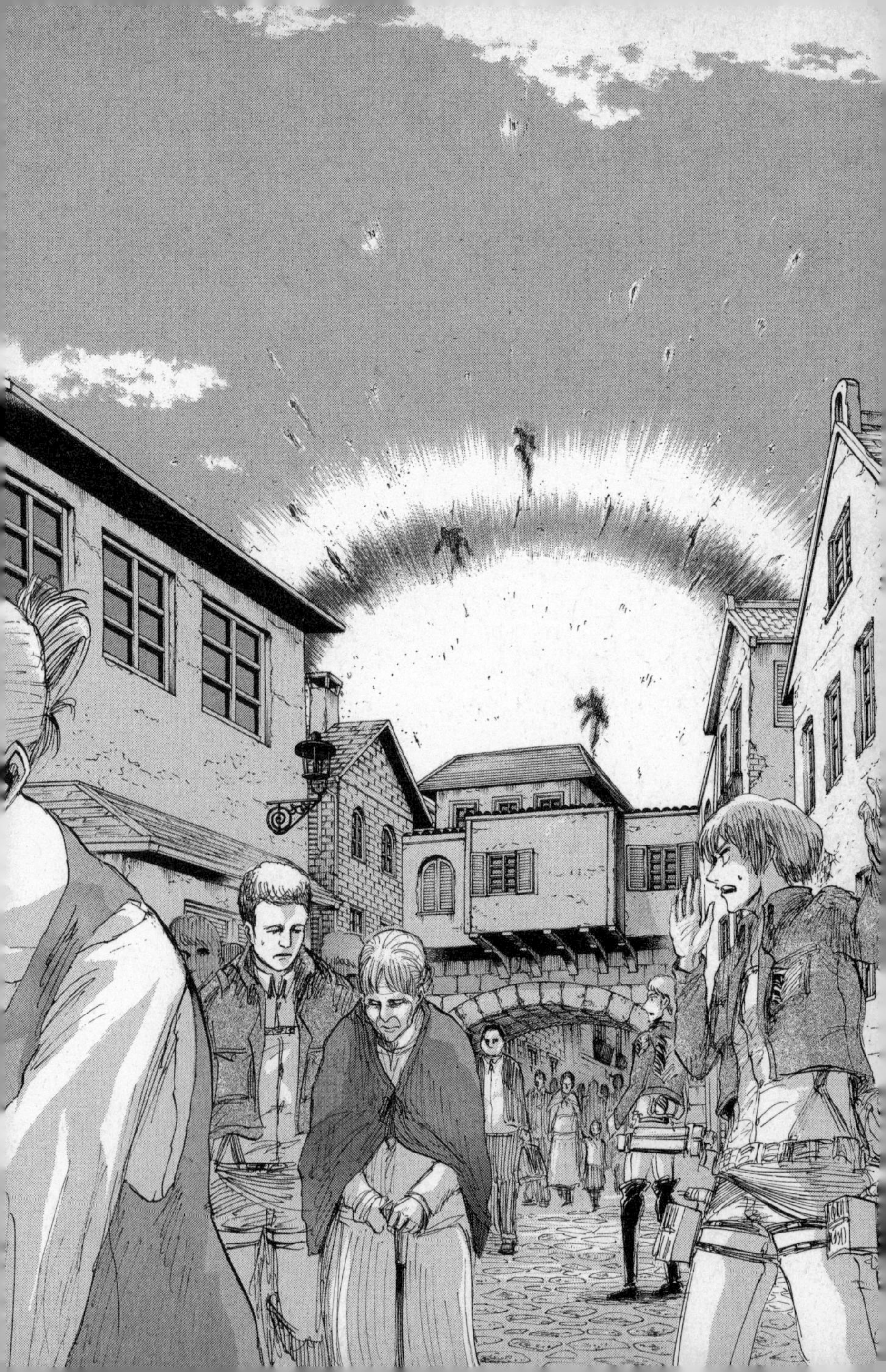

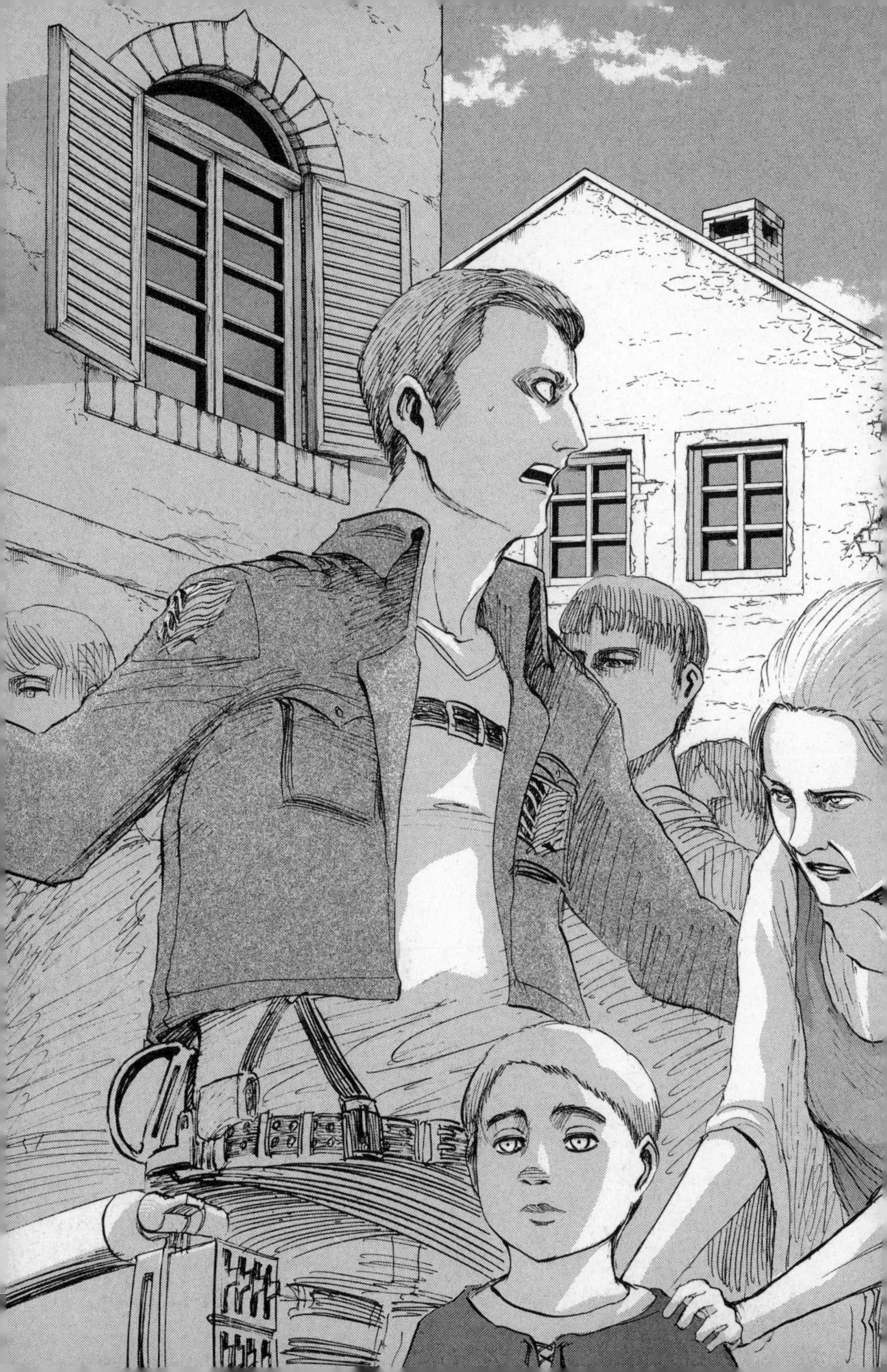

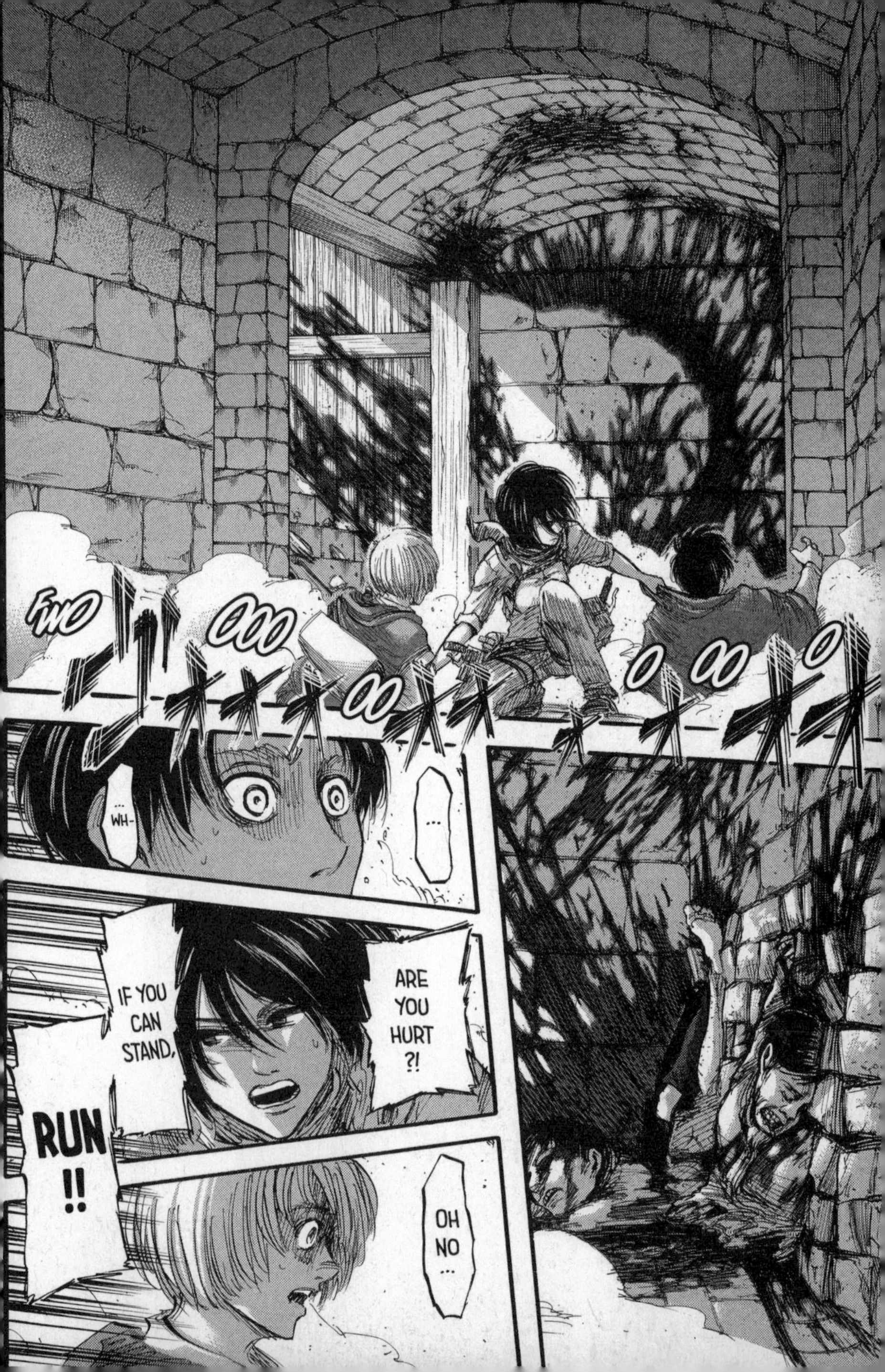
FWOOOOOOOOOO
...
... WH-
ARE YOU HURT ?!
IF YOU CAN STAND,
RUN !!
OH NO ...

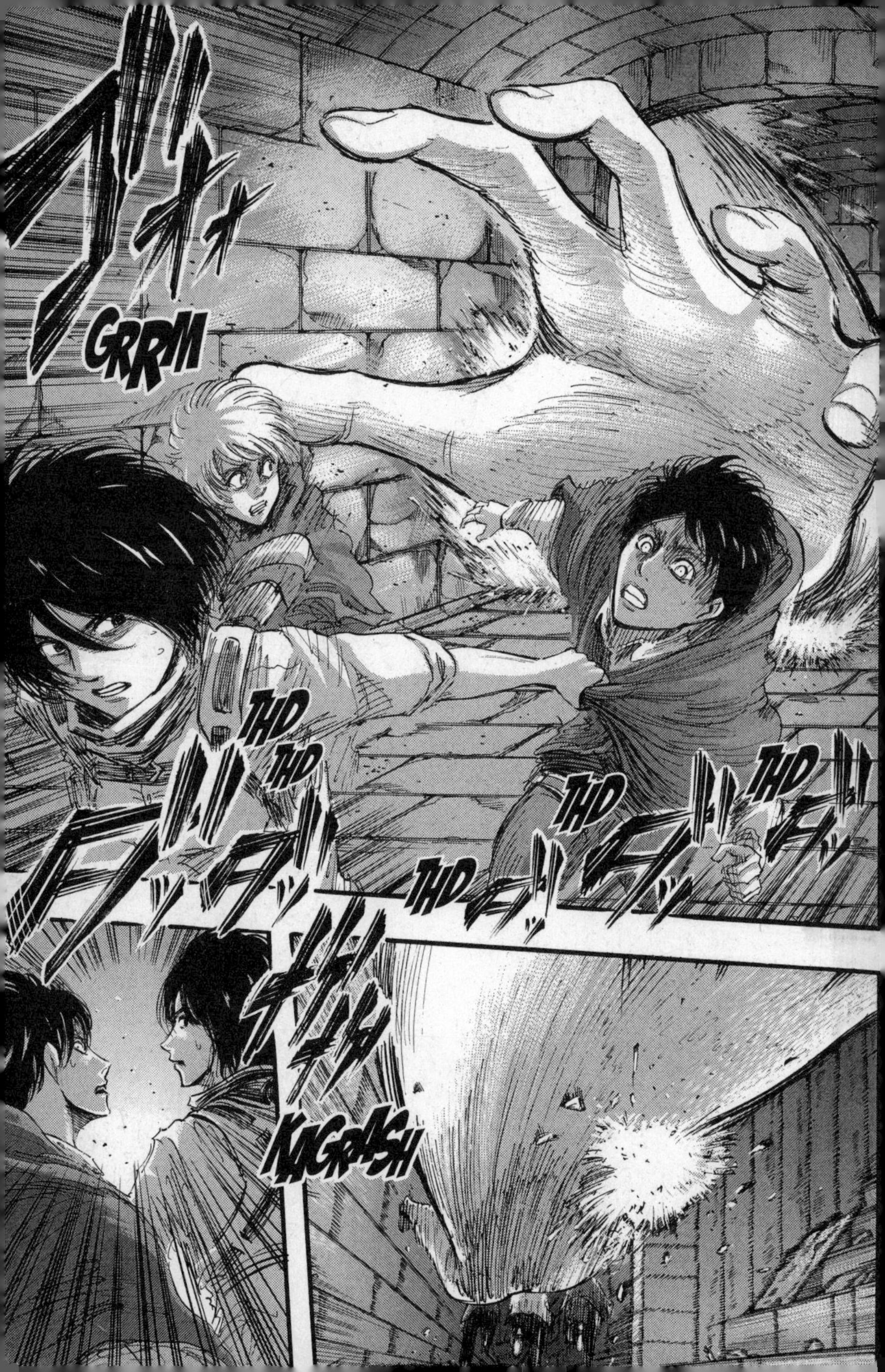
GRRM
THD
THD
THD
THD
THD
KAGRASH

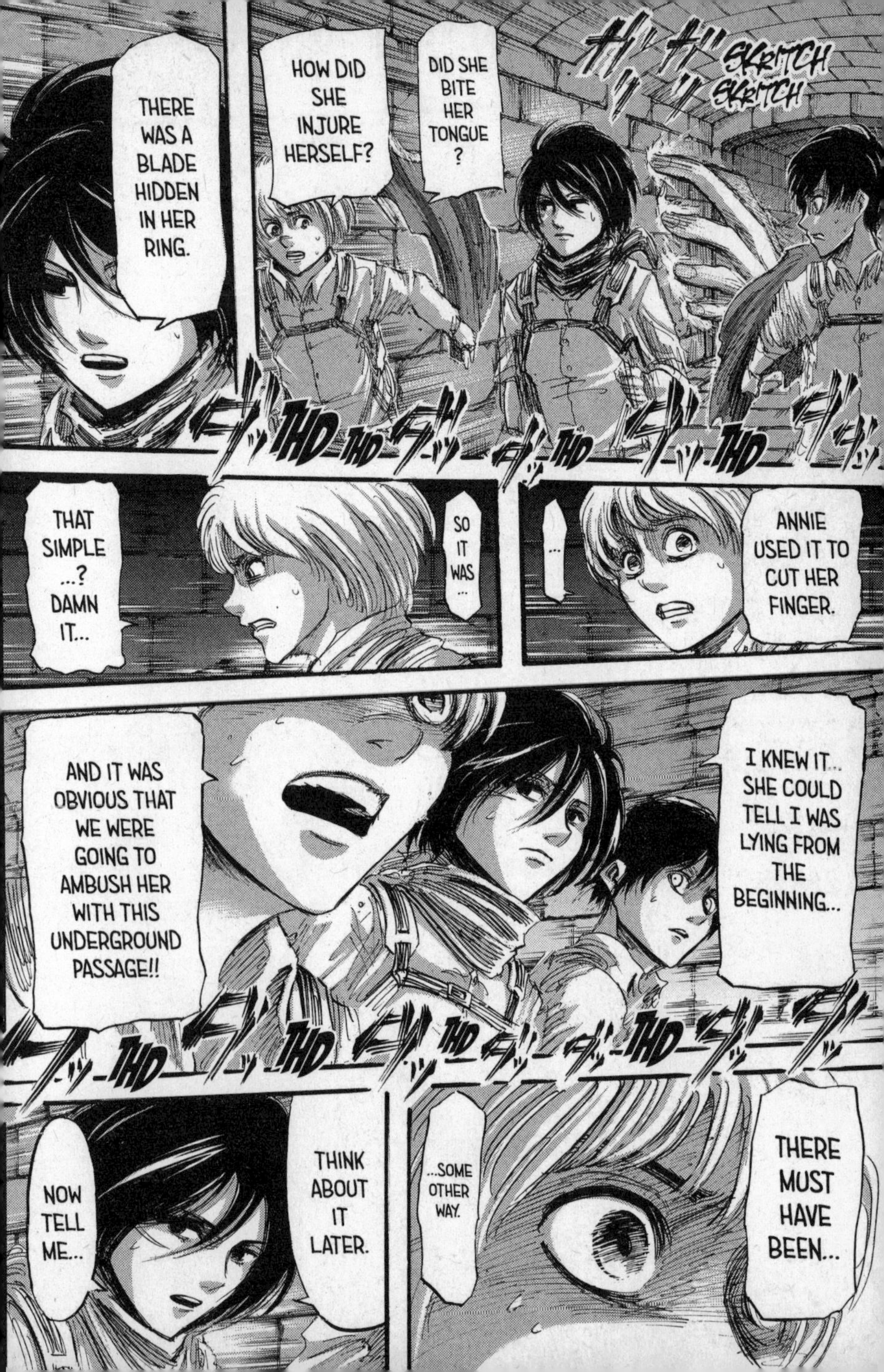
SKRITCH SKRITCH
DID SHE BITE HER TONGUE?
HOW DID SHE INJURE HERSELF?
THD THD THD THD
THERE WAS A BLADE HIDDEN IN HER RING.
ANNIE USED IT TO CUT HER FINGER.
...
SO IT WAS...
THAT SIMPLE ...? DAMN IT...
I KNEW IT... SHE COULD TELL I WAS LYING FROM THE BEGINNING...
AND IT WAS OBVIOUS THAT WE WERE GOING TO AMBUSH HER WITH THIS UNDERGROUND PASSAGE!!
THD THD THD THD
THERE MUST HAVE BEEN...
...SOME OTHER WAY.
THINK ABOUT IT LATER.
NOW TELL ME...

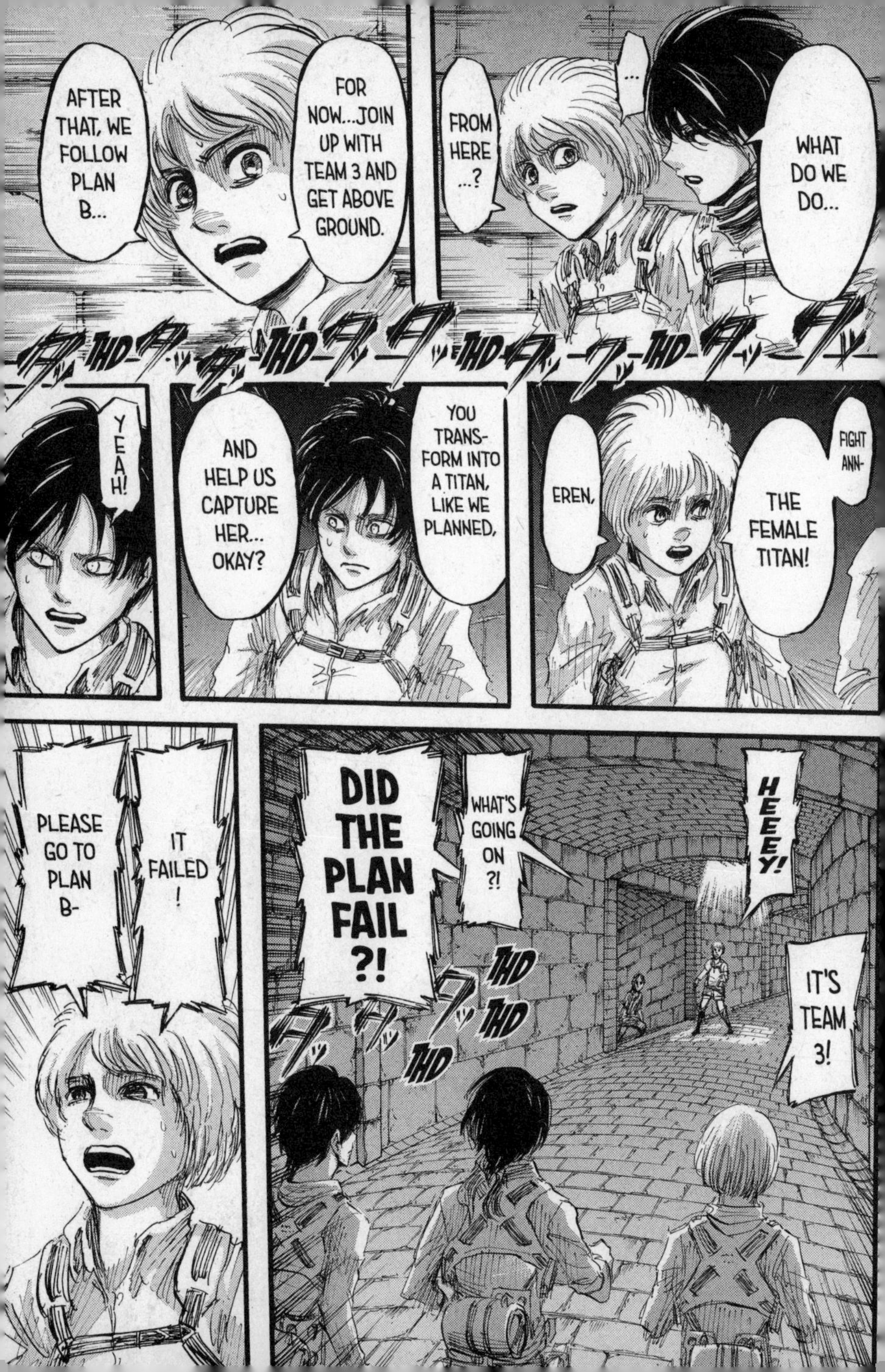
WHAT DO WE DO...
...
FROM HERE ...?
FOR NOW...JOIN UP WITH TEAM 3 AND GET ABOVE GROUND.
AFTER THAT, WE FOLLOW PLAN B...
THD THD THD THD THD
FIGHT ANN-
THE FEMALE TITAN!
EREN,
YOU TRANSFORM INTO A TITAN, LIKE WE PLANNED,
AND HELP US CAPTURE HER... OKAY?
YEAH!
HEEEEY!
IT'S TEAM 3!
WHAT'S GOING ON ?!
DID THE PLAN FAIL ?!
THD THD THD
IT FAILED !
PLEASE GO TO PLAN B-

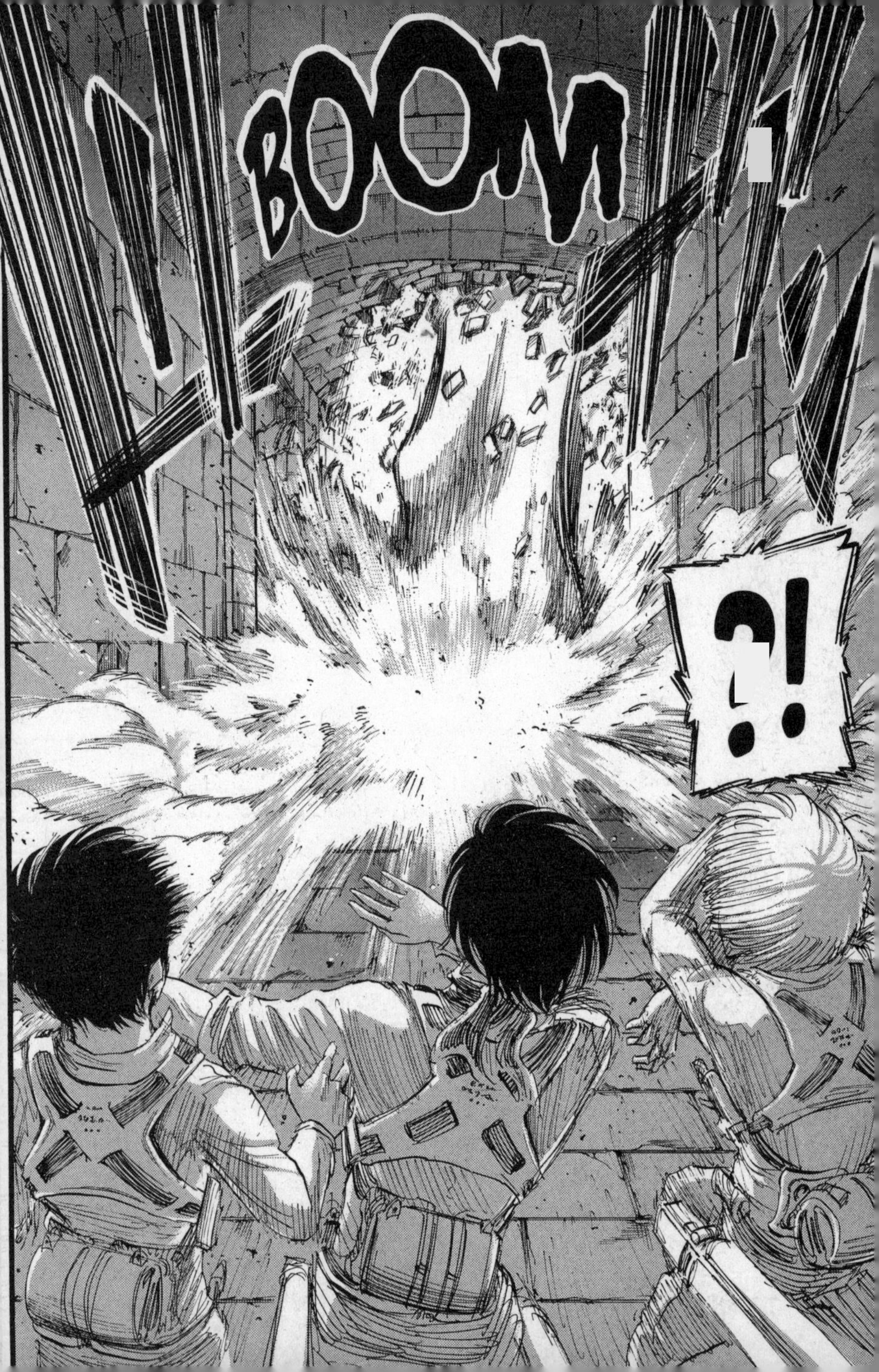
BOOM!
?!

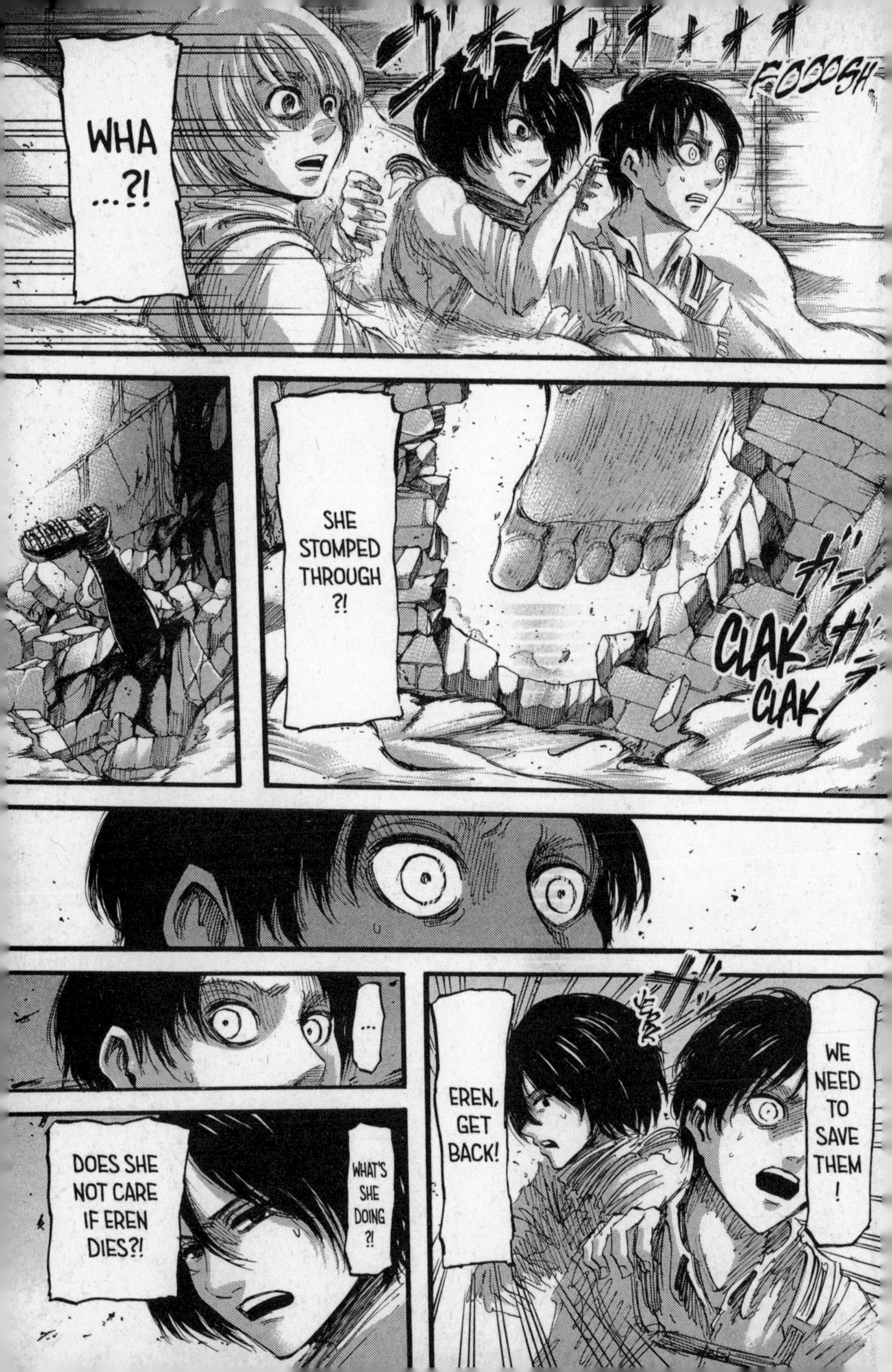
FOOOSH
WHA ...?!
SHE STOMPED THROUGH ?!
CLAK CLAK
WE NEED TO SAVE THEM !
EREN, GET BACK!
...
WHAT'S SHE DOING ?!
DOES SHE NOT CARE IF EREN DIES?!

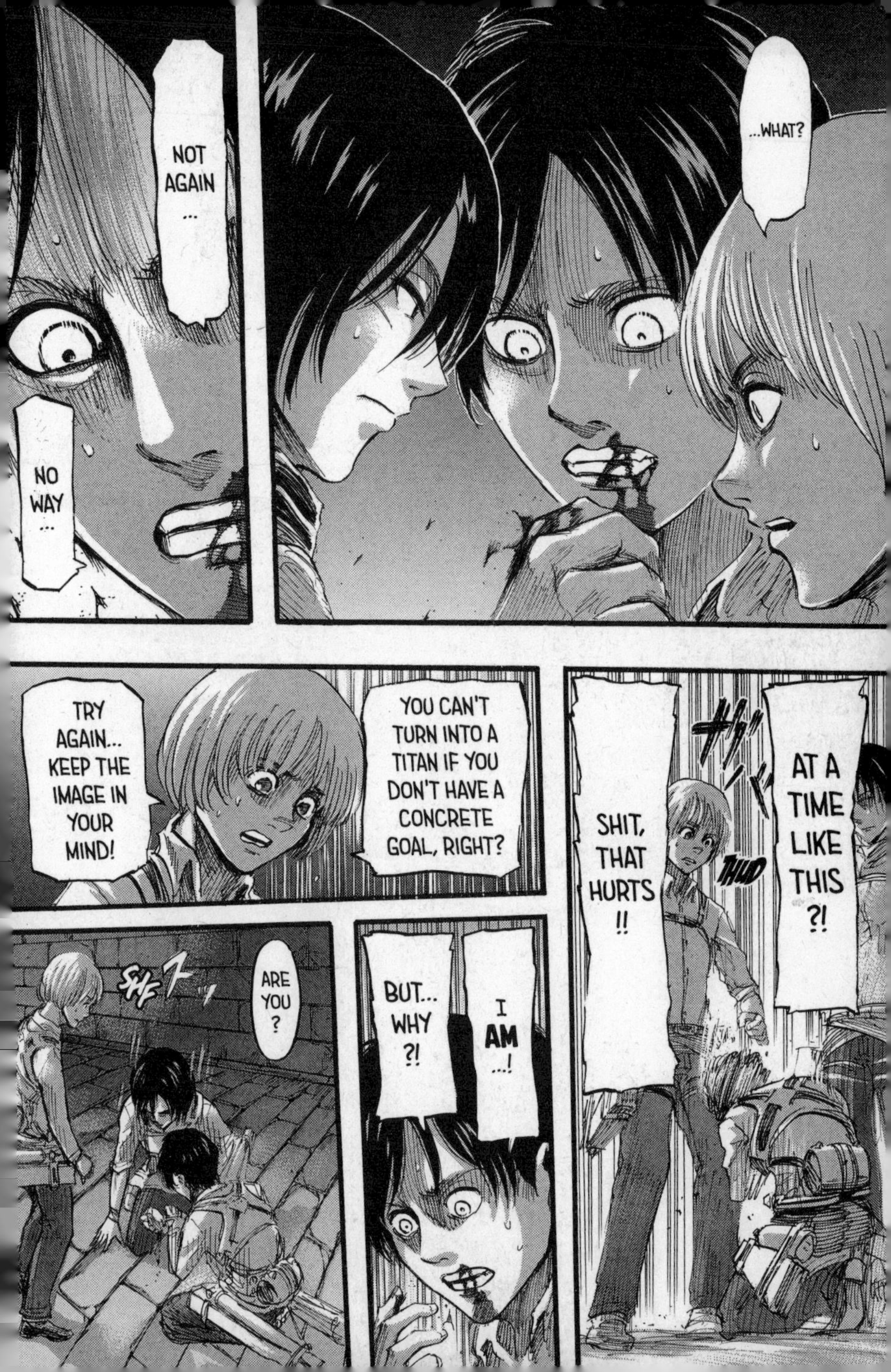
...WHAT?
NOT AGAIN ...
NO WAY ...
AT A TIME LIKE THIS ?!
THUD
SHIT, THAT HURTS !!
YOU CAN'T TURN INTO A TITAN IF YOU DON'T HAVE A CONCRETE GOAL, RIGHT?
TRY AGAIN... KEEP THE IMAGE IN YOUR MIND!
I AM ...!
BUT... WHY ?!
ARE YOU ?
SHF

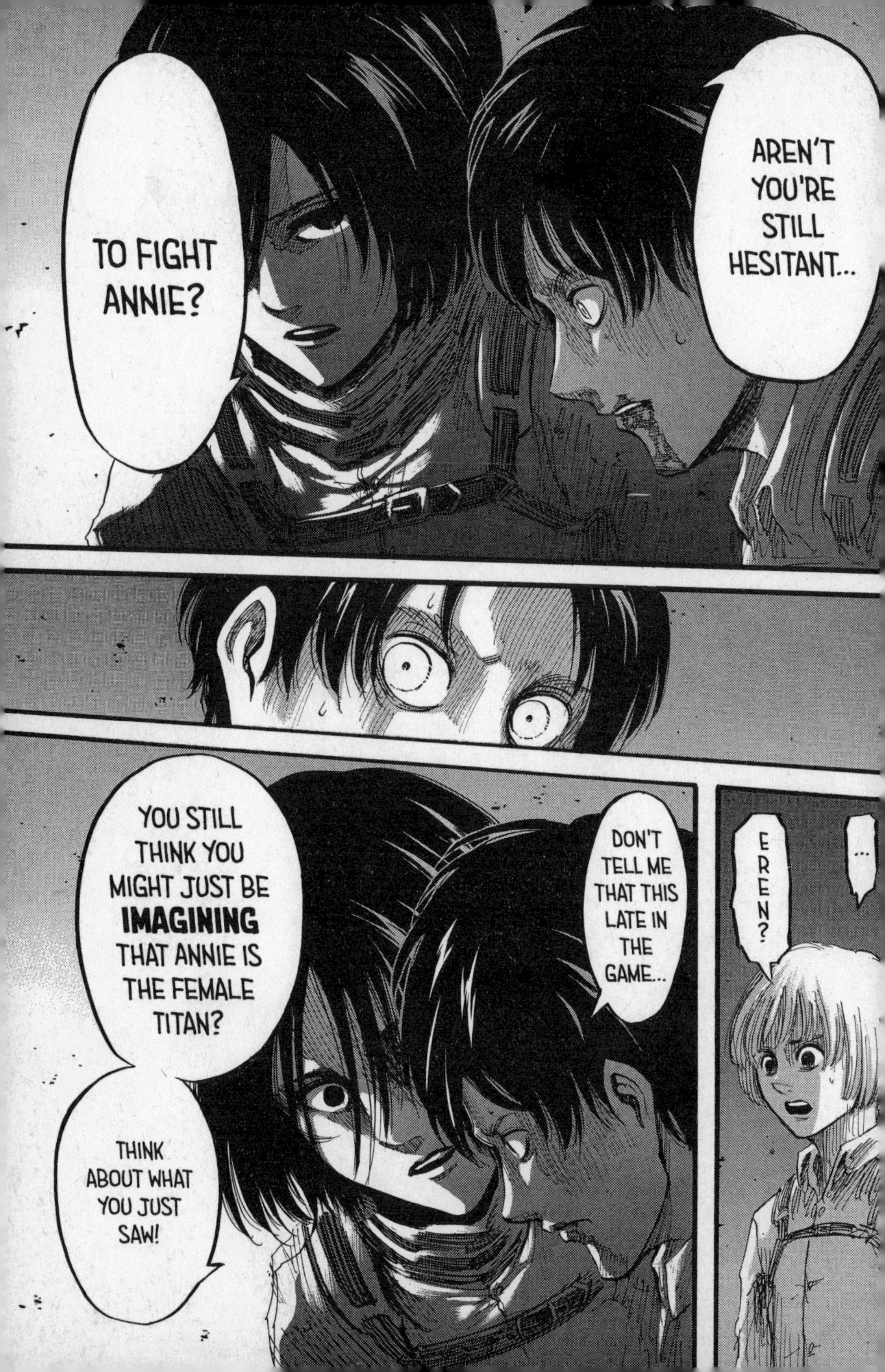
AREN'T YOU'RE STILL HESITANT...
TO FIGHT ANNIE?
...
EREN?
DON'T TELL ME THAT THIS LATE IN THE GAME...
YOU STILL THINK YOU MIGHT JUST BE **IMAGINING** THAT ANNIE IS THE FEMALE TITAN?
THINK ABOUT WHAT YOU JUST SAW!

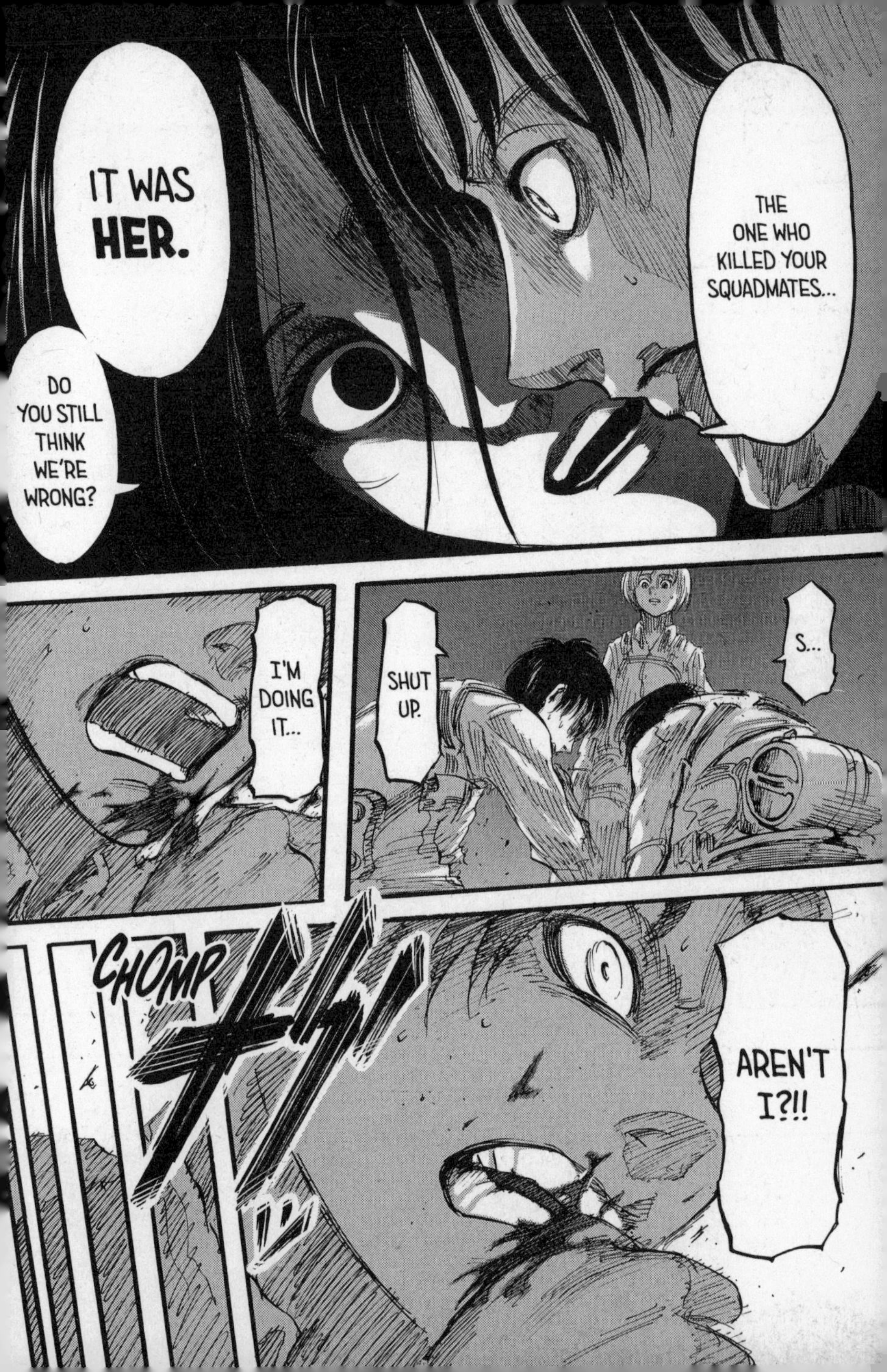
THE ONE WHO KILLED YOUR SQUADMATES...
IT WAS HER.
DO YOU STILL THINK WE'RE WRONG?
S...
SHUT UP.
I'M DOING IT...
AREN'T I?!!
CHOMP

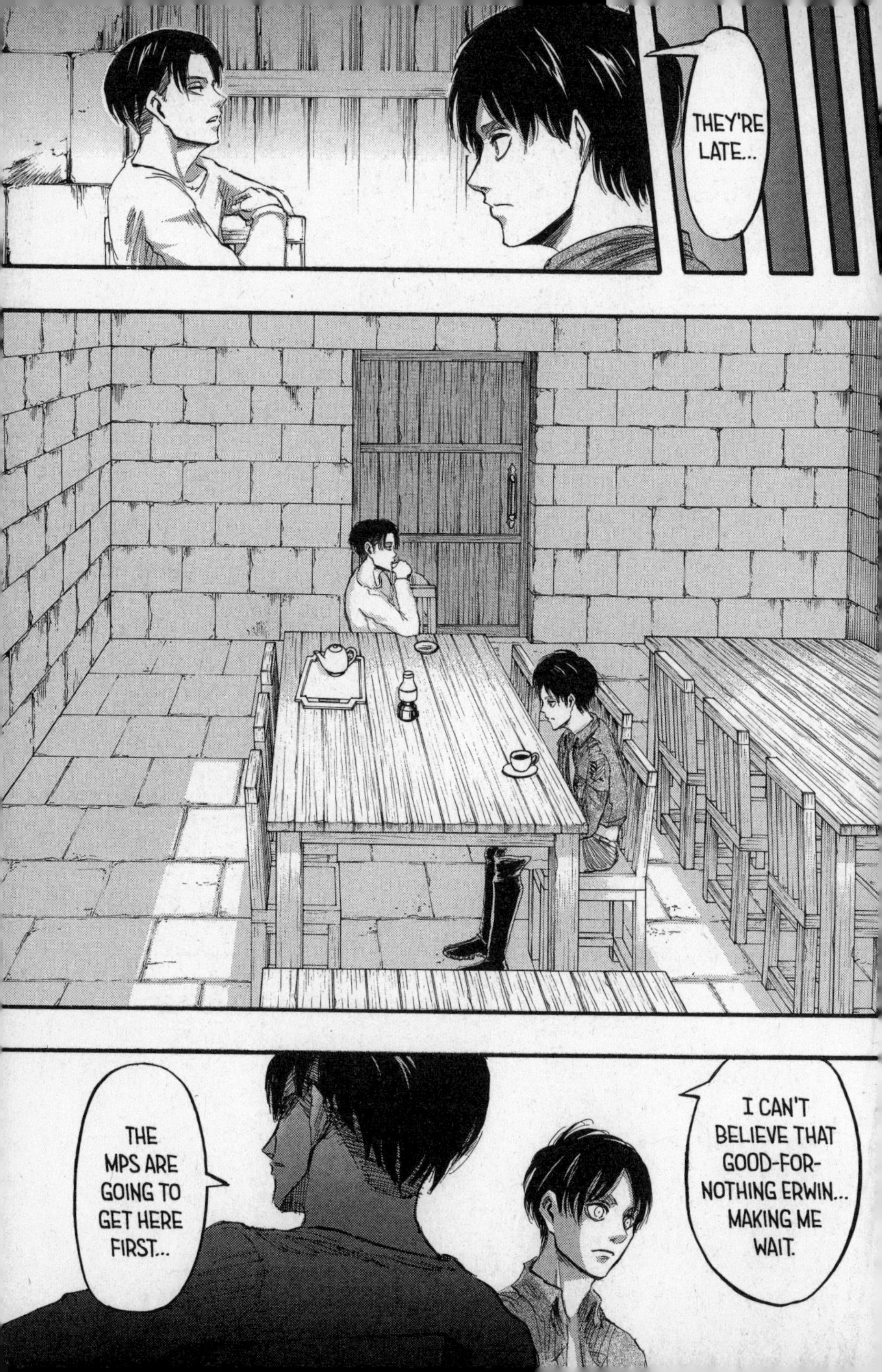
THEY'RE LATE...
I CAN'T BELIEVE THAT GOOD-FOR-NOTHING ERWIN... MAKING ME WAIT.
THE MPS ARE GOING TO GET HERE FIRST...

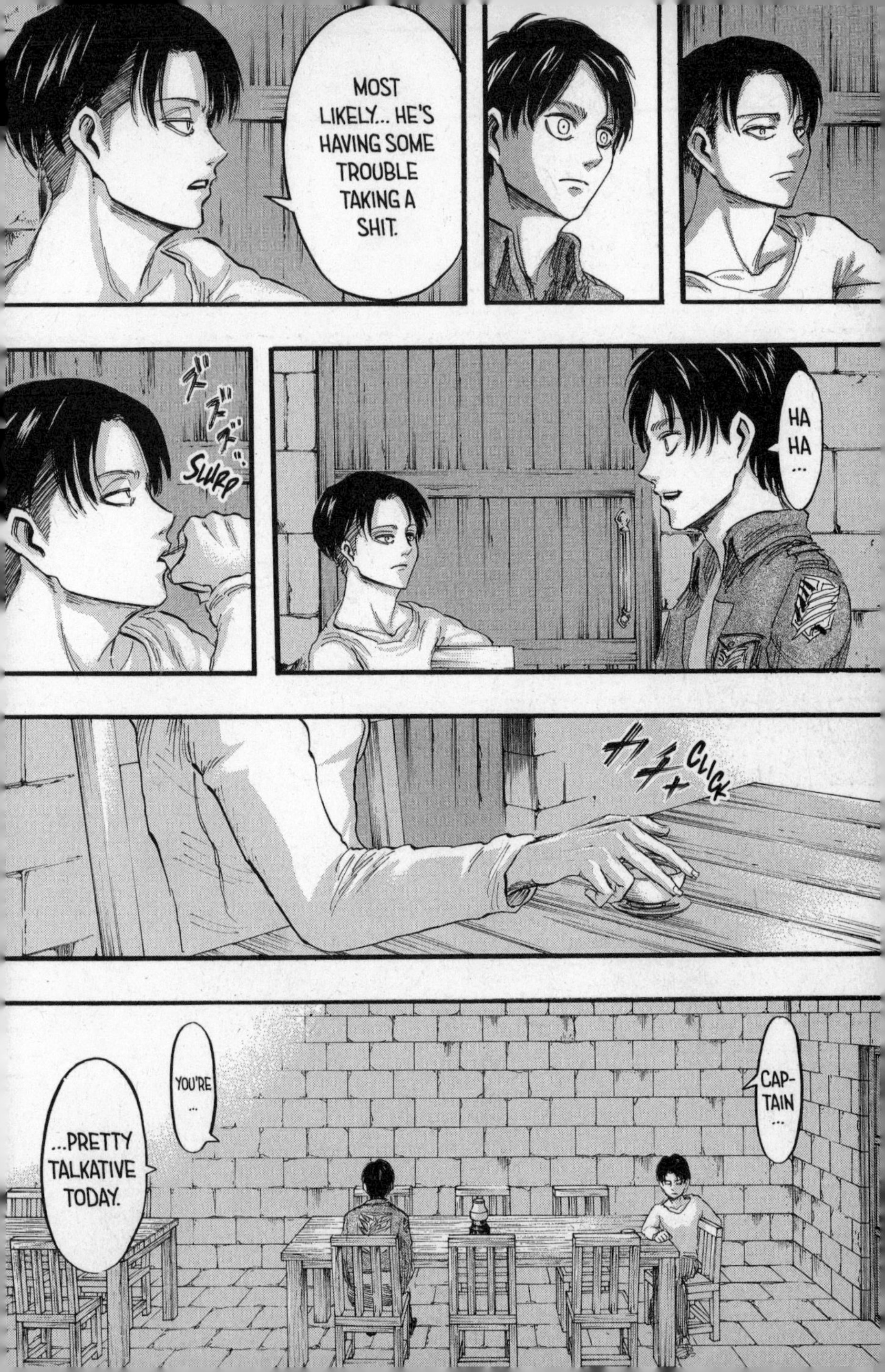
MOST LIKELY... HE'S HAVING SOME TROUBLE TAKING A SHIT.
HA HA ...
ズズズ..
SLURP
カチャ
CLICK
CAP-TAIN ...
YOU'RE ...
...PRETTY TALKATIVE TODAY.

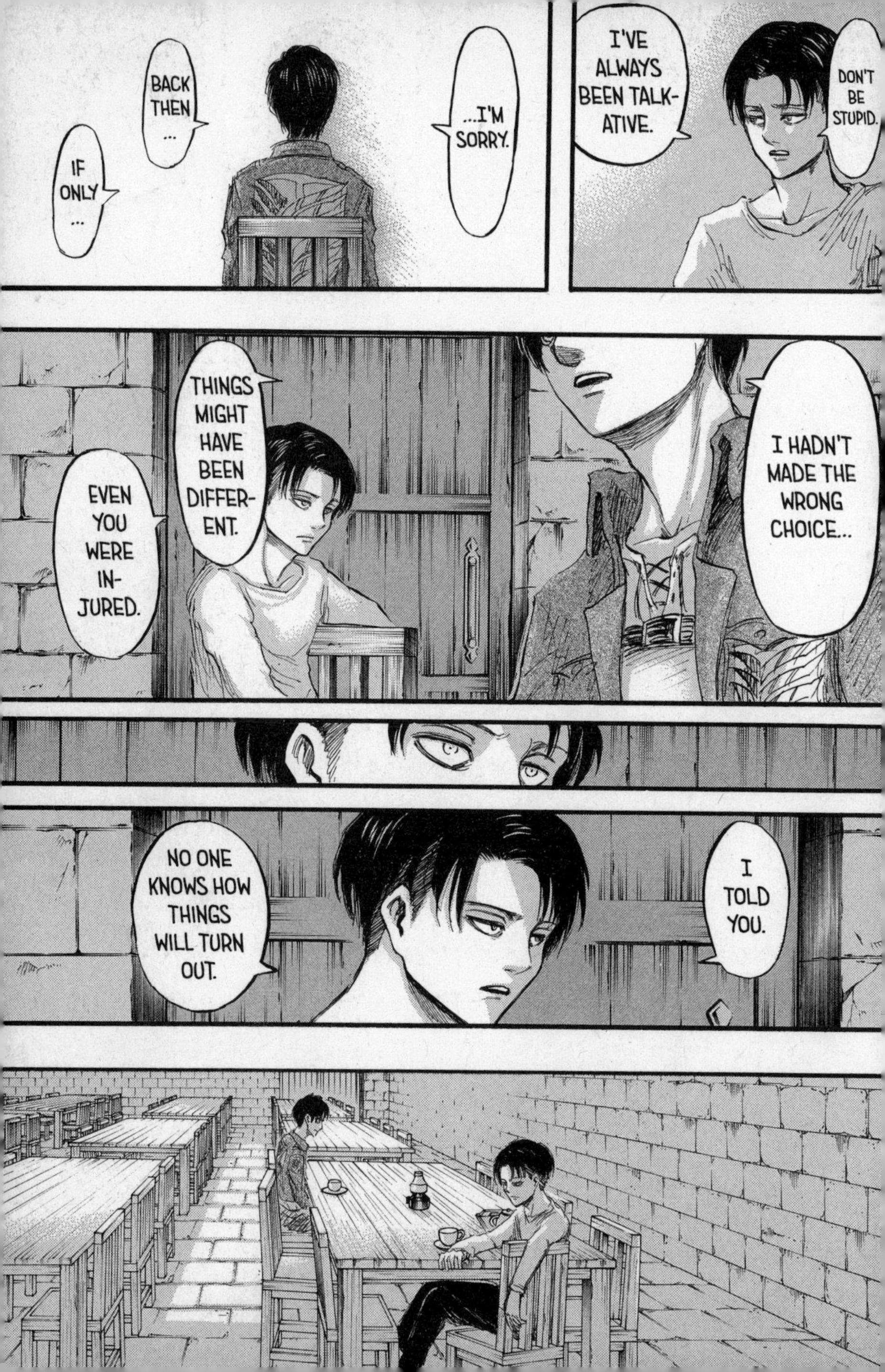

DON'T BE STUPID.
I'VE ALWAYS BEEN TALKATIVE.
...I'M SORRY.
BACK THEN...
IF ONLY...
I HADN'T MADE THE WRONG CHOICE...
THINGS MIGHT HAVE BEEN DIFFERENT.
EVEN YOU WERE INJURED.
I TOLD YOU.
NO ONE KNOWS HOW THINGS WILL TURN OUT.

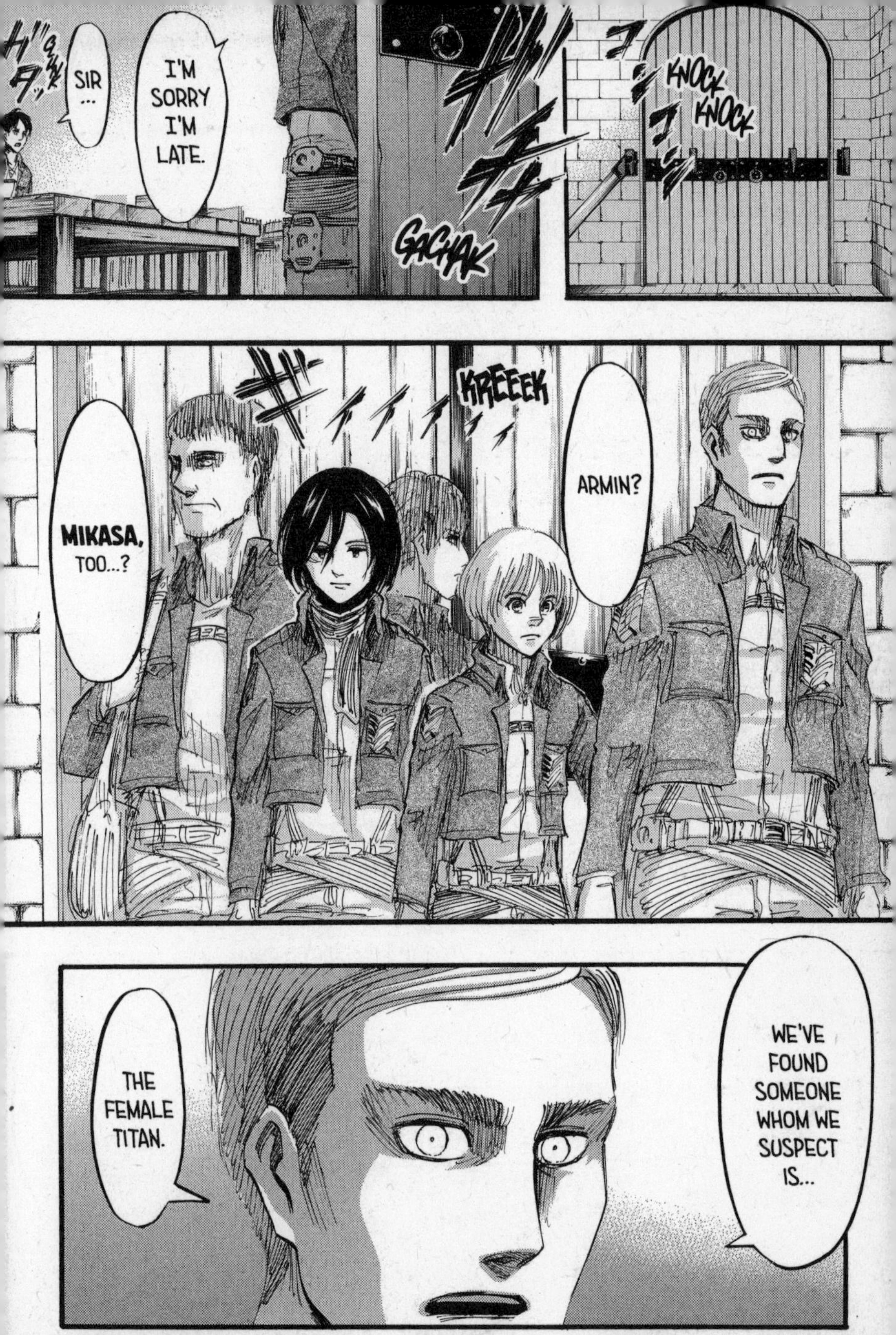
KNOCK KNOCK
GACHAK
I'M SORRY I'M LATE.
SIR ...
KREEEK
ARMIN?
MIKASA, TOO...?
WE'VE FOUND SOMEONE WHOM WE SUSPECT IS...
THE FEMALE TITAN.

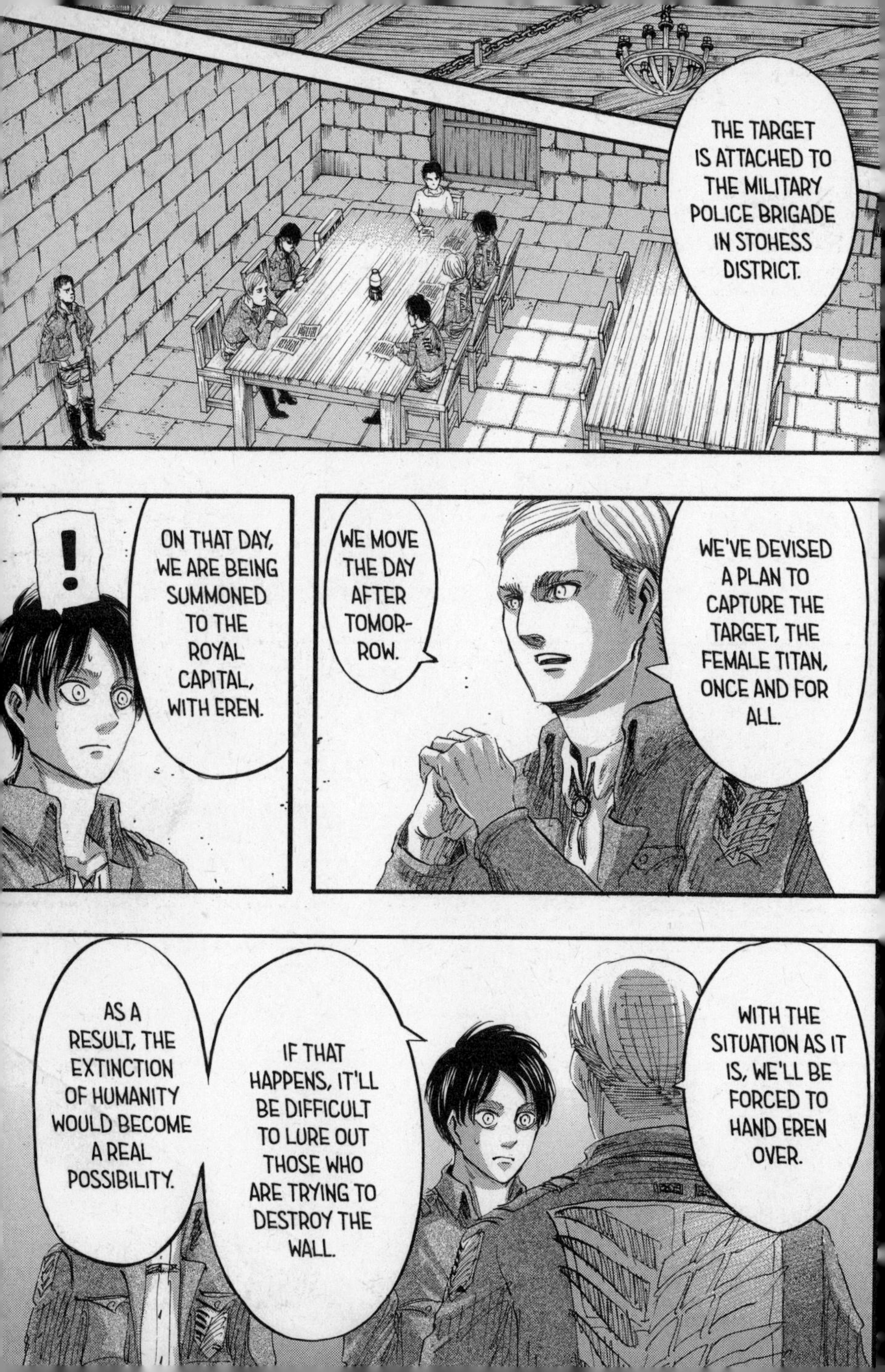
THE TARGET IS ATTACHED TO THE MILITARY POLICE BRIGADE IN STOHESS DISTRICT.
WE'VE DEVISED A PLAN TO CAPTURE THE TARGET, THE FEMALE TITAN, ONCE AND FOR ALL.
WE MOVE THE DAY AFTER TOMOR-ROW.
!
ON THAT DAY, WE ARE BEING SUMMONED TO THE ROYAL CAPITAL, WITH EREN.
WITH THE SITUATION AS IT IS, WE'LL BE FORCED TO HAND EREN OVER.
IF THAT HAPPENS, IT'LL BE DIFFICULT TO LURE OUT THOSE WHO ARE TRYING TO DESTROY THE WALL.
AS A RESULT, THE EXTINCTION OF HUMANITY WOULD BECOME A REAL POSSIBILITY.

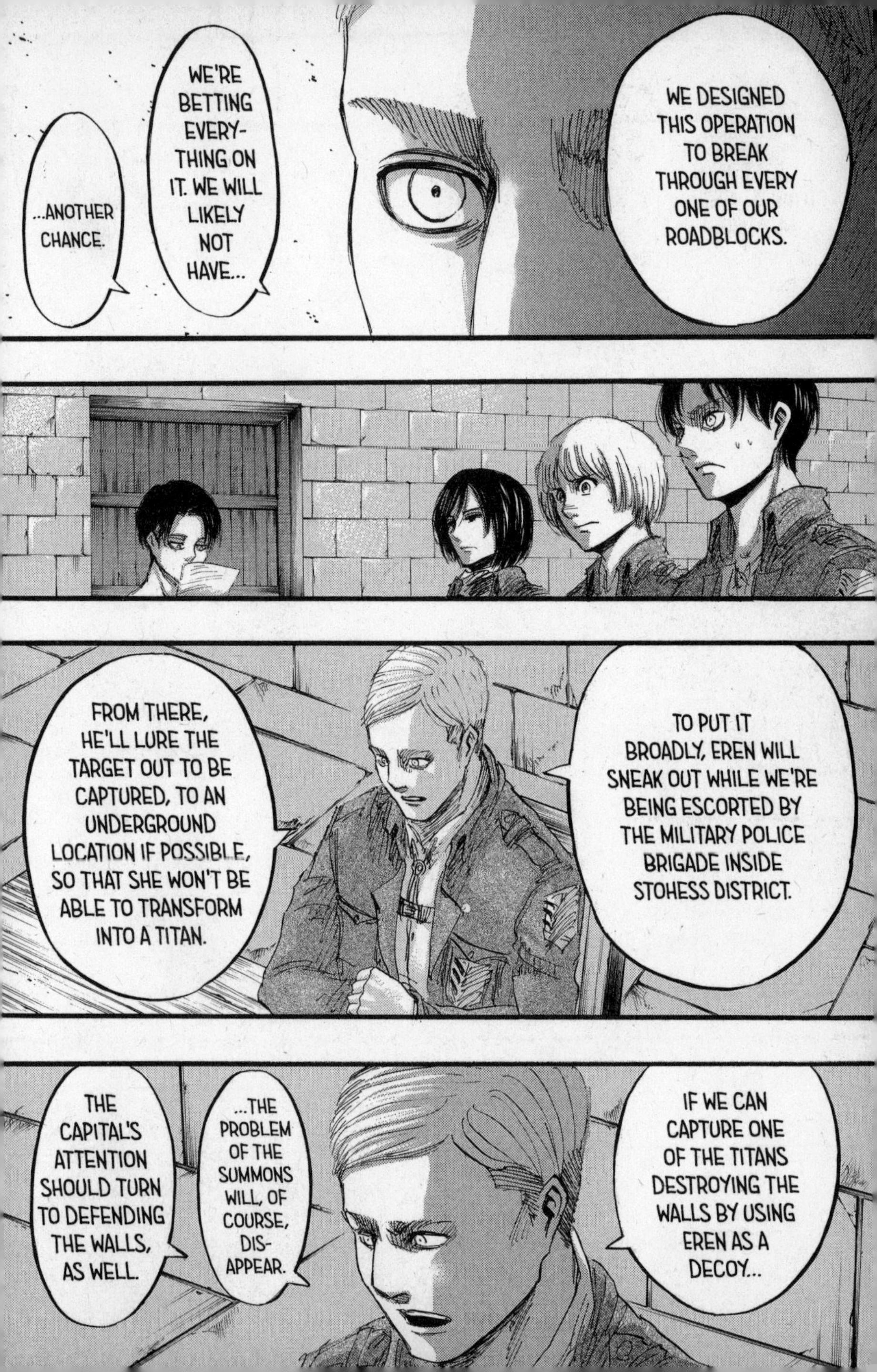
WE DESIGNED THIS OPERATION TO BREAK THROUGH EVERY ONE OF OUR ROADBLOCKS.
WE'RE BETTING EVERYTHING ON IT. WE WILL LIKELY NOT HAVE...
...ANOTHER CHANCE.
TO PUT IT BROADLY, EREN WILL SNEAK OUT WHILE WE'RE BEING ESCORTED BY THE MILITARY POLICE BRIGADE INSIDE STOHESS DISTRICT.
FROM THERE, HE'LL LURE THE TARGET OUT TO BE CAPTURED, TO AN UNDERGROUND LOCATION IF POSSIBLE, SO THAT SHE WON'T BE ABLE TO TRANSFORM INTO A TITAN.
IF WE CAN CAPTURE ONE OF THE TITANS DESTROYING THE WALLS BY USING EREN AS A DECOY...
...THE PROBLEM OF THE SUMMONS WILL, OF COURSE, DISAPPEAR.
THE CAPITAL'S ATTENTION SHOULD TURN TO DEFENDING THE WALLS, AS WELL.

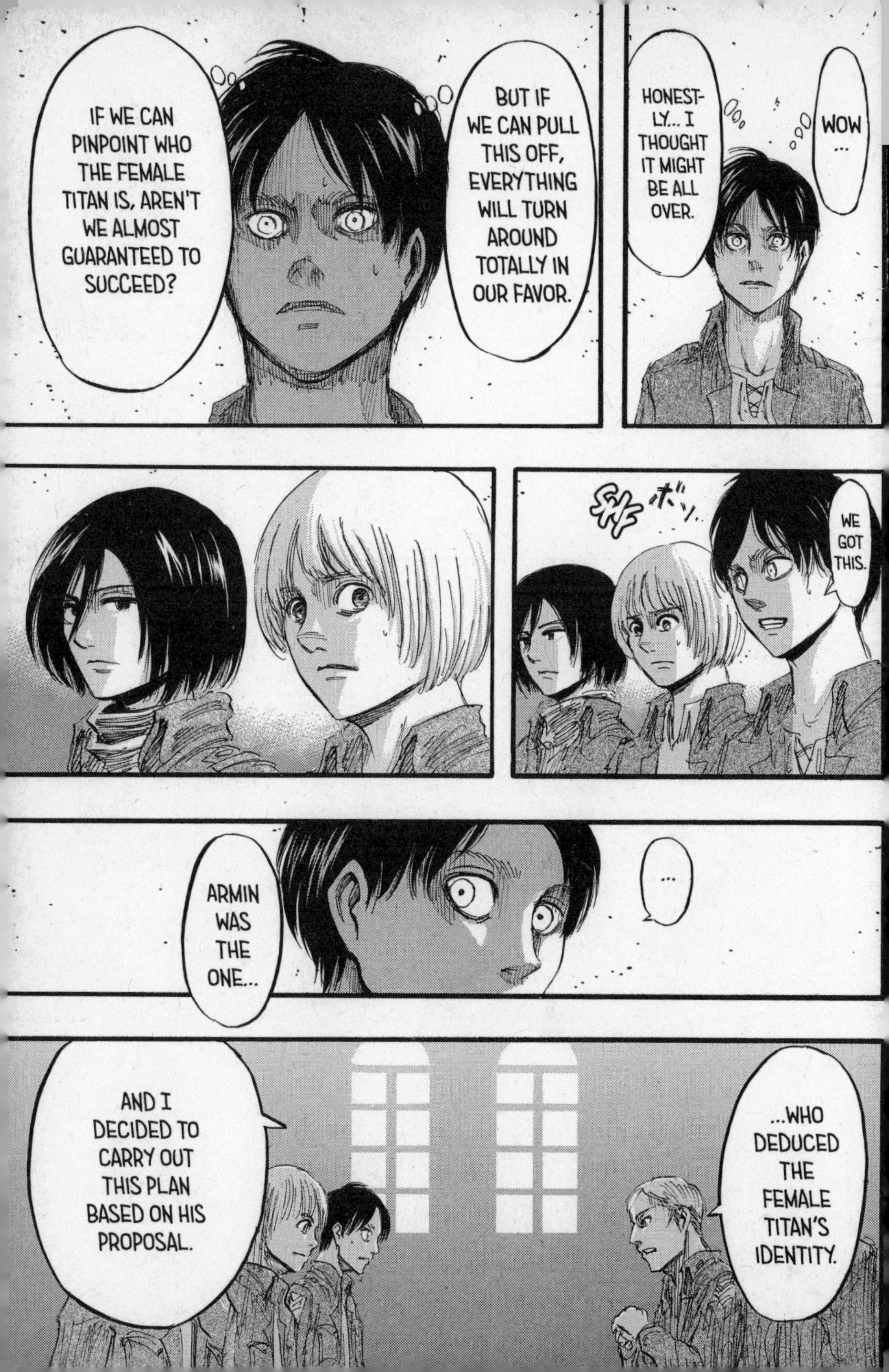

IF WE CAN PINPOINT WHO THE FEMALE TITAN IS, AREN'T WE ALMOST GUARANTEED TO SUCCEED?
BUT IF WE CAN PULL THIS OFF, EVERYTHING WILL TURN AROUND TOTALLY IN OUR FAVOR.
HONEST-LY... I THOUGHT IT MIGHT BE ALL OVER.
WOW...
SHK
ボッ..
WE GOT THIS.
ARMIN WAS THE ONE...
...
...WHO DEDUCED THE FEMALE TITAN'S IDENTITY.
AND I DECIDED TO CARRY OUT THIS PLAN BASED ON HIS PROPOSAL.

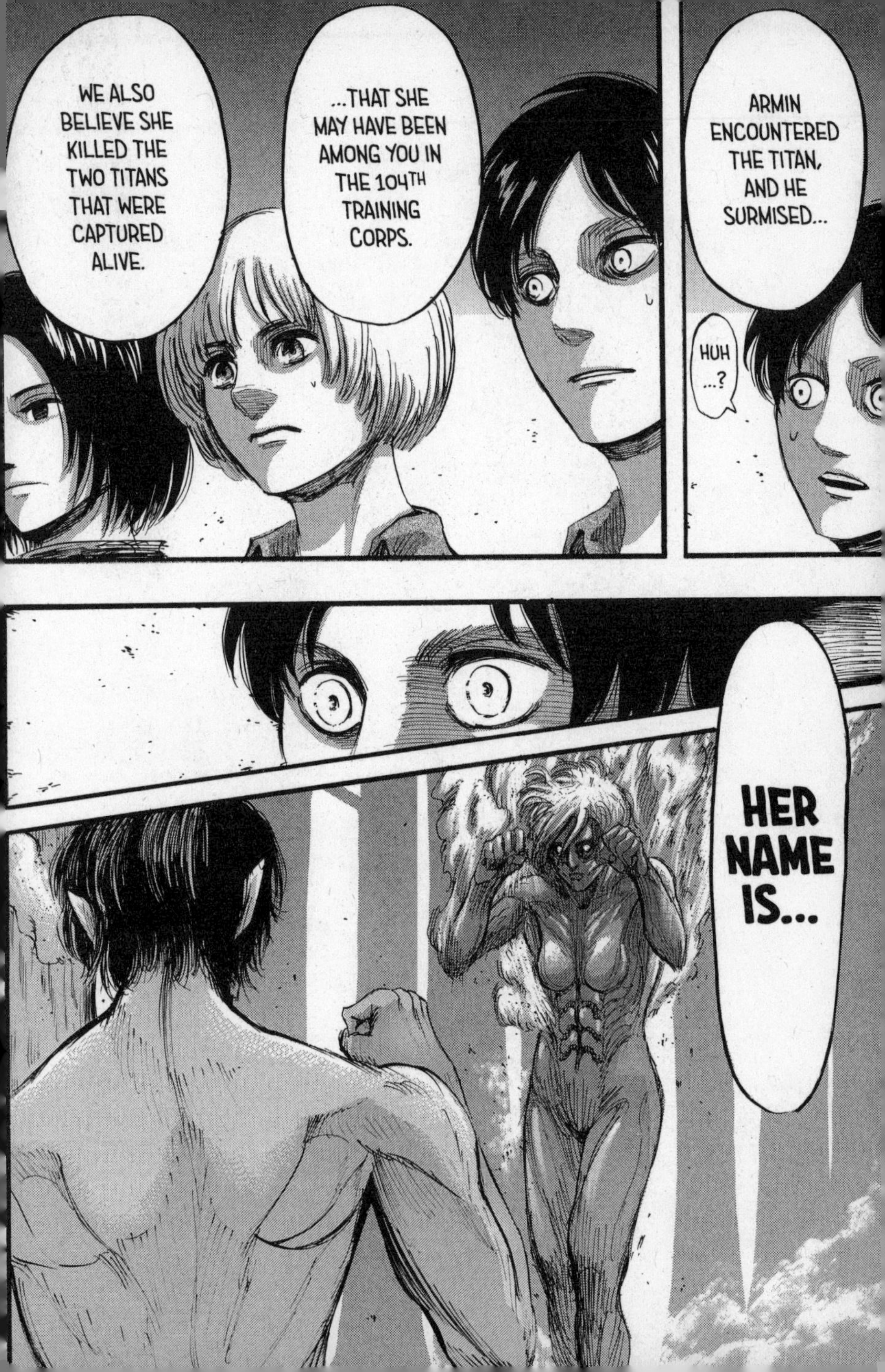
ARMIN ENCOUNTERED THE TITAN, AND HE SURMISED...
HUH ...?
...THAT SHE MAY HAVE BEEN AMONG YOU IN THE 104TH TRAINING CORPS.
WE ALSO BELIEVE SHE KILLED THE TWO TITANS THAT WERE CAPTURED ALIVE.
HER NAME IS...

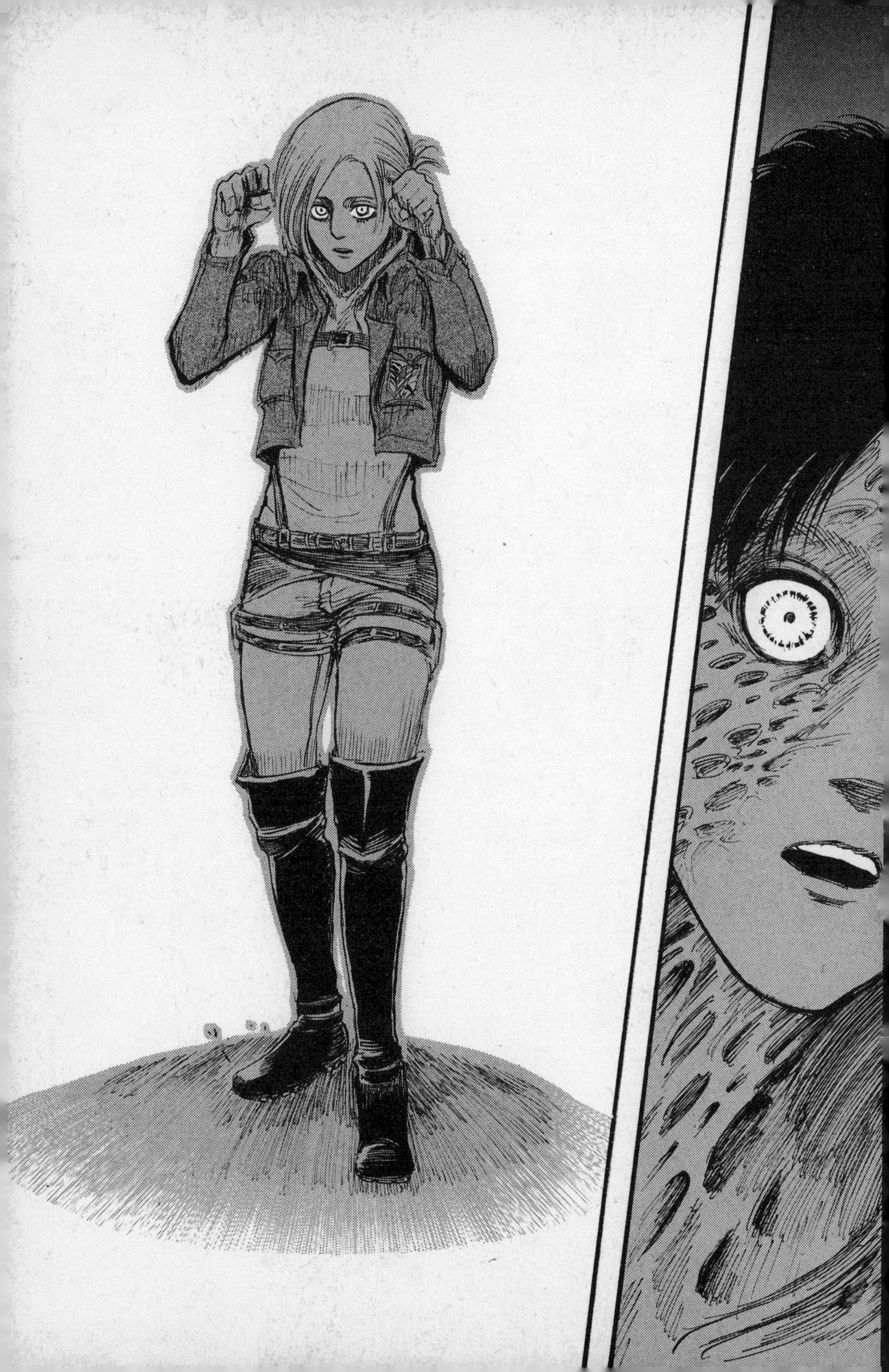

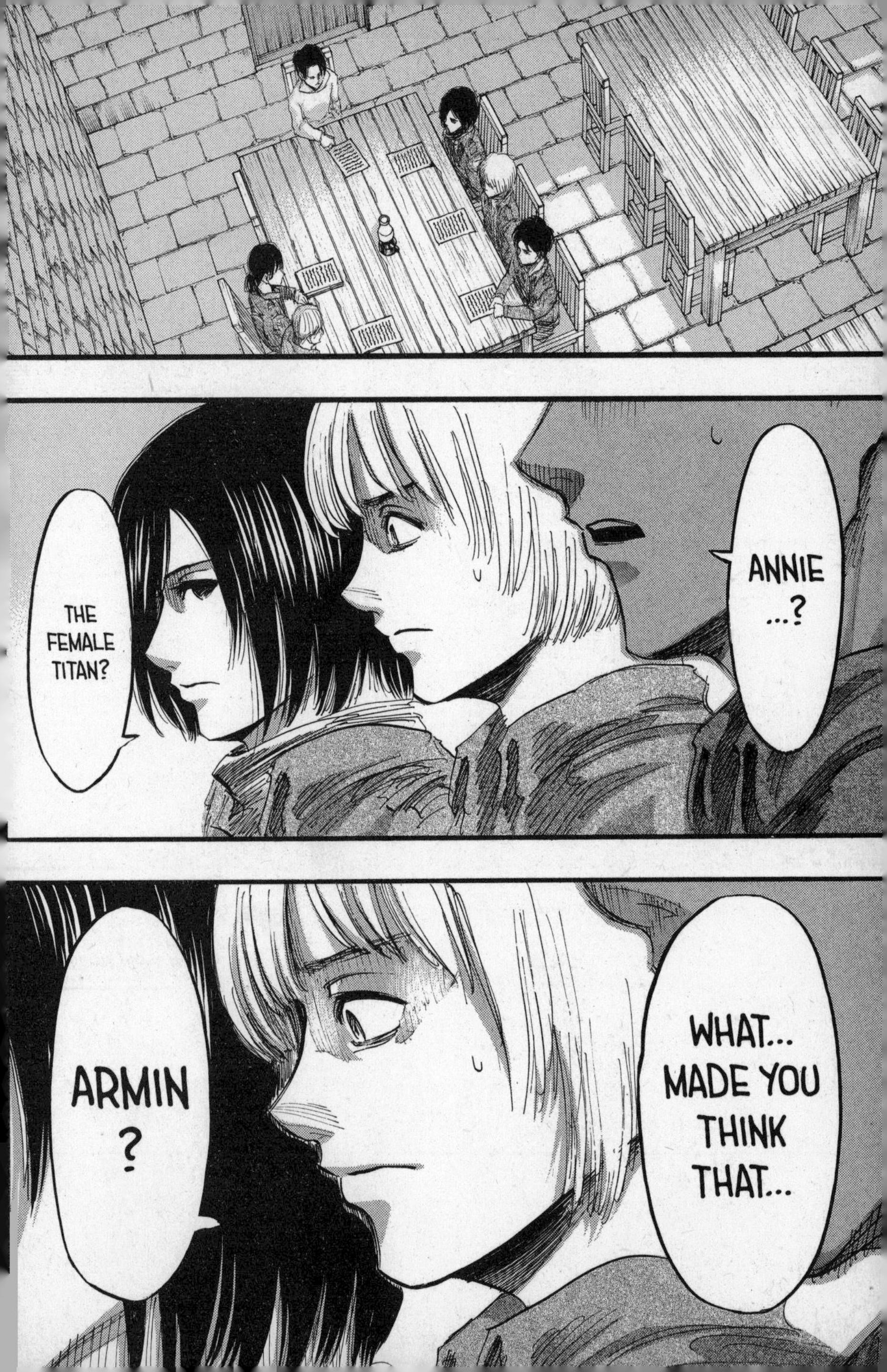
ANNIE ...?
THE FEMALE TITAN?
WHAT... MADE YOU THINK THAT...
ARMIN ?

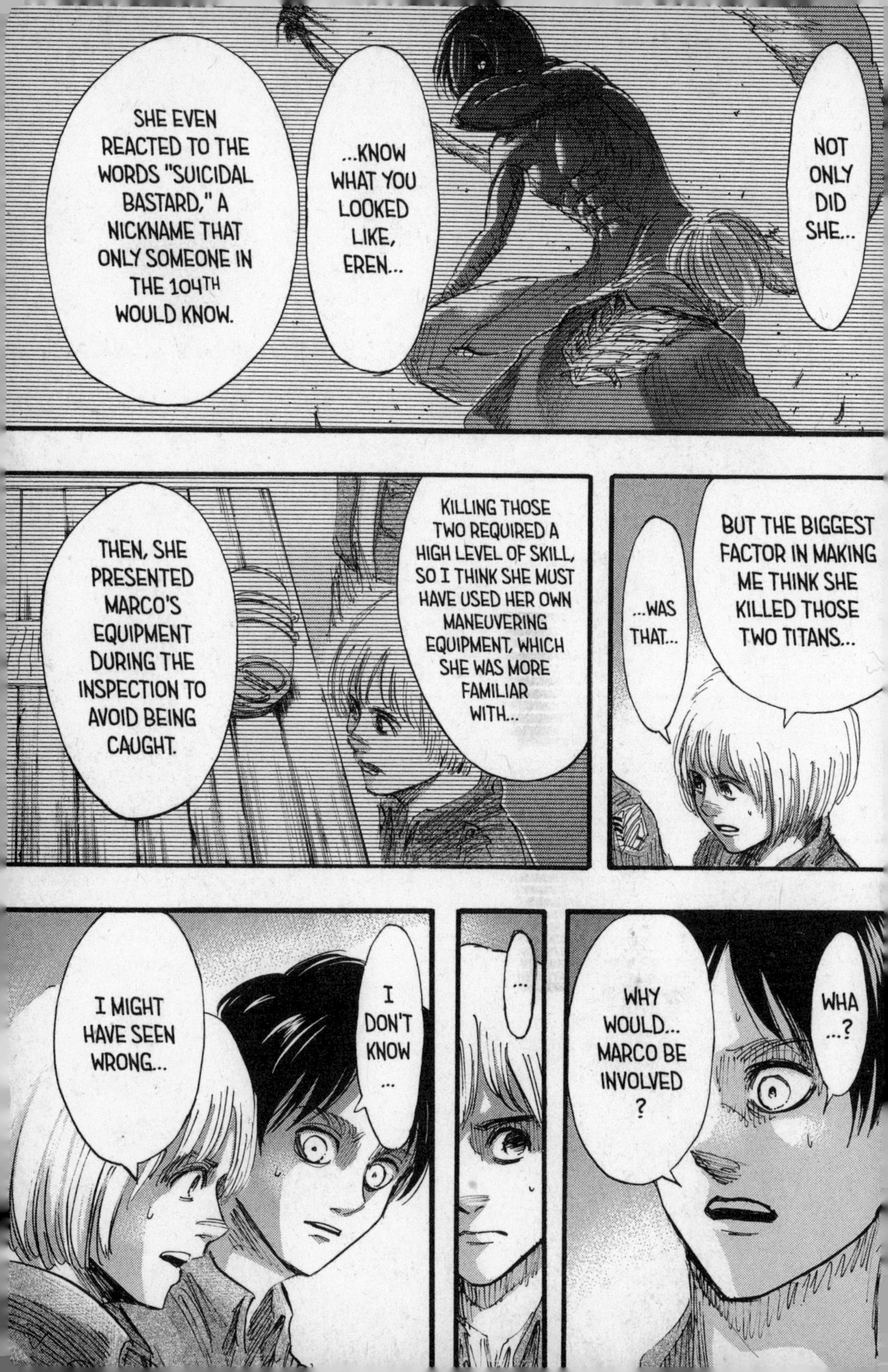
NOT ONLY DID SHE...
...KNOW WHAT YOU LOOKED LIKE, EREN...
SHE EVEN REACTED TO THE WORDS "SUICIDAL BASTARD," A NICKNAME THAT ONLY SOMEONE IN THE 104TH WOULD KNOW.
BUT THE BIGGEST FACTOR IN MAKING ME THINK SHE KILLED THOSE TWO TITANS...
...WAS THAT...
KILLING THOSE TWO REQUIRED A HIGH LEVEL OF SKILL, SO I THINK SHE MUST HAVE USED HER OWN MANEUVERING EQUIPMENT, WHICH SHE WAS MORE FAMILIAR WITH...
THEN, SHE PRESENTED MARCO'S EQUIPMENT DURING THE INSPECTION TO AVOID BEING CAUGHT.
WHA ...?
WHY WOULD... MARCO BE INVOLVED ?
...
I DON'T KNOW ...
I MIGHT HAVE SEEN WRONG...

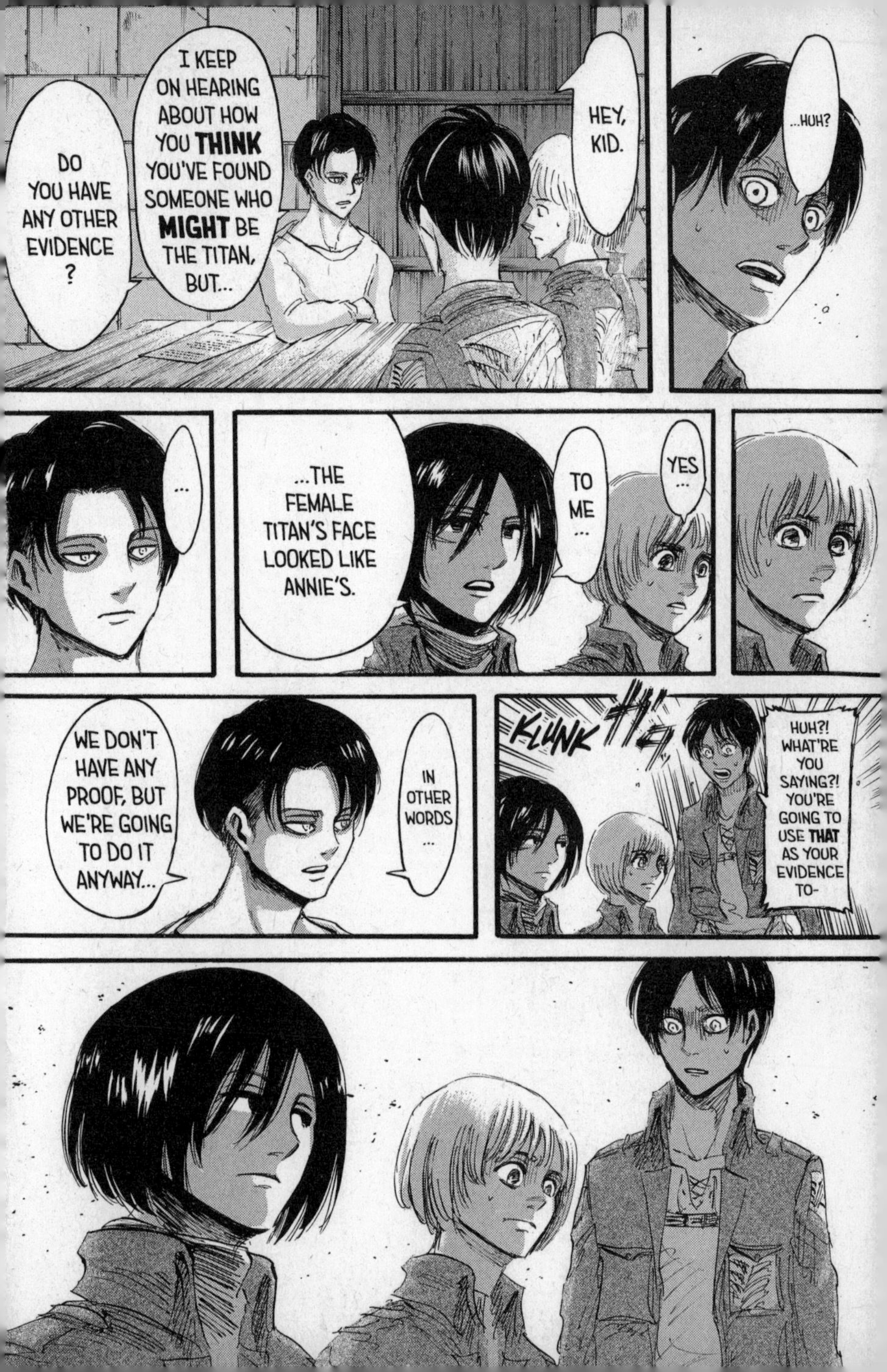
...HUH?
HEY, KID.
I KEEP ON HEARING ABOUT HOW YOU **THINK** YOU'VE FOUND SOMEONE WHO **MIGHT** BE THE TITAN, BUT...
DO YOU HAVE ANY OTHER EVIDENCE ?
YES ...
TO ME ...
...THE FEMALE TITAN'S FACE LOOKED LIKE ANNIE'S.
...
HUH?! WHAT'RE YOU SAYING?! YOU'RE GOING TO USE **THAT** AS YOUR EVIDENCE TO-
KLUNK
IN OTHER WORDS ...
WE DON'T HAVE ANY PROOF, BUT WE'RE GOING TO DO IT ANYWAY...

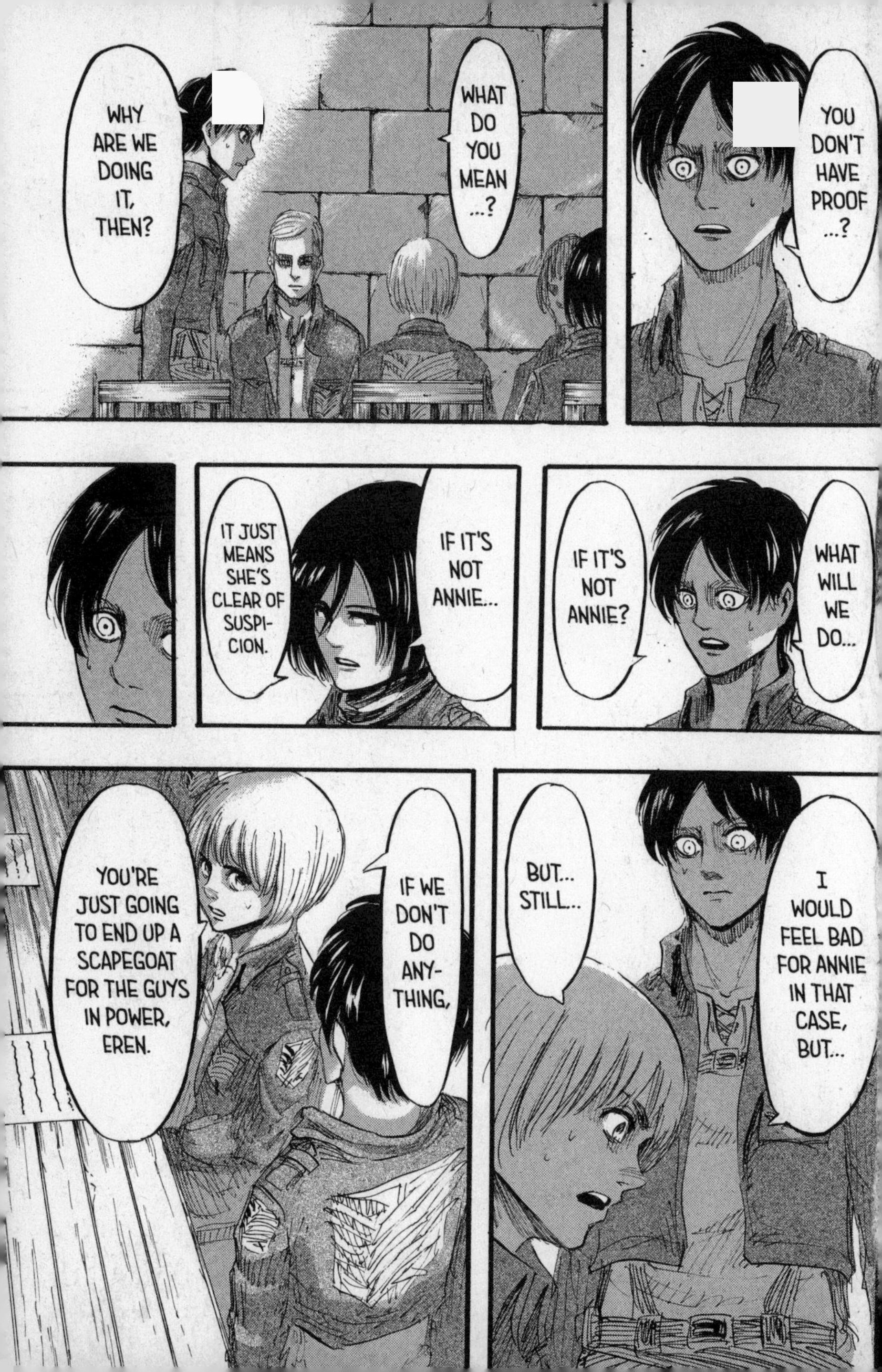
YOU DON'T HAVE PROOF ...?
WHAT DO YOU MEAN ...?
WHY ARE WE DOING IT, THEN?
WHAT WILL WE DO...
IF IT'S NOT ANNIE?
IF IT'S NOT ANNIE...
IT JUST MEANS SHE'S CLEAR OF SUSPICION.
I WOULD FEEL BAD FOR ANNIE IN THAT CASE, BUT...
BUT... STILL...
IF WE DON'T DO ANYTHING,
YOU'RE JUST GOING TO END UP A SCAPEGOAT FOR THE GUYS IN POWER, EREN.

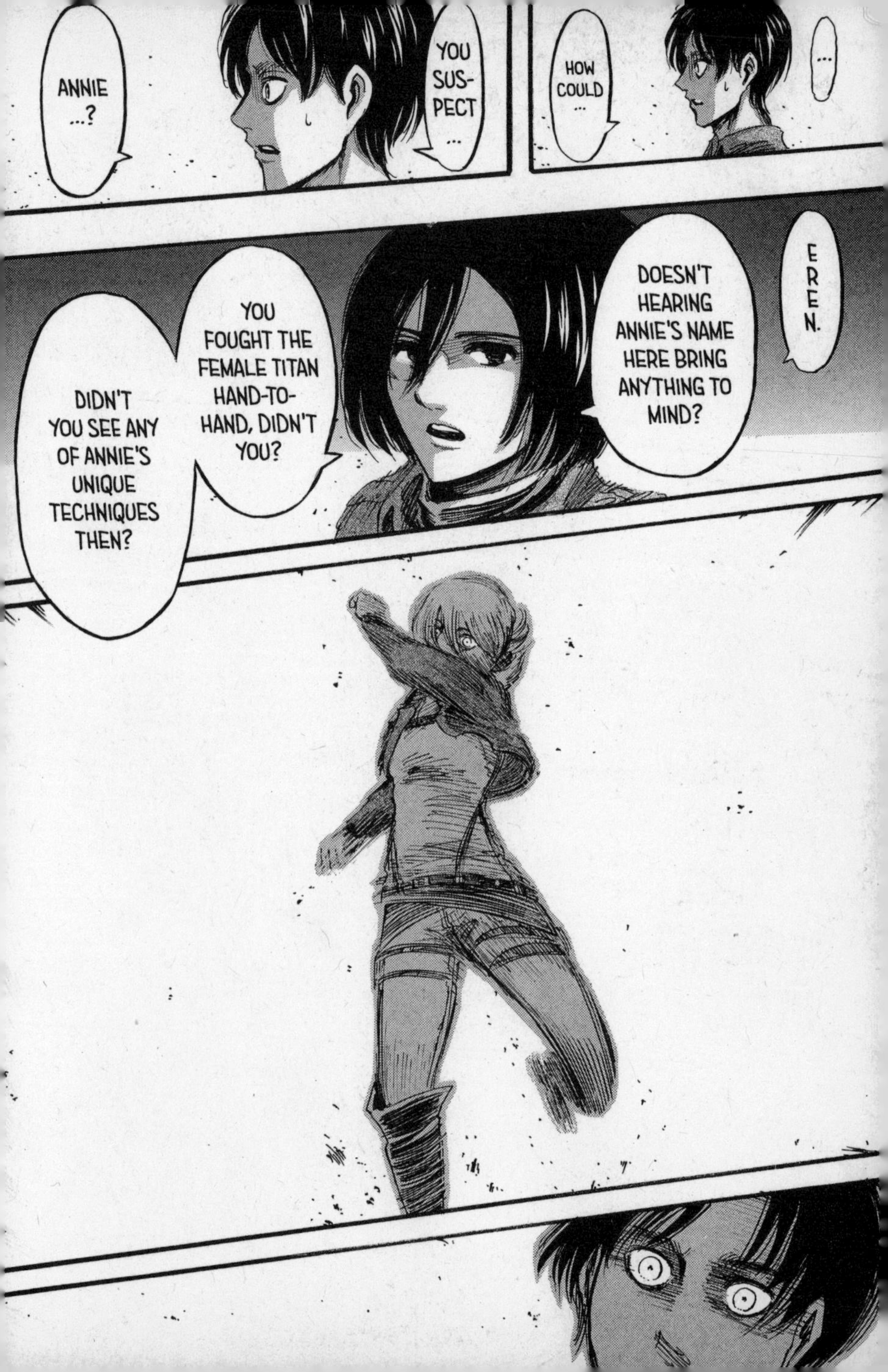
...
HOW COULD ...
YOU SUS-PECT ...
ANNIE ...?
EREN.
DOESN'T HEARING ANNIE'S NAME HERE BRING ANYTHING TO MIND?
YOU FOUGHT THE FEMALE TITAN HAND-TO-HAND, DIDN'T YOU?
DIDN'T YOU SEE ANY OF ANNIE'S UNIQUE TECHNIQUES THEN?

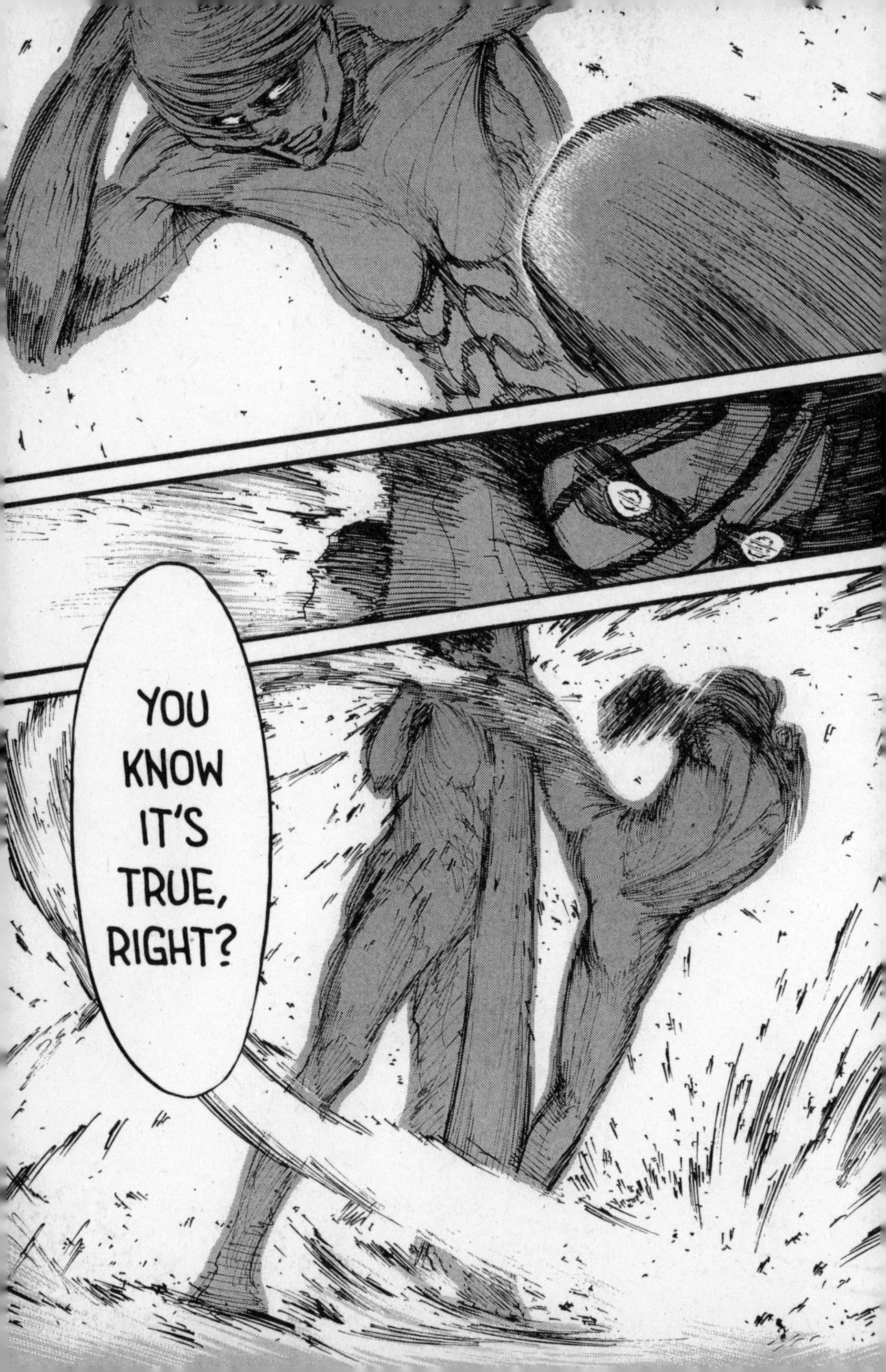
YOU KNOW IT'S TRUE, RIGHT?

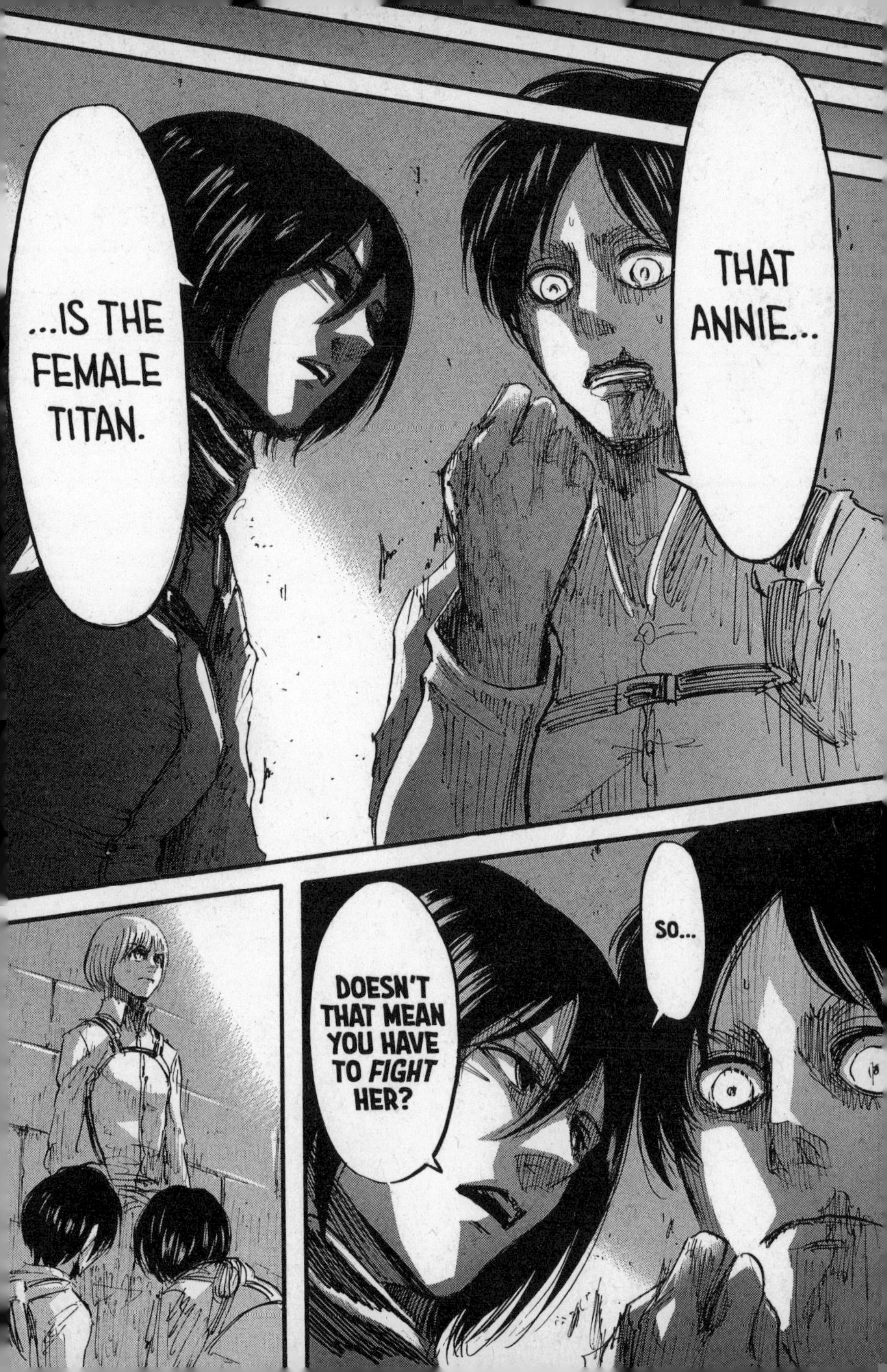
THAT ANNIE...
...IS THE FEMALE TITAN.
SO...
DOESN'T THAT MEAN YOU HAVE TO *FIGHT* HER?

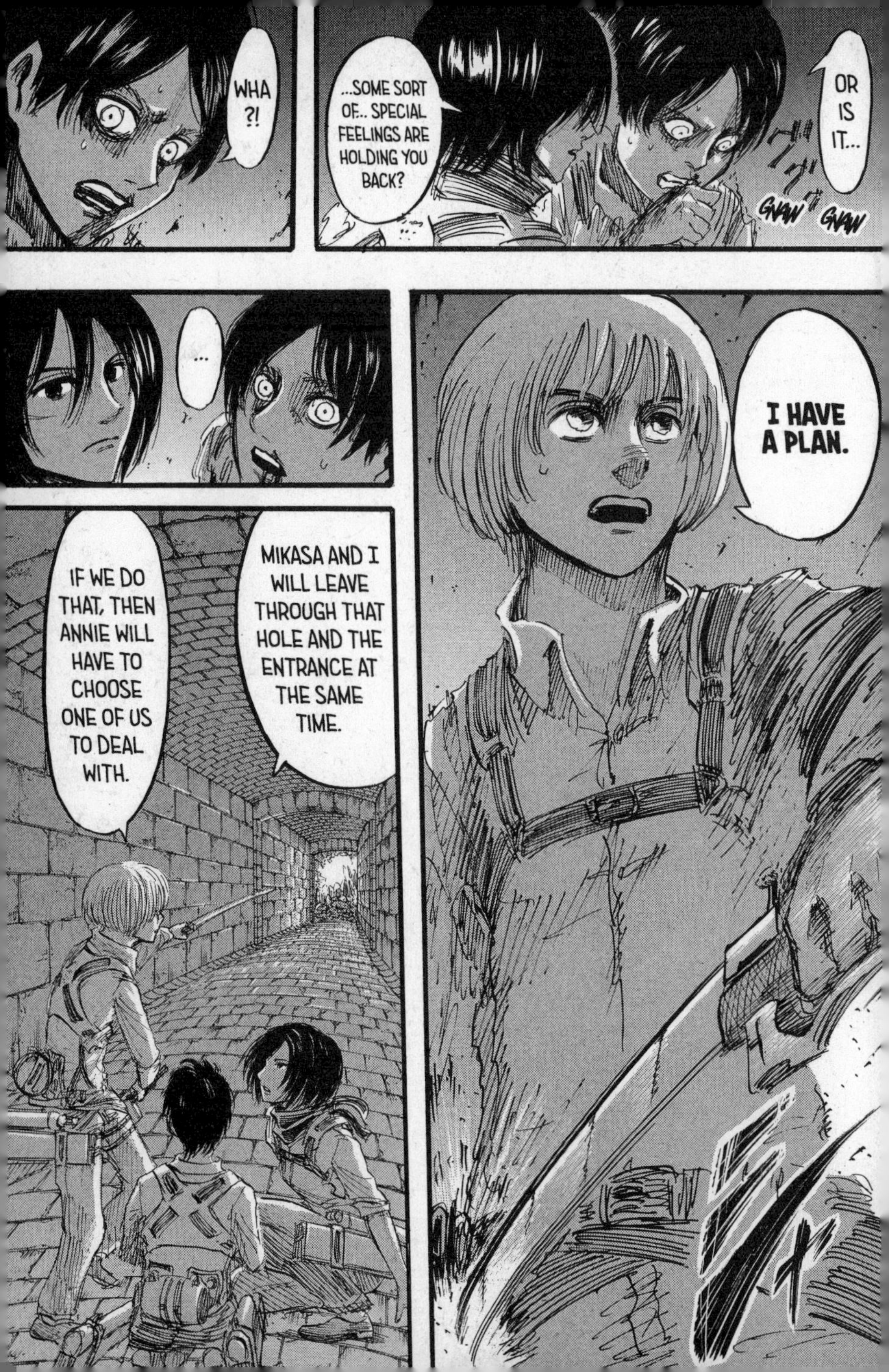
OR IS IT...
...SOME SORT OF.. SPECIAL FEELINGS ARE HOLDING YOU BACK?
GNAW GNAW
WHA ?!
I HAVE A PLAN.
...
MIKASA AND I WILL LEAVE THROUGH THAT HOLE AND THE ENTRANCE AT THE SAME TIME.
IF WE DO THAT, THEN ANNIE WILL HAVE TO CHOOSE ONE OF US TO DEAL WITH.

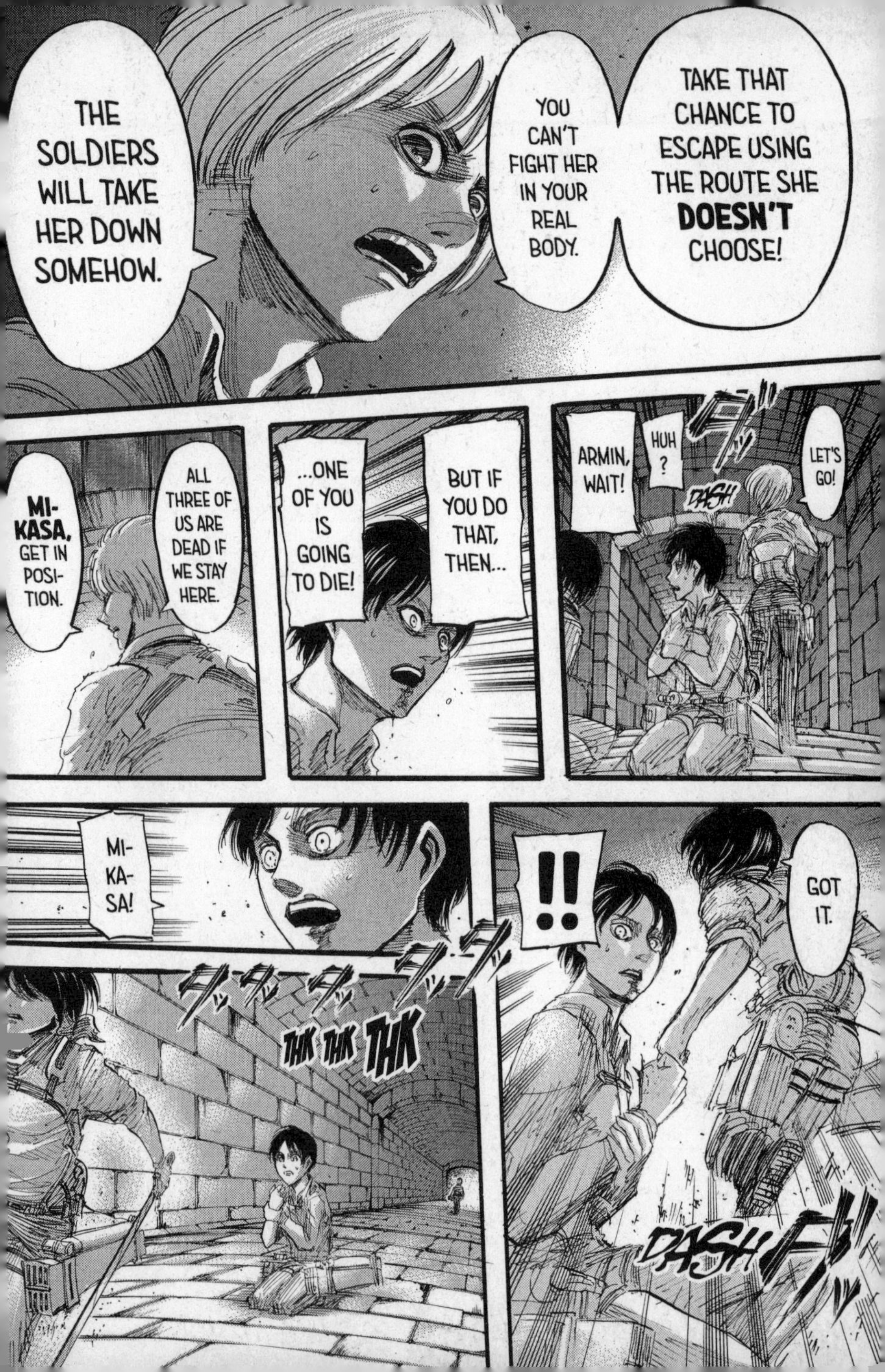
TAKE THAT CHANCE TO ESCAPE USING THE ROUTE SHE **DOESN'T** CHOOSE!
YOU CAN'T FIGHT HER IN YOUR REAL BODY.
THE SOLDIERS WILL TAKE HER DOWN SOMEHOW.
LET'S GO!
DASH
HUH ?
ARMIN, WAIT!
BUT IF YOU DO THAT, THEN...
...ONE OF YOU IS GOING TO DIE!
ALL THREE OF US ARE DEAD IF WE STAY HERE.
MI-KASA, GET IN POSI-TION.
GOT IT.
!!
DASH
MI-KA-SA!
THK THK THK

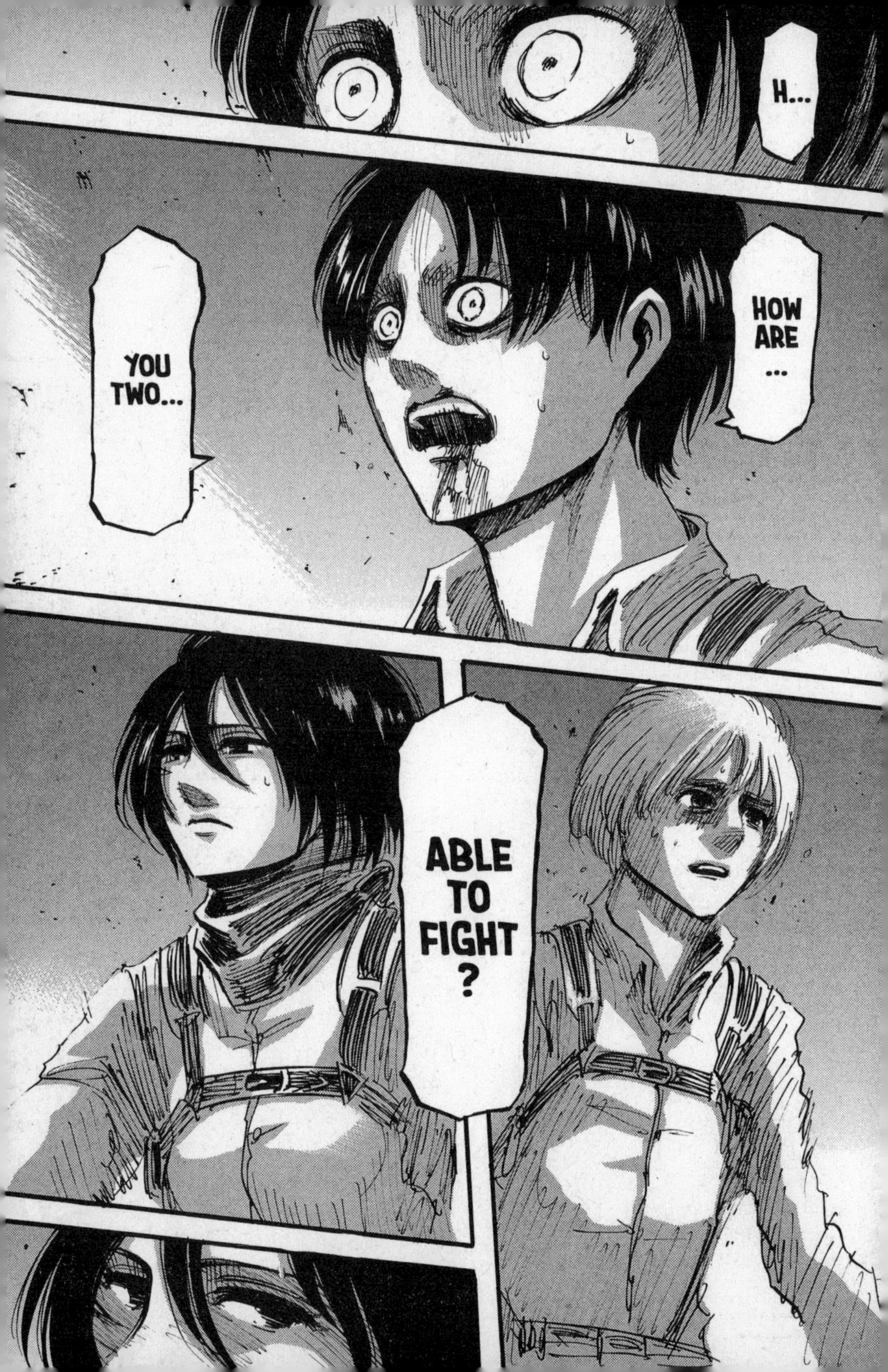
H...
HOW ARE ...
YOU TWO...
ABLE TO FIGHT ?

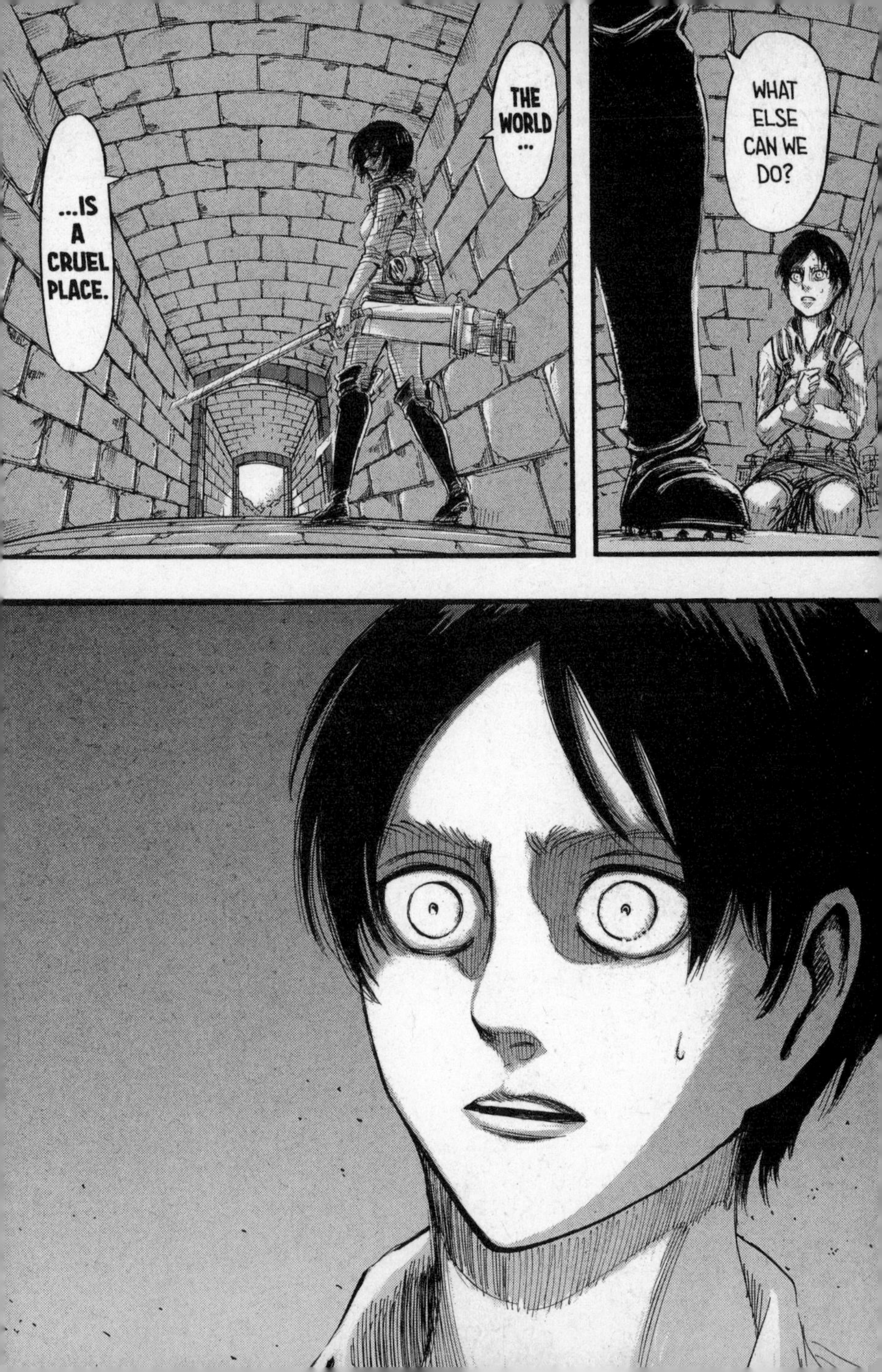
WHAT ELSE CAN WE DO?
THE WORLD...
...IS A CRUEL PLACE.

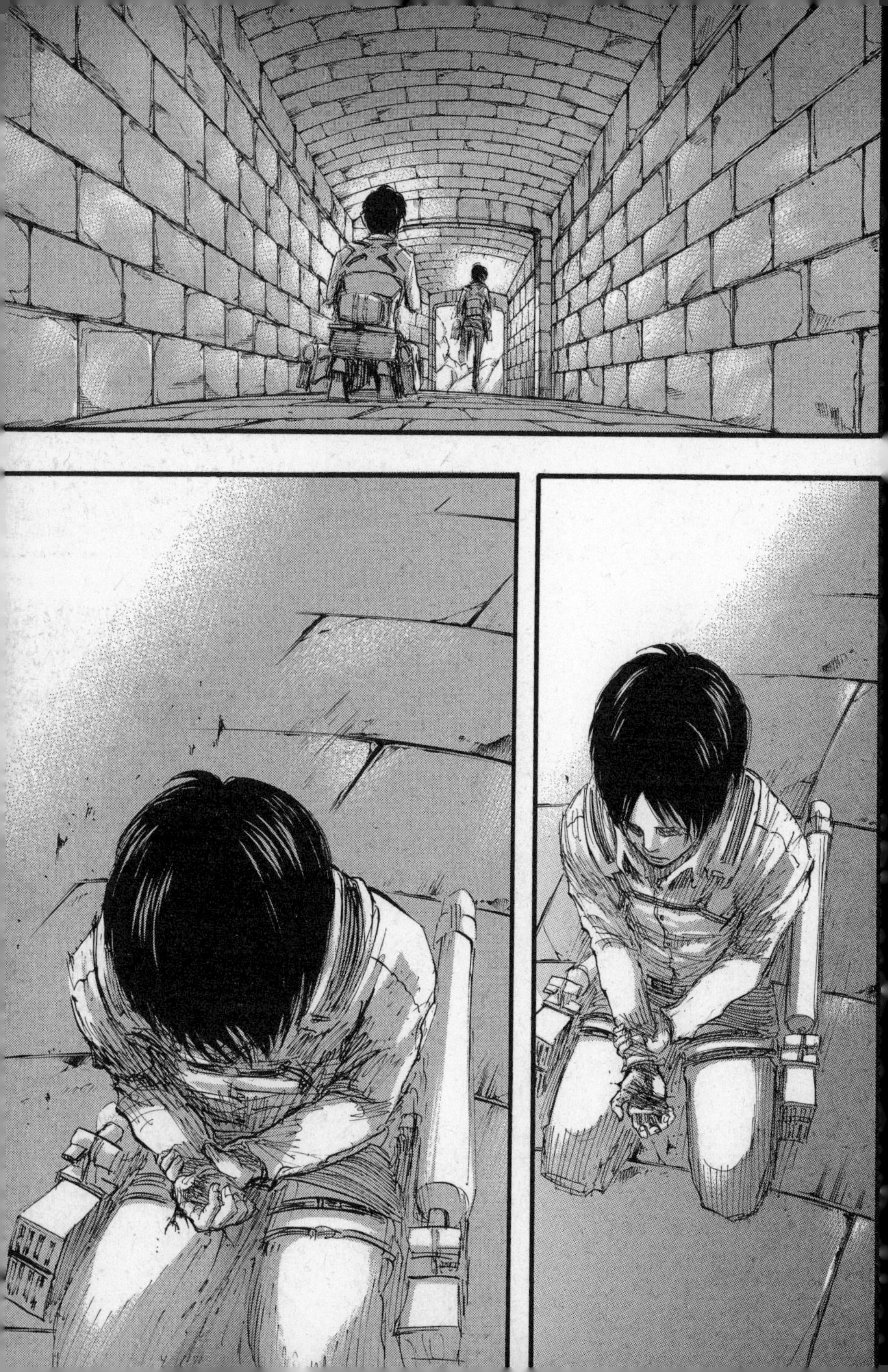

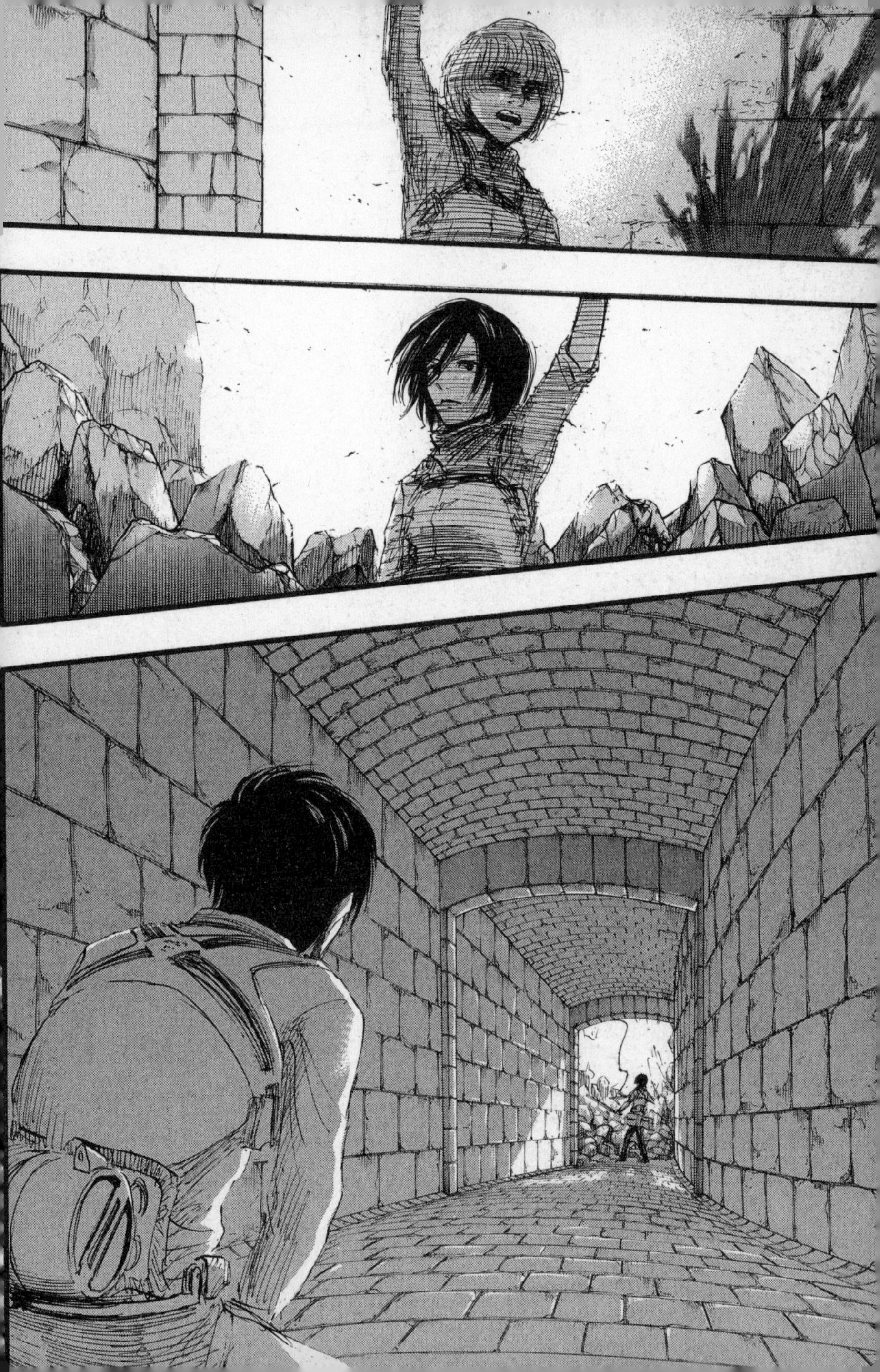

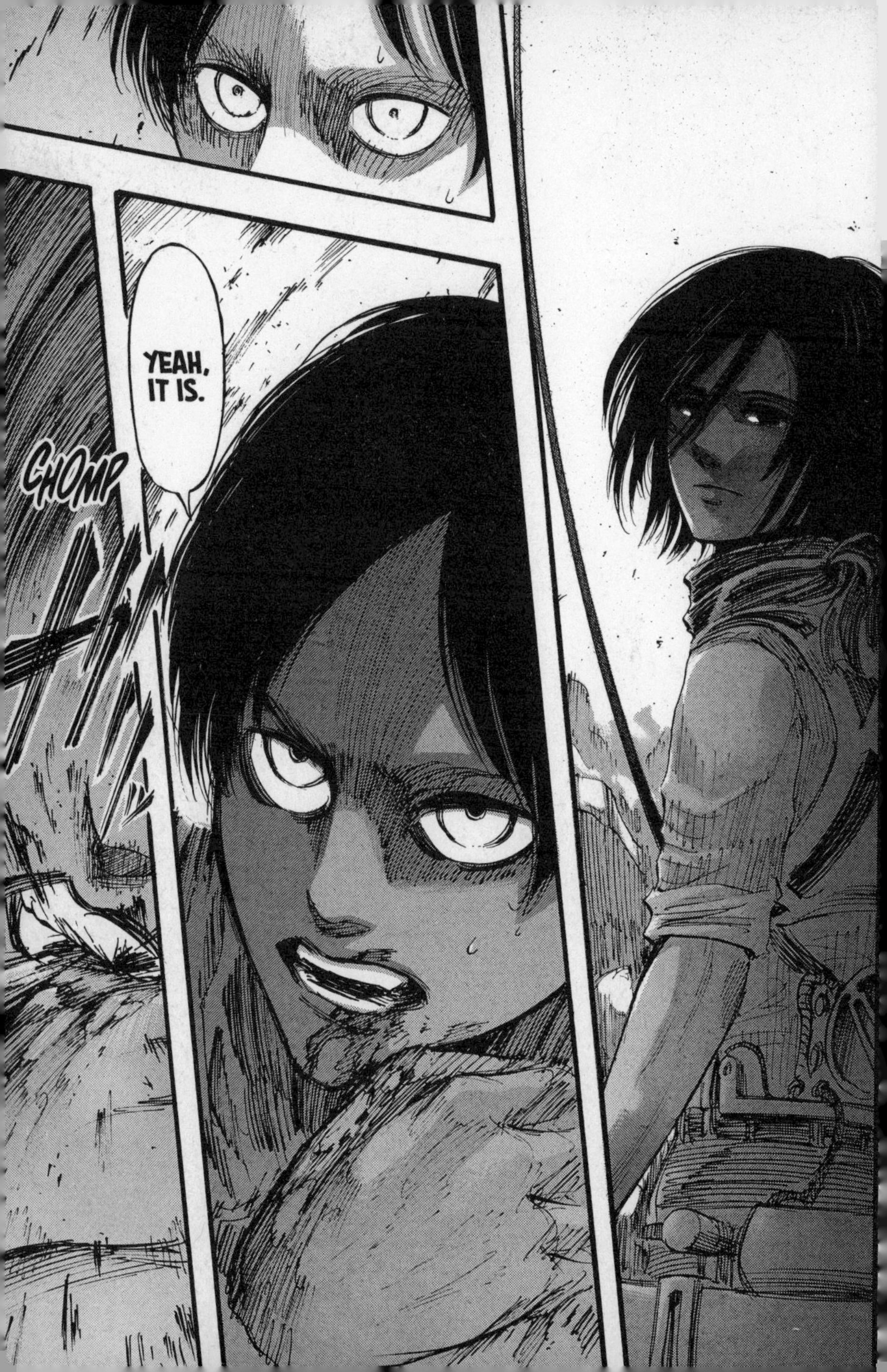
YEAH, IT IS.
CHOMP

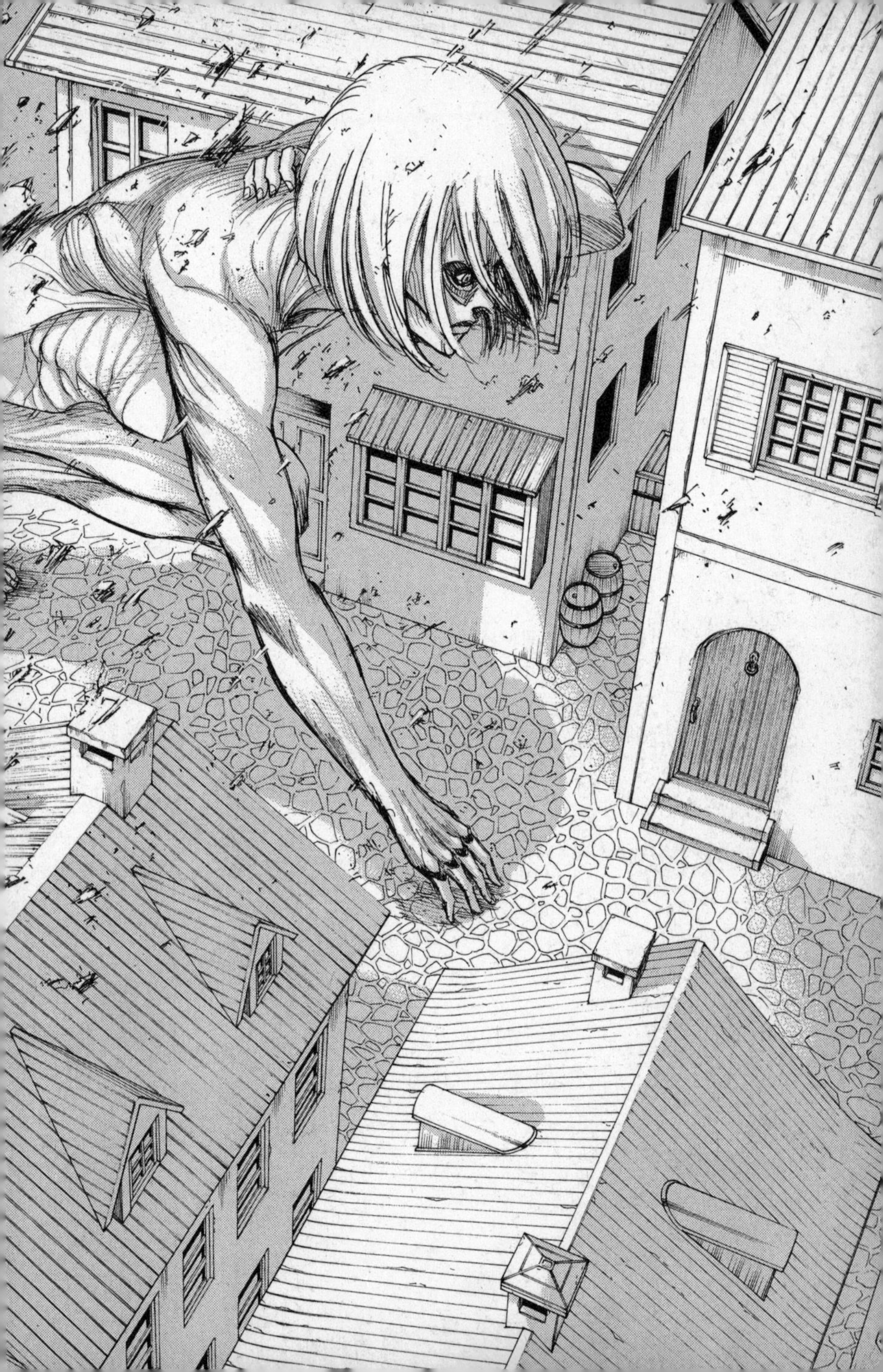

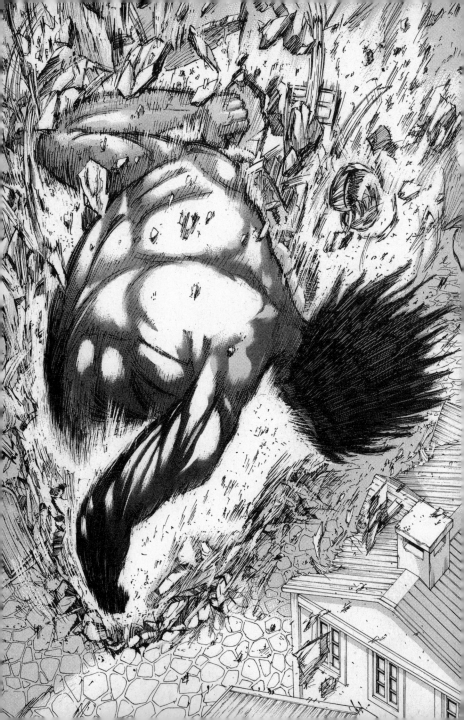

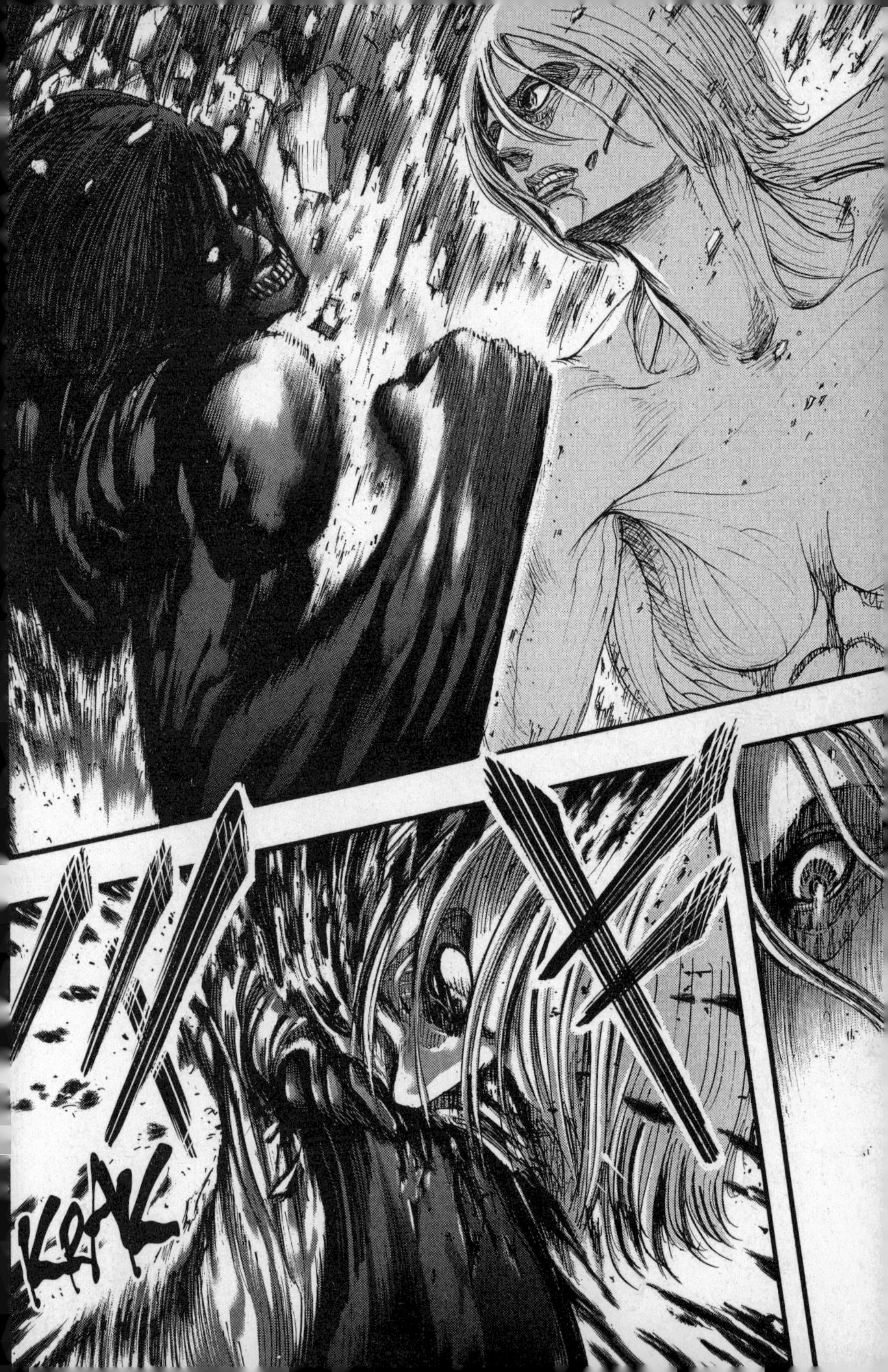
KRAK

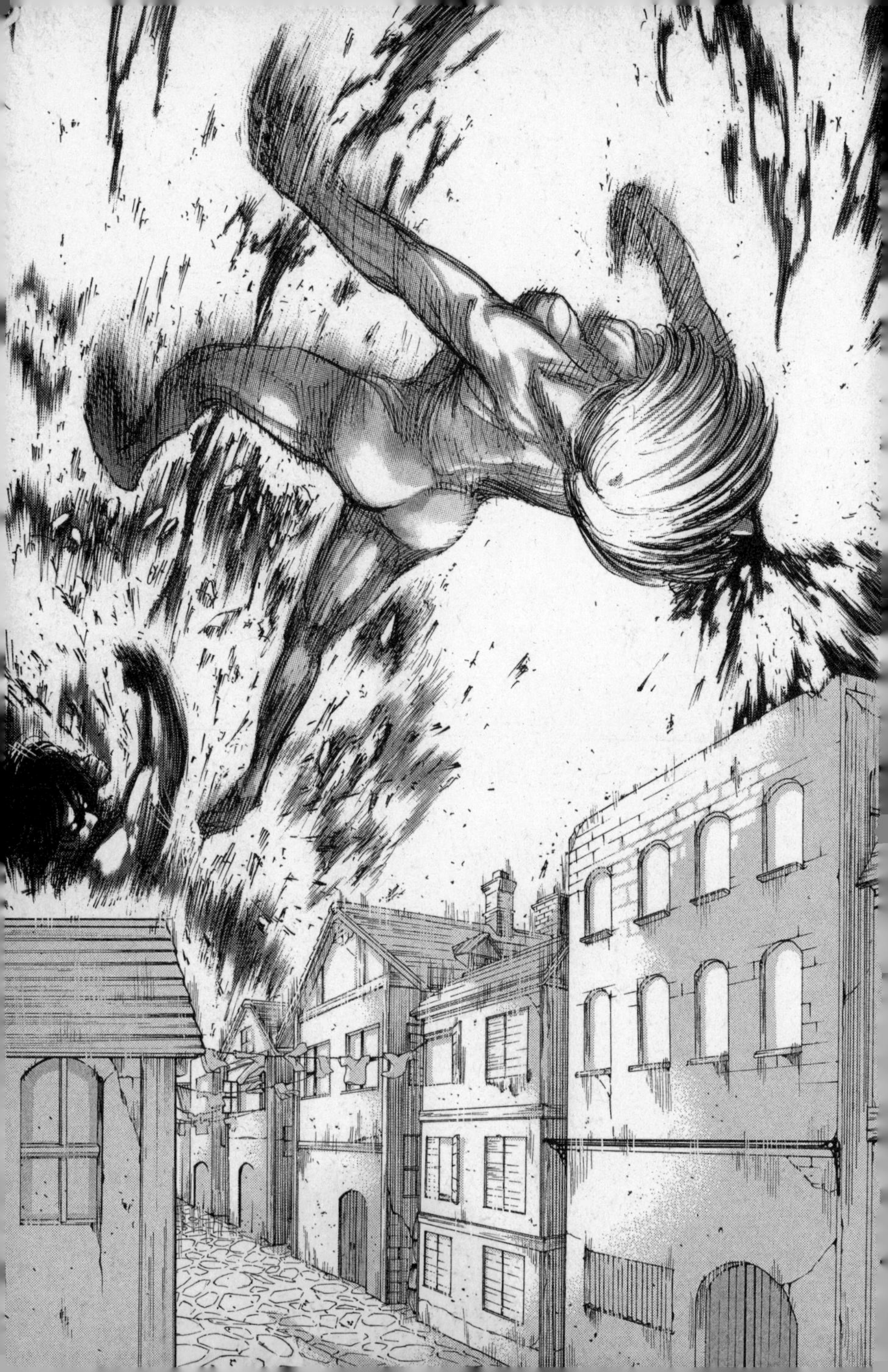

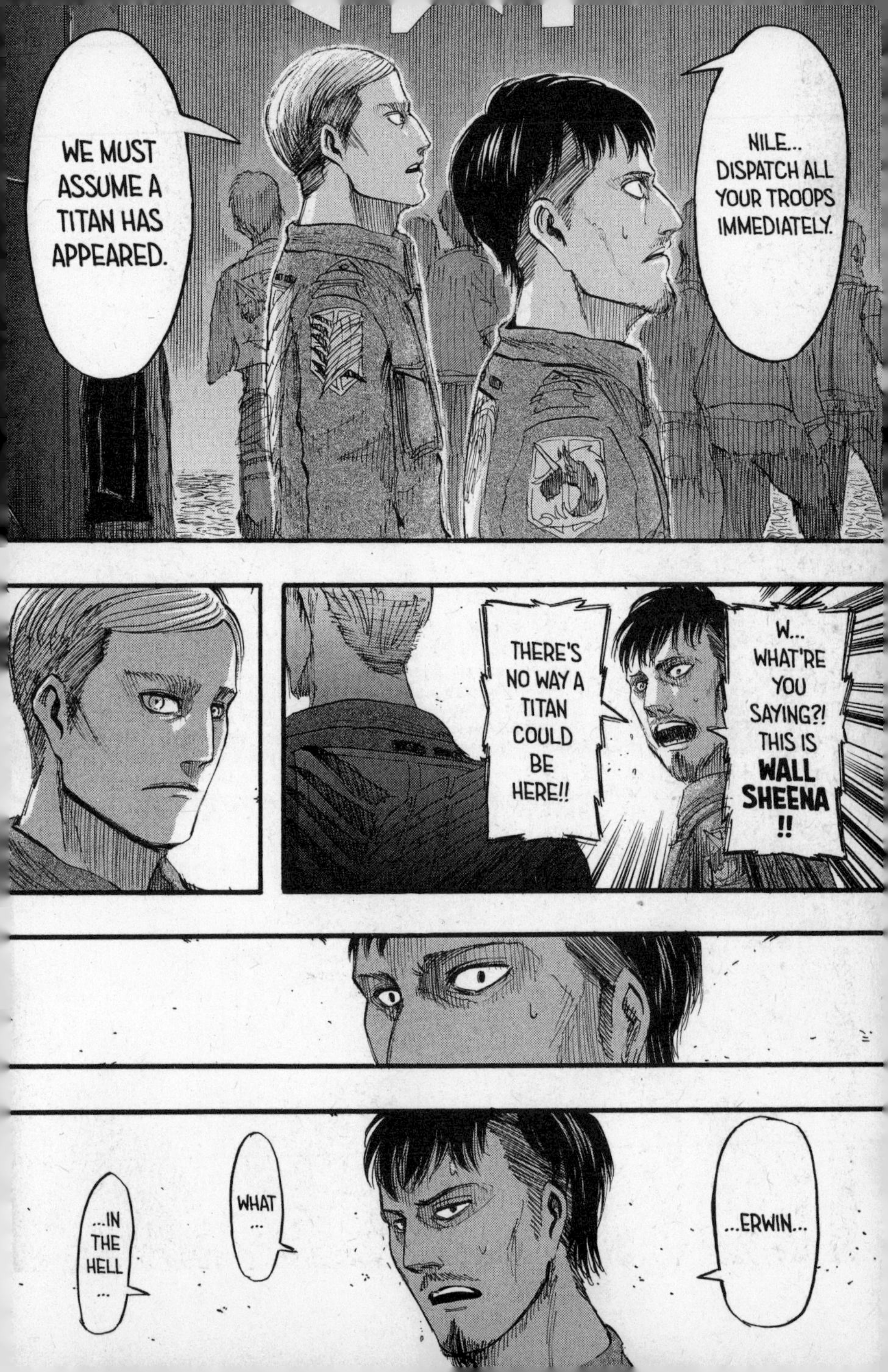
WE MUST ASSUME A TITAN HAS APPEARED.
NILE... DISPATCH ALL YOUR TROOPS IMMEDIATELY.
THERE'S NO WAY A TITAN COULD BE HERE!!
W... WHAT'RE YOU SAYING?! THIS IS **WALL SHEENA**!!
...ERWIN...
WHAT ...
...IN THE HELL ...

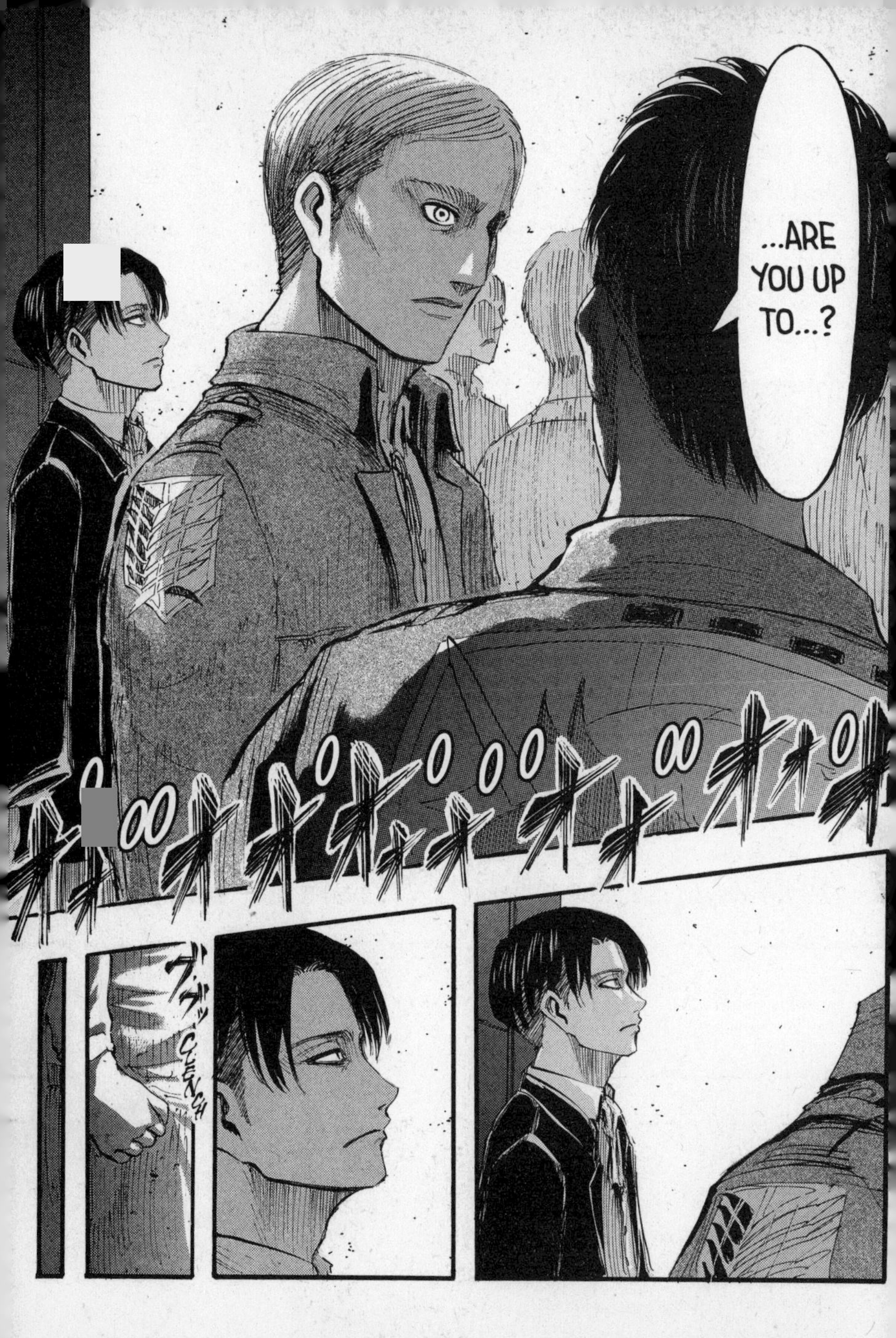
...ARE YOU UP TO...?
CLENCH

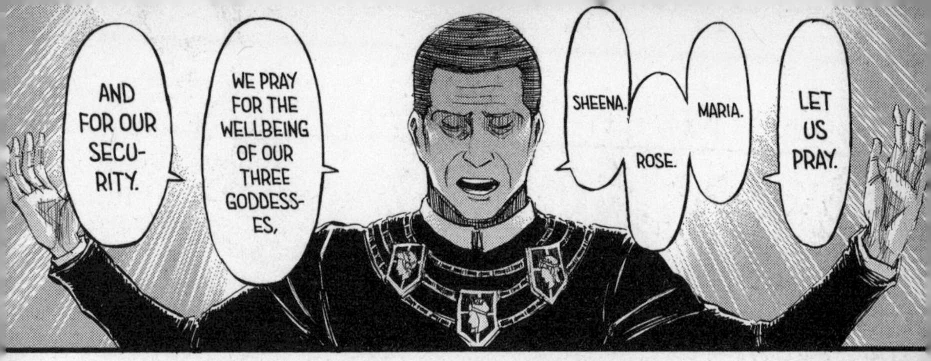
LET US PRAY.
MARIA.
ROSE.
SHEENA.
WE PRAY FOR THE WELLBEING OF OUR THREE GODDESS-ES,
AND FOR OUR SECU-RITY.

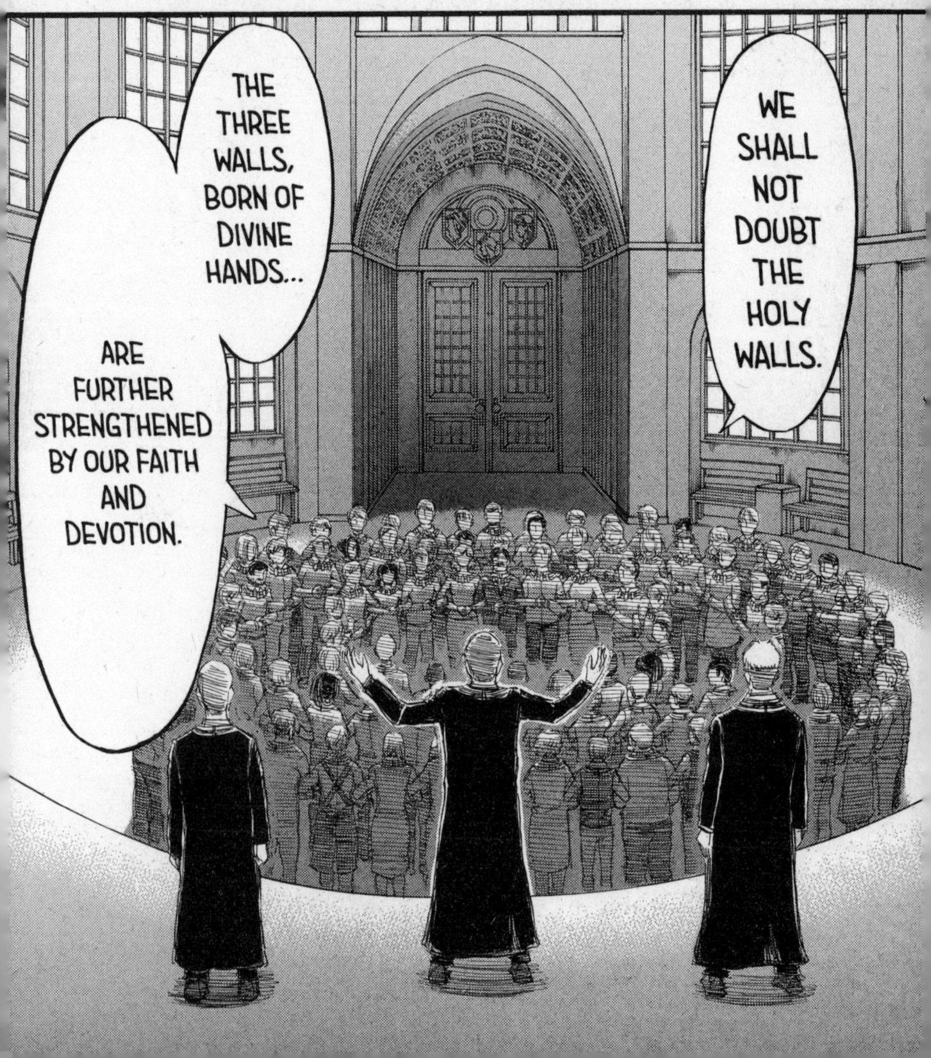
WE SHALL NOT DOUBT THE HOLY WALLS.
THE THREE WALLS, BORN OF DIVINE HANDS...
ARE FURTHER STRENGTHENED BY OUR FAITH AND DEVOTION.

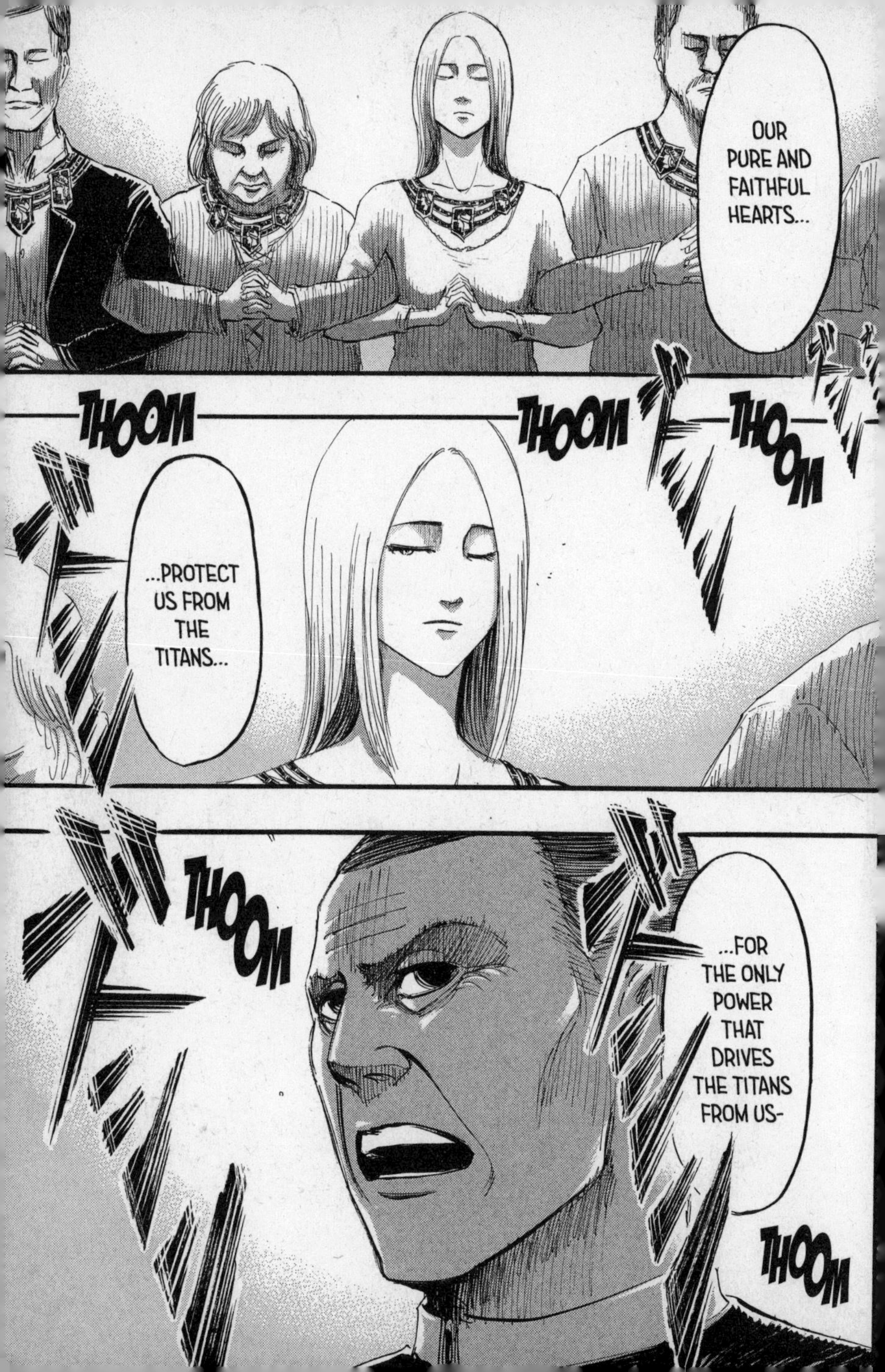
OUR PURE AND FAITHFUL HEARTS...
THOOM
THOOM
THOOM
...PROTECT US FROM THE TITANS...
...FOR THE ONLY POWER THAT DRIVES THE TITANS FROM US-
THOOM
THOOM

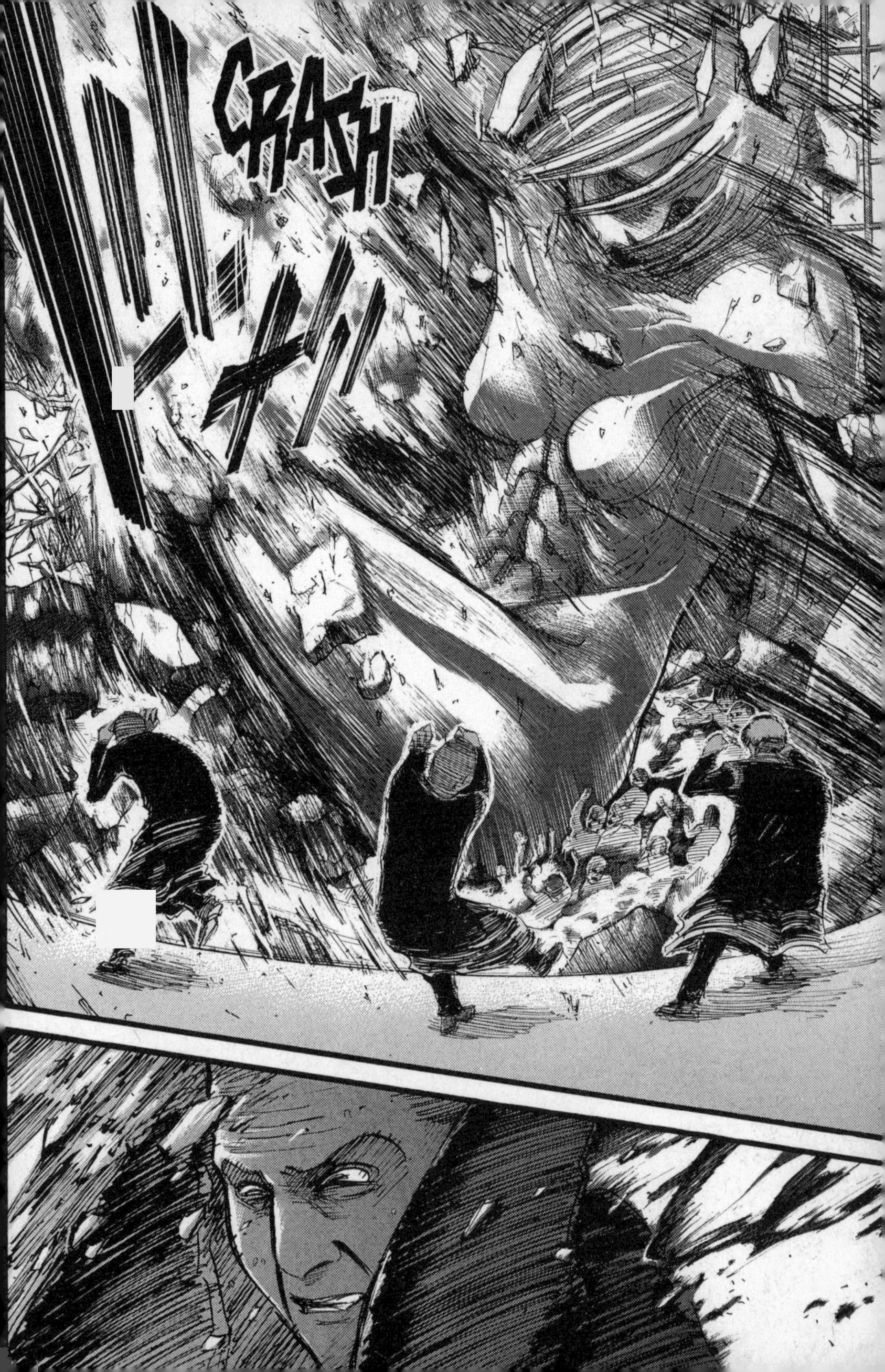
CRASH

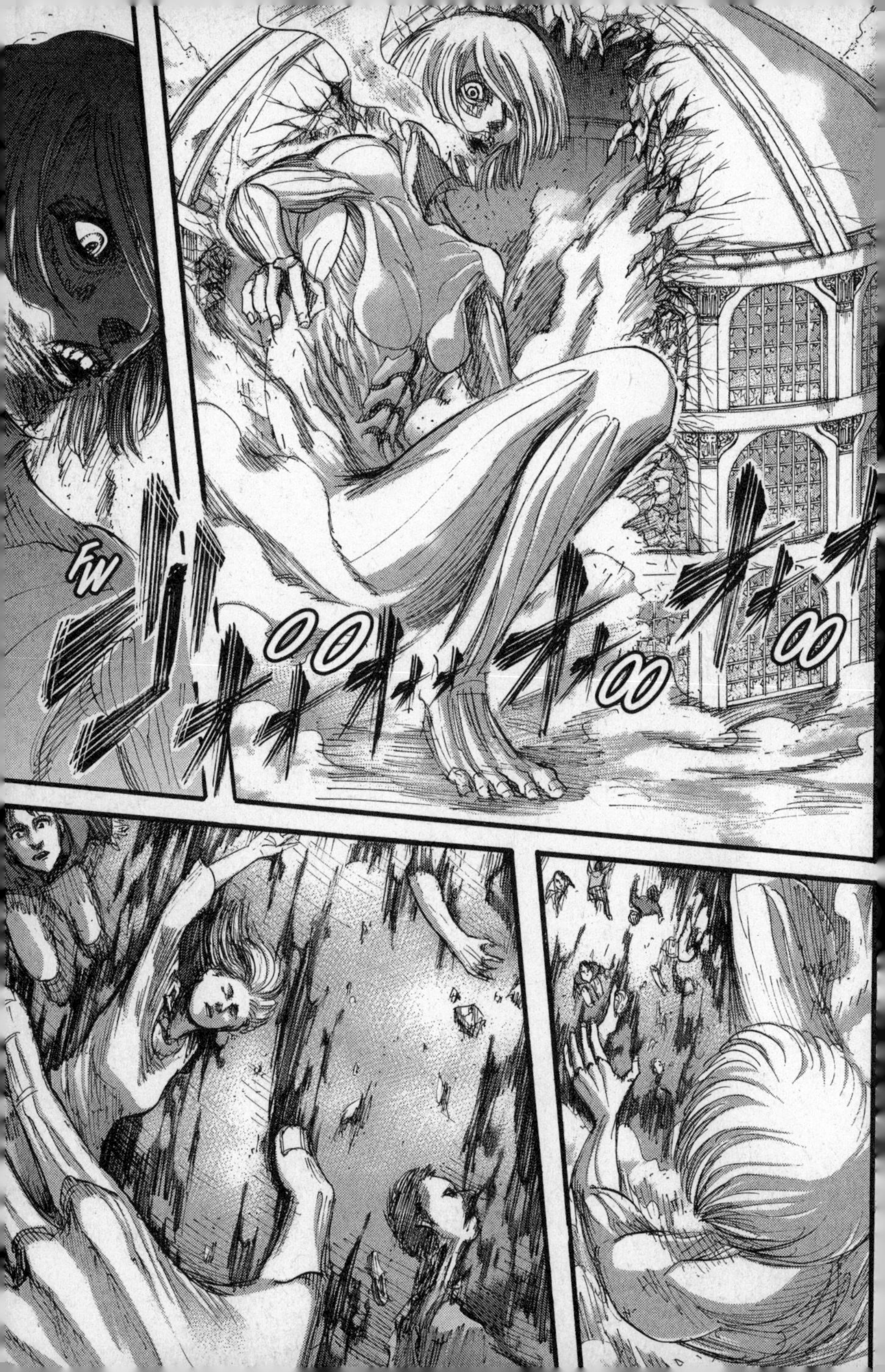
FWOOOOOOOO

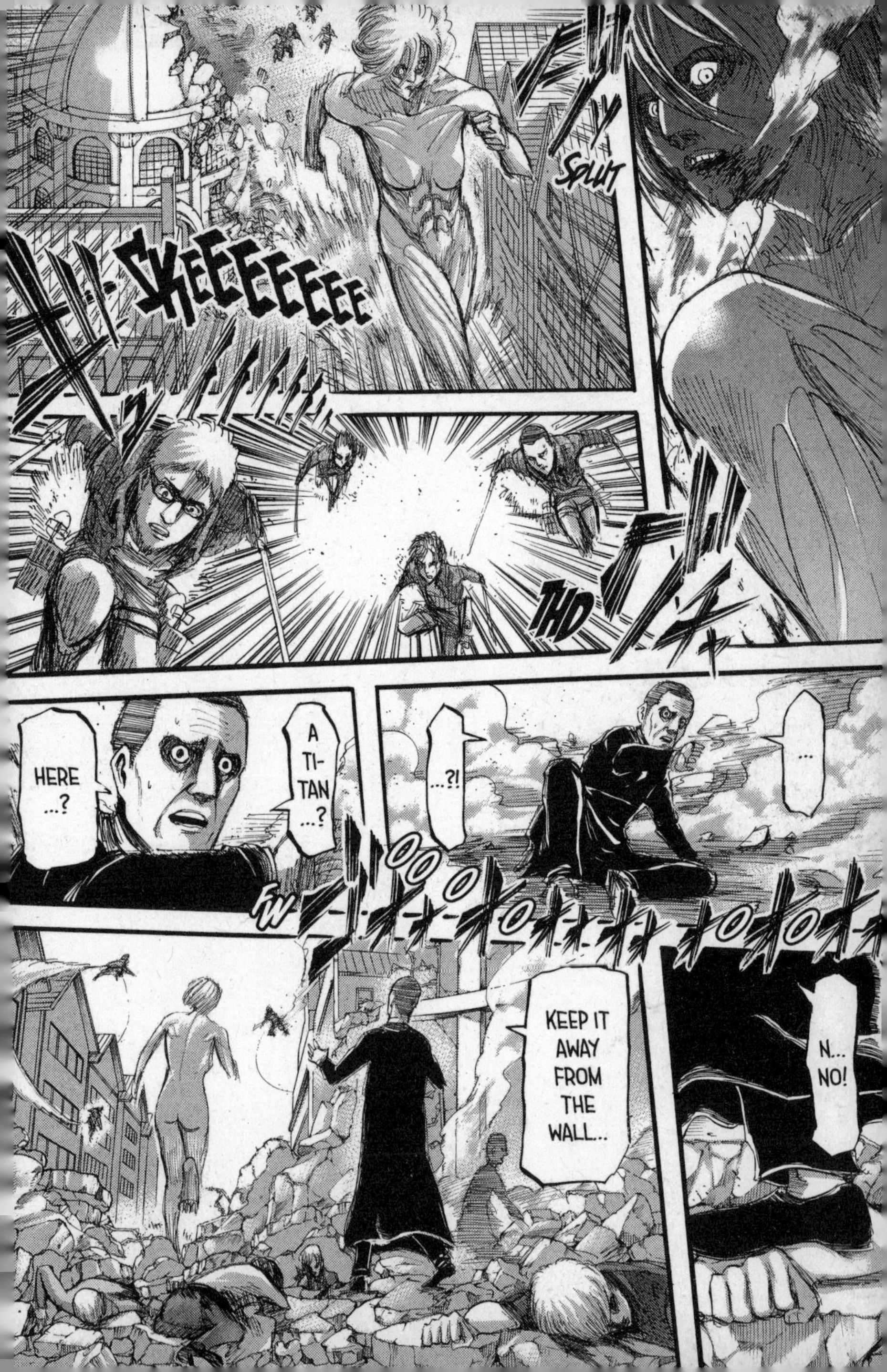
SPLUT
SKEEEEEEEE
THD
...
...?!
A TI-TAN ...?
HERE ...?
FWOOOO
N... NO!
KEEP IT AWAY FROM THE WALL...

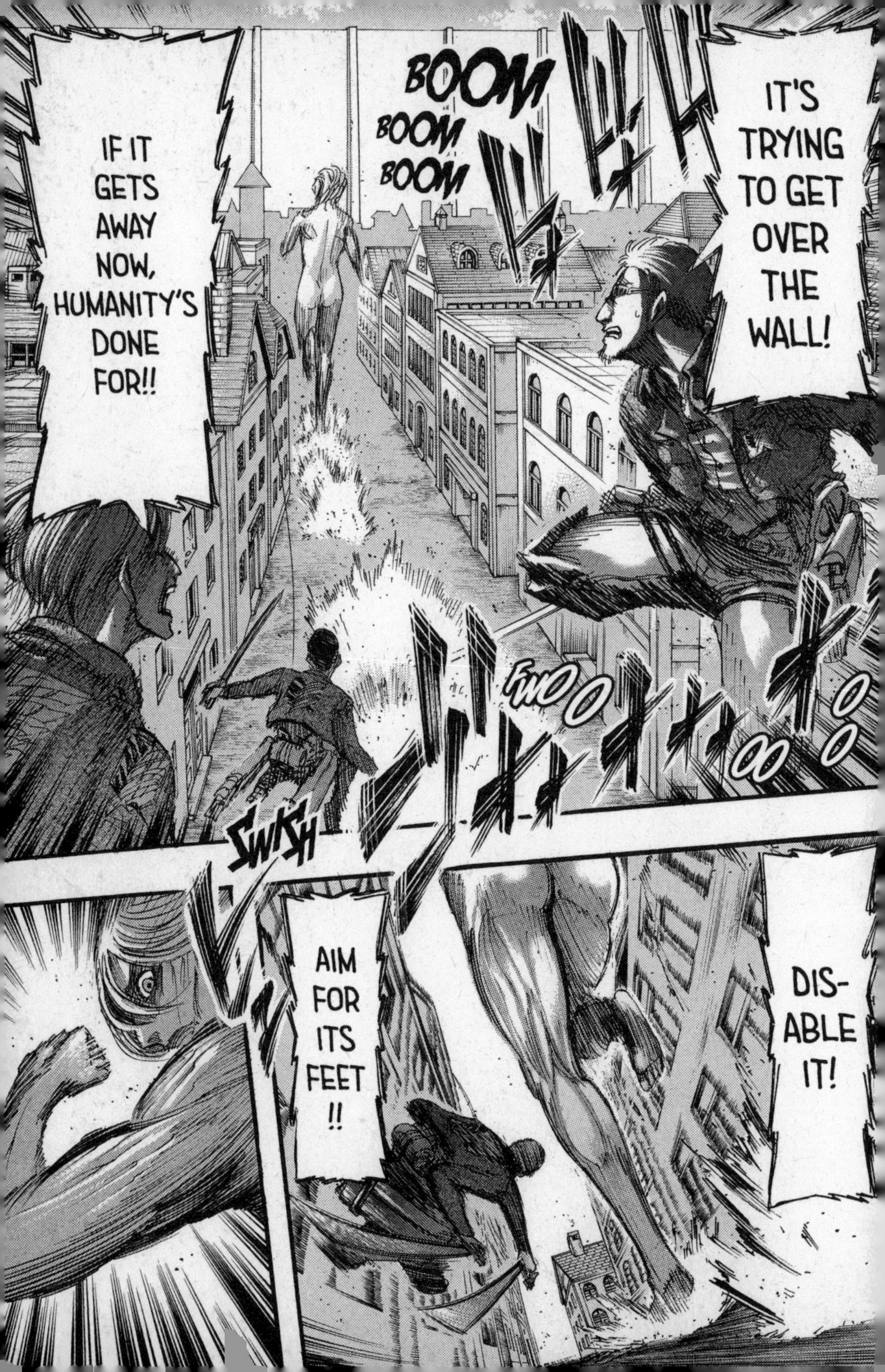

IT'S TRYING TO GET OVER THE WALL!
BOOM
BOOM
BOOM
IF IT GETS AWAY NOW, HUMANITY'S DONE FOR!!
FWOOO
SWSH
DIS-ABLE IT!
AIM FOR ITS FEET!!

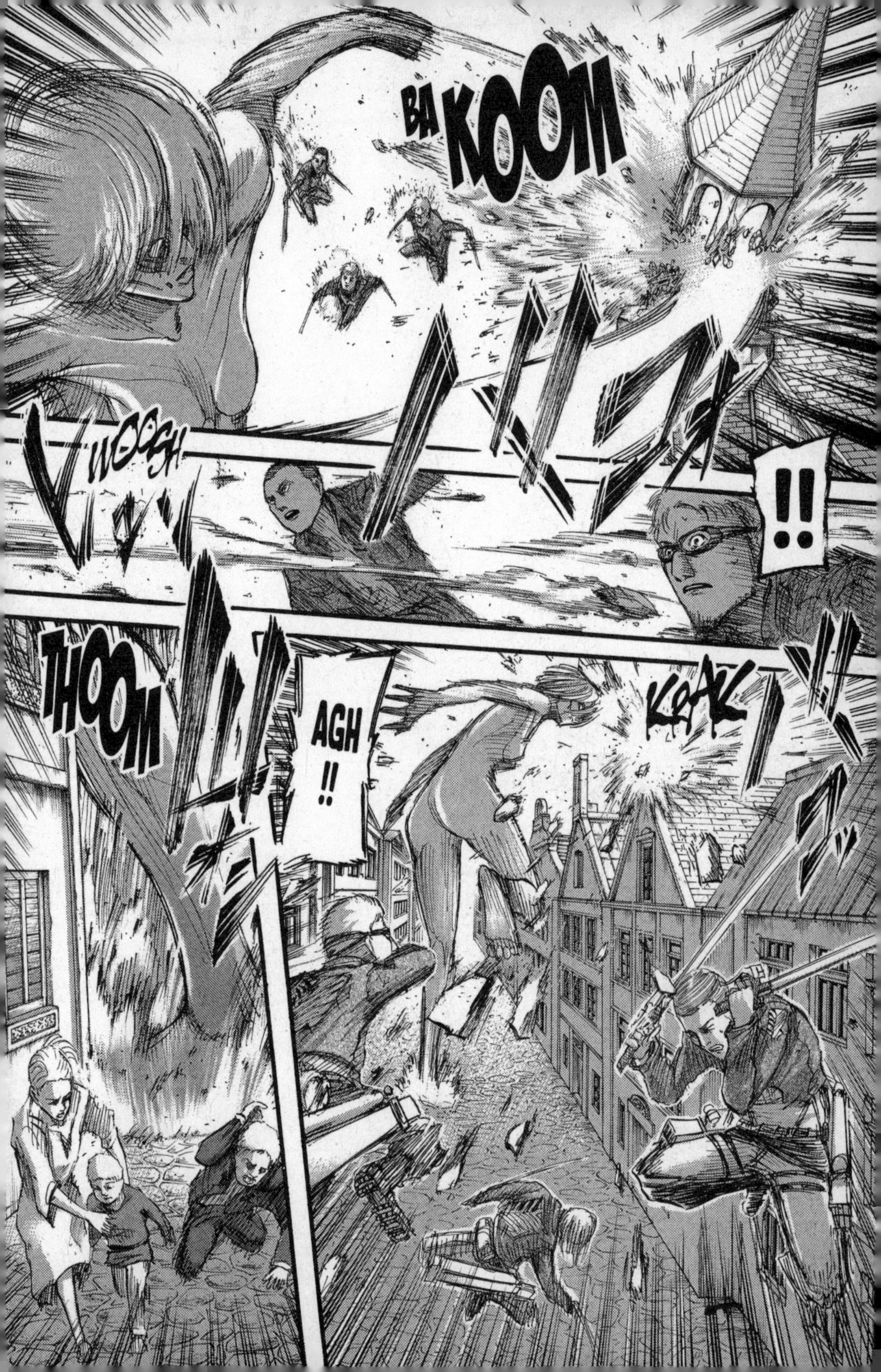
BA KOOM
!!
WOOSH
KRAK
AGH !!
THOOM

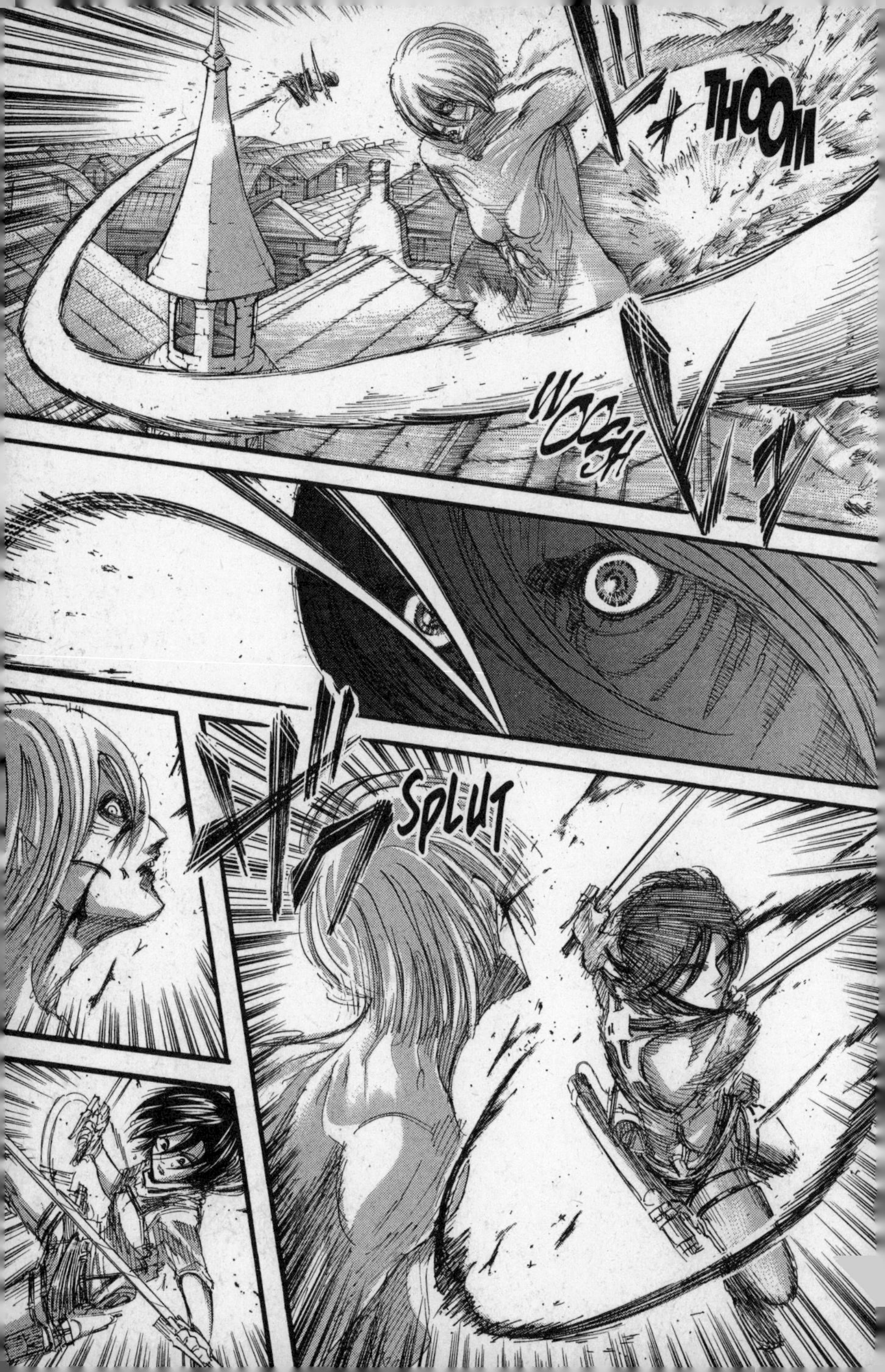
THOOM
WOOSH
SPLUT

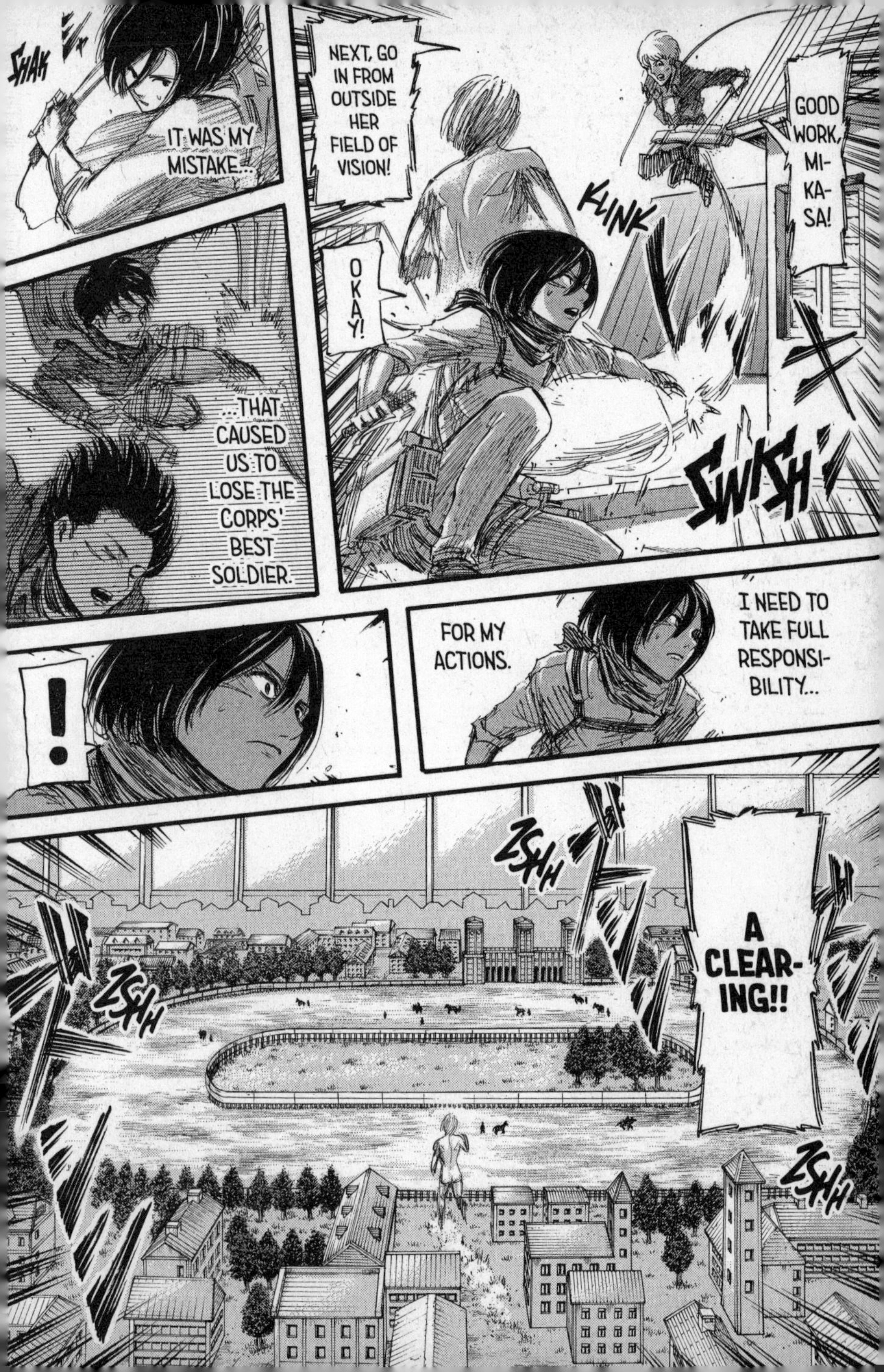
GOOD WORK, MI-KA-SA!
NEXT, GO IN FROM OUTSIDE HER FIELD OF VISION!
KLINK
OKAY!
SWISH
SHAK
IT WAS MY MISTAKE...
...THAT CAUSED US TO LOSE THE CORPS' BEST SOLDIER.
I NEED TO TAKE FULL RESPONSI-BILITY...
FOR MY ACTIONS.
!
A CLEAR-ING!!
ZSHH
ZSHH
ZSHH

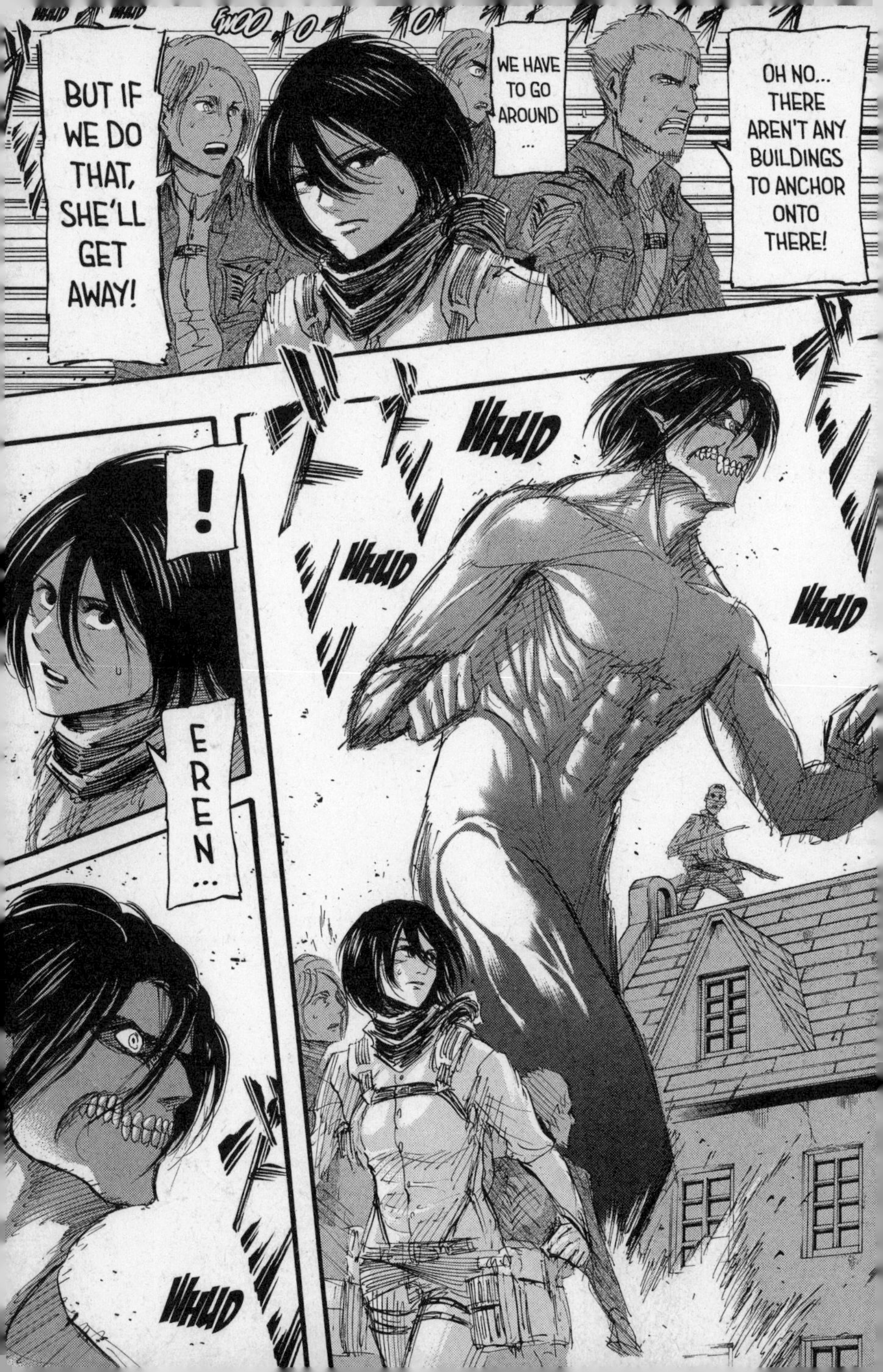

OH NO... THERE AREN'T ANY BUILDINGS TO ANCHOR ONTO THERE!
WE HAVE TO GO AROUND ...
BUT IF WE DO THAT, SHE'LL GET AWAY!
WHUD
WHUD
WHUD
!
EREN...
WHUD

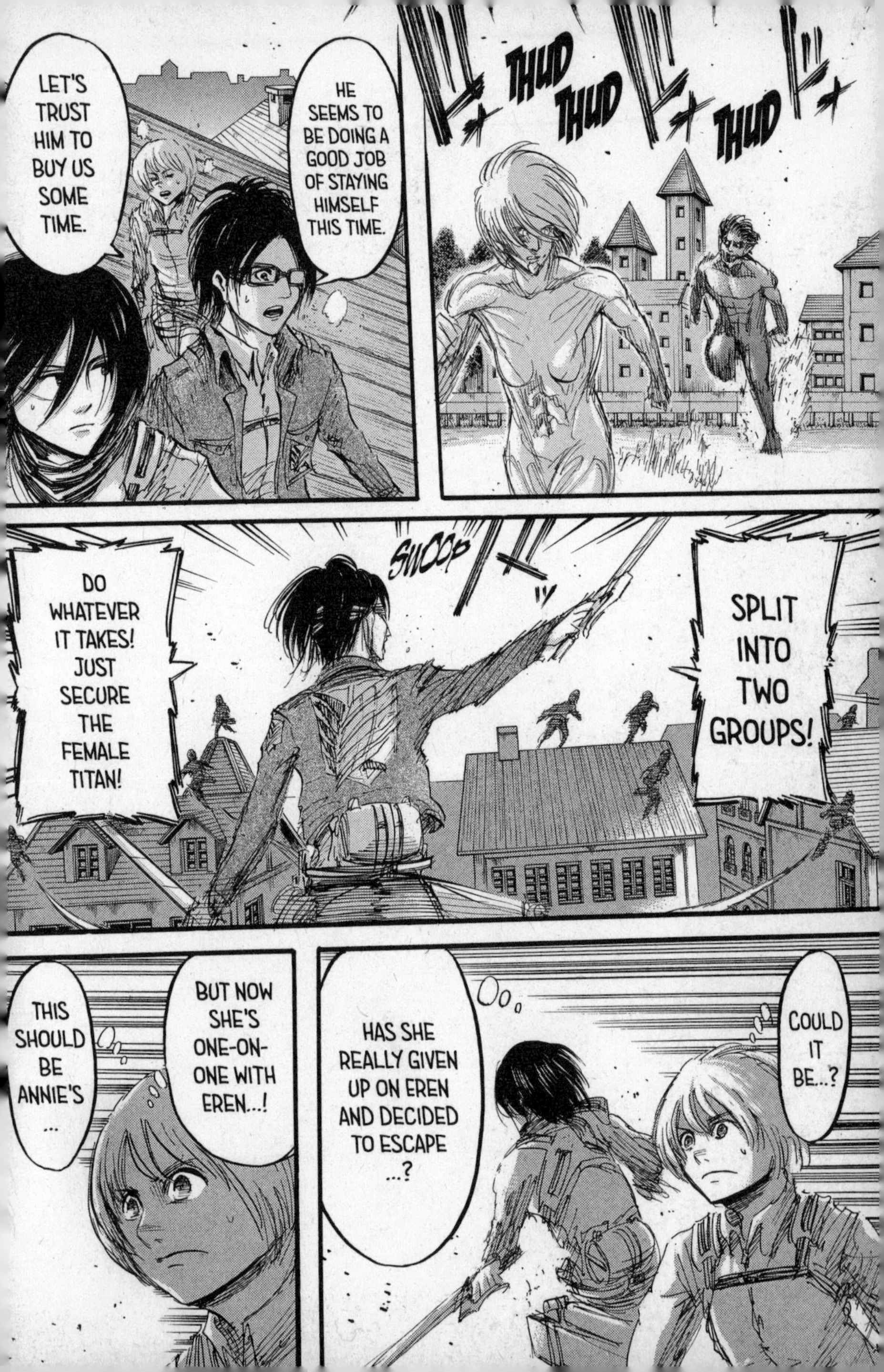
THUD
THUD
THUD
HE SEEMS TO BE DOING A GOOD JOB OF STAYING HIMSELF THIS TIME.
LET'S TRUST HIM TO BUY US SOME TIME.
SPLIT INTO TWO GROUPS!
SWOOP
DO WHATEVER IT TAKES! JUST SECURE THE FEMALE TITAN!
COULD IT BE...?
HAS SHE REALLY GIVEN UP ON EREN AND DECIDED TO ESCAPE ...?
BUT NOW SHE'S ONE-ON-ONE WITH EREN...!
THIS SHOULD BE ANNIE'S ...

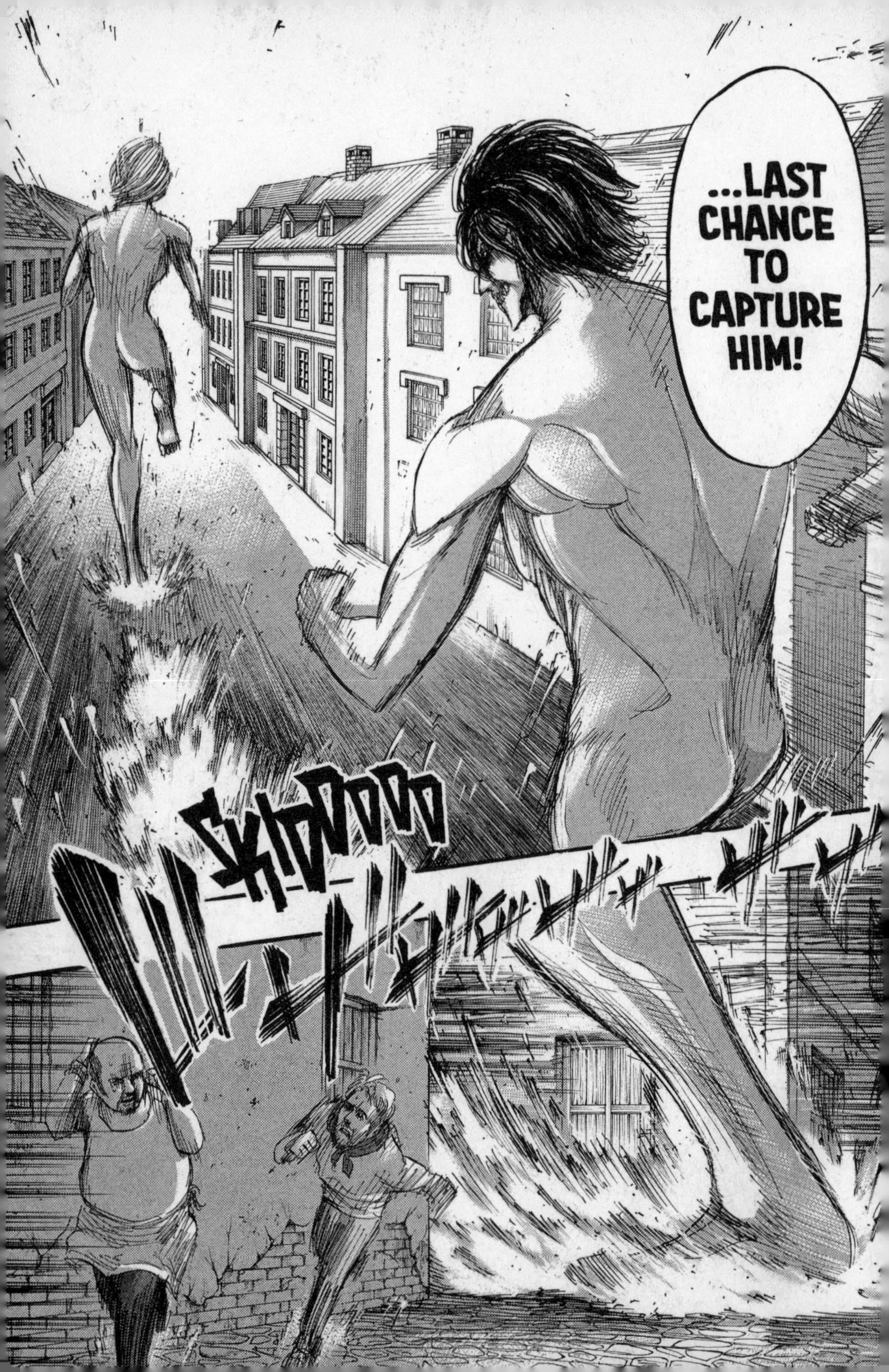
...LAST CHANCE TO CAPTURE HIM!
SKIDOOOO

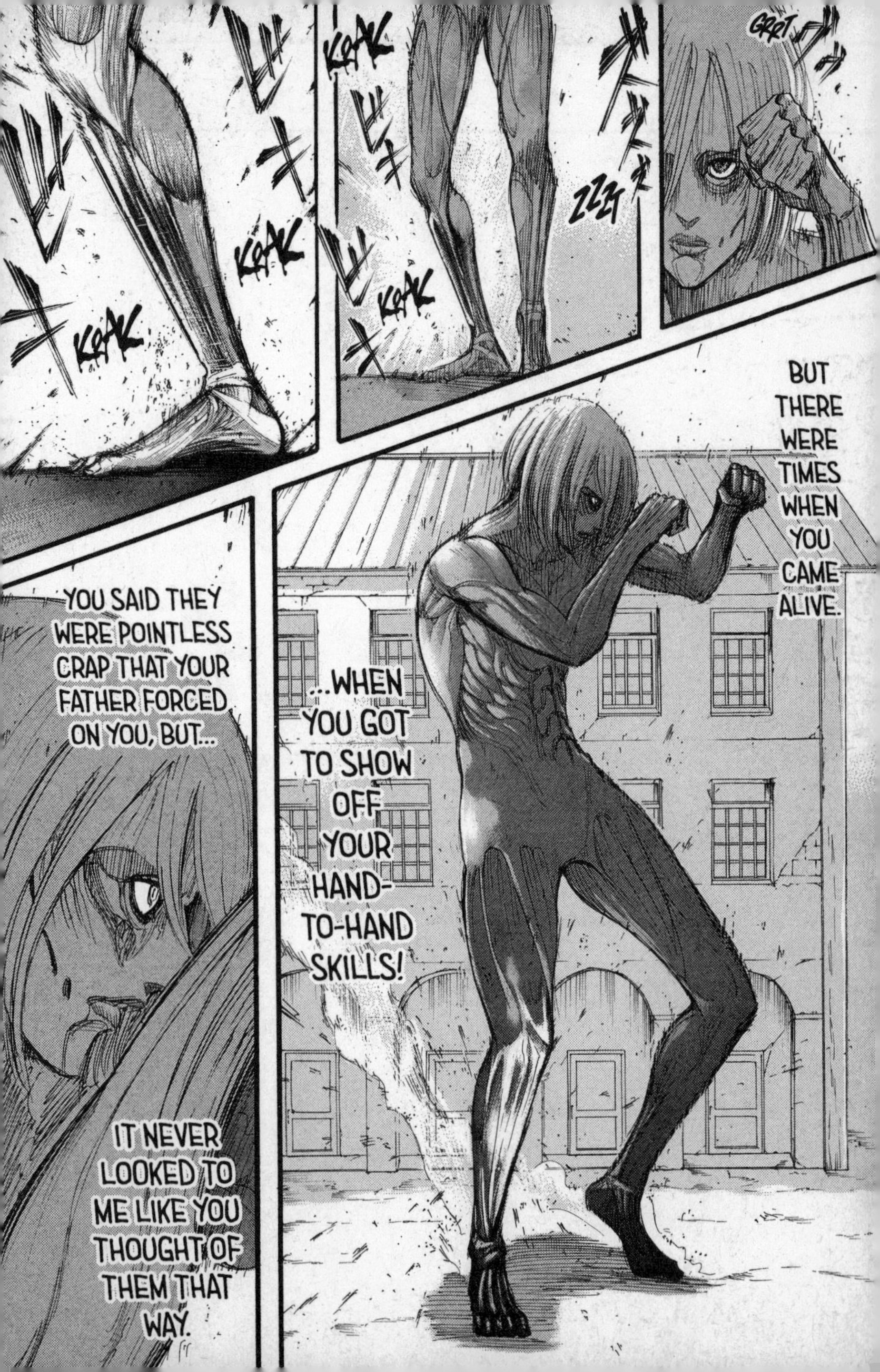
GRRT
ZZZT
KRAK
KRAK
KRAK
KRAK
BUT THERE WERE TIMES WHEN YOU CAME ALIVE.
...WHEN YOU GOT TO SHOW OFF YOUR HAND-TO-HAND SKILLS!
YOU SAID THEY WERE POINTLESS CRAP THAT YOUR FATHER FORCED ON YOU, BUT...
IT NEVER LOOKED TO ME LIKE YOU THOUGHT OF THEM THAT WAY.

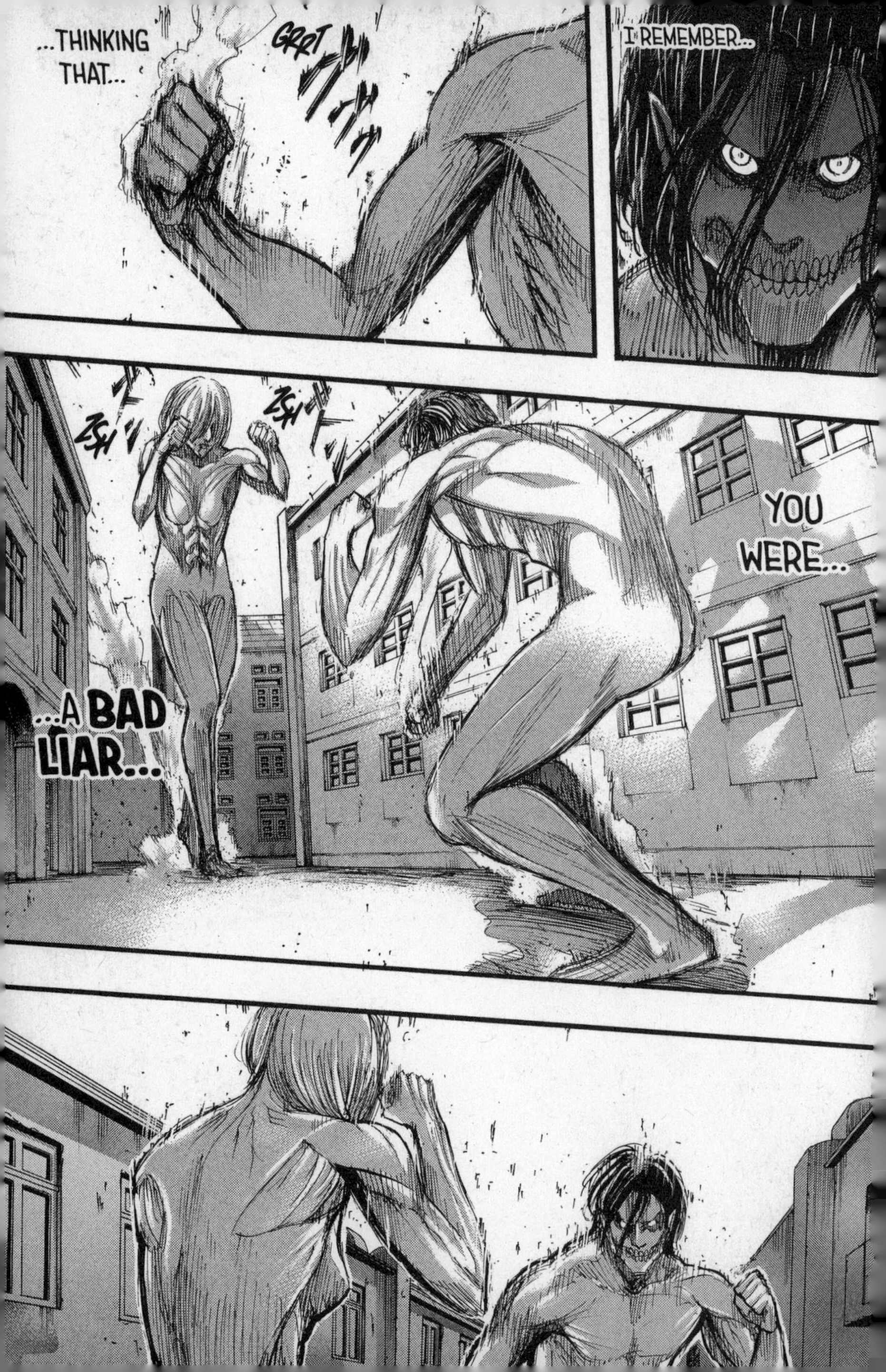
I REMEMBER...
...THINKING THAT...
GRRT
YOU WERE...
ZSH
ZSH
...A BAD LIAR...

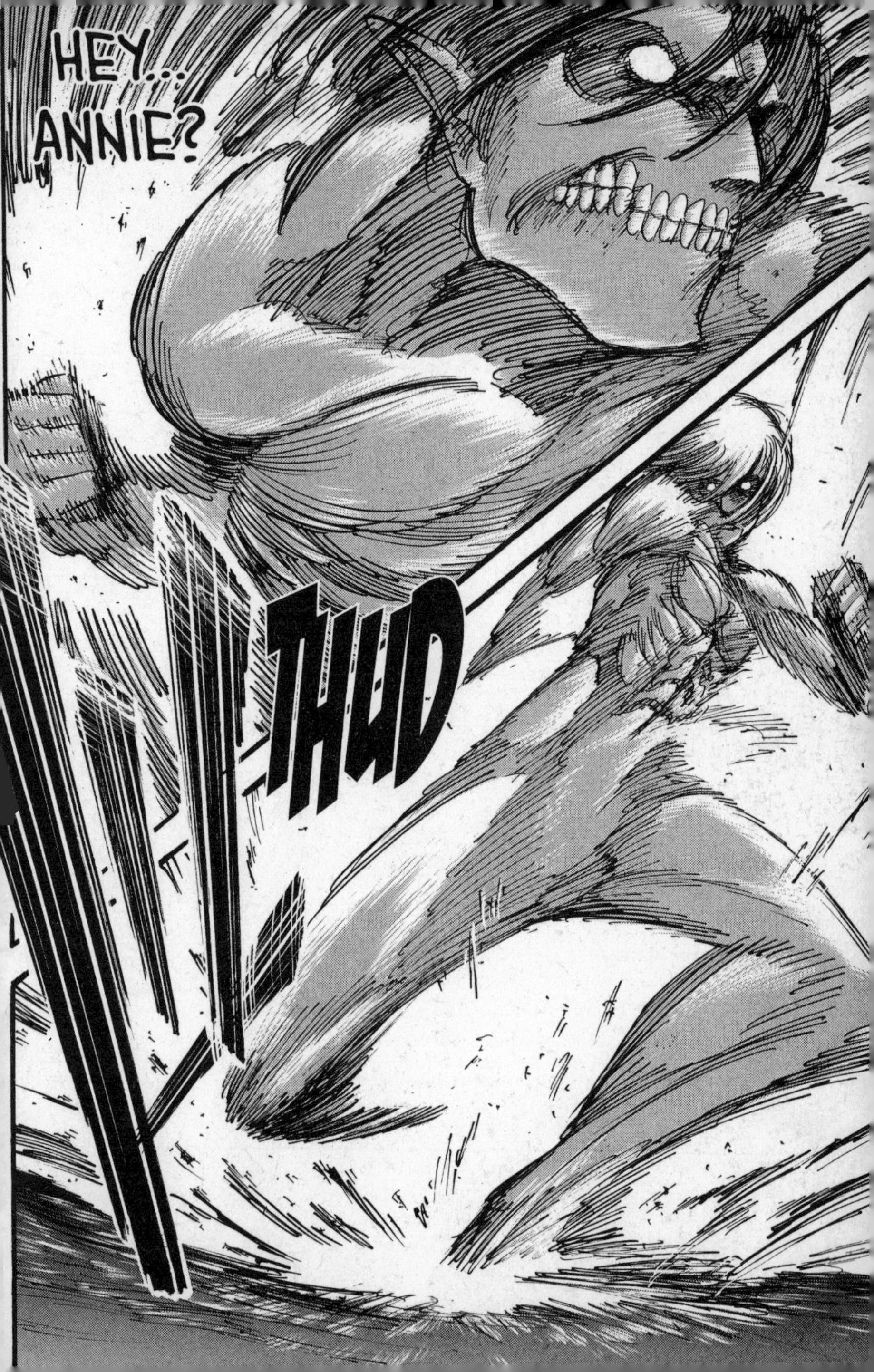
HEY... ANNIE?
THUD

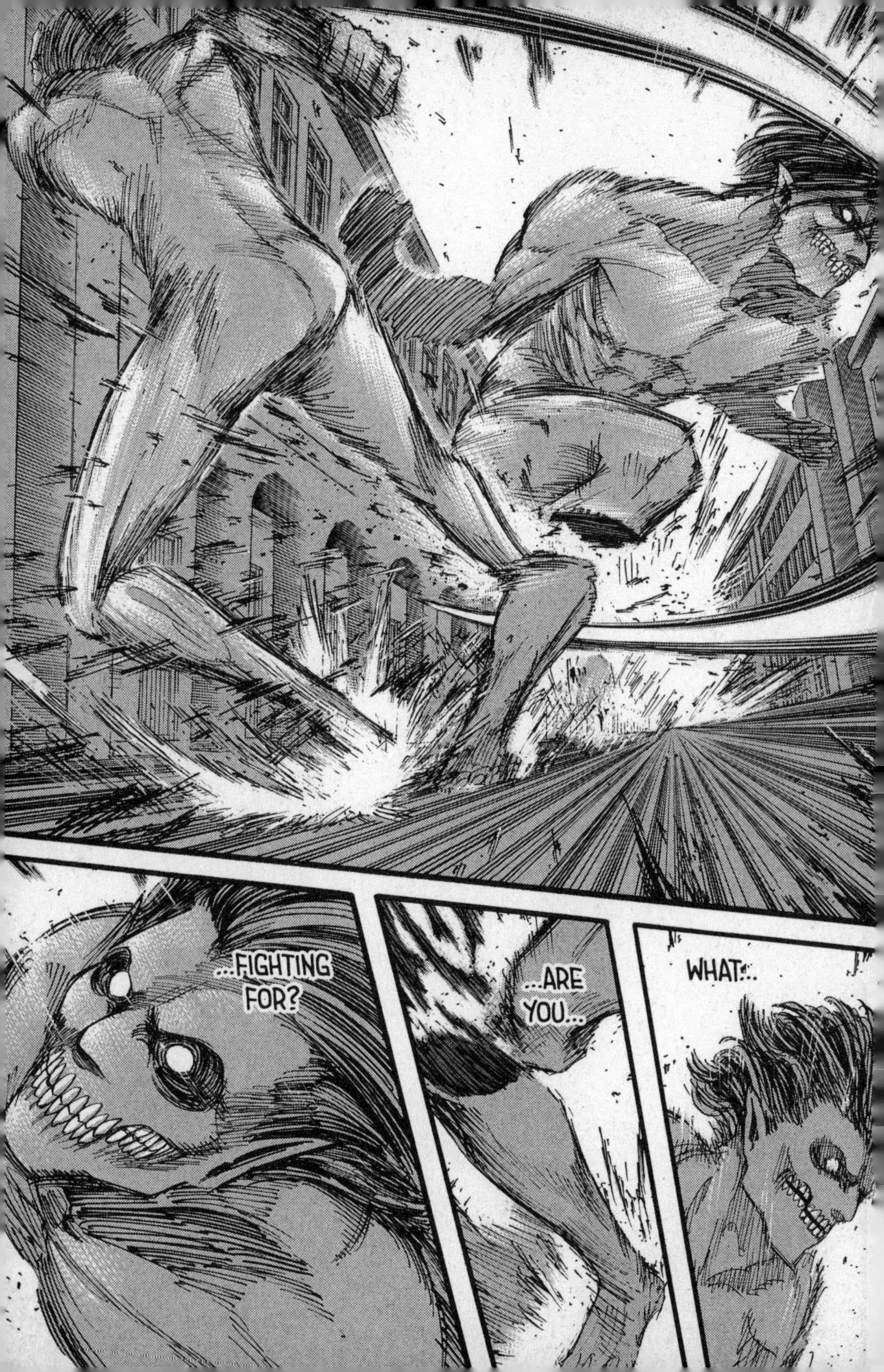
WHAT...
...ARE YOU...
...FIGHTING FOR?

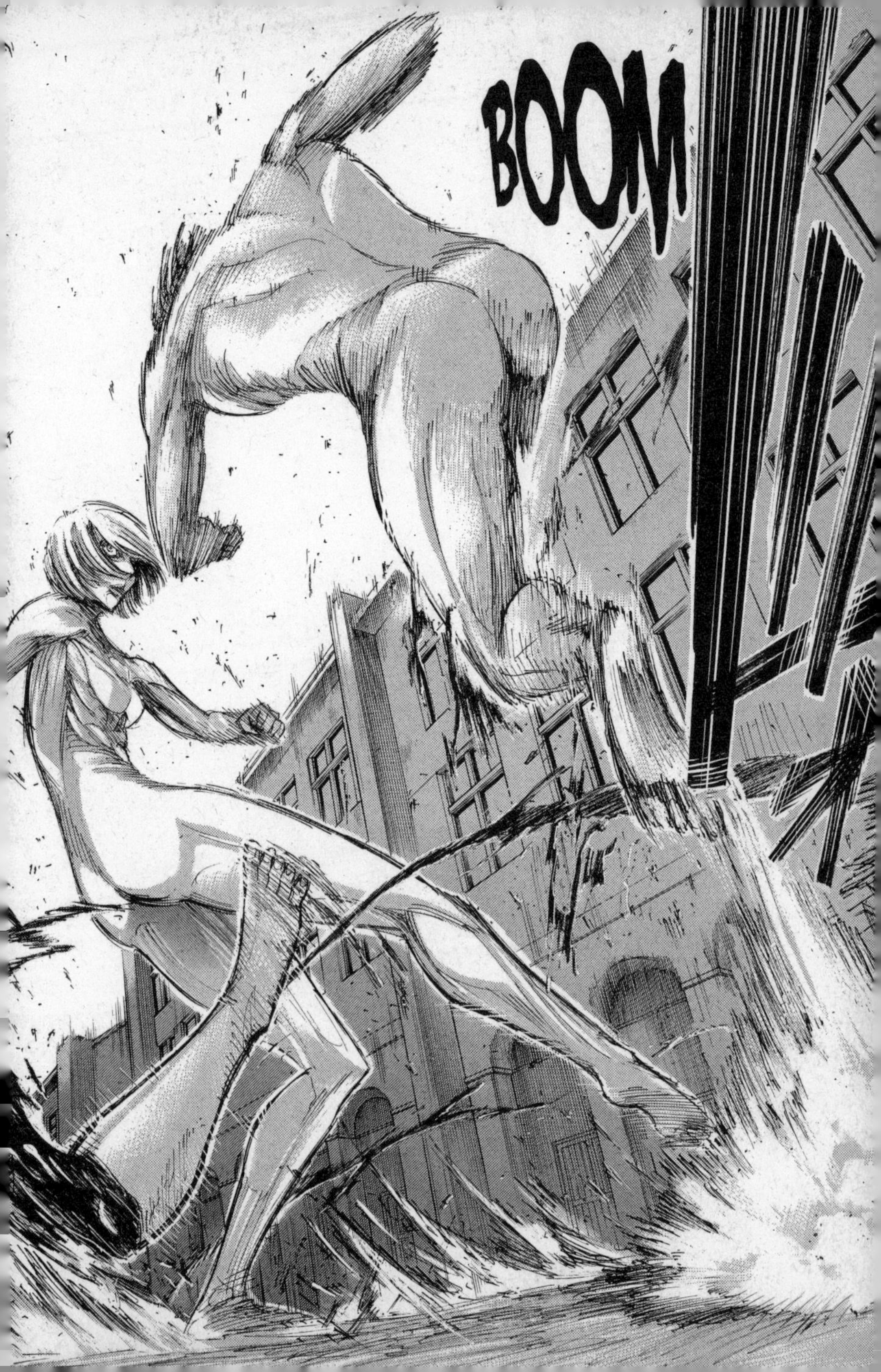
BOOM

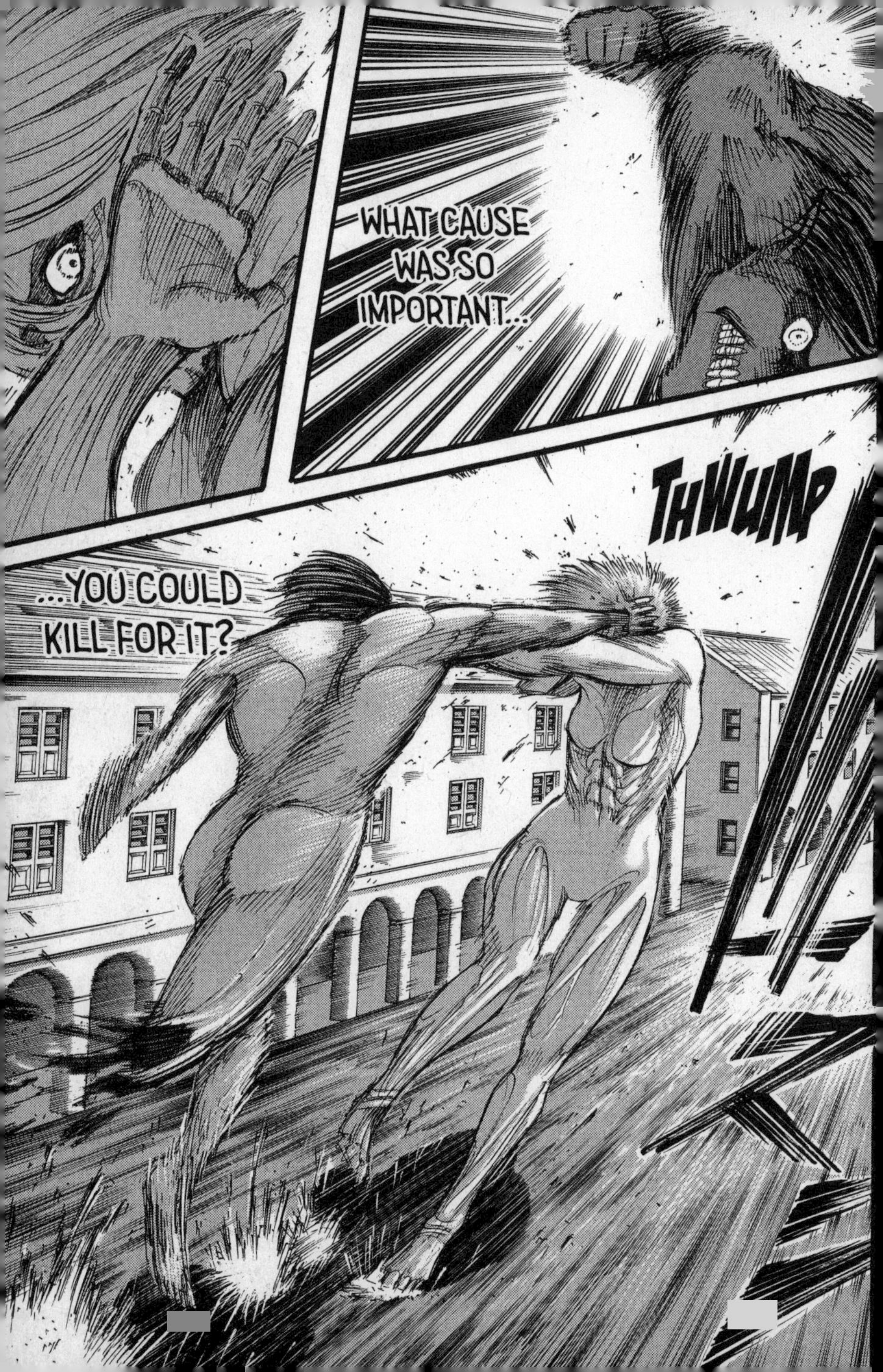
WHAT CAUSE WAS SO IMPORTANT...
THWUMP
...YOU COULD KILL FOR IT?

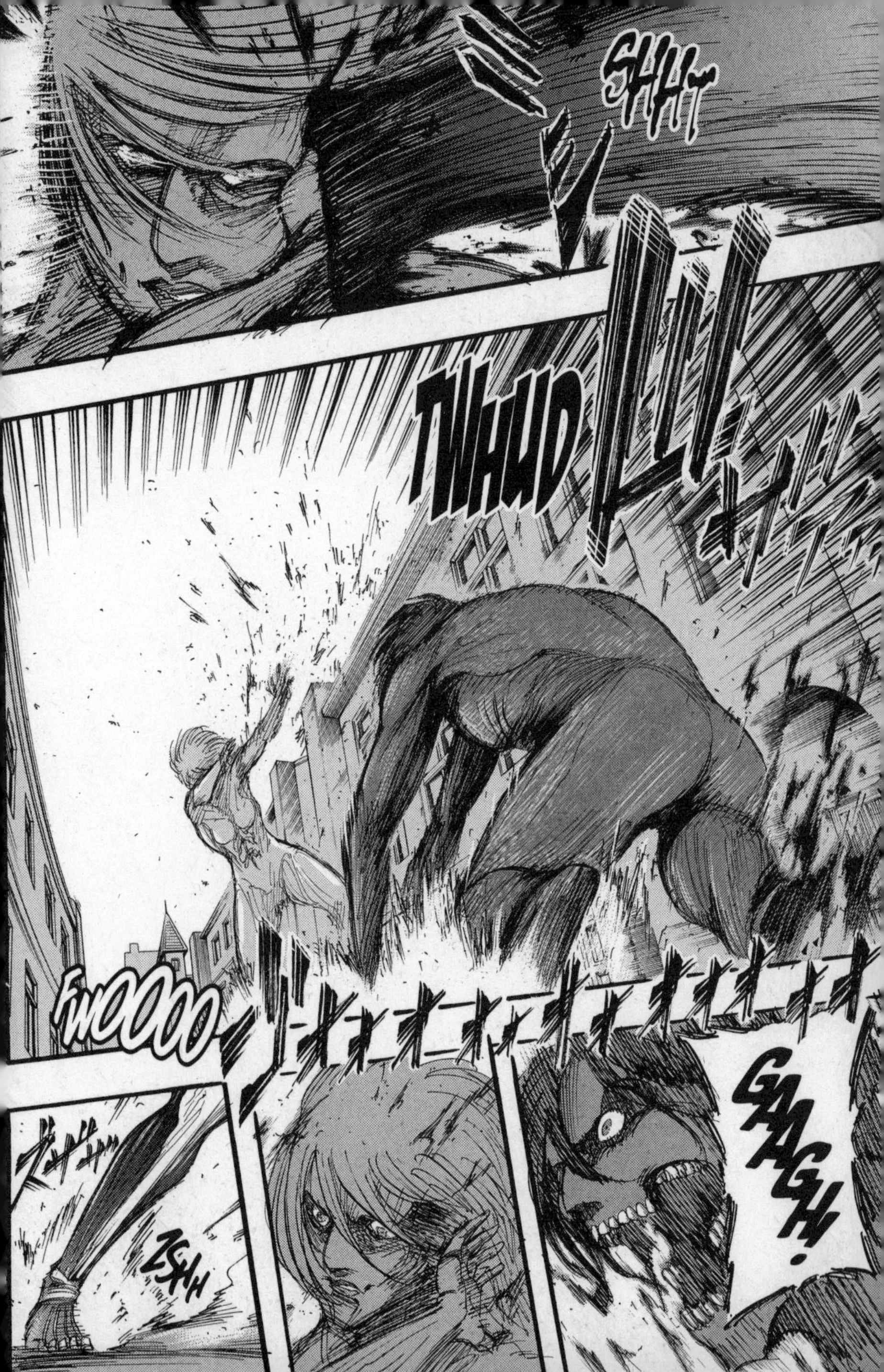
SHHH
THUD
FWOOOO
GAAGH!
TSHH

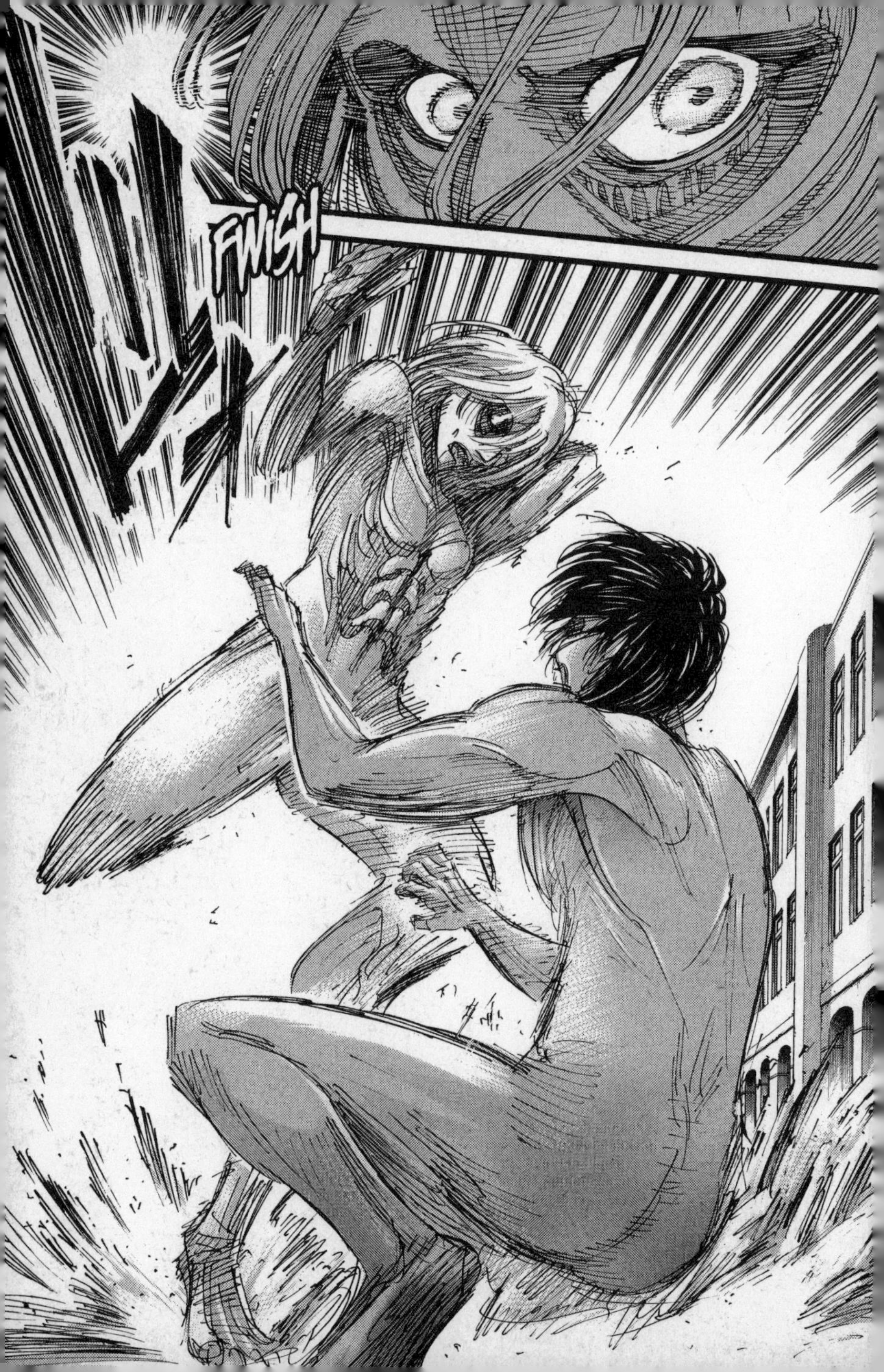
FWISH

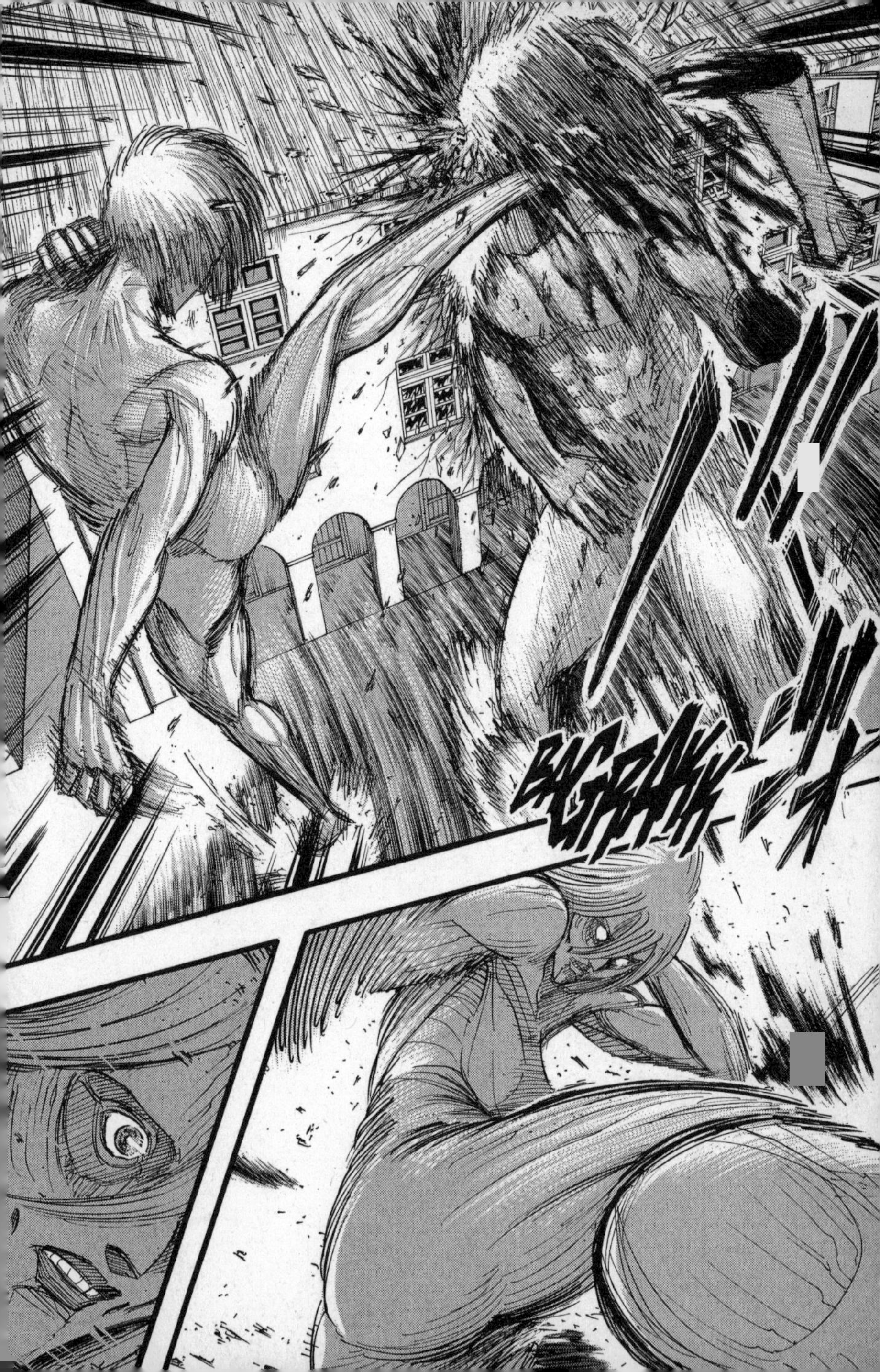
BAGRAK

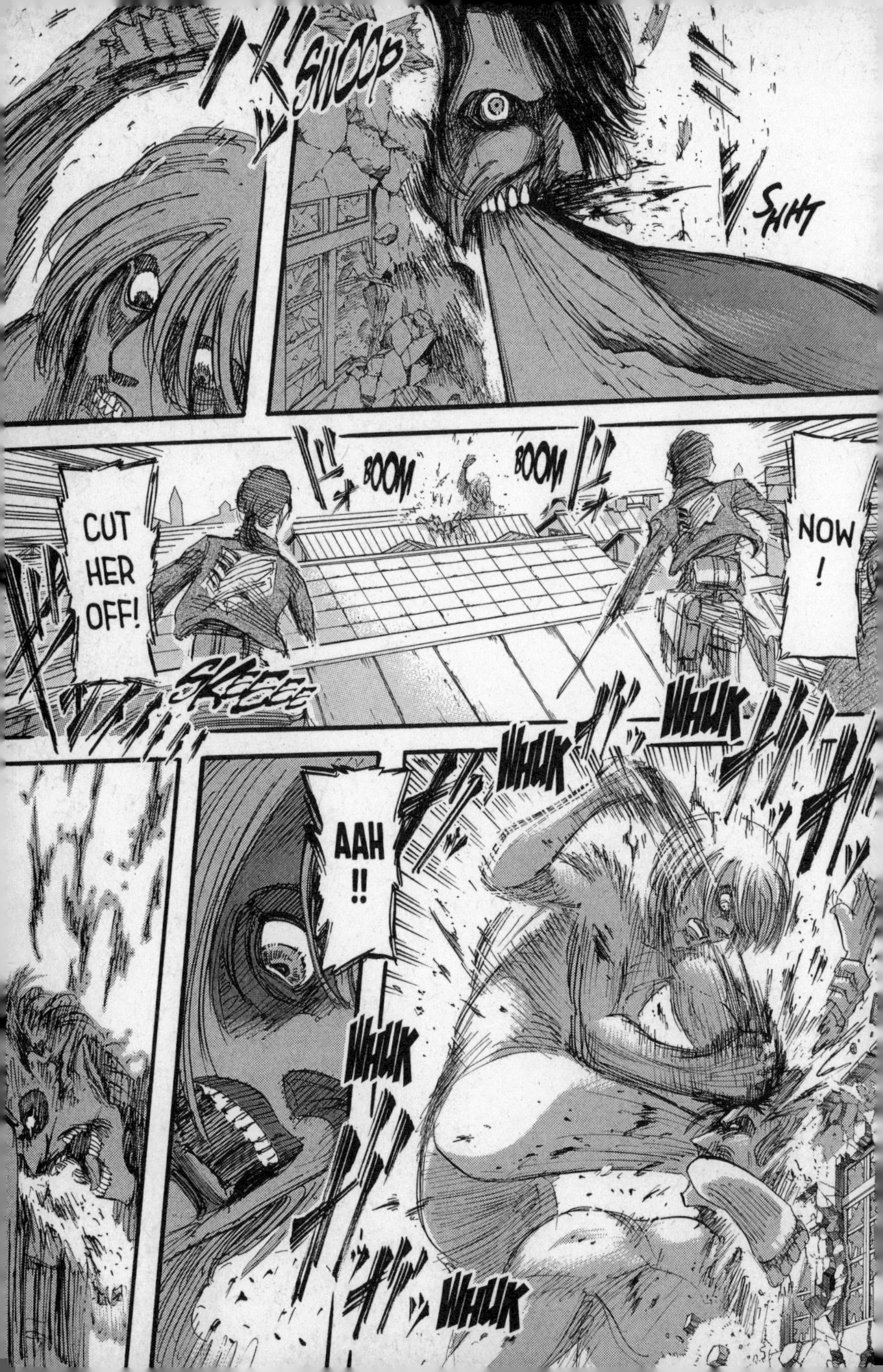
SWOOP
SHHT
NOW!
BOOM
BOOM
CUT HER OFF!
SKREEE
WHUK
WHUK
AAH!!
WHUK
WHUK

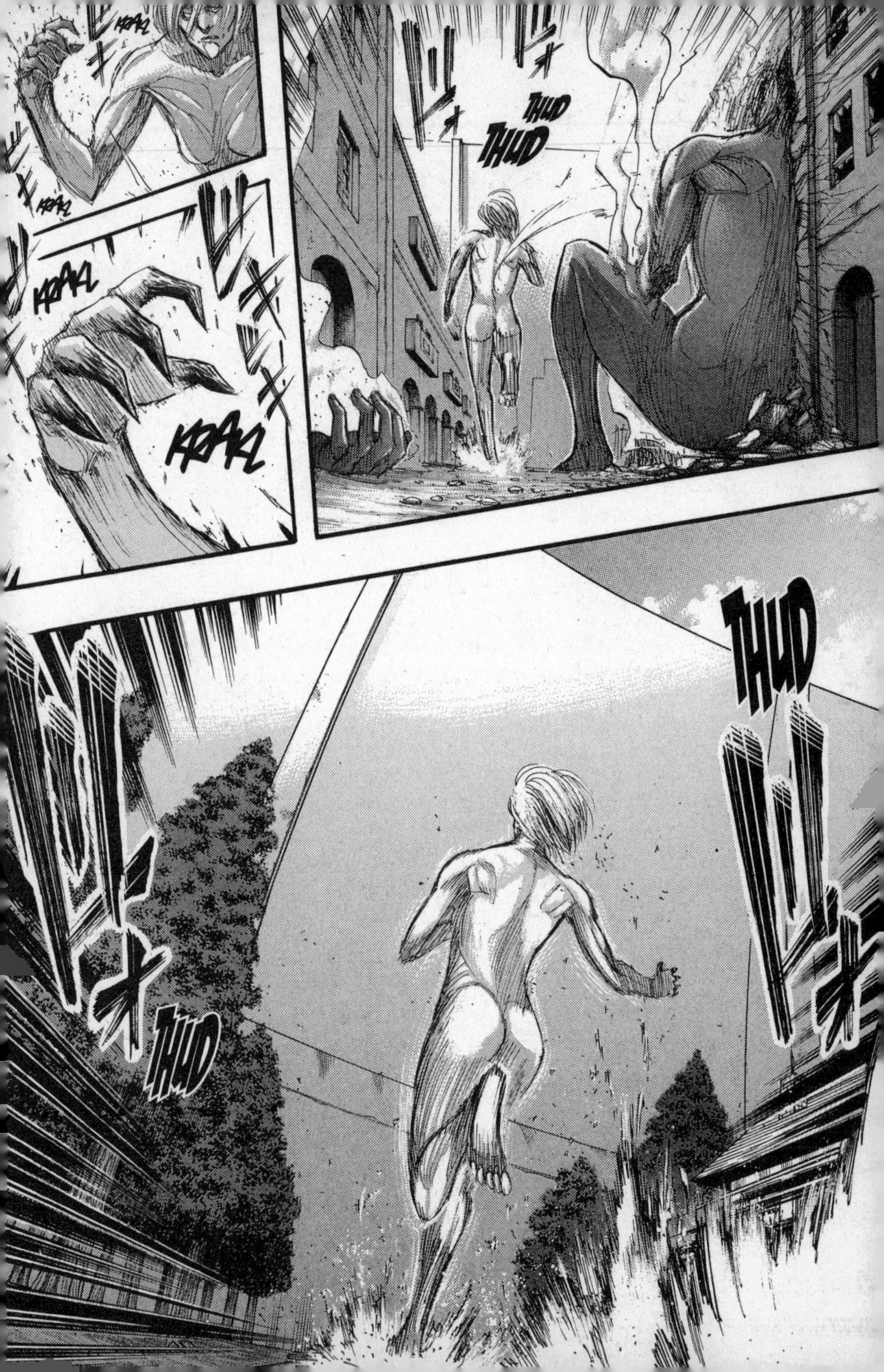
THUD
THUD
KRAKL
KRAKL
KRAKL
KRAKL
THUD
THUD

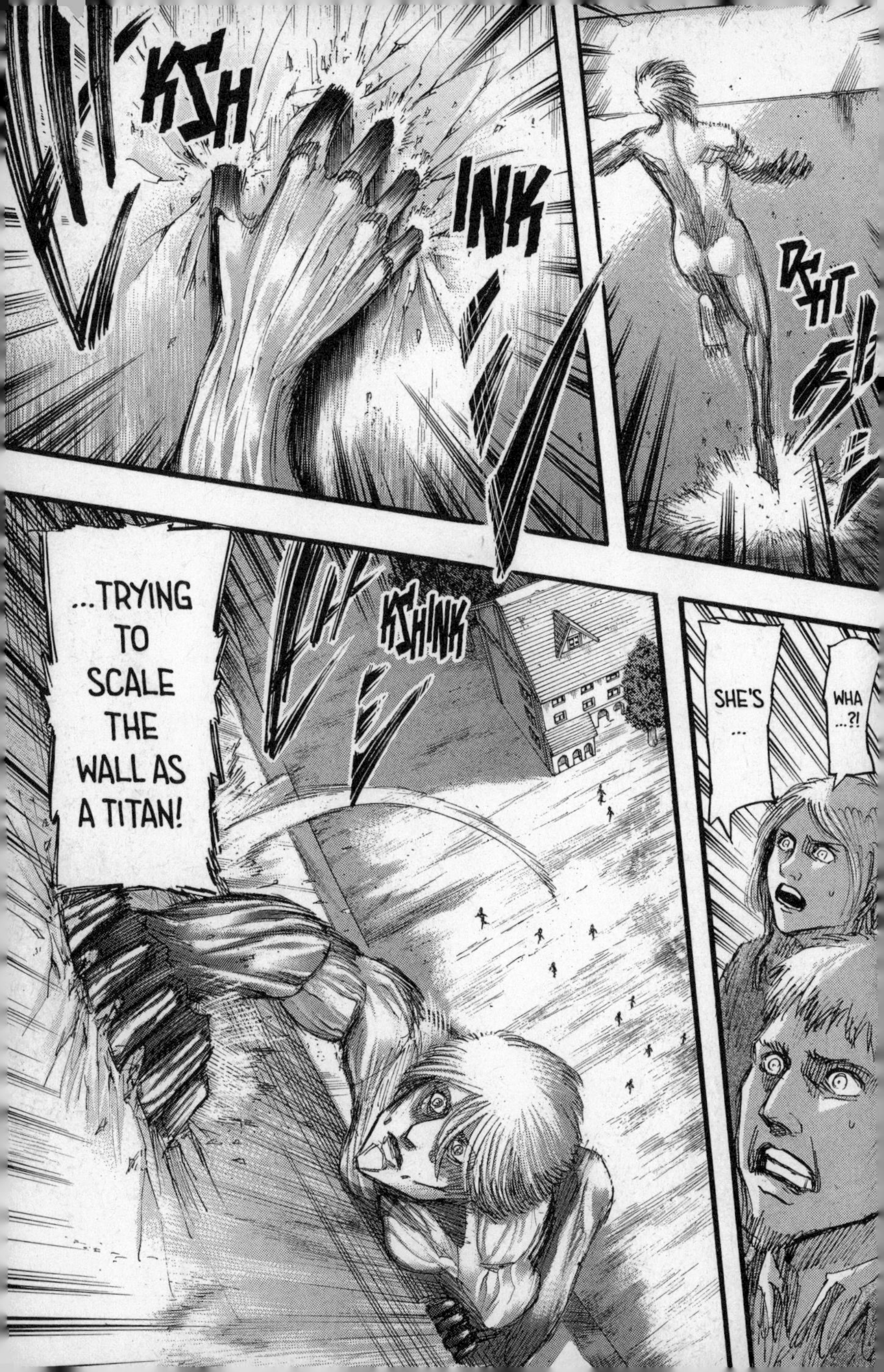
DSHT
KSH
INK
SHE'S ...
WHA ...?!
...TRYING TO SCALE THE WALL AS A TITAN!
KSHINK

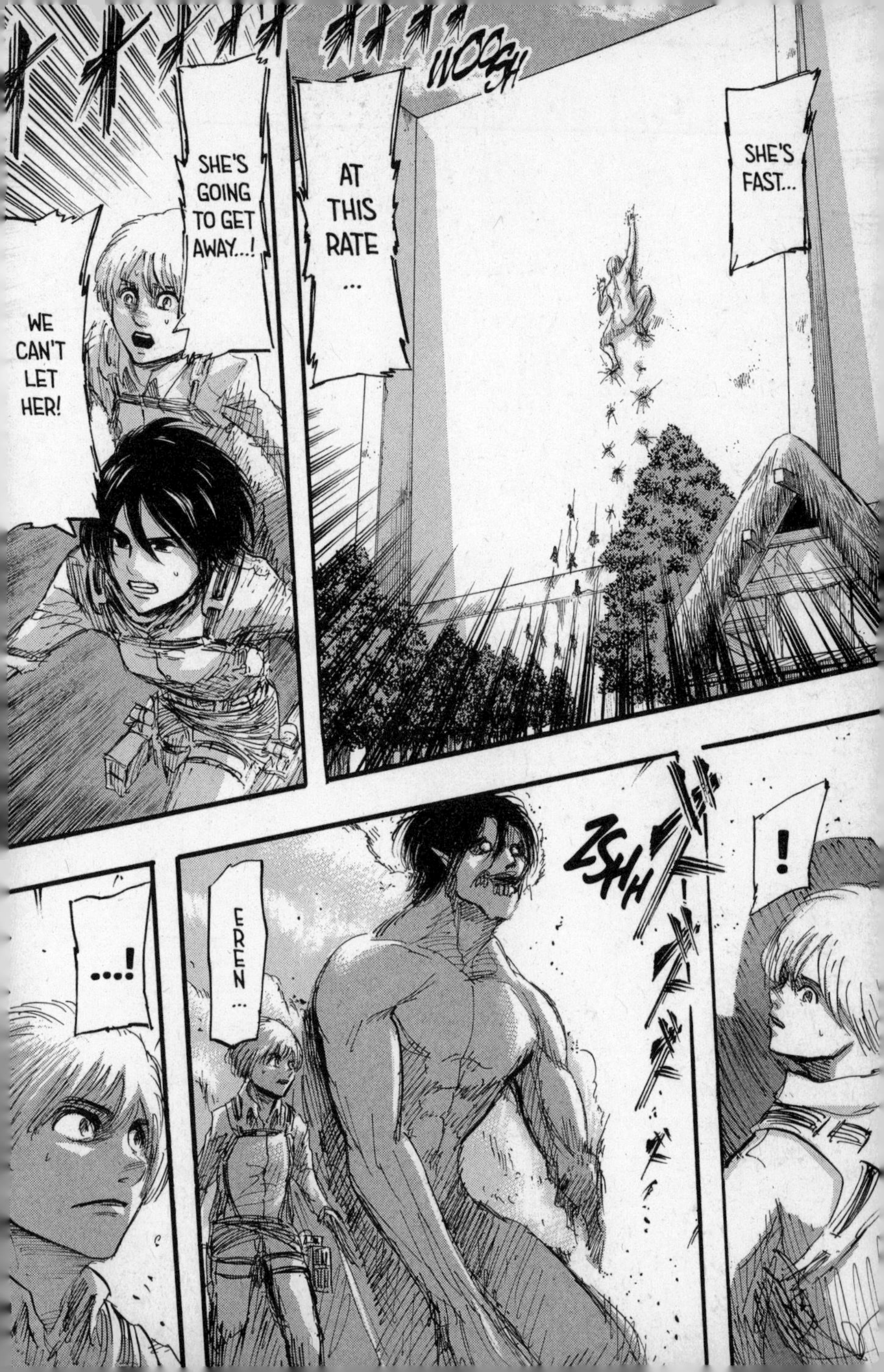
WOOSH
SHE'S FAST...
AT THIS RATE...
SHE'S GOING TO GET AWAY...!
WE CAN'T LET HER!
ZSHH
!
EREN...
...!

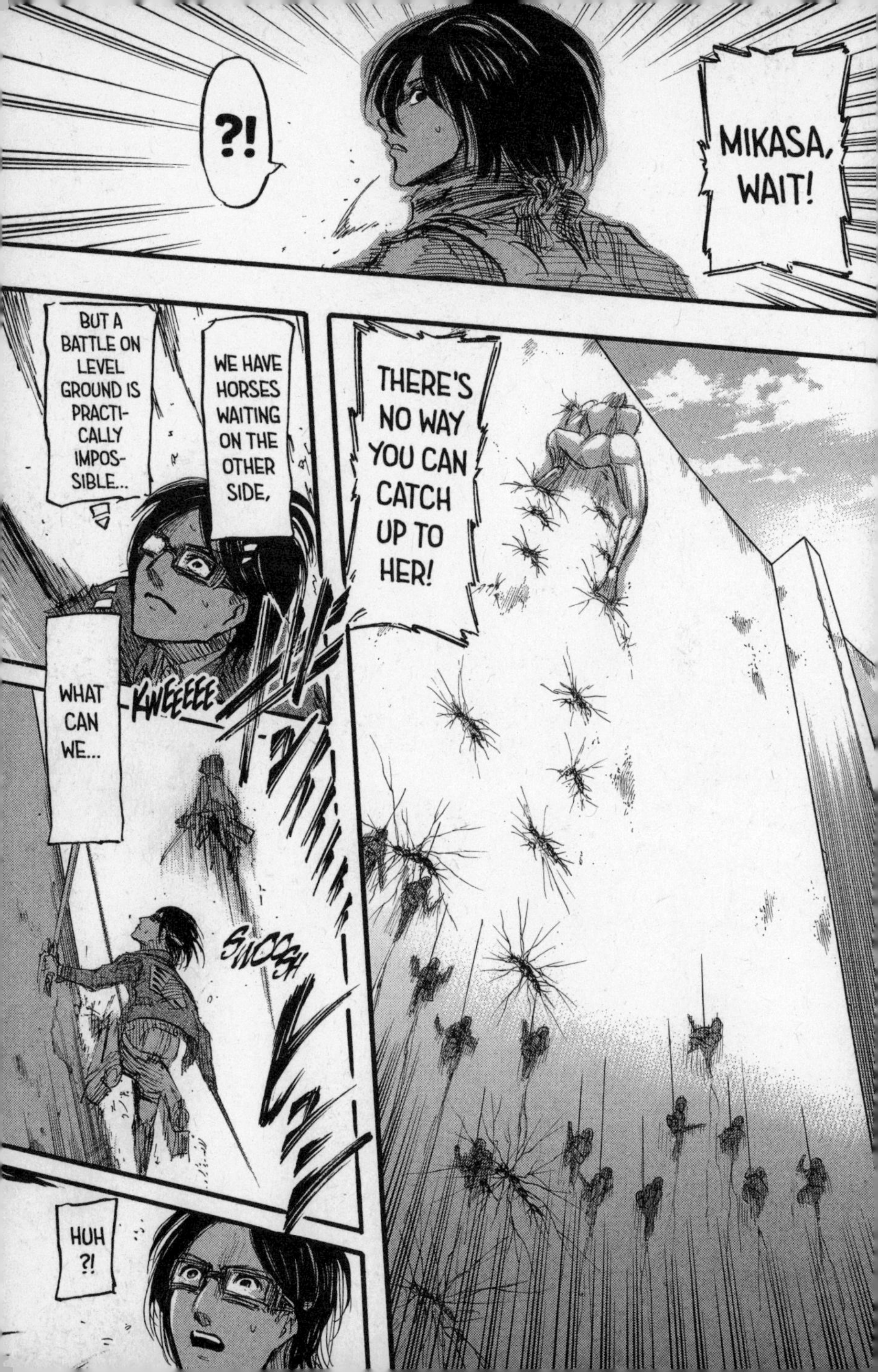
MIKASA, WAIT!
?!
THERE'S NO WAY YOU CAN CATCH UP TO HER!
WE HAVE HORSES WAITING ON THE OTHER SIDE,
BUT A BATTLE ON LEVEL GROUND IS PRACTICALLY IMPOSSIBLE...
WHAT CAN WE...
KWEEEEE
SWOOSH
HUH ?!

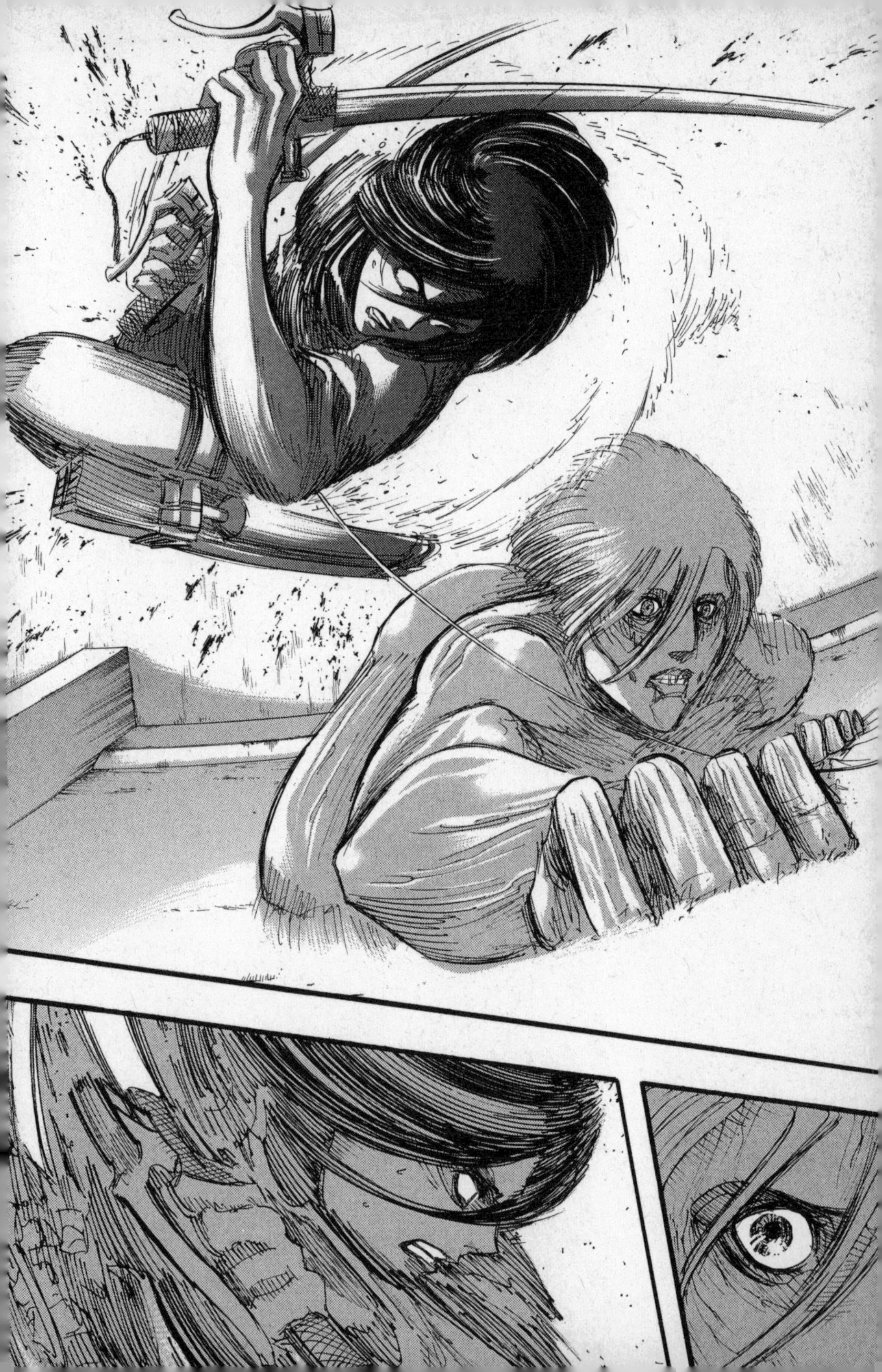

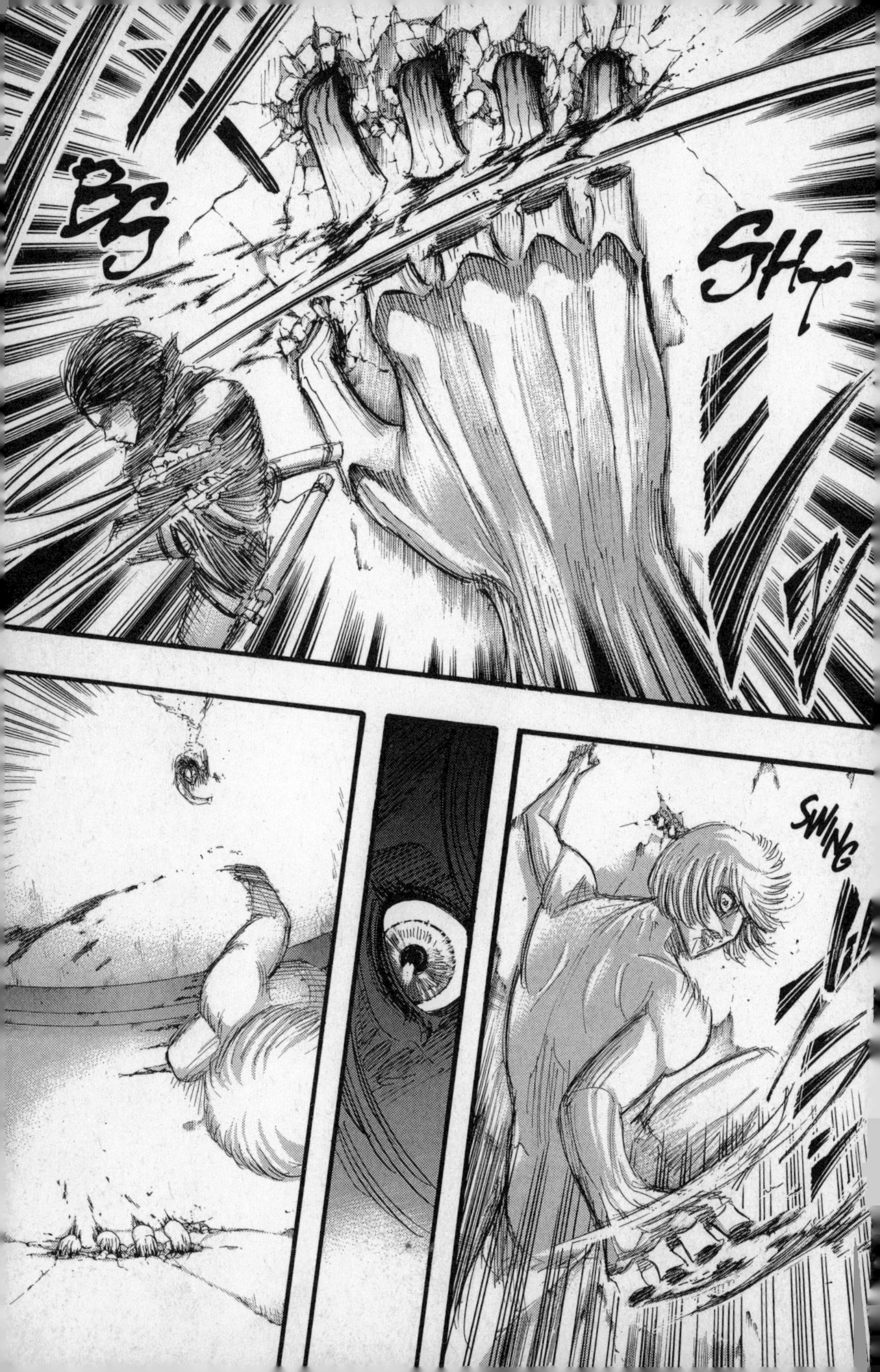
BG
SWING

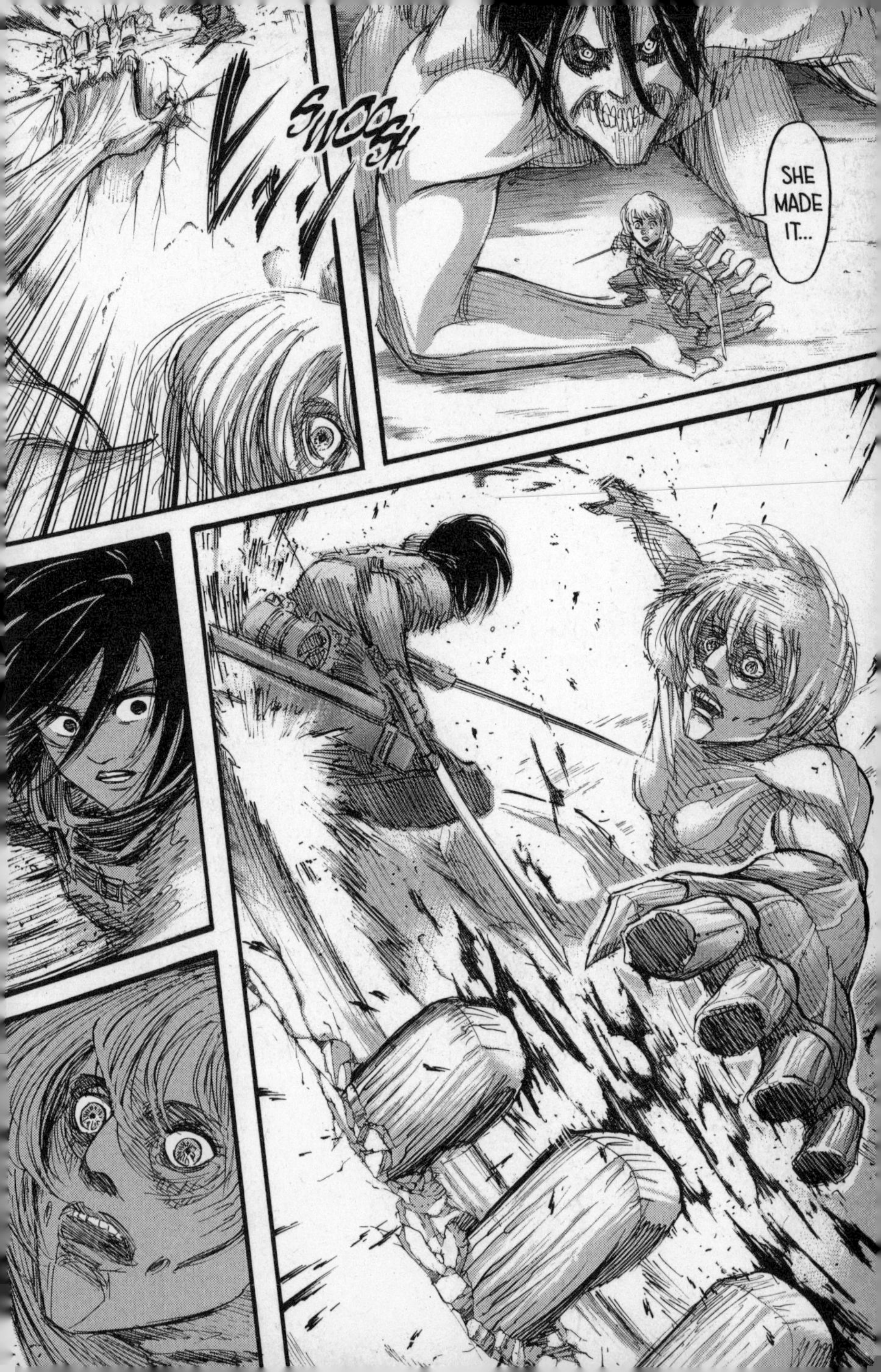
SHE MADE IT...
SWOOSH

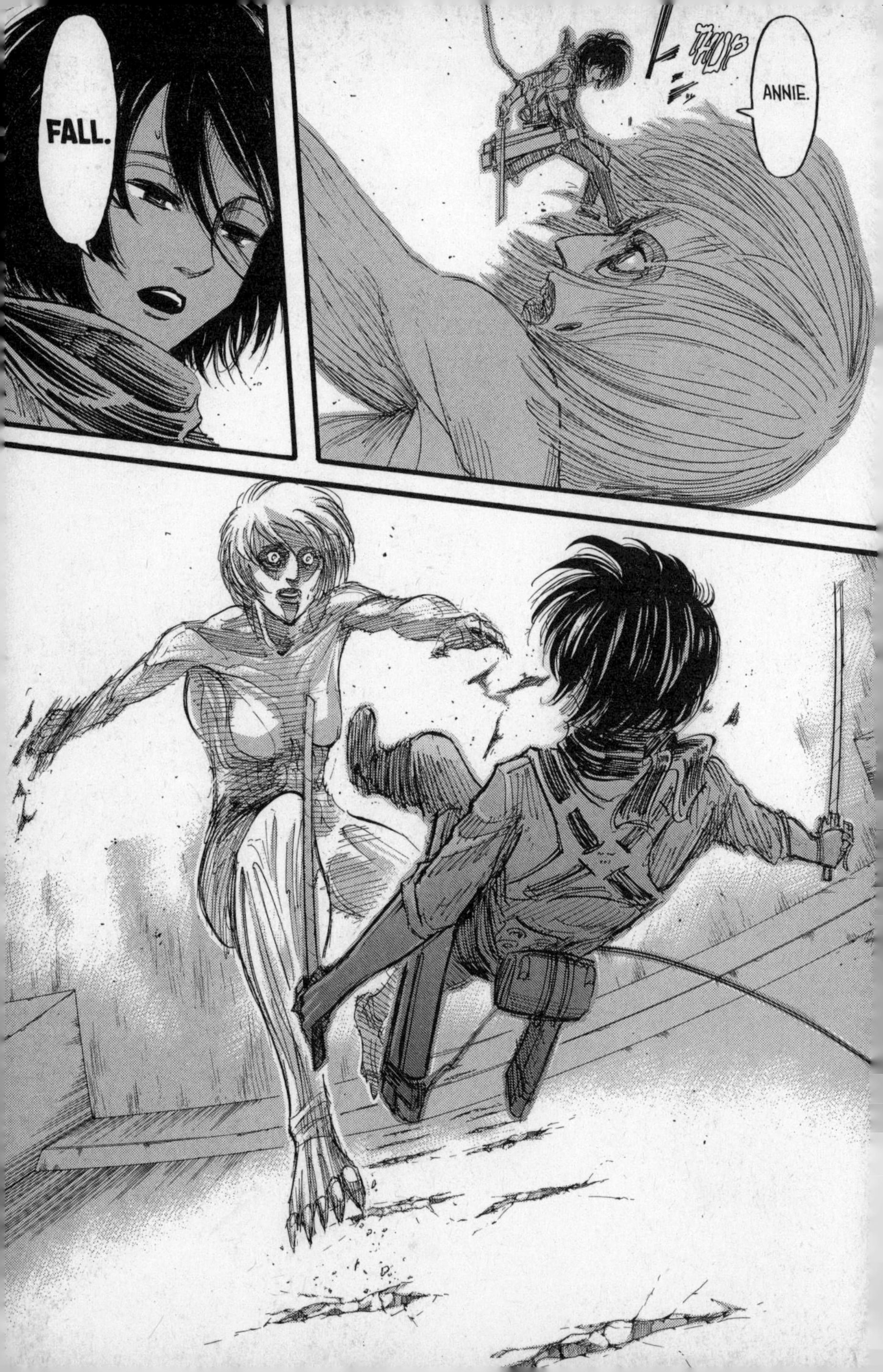

ANNIE.
THUP
FALL.

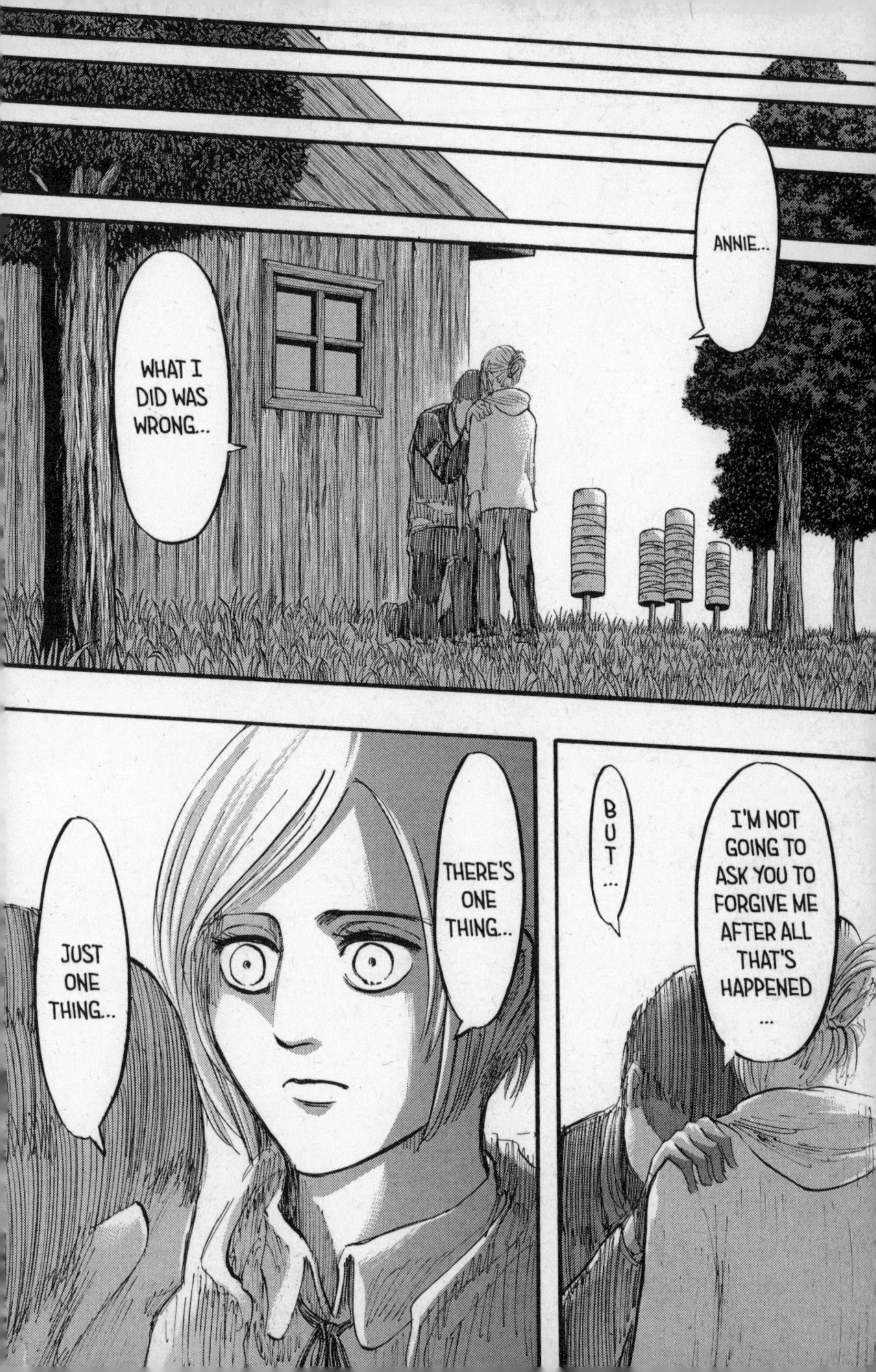
ANNIE...
WHAT I DID WAS WRONG...
I'M NOT GOING TO ASK YOU TO FORGIVE ME AFTER ALL THAT'S HAPPENED ...
BUT...
THERE'S ONE THING...
JUST ONE THING...

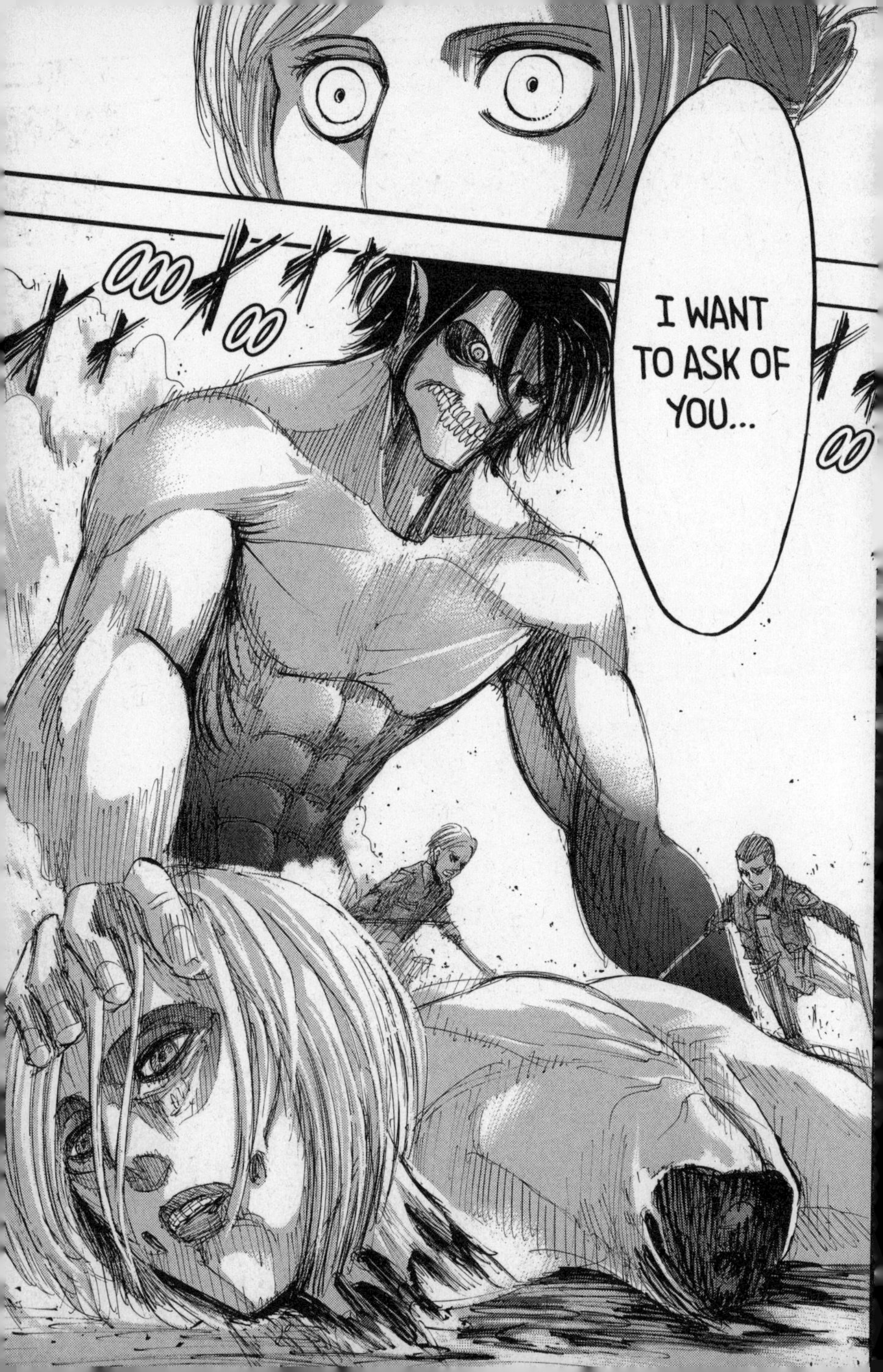
I WANT TO ASK OF YOU...

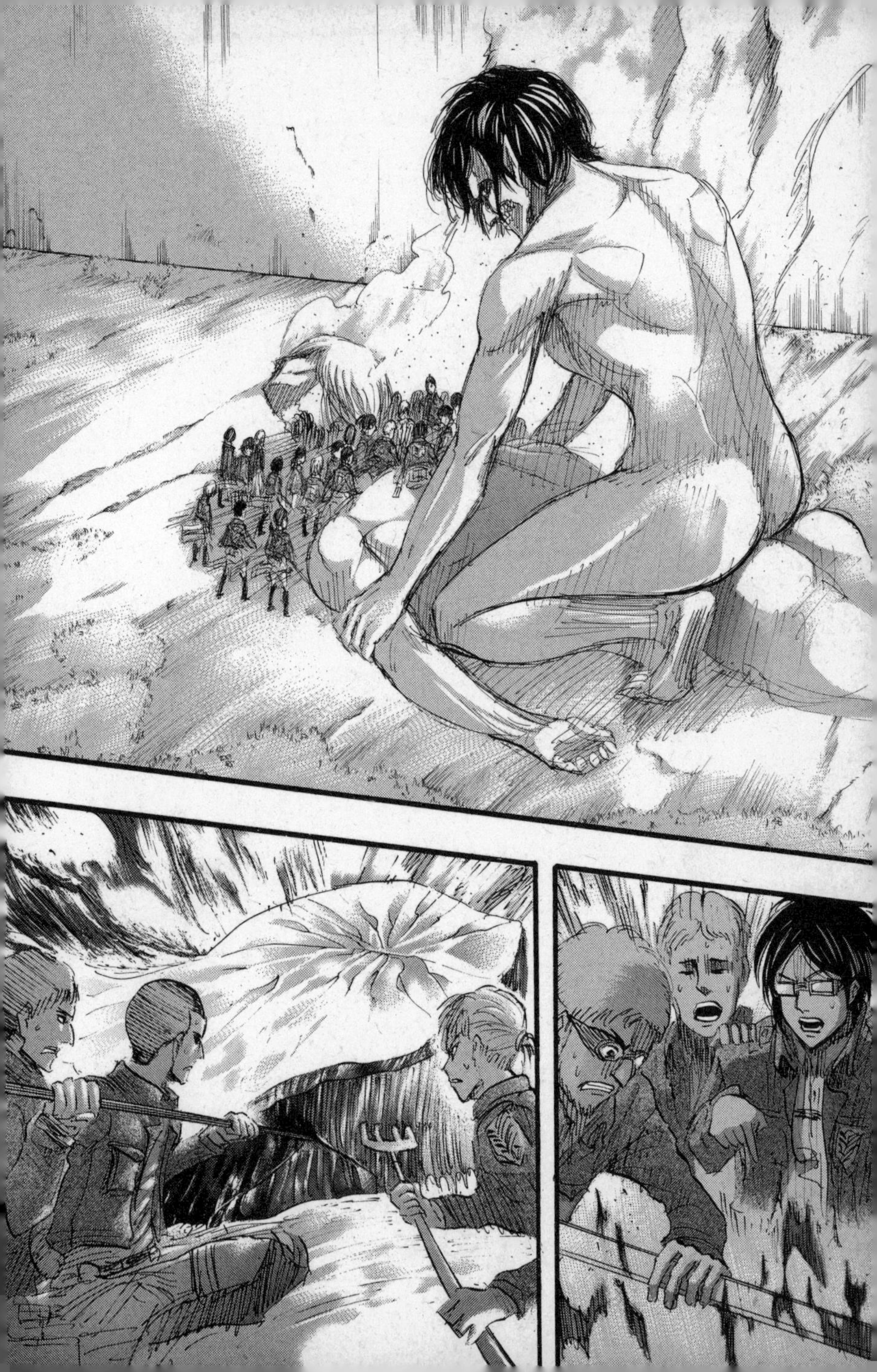

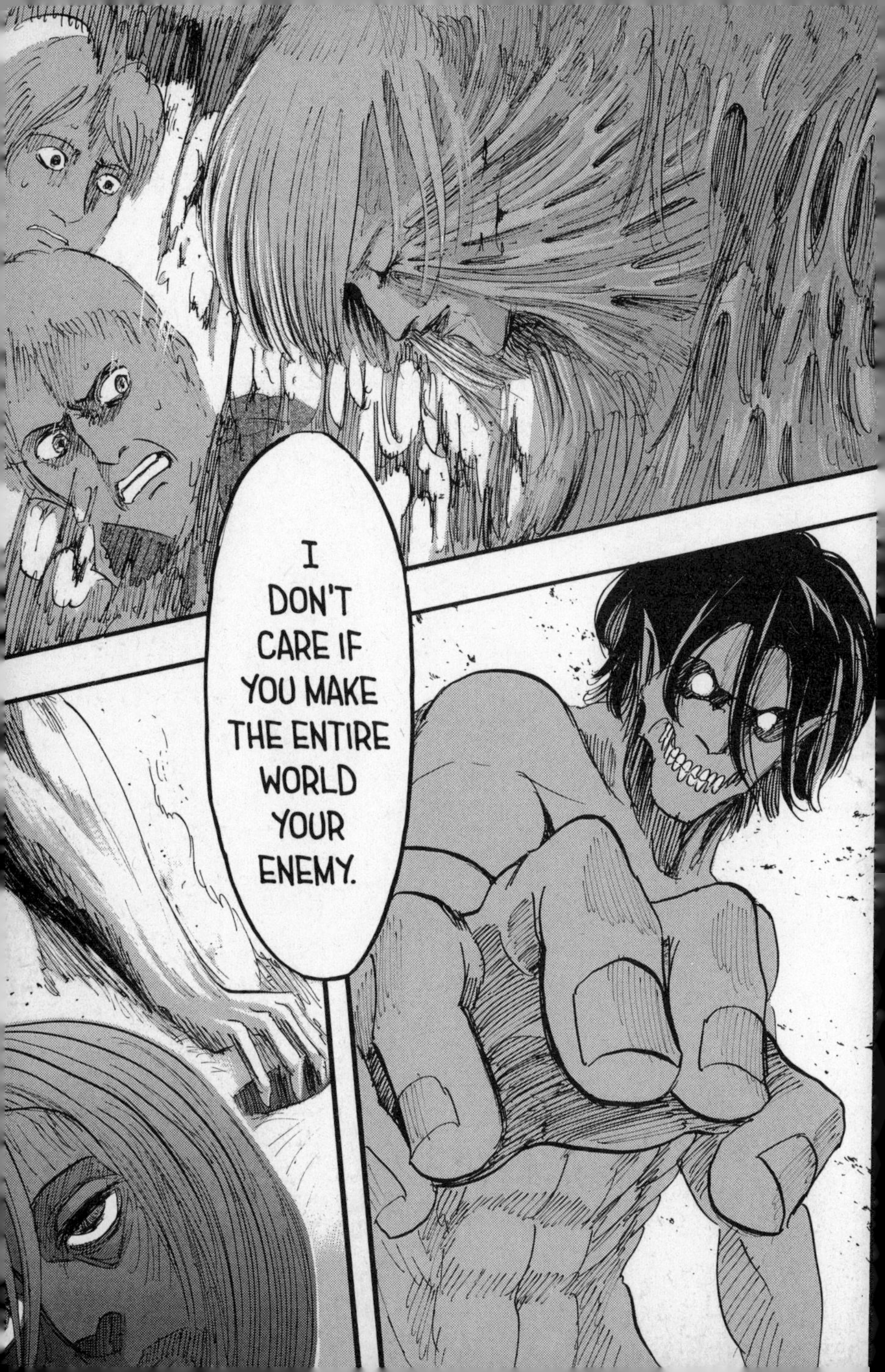
I DON'T CARE IF YOU MAKE THE ENTIRE WORLD YOUR ENEMY.

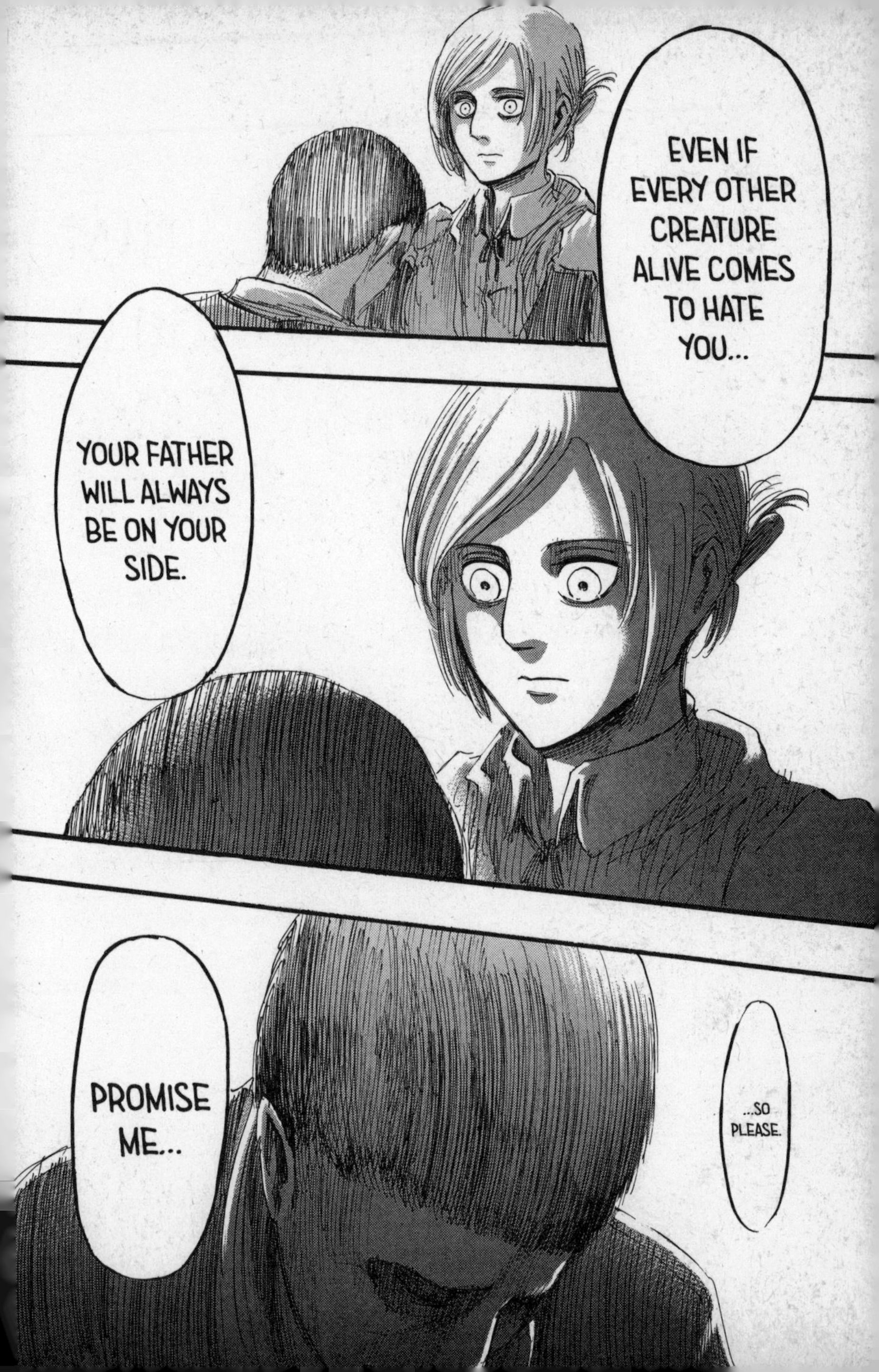
EVEN IF EVERY OTHER CREATURE ALIVE COMES TO HATE YOU...
YOUR FATHER WILL ALWAYS BE ON YOUR SIDE.
...SO PLEASE.
PROMISE ME...

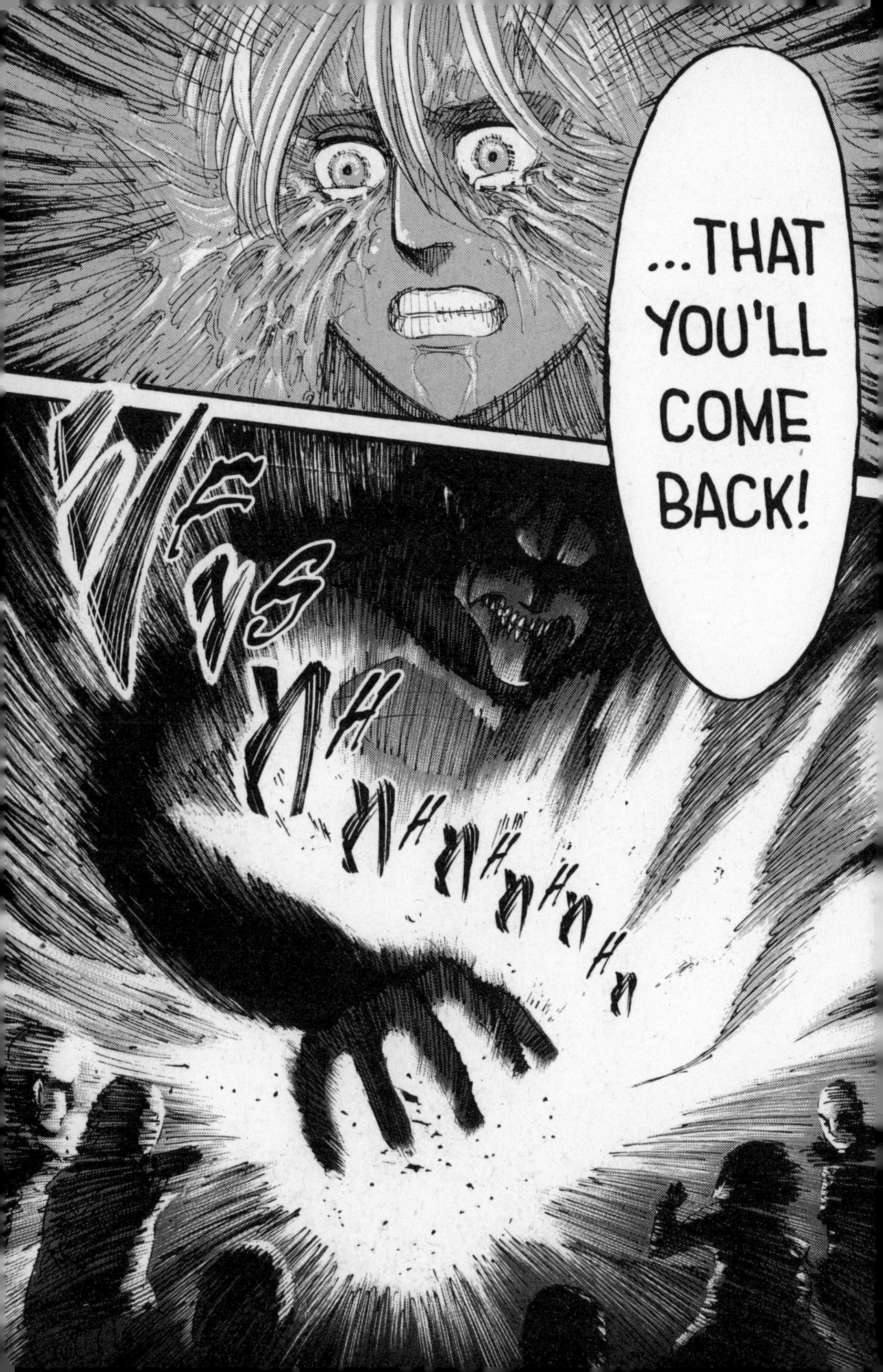
...THAT YOU'LL COME BACK!

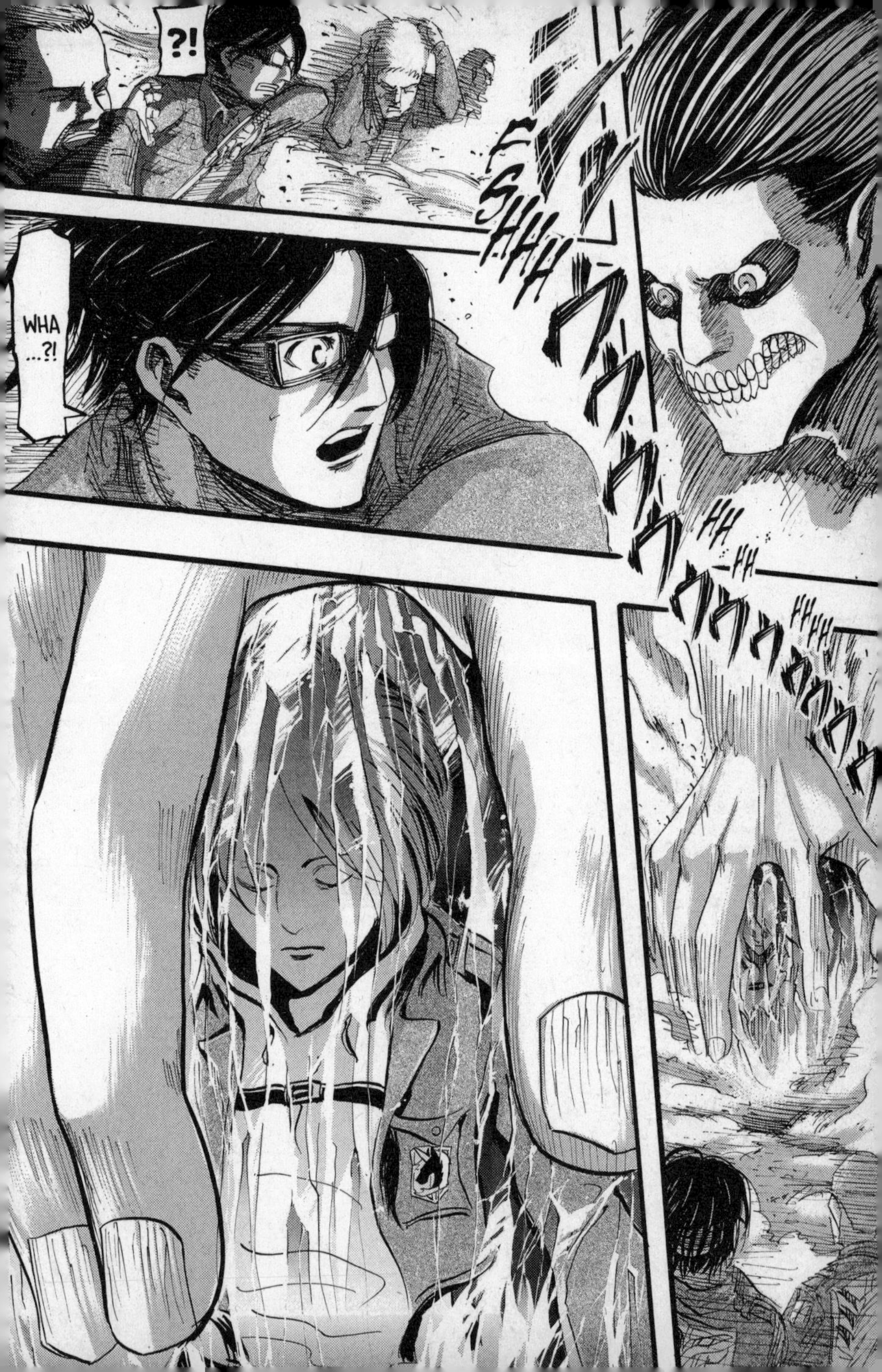
FSHHH
?!
WHA ...?!

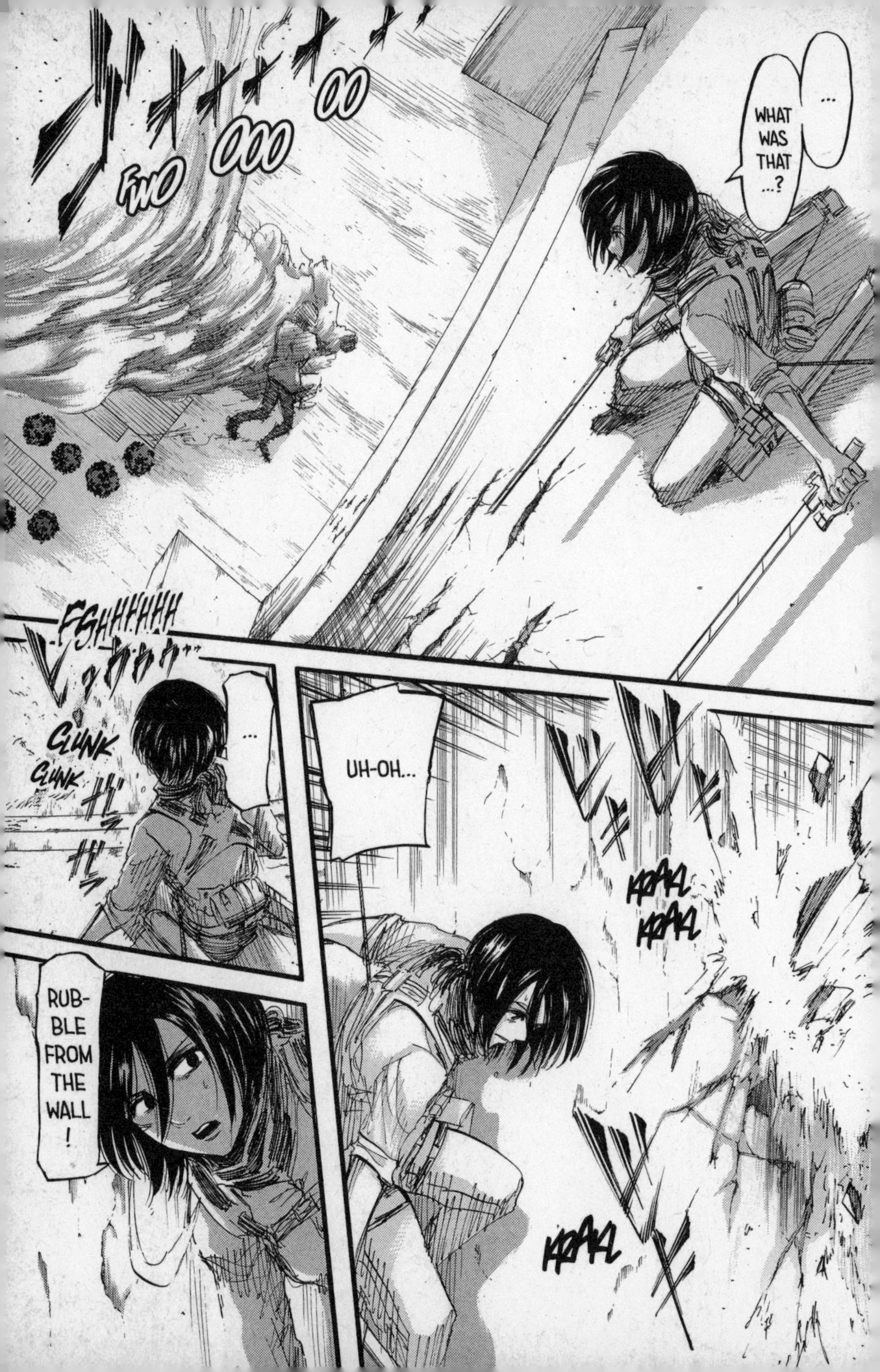
...
WHAT WAS THAT ...?
FWOOOOOO
UH-OH...
KRAK KRAK
KRAK
FSHHHHHH
...
CLUNK CLUNK
RUB-BLE FROM THE WALL!

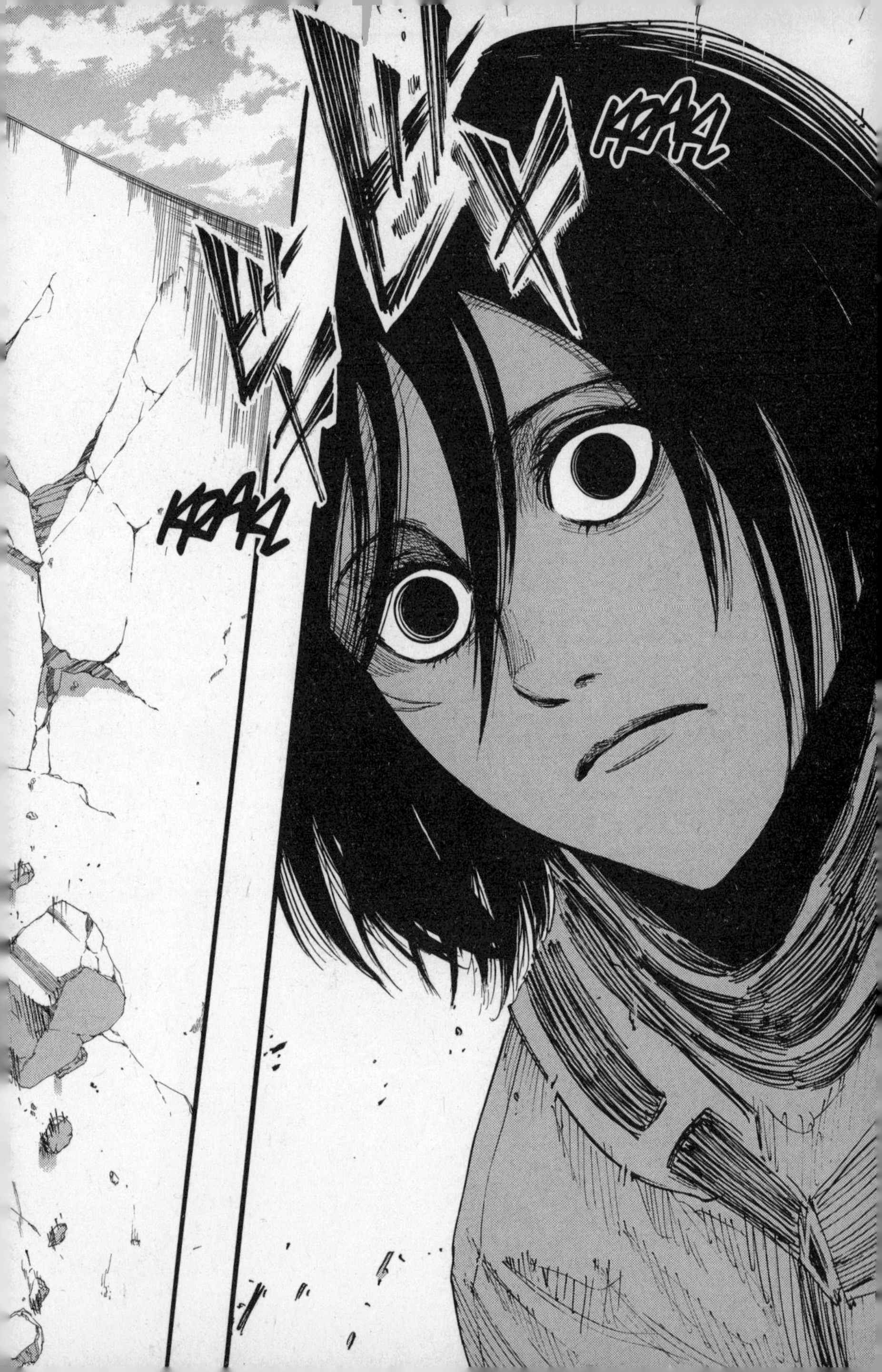

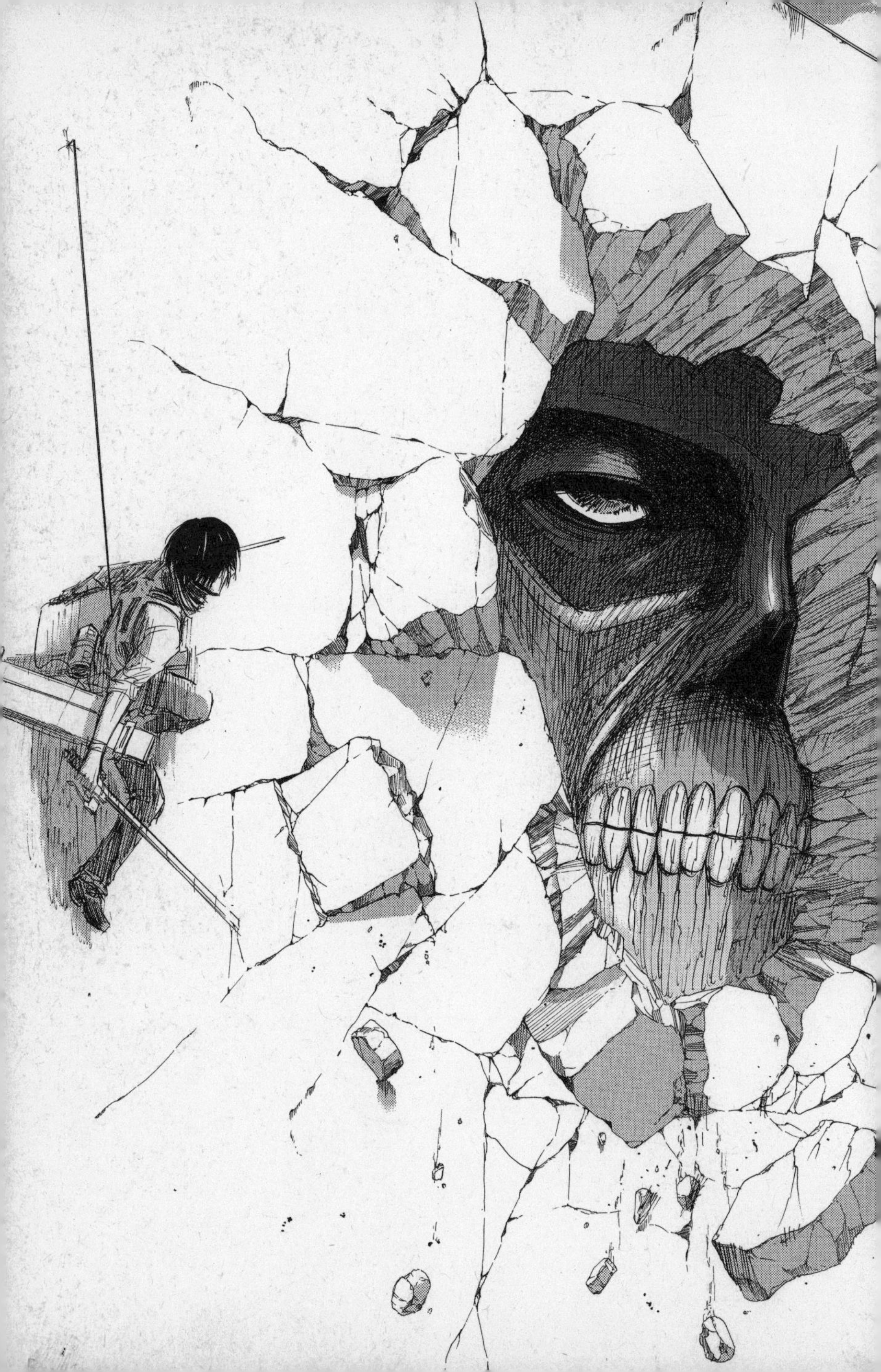

ATTACK on TITAN

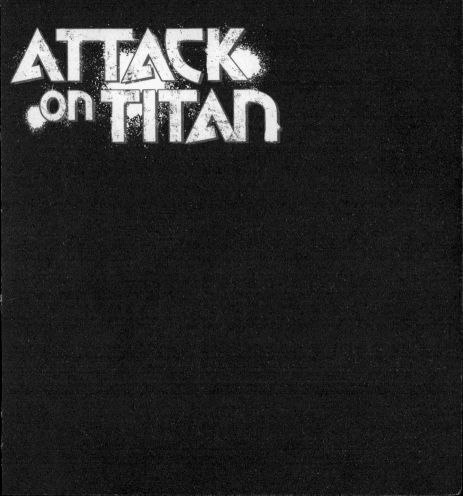

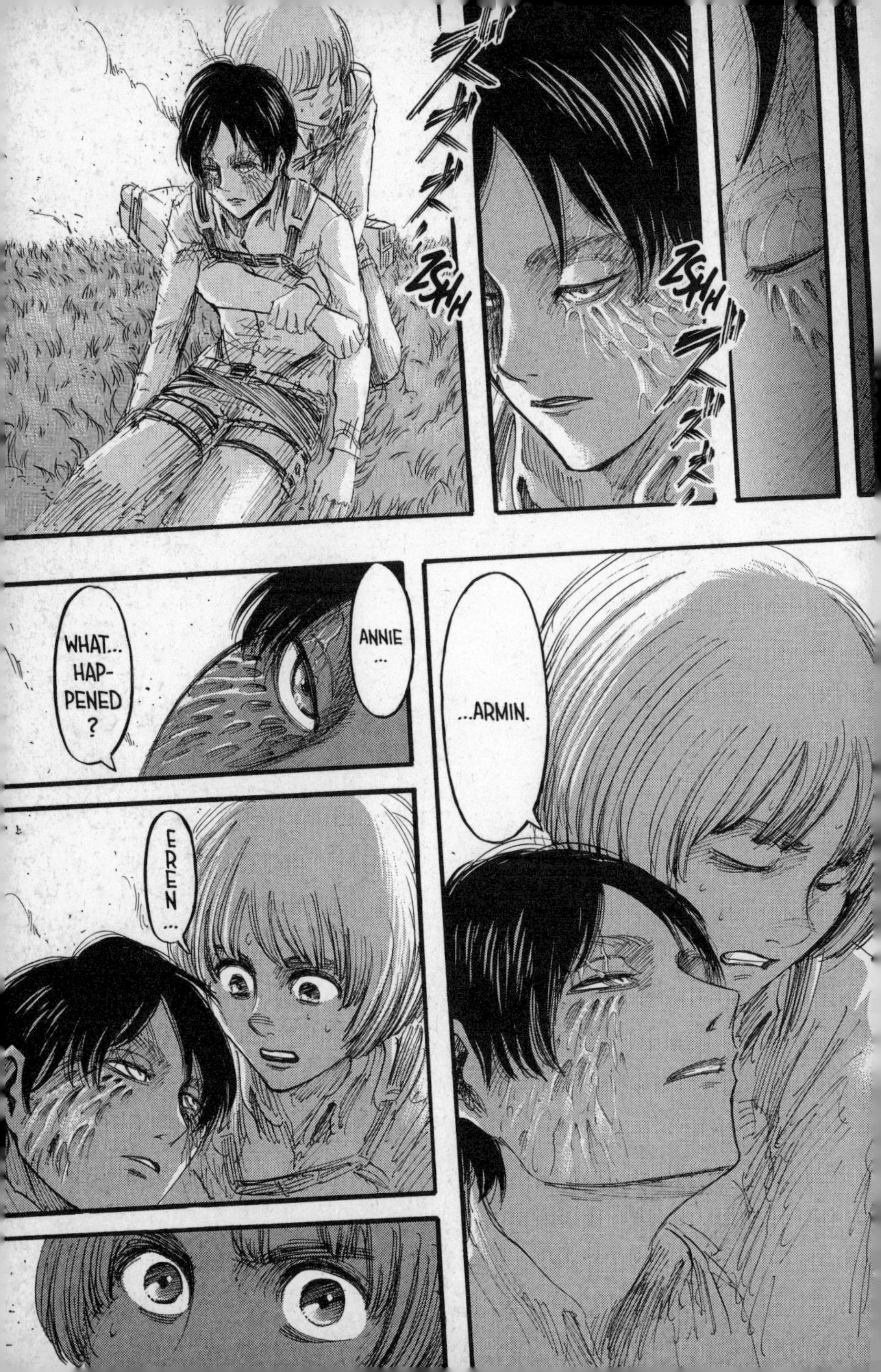
ZSHH
ZSHH
...ARMIN.
ANNIE...
WHAT... HAP-PENED?
EREN...

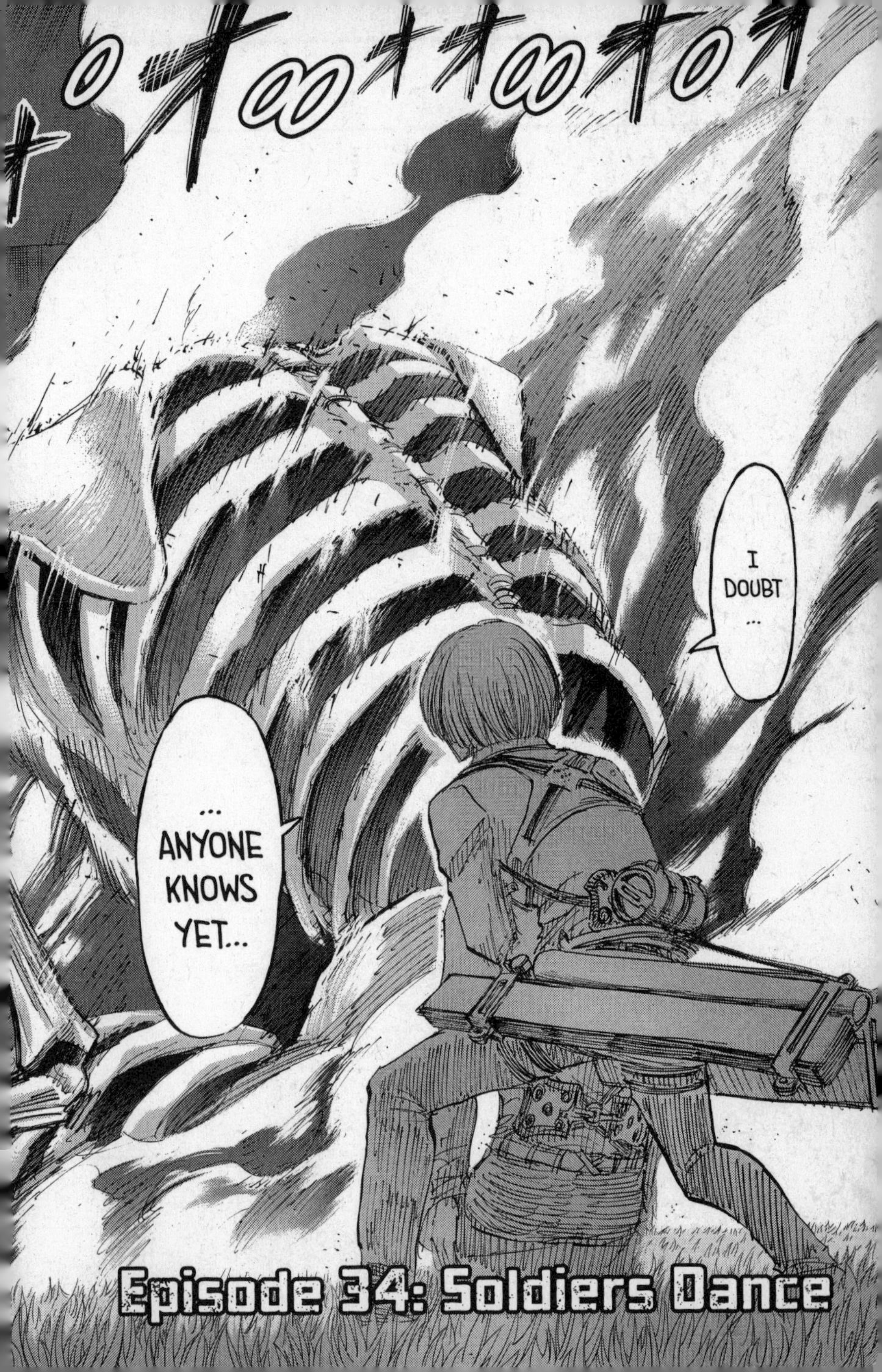
I DOUBT ...
... ANYONE KNOWS YET...

Episode 34: Soldiers Dance

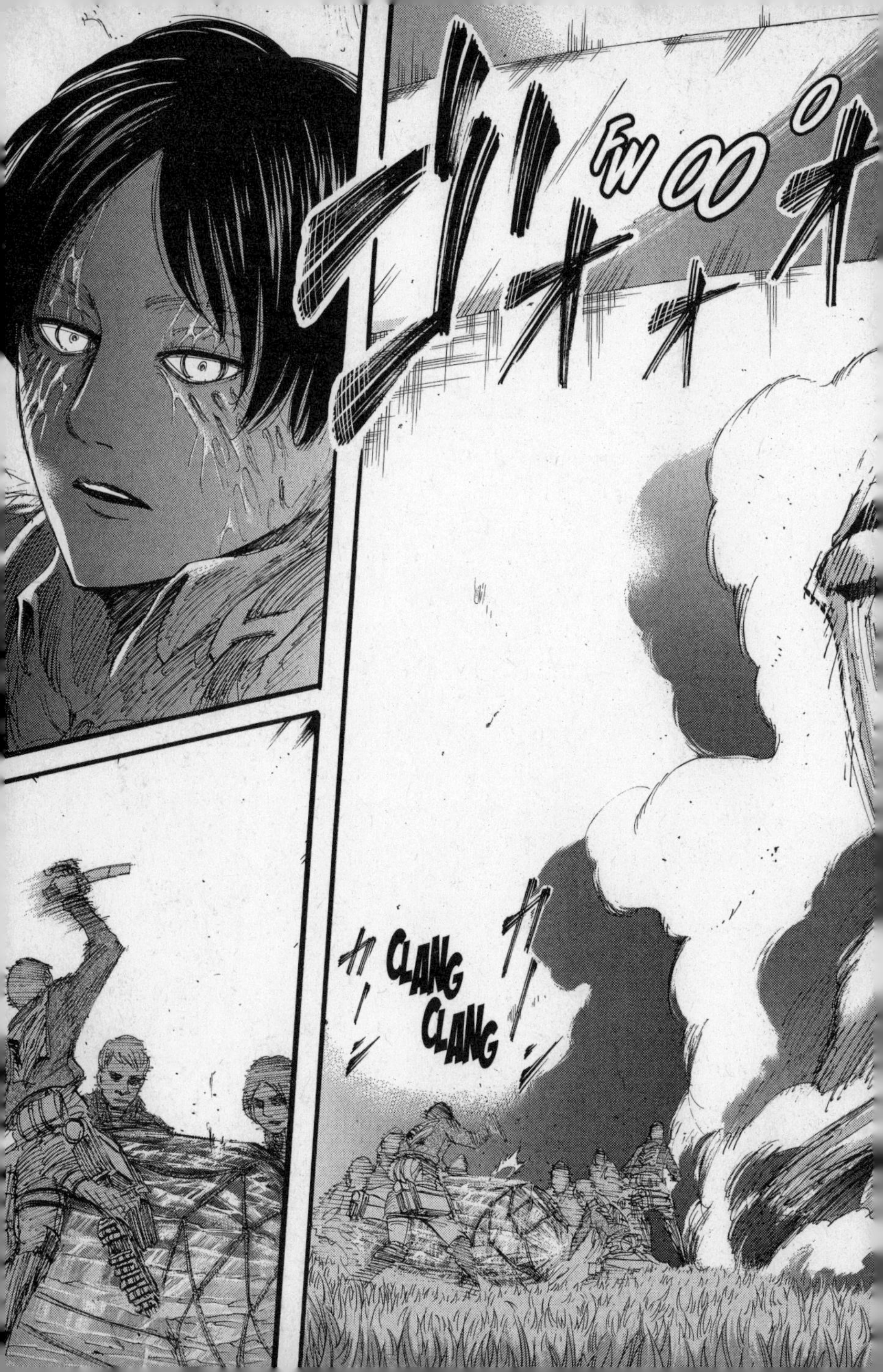
FWOOO
CLANG
CLANG

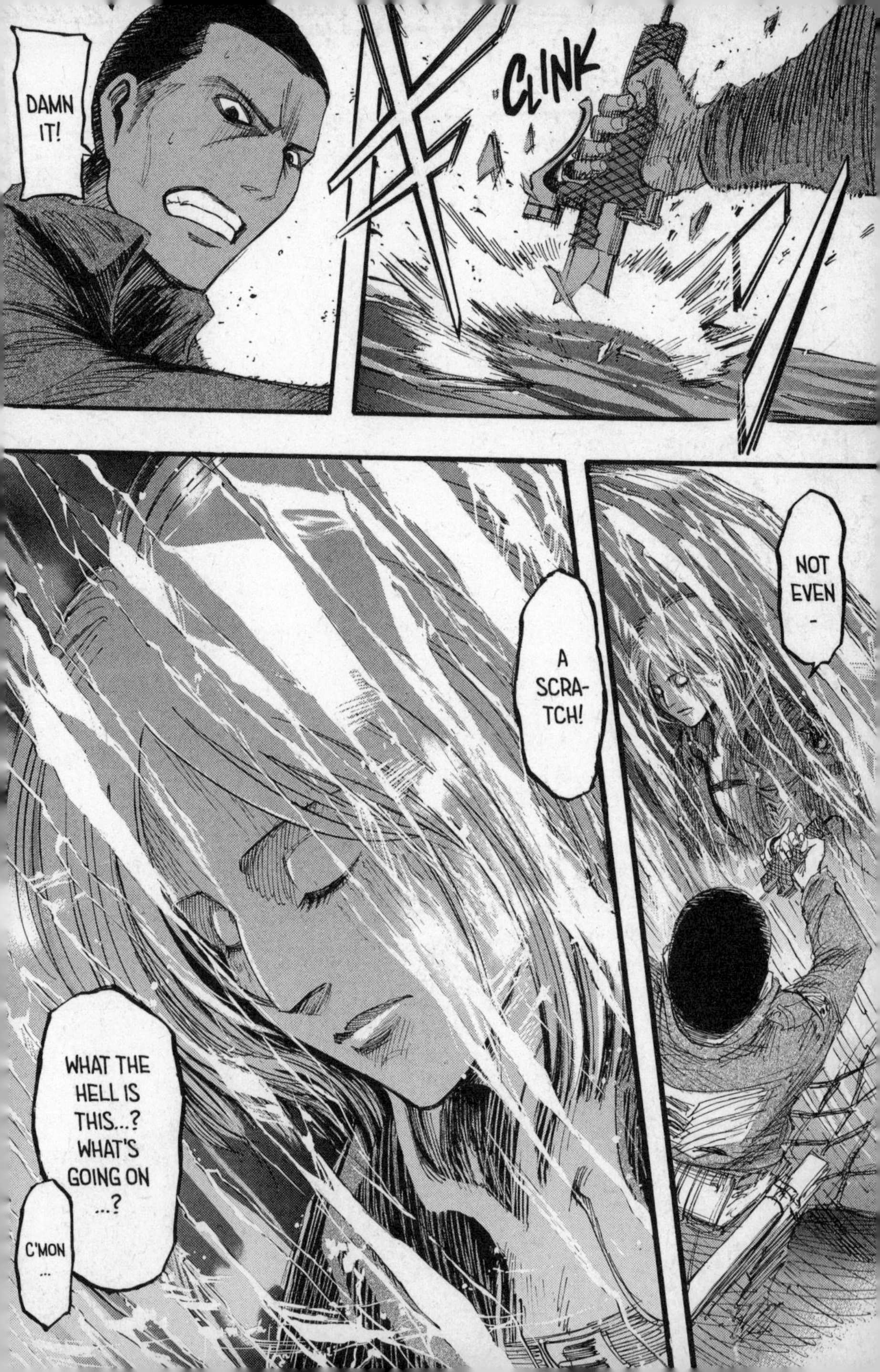
CLINK
DAMN IT!
NOT EVEN -
A SCRA-TCH!
WHAT THE HELL IS THIS...? WHAT'S GOING ON ...?
C'MON ...

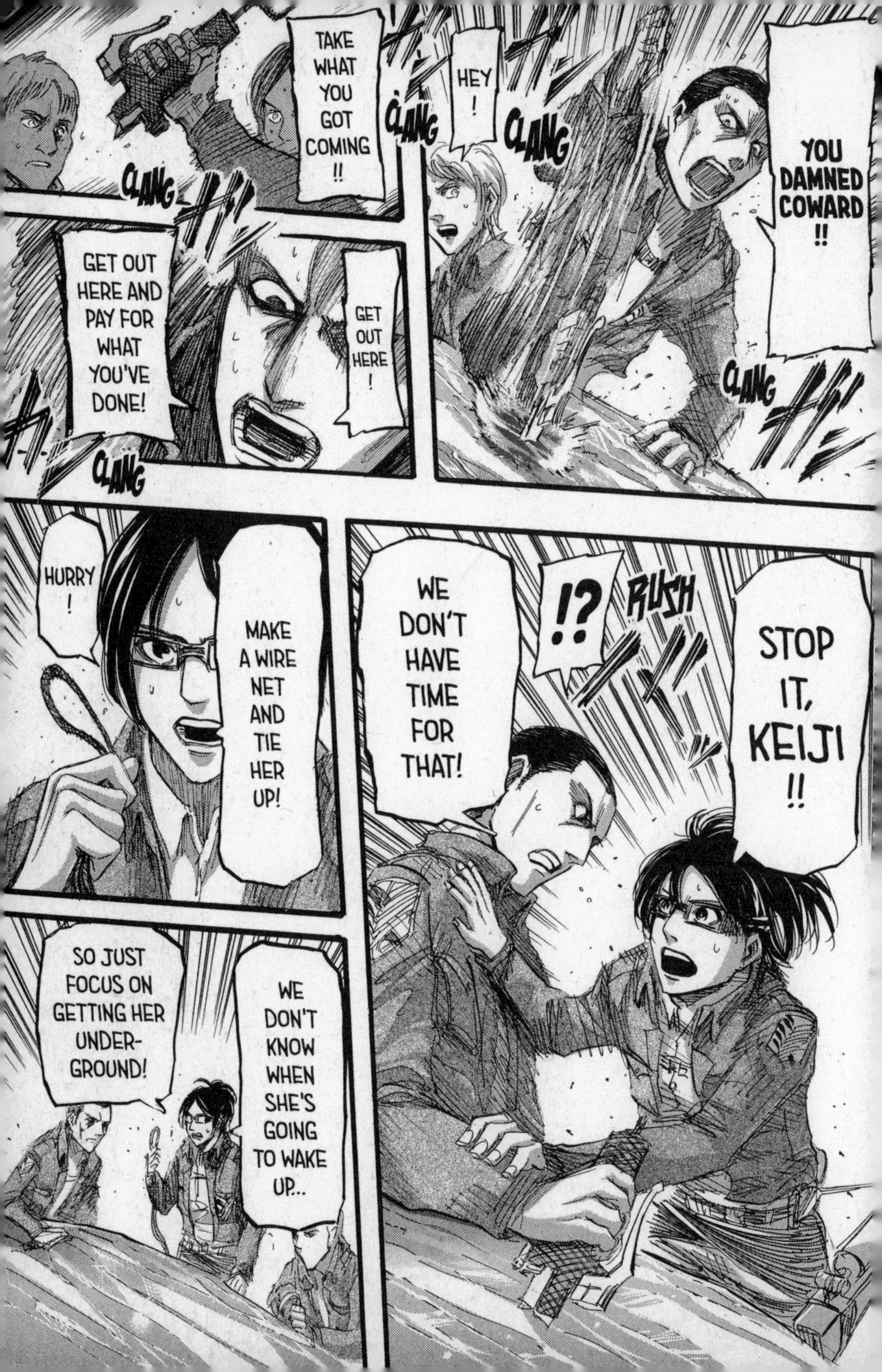
YOU DAMNED COWARD!!
CLANG
CLANG
HEY!
CLANG
TAKE WHAT YOU GOT COMING!!
CLANG
GET OUT HERE!
GET OUT HERE AND PAY FOR WHAT YOU'VE DONE!
CLANG
STOP IT, KEIJI!!
RUSH
!?
WE DON'T HAVE TIME FOR THAT!
MAKE A WIRE NET AND TIE HER UP!
HURRY!
WE DON'T KNOW WHEN SHE'S GOING TO WAKE UP...
SO JUST FOCUS ON GETTING HER UNDERGROUND!

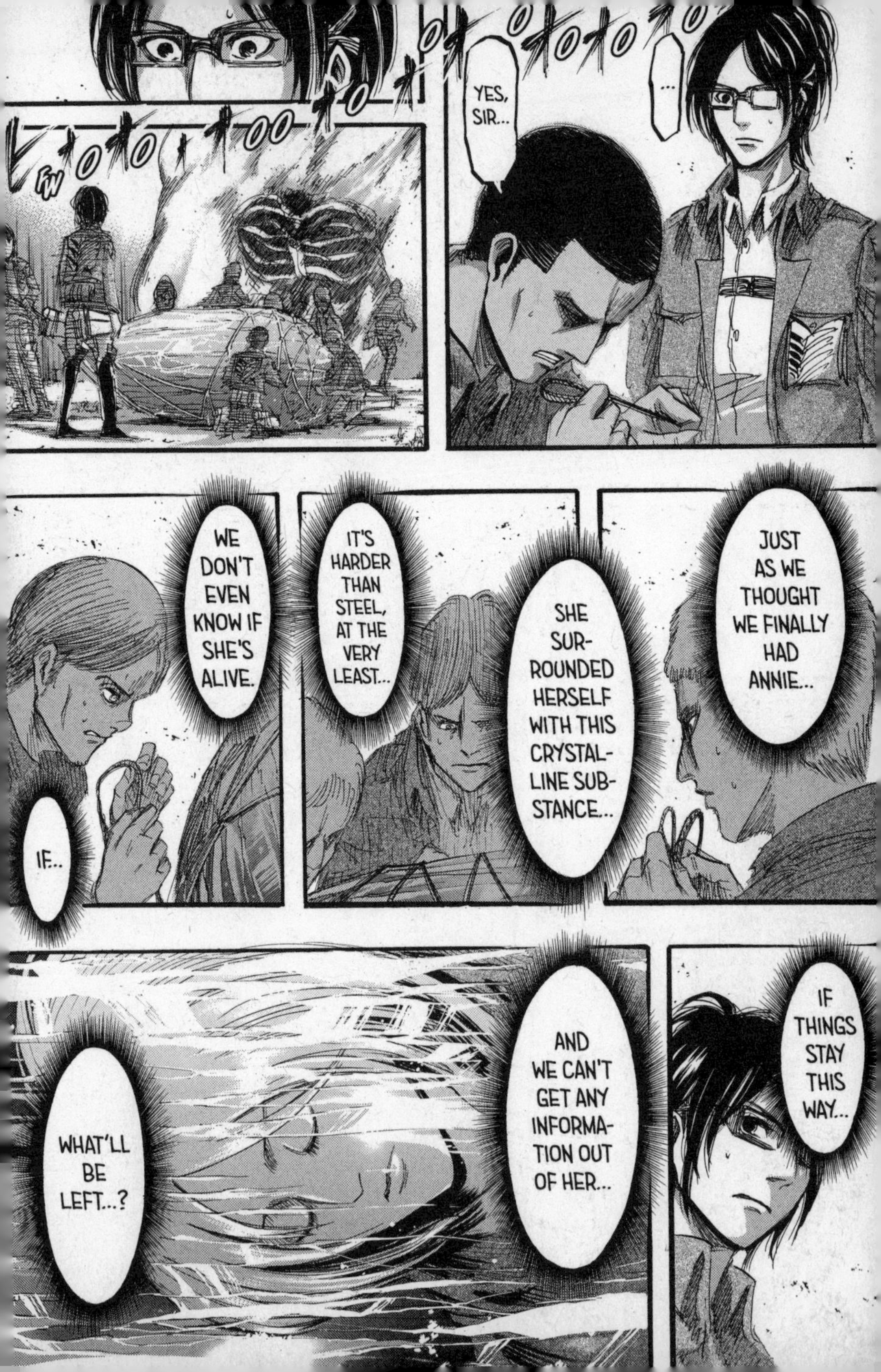
...
YES, SIR...
JUST AS WE THOUGHT WE FINALLY HAD ANNIE...
SHE SURROUNDED HERSELF WITH THIS CRYSTALLINE SUBSTANCE...
IT'S HARDER THAN STEEL, AT THE VERY LEAST...
WE DON'T EVEN KNOW IF SHE'S ALIVE.
IF...
IF THINGS STAY THIS WAY...
AND WE CAN'T GET ANY INFORMATION OUT OF HER...
WHAT'LL BE LEFT...?

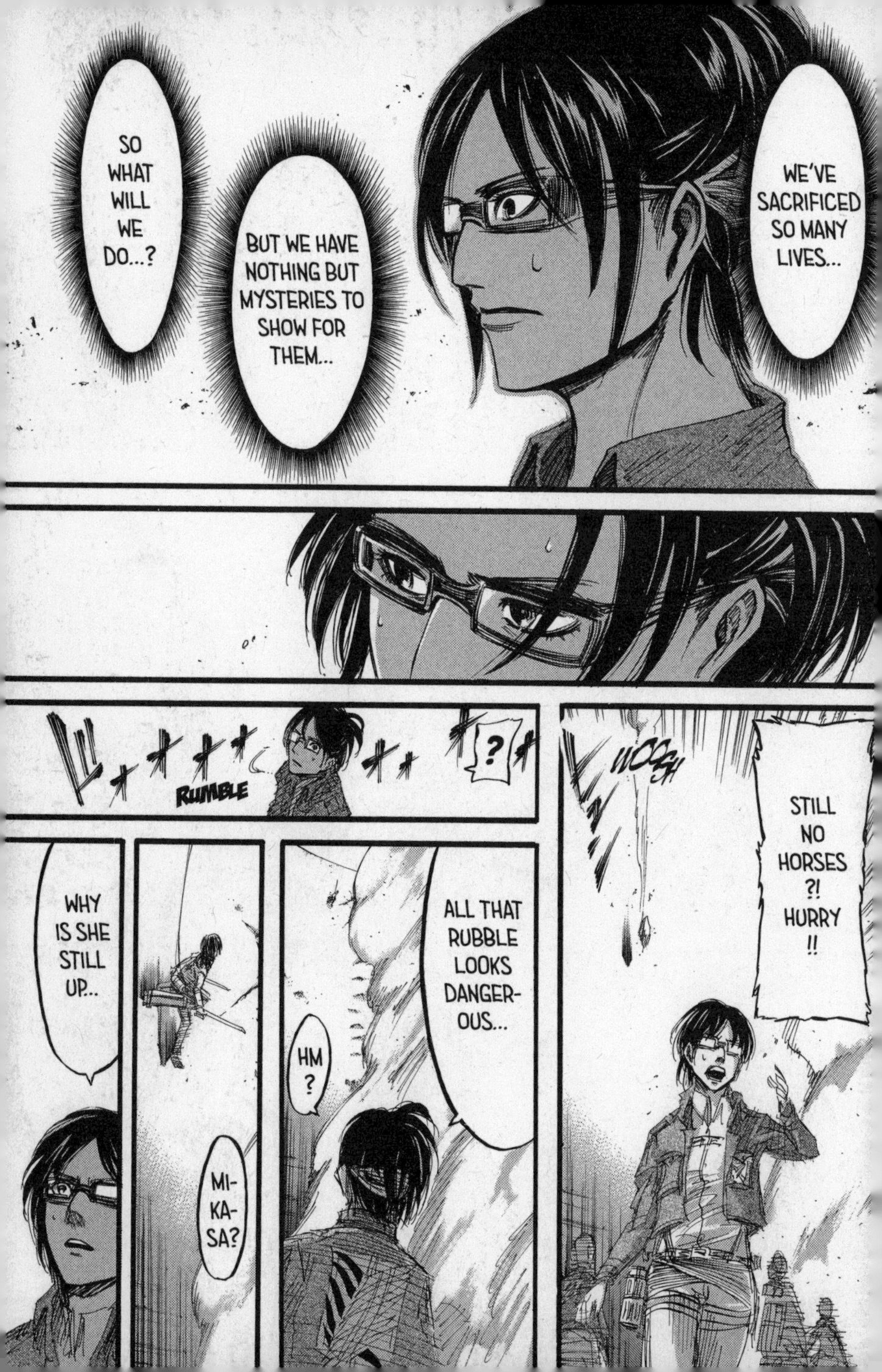
WE'VE SACRIFICED SO MANY LIVES...
BUT WE HAVE NOTHING BUT MYSTERIES TO SHOW FOR THEM...
SO WHAT WILL WE DO...?
WOOSH
STILL NO HORSES?! HURRY!!
?
RUMBLE
ALL THAT RUBBLE LOOKS DANGER-OUS...
HM?
MI-KA-SA?
WHY IS SHE STILL UP...

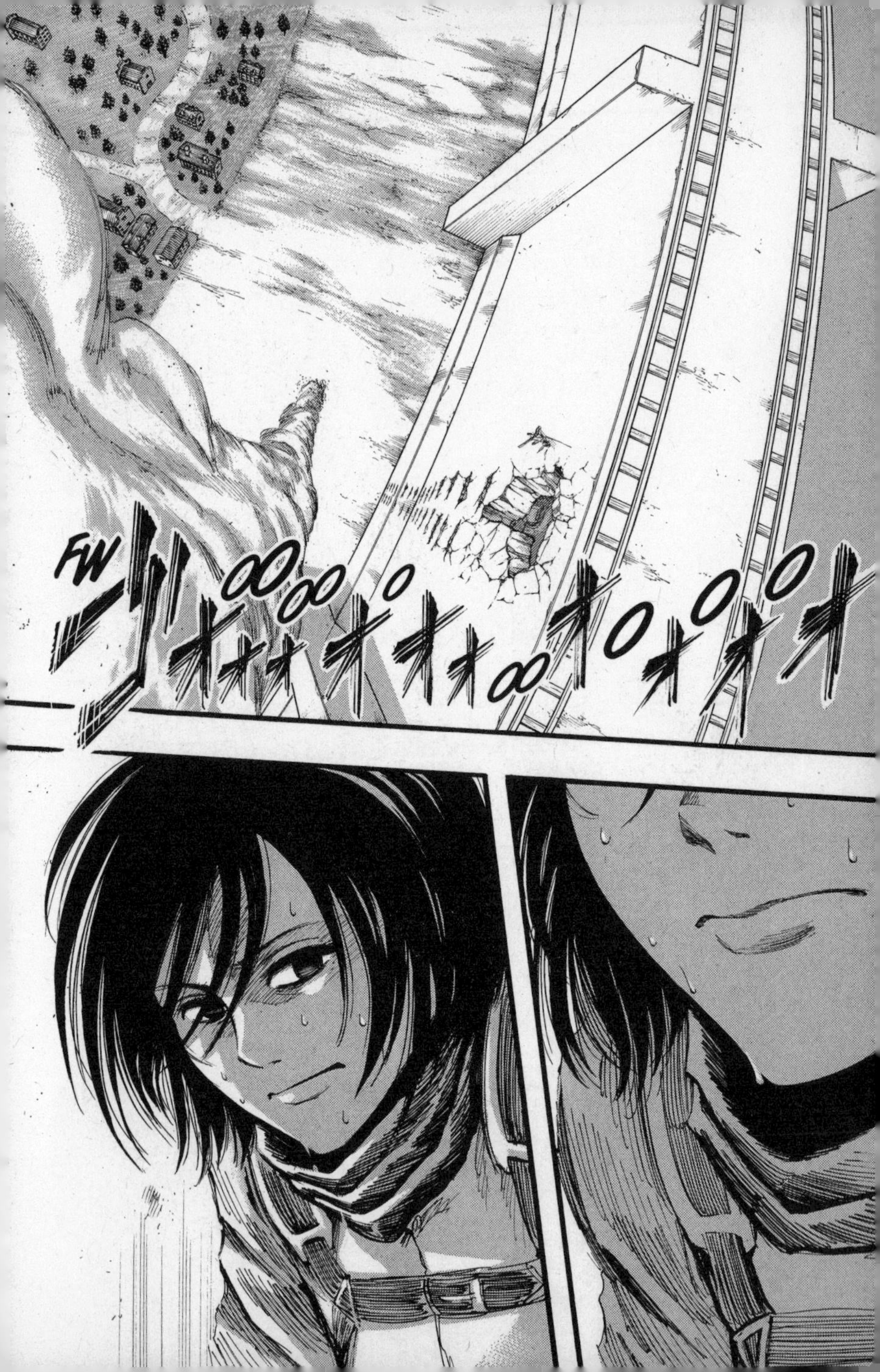
FW

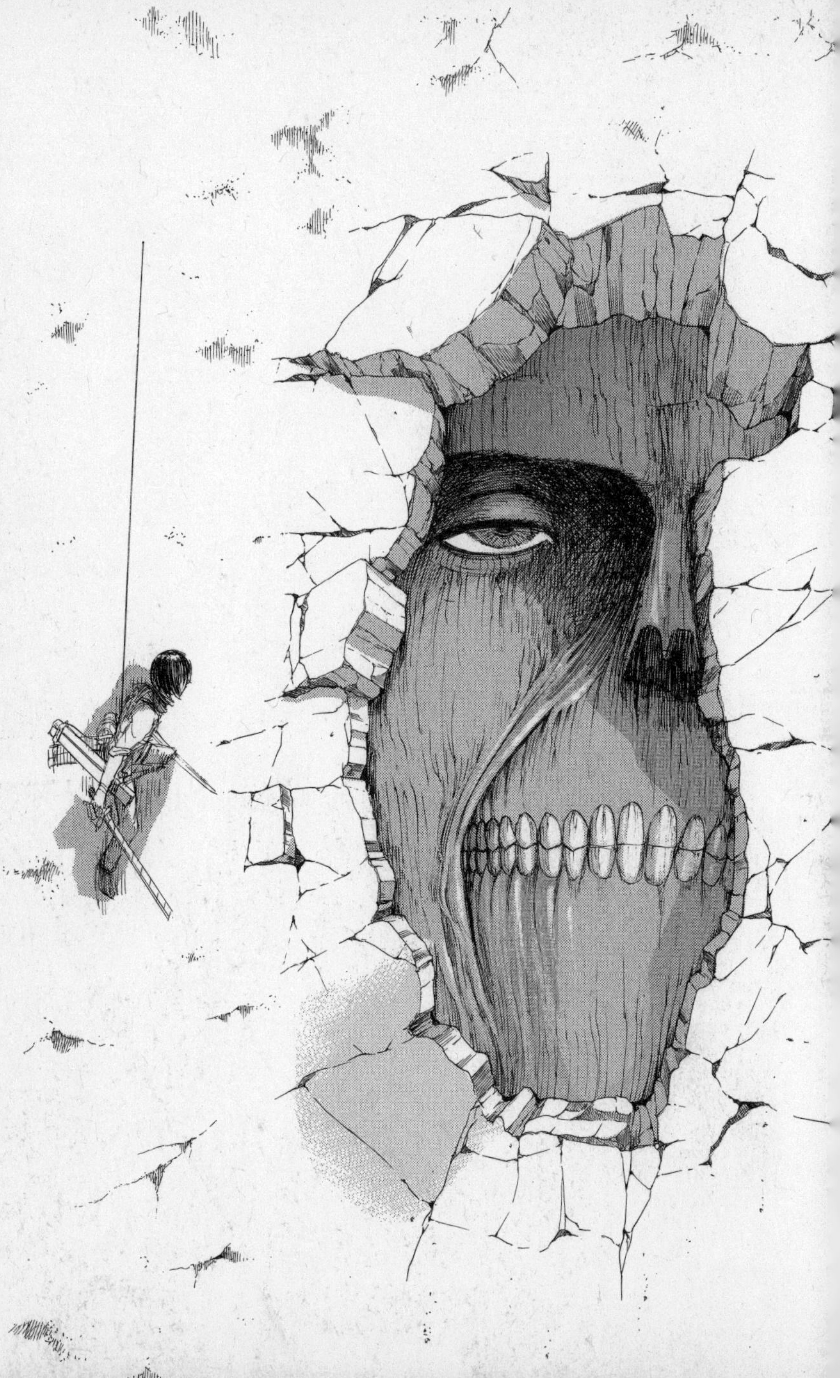

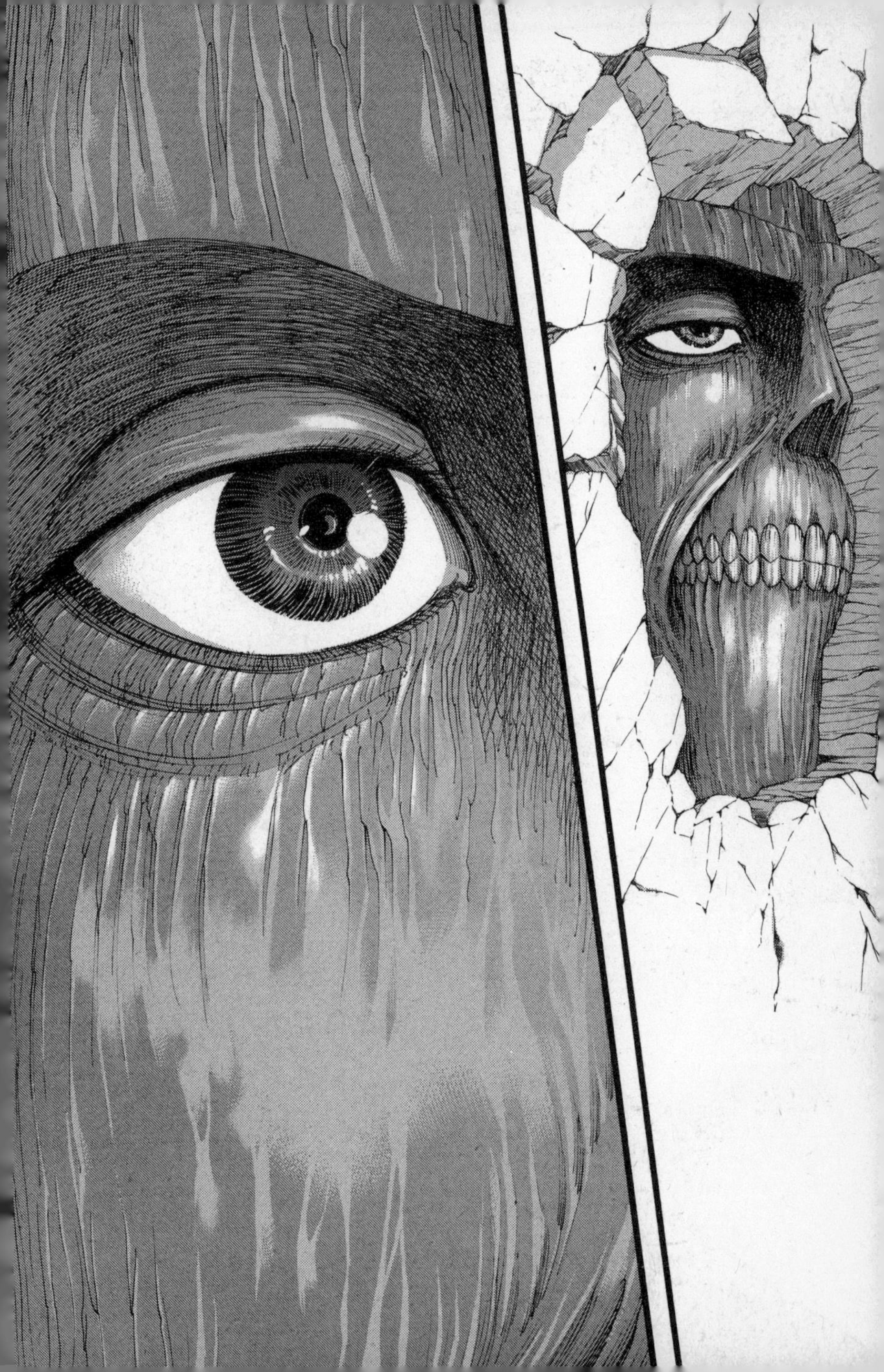

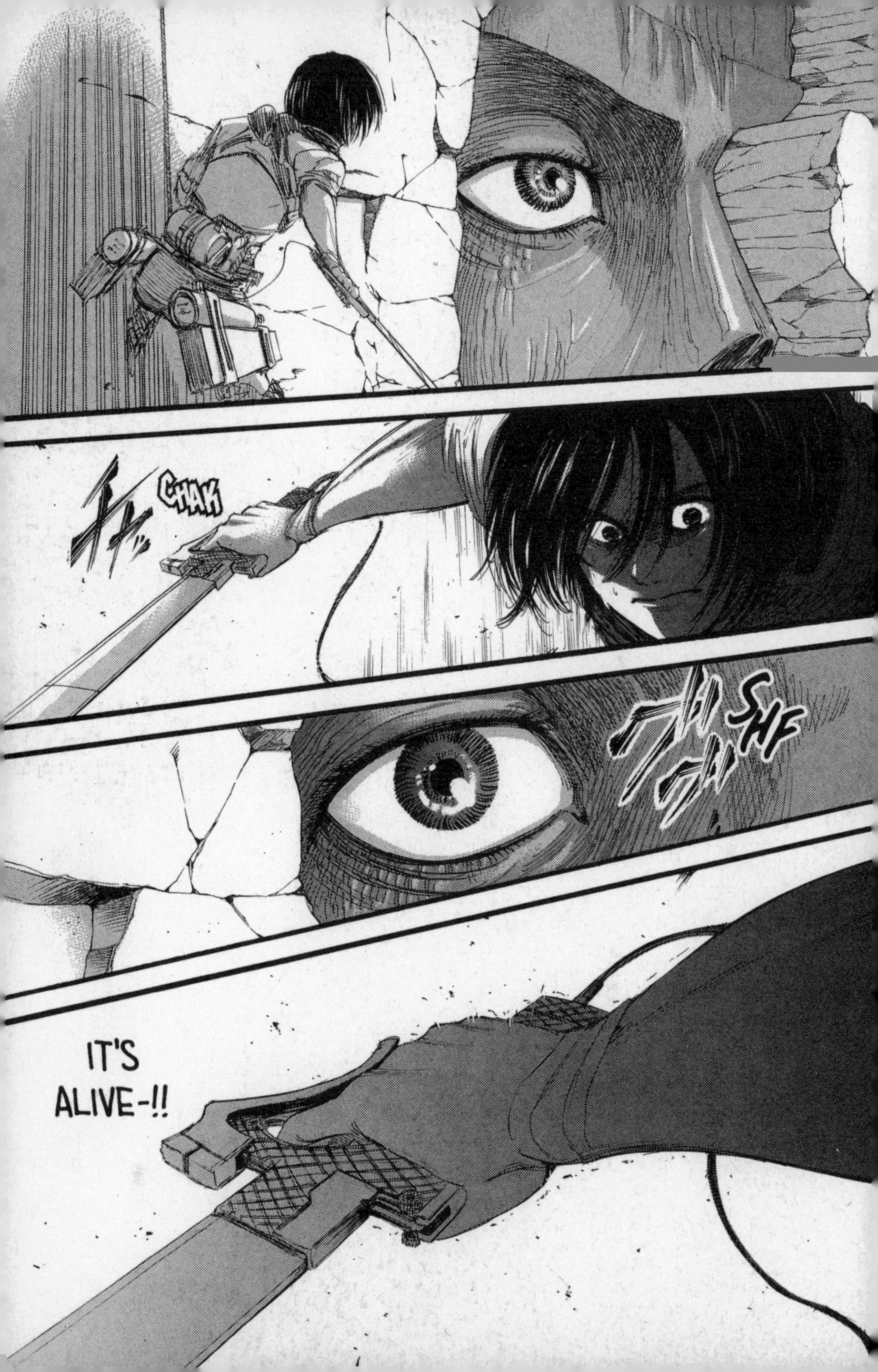
CHAK
SHF
IT'S ALIVE-!!

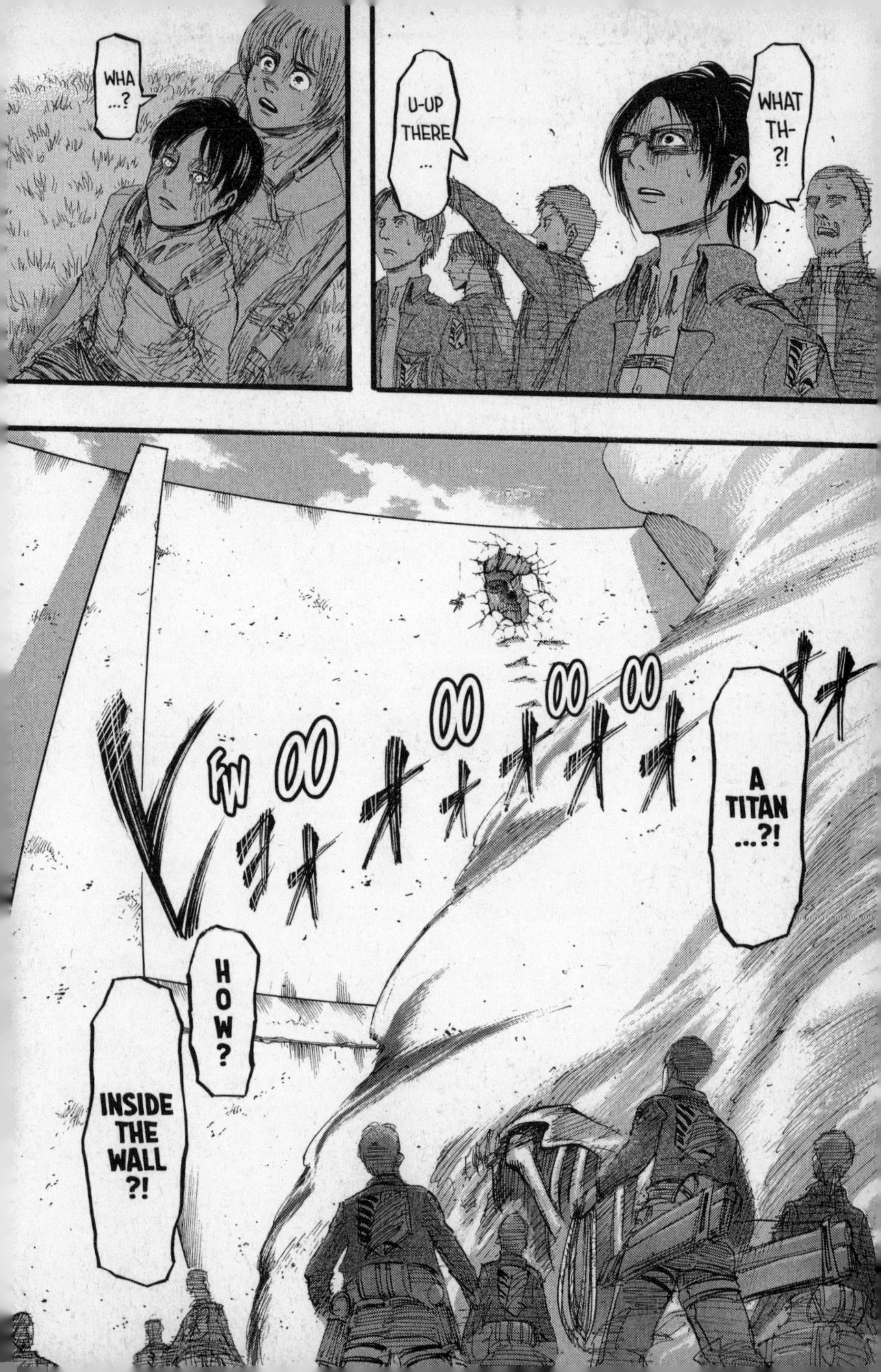
WHAT TH- ?!
U-UP THERE ...
WHA ...?
A TITAN ...?!
FWOOOOOOOO
HOW?
INSIDE THE WALL ?!

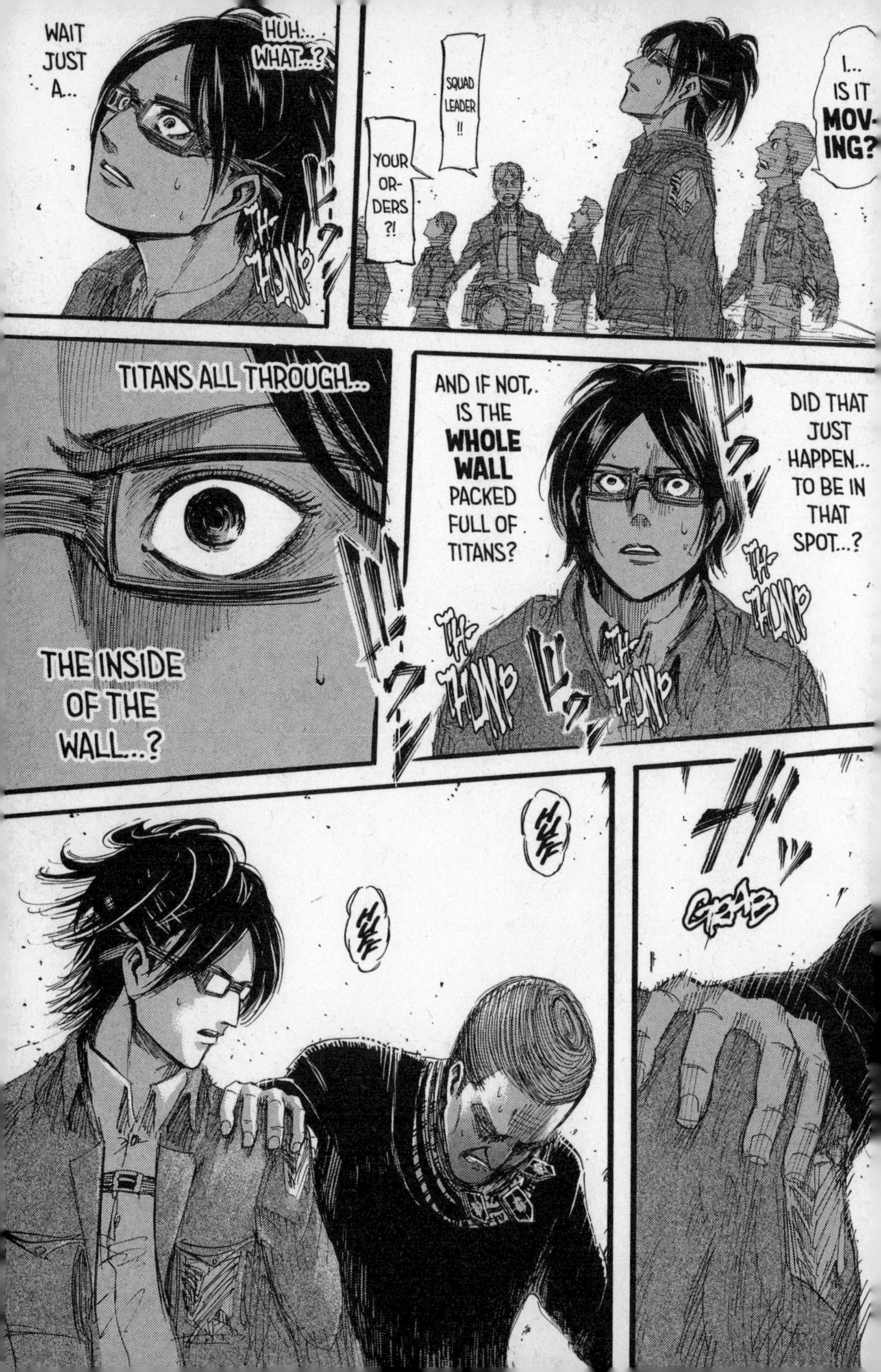
I... IS IT MOVING?
SQUAD LEADER!!
YOUR ORDERS?!
HUH... WHAT...?
WAIT JUST A...
THA-THUMP
DID THAT JUST HAPPEN... TO BE IN THAT SPOT...?
THA-THUMP
AND IF NOT, IS THE WHOLE WALL PACKED FULL OF TITANS?
THA-THUMP
THA-THUMP
TITANS ALL THROUGH...
THE INSIDE OF THE WALL...?
GRAB

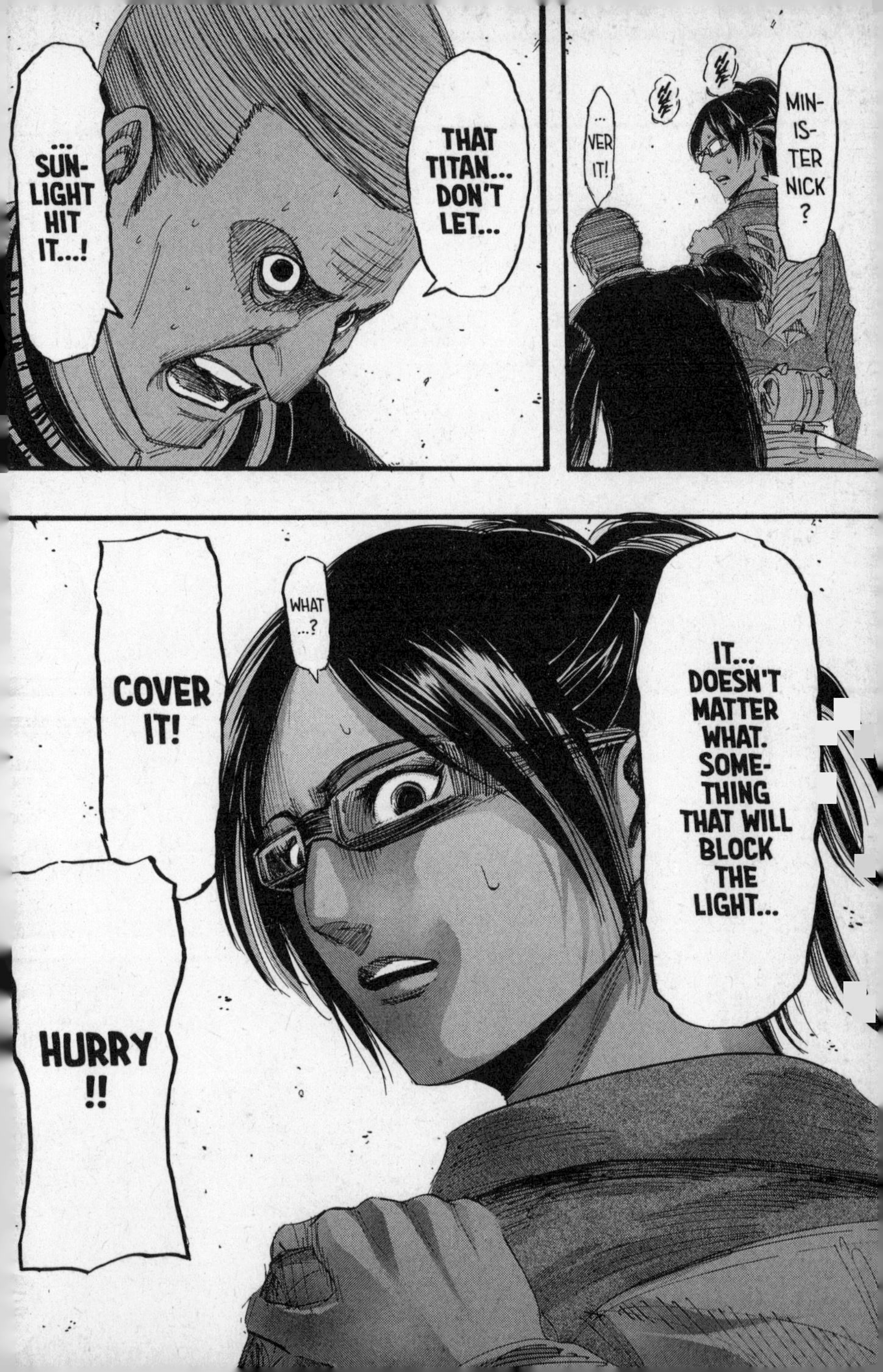
MIN-IS-TER NICK?
...VER IT!
THAT TITAN... DON'T LET...
...SUN-LIGHT HIT IT...!
IT... DOESN'T MATTER WHAT. SOME-THING THAT WILL BLOCK THE LIGHT...
WHAT...?
COVER IT!
HURRY!!

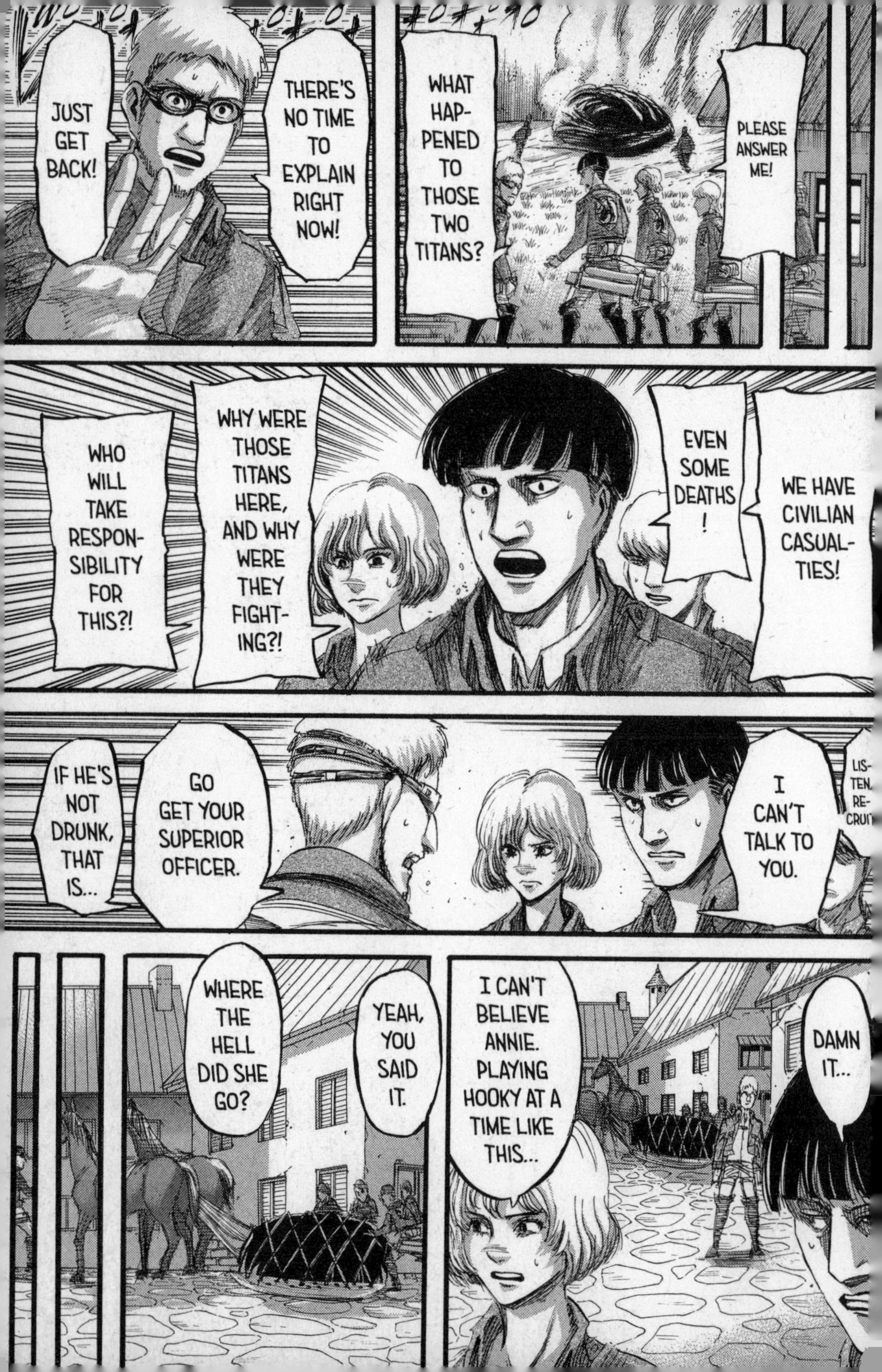
PLEASE ANSWER ME!
WHAT HAPPENED TO THOSE TWO TITANS?
THERE'S NO TIME TO EXPLAIN RIGHT NOW!
JUST GET BACK!
WE HAVE CIVILIAN CASUALTIES!
EVEN SOME DEATHS!
WHY WERE THOSE TITANS HERE, AND WHY WERE THEY FIGHTING?!
WHO WILL TAKE RESPONSIBILITY FOR THIS?!
LISTEN, RECRUI
I CAN'T TALK TO YOU.
GO GET YOUR SUPERIOR OFFICER.
IF HE'S NOT DRUNK, THAT IS...
DAMN IT...
I CAN'T BELIEVE ANNIE. PLAYING HOOKY AT A TIME LIKE THIS...
YEAH, YOU SAID IT.
WHERE THE HELL DID SHE GO?

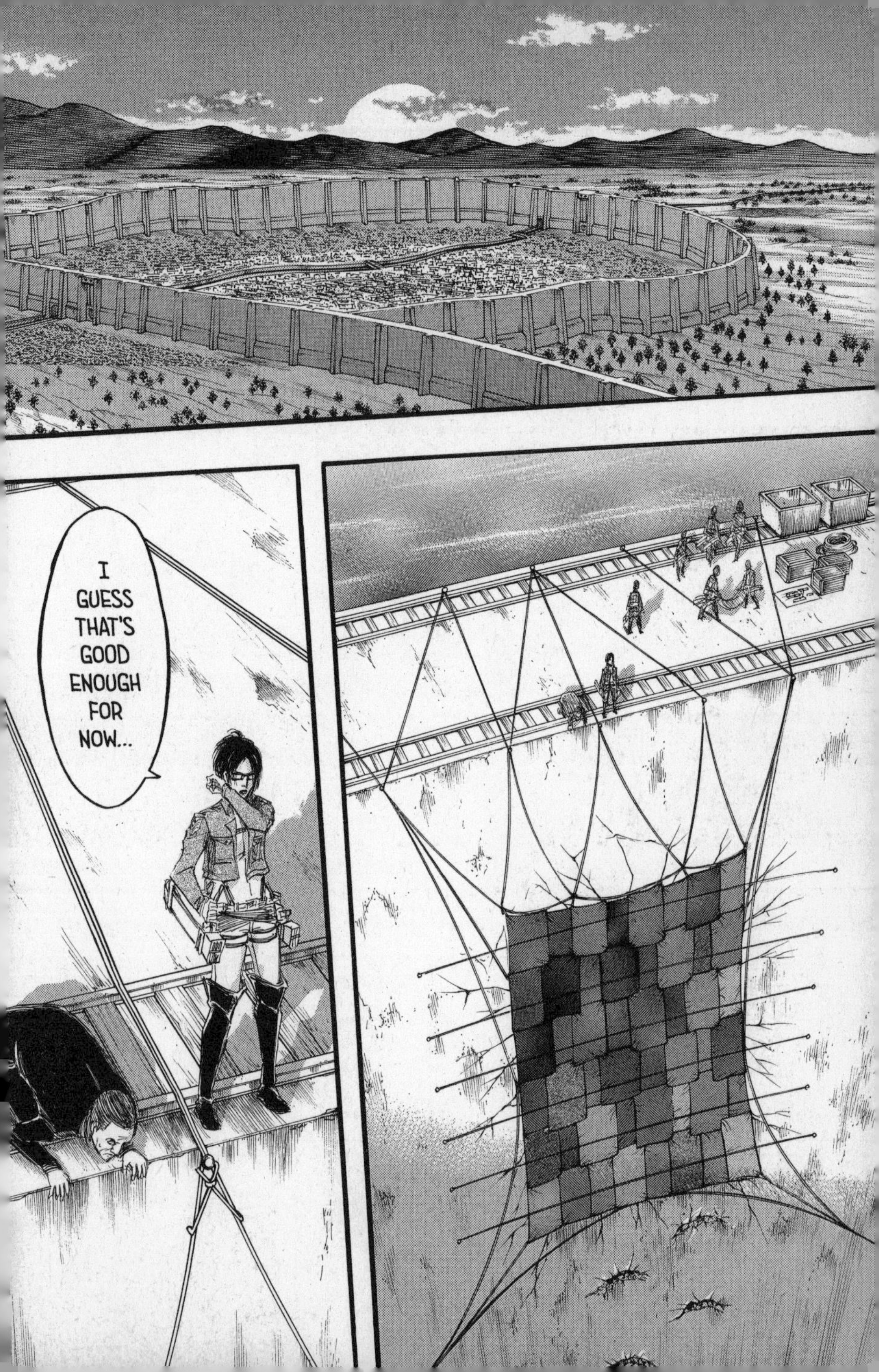
I GUESS THAT'S GOOD ENOUGH FOR NOW...

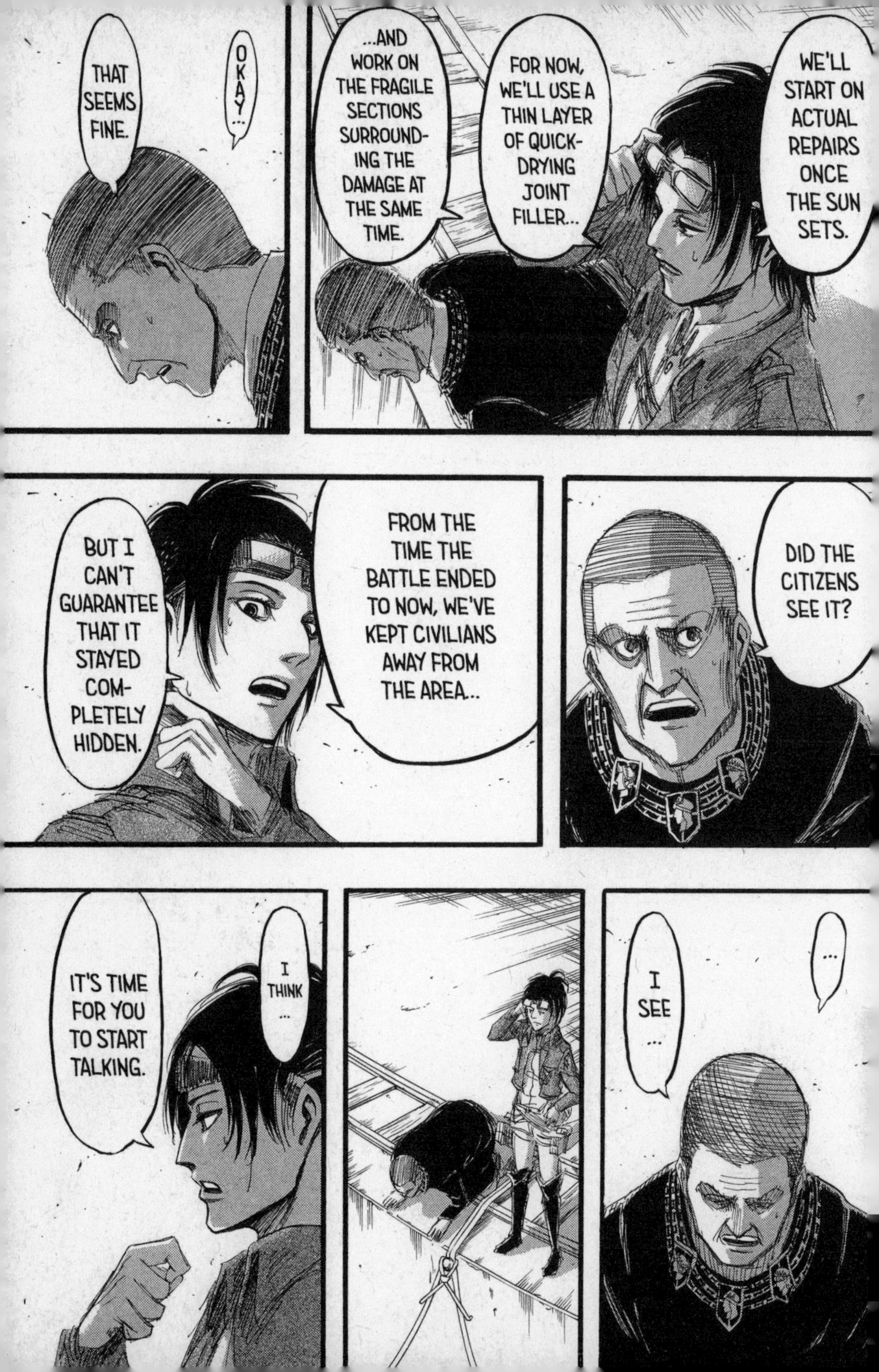
WE'LL START ON ACTUAL REPAIRS ONCE THE SUN SETS.
FOR NOW, WE'LL USE A THIN LAYER OF QUICK-DRYING JOINT FILLER...
...AND WORK ON THE FRAGILE SECTIONS SURROUNDING THE DAMAGE AT THE SAME TIME.
OKAY...
THAT SEEMS FINE.
DID THE CITIZENS SEE IT?
FROM THE TIME THE BATTLE ENDED TO NOW, WE'VE KEPT CIVILIANS AWAY FROM THE AREA...
BUT I CAN'T GUARANTEE THAT IT STAYED COMPLETELY HIDDEN.
...
I SEE...
I THINK...
IT'S TIME FOR YOU TO START TALKING.

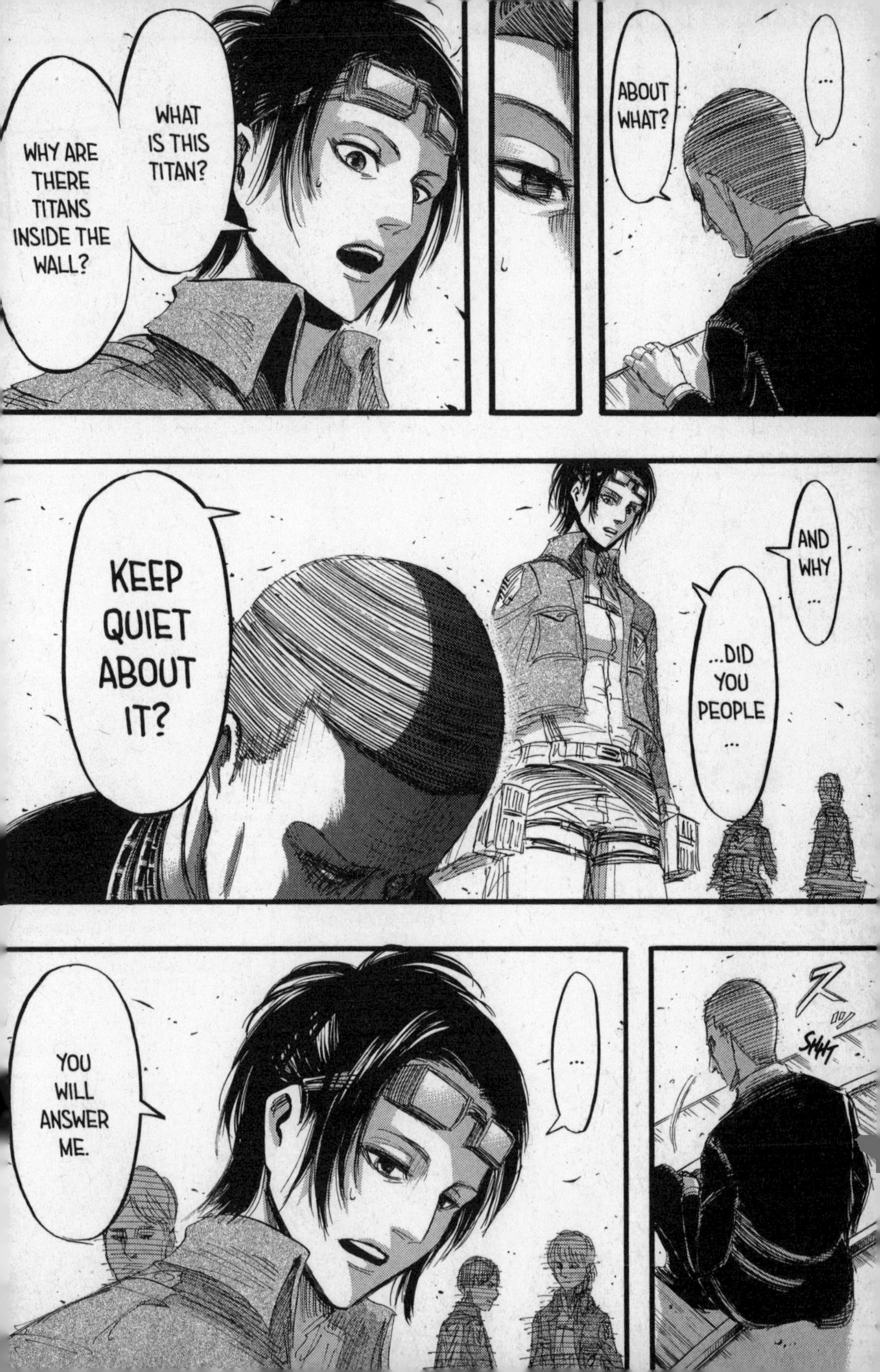
...
ABOUT WHAT?
WHAT IS THIS TITAN?
WHY ARE THERE TITANS INSIDE THE WALL?
AND WHY ...
...DID YOU PEOPLE ...
KEEP QUIET ABOUT IT?
SHHT
...
YOU WILL ANSWER ME.

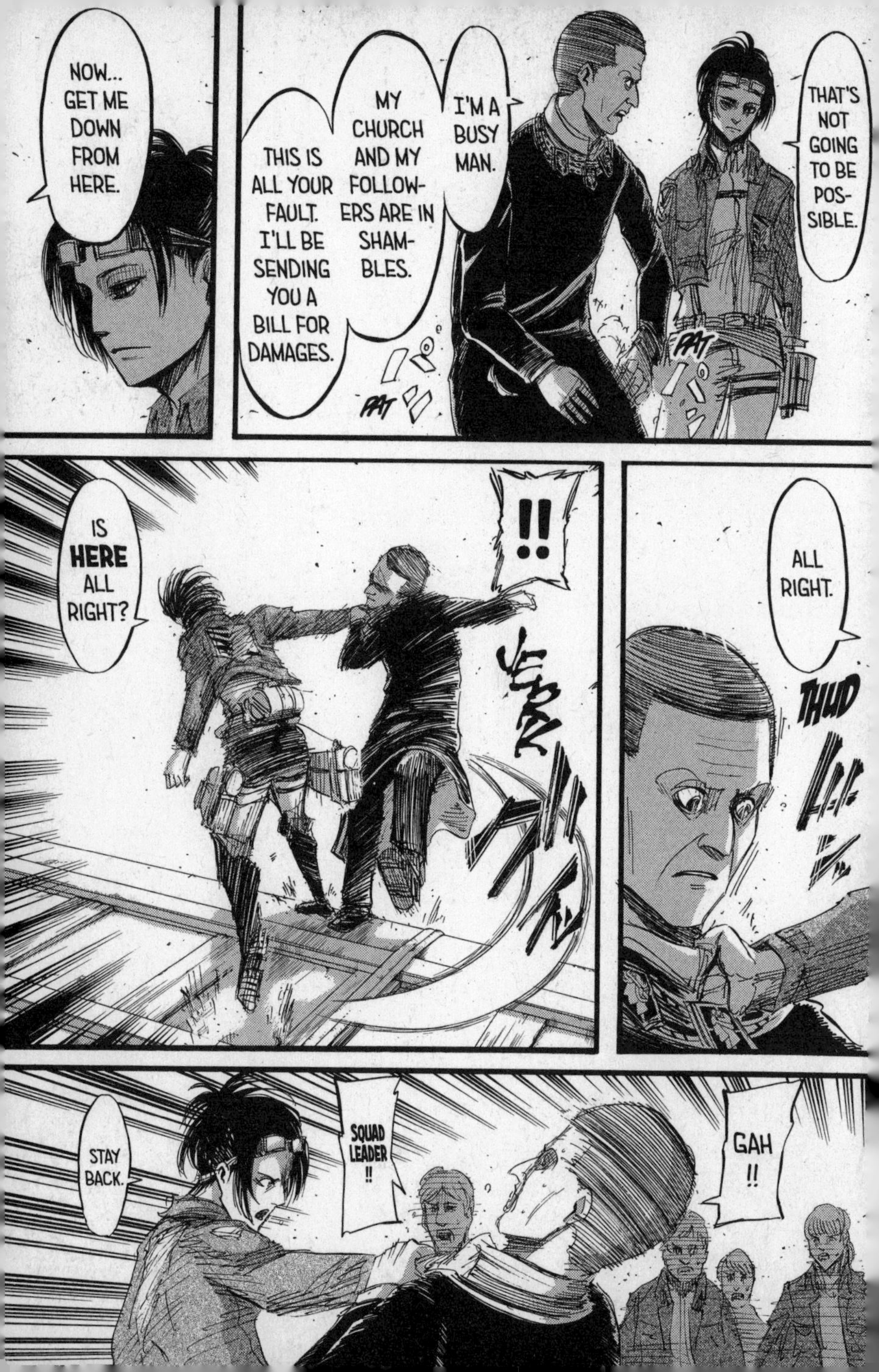
THAT'S NOT GOING TO BE POSSIBLE.
I'M A BUSY MAN.
MY CHURCH AND MY FOLLOWERS ARE IN SHAMBLES.
THIS IS ALL YOUR FAULT. I'LL BE SENDING YOU A BILL FOR DAMAGES.
PAT
PAT
NOW... GET ME DOWN FROM HERE.
ALL RIGHT.
THUD
!!
JERK
IS **HERE** ALL RIGHT?
GAH !!
SQUAD LEADER !!
STAY BACK.

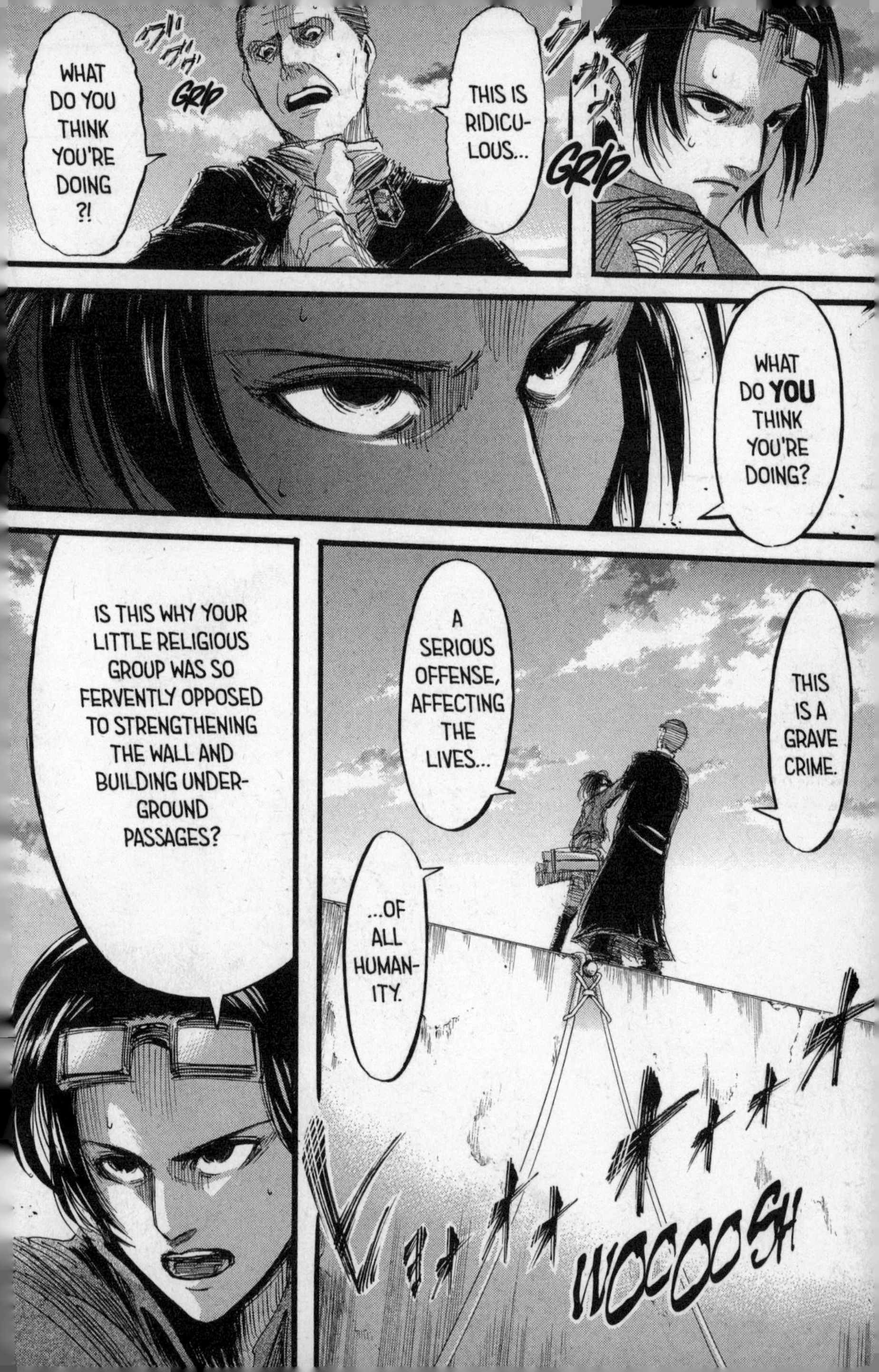
GRIP
THIS IS RIDICULOUS...
GRIP
WHAT DO YOU THINK YOU'RE DOING ?!
WHAT DO **YOU** THINK YOU'RE DOING?
THIS IS A GRAVE CRIME.
A SERIOUS OFFENSE, AFFECTING THE LIVES...
...OF ALL HUMANITY.
WOOOOSH
IS THIS WHY YOUR LITTLE RELIGIOUS GROUP WAS SO FERVENTLY OPPOSED TO STRENGTHENING THE WALL AND BUILDING UNDERGROUND PASSAGES?

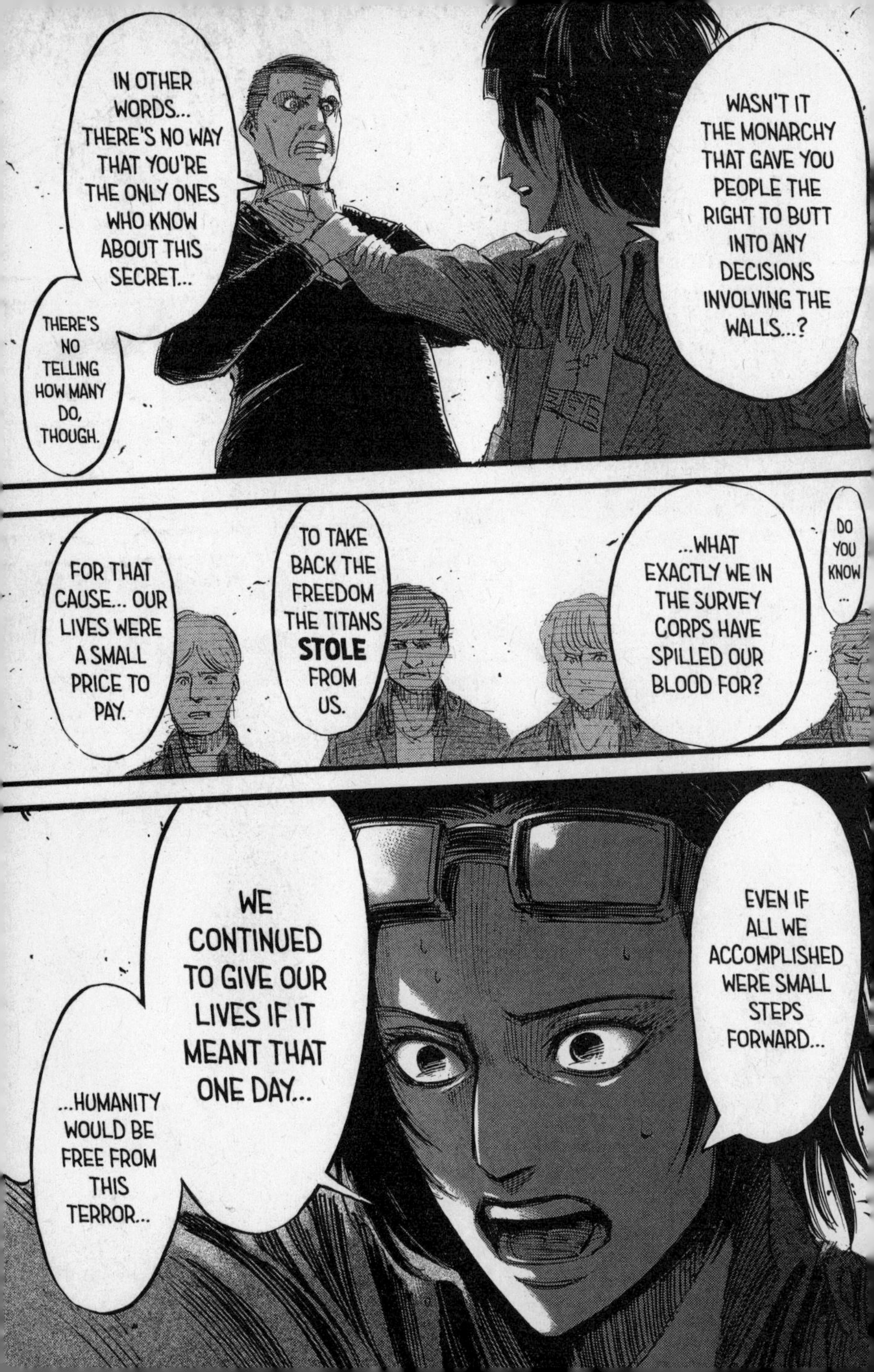
WASN'T IT THE MONARCHY THAT GAVE YOU PEOPLE THE RIGHT TO BUTT INTO ANY DECISIONS INVOLVING THE WALLS...?
IN OTHER WORDS... THERE'S NO WAY THAT YOU'RE THE ONLY ONES WHO KNOW ABOUT THIS SECRET...
THERE'S NO TELLING HOW MANY DO, THOUGH.
DO YOU KNOW...
...WHAT EXACTLY WE IN THE SURVEY CORPS HAVE SPILLED OUR BLOOD FOR?
TO TAKE BACK THE FREEDOM THE TITANS **STOLE** FROM US.
FOR THAT CAUSE... OUR LIVES WERE A SMALL PRICE TO PAY.
EVEN IF ALL WE ACCOMPLISHED WERE SMALL STEPS FORWARD...
WE CONTINUED TO GIVE OUR LIVES IF IT MEANT THAT ONE DAY...
...HUMANITY WOULD BE FREE FROM THIS TERROR...

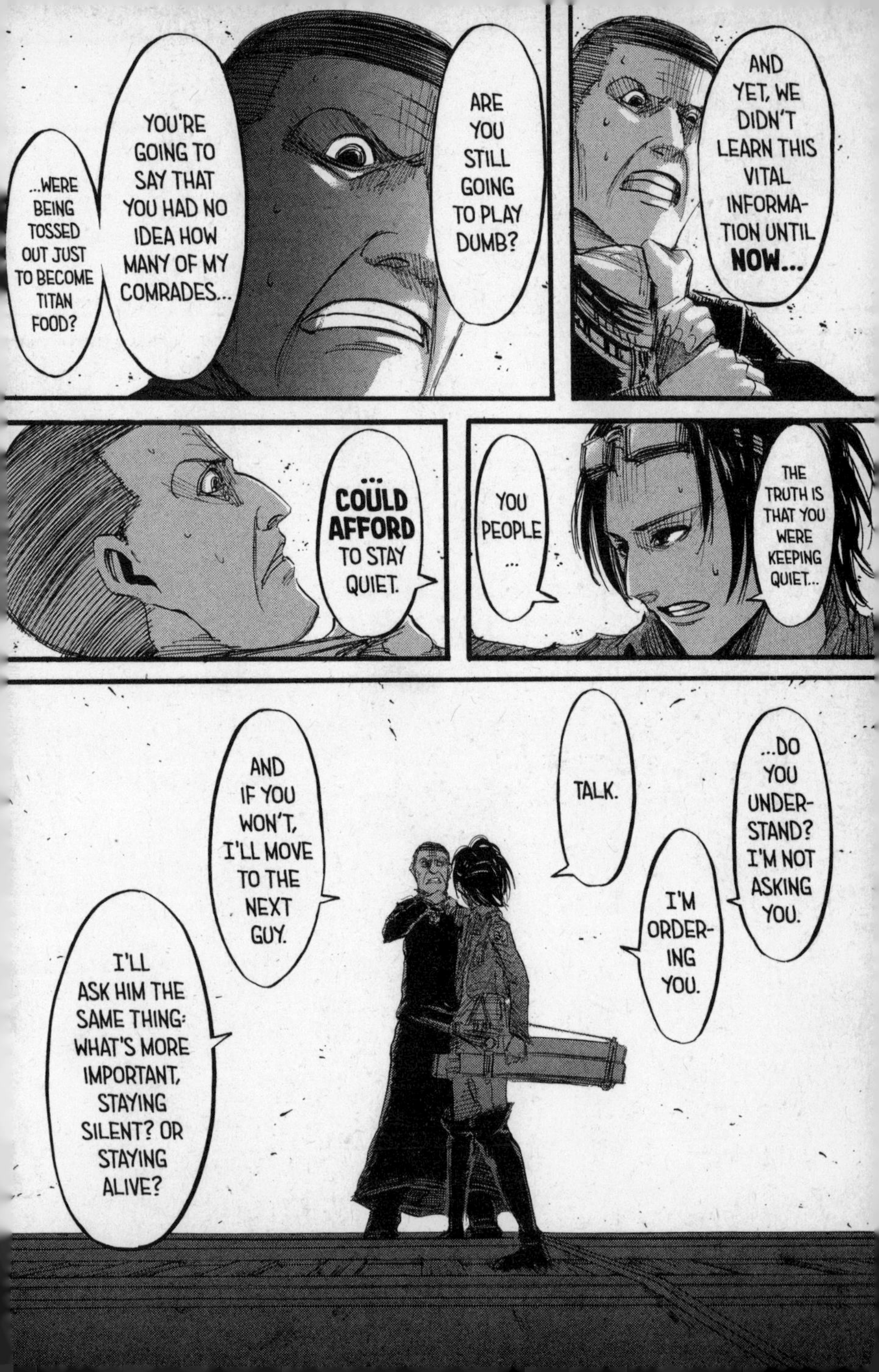
AND YET, WE DIDN'T LEARN THIS VITAL INFORMATION UNTIL **NOW...**
ARE YOU STILL GOING TO PLAY DUMB?
YOU'RE GOING TO SAY THAT YOU HAD NO IDEA HOW MANY OF MY COMRADES...
...WERE BEING TOSSED OUT JUST TO BECOME TITAN FOOD?
THE TRUTH IS THAT YOU WERE KEEPING QUIET...
YOU PEOPLE...
...**COULD AFFORD** TO STAY QUIET.
...DO YOU UNDERSTAND? I'M NOT ASKING YOU.
I'M ORDERING YOU.
TALK.
AND IF YOU WON'T, I'LL MOVE TO THE NEXT GUY.
I'LL ASK HIM THE SAME THING: WHAT'S MORE IMPORTANT, STAYING SILENT? OR STAYING ALIVE?

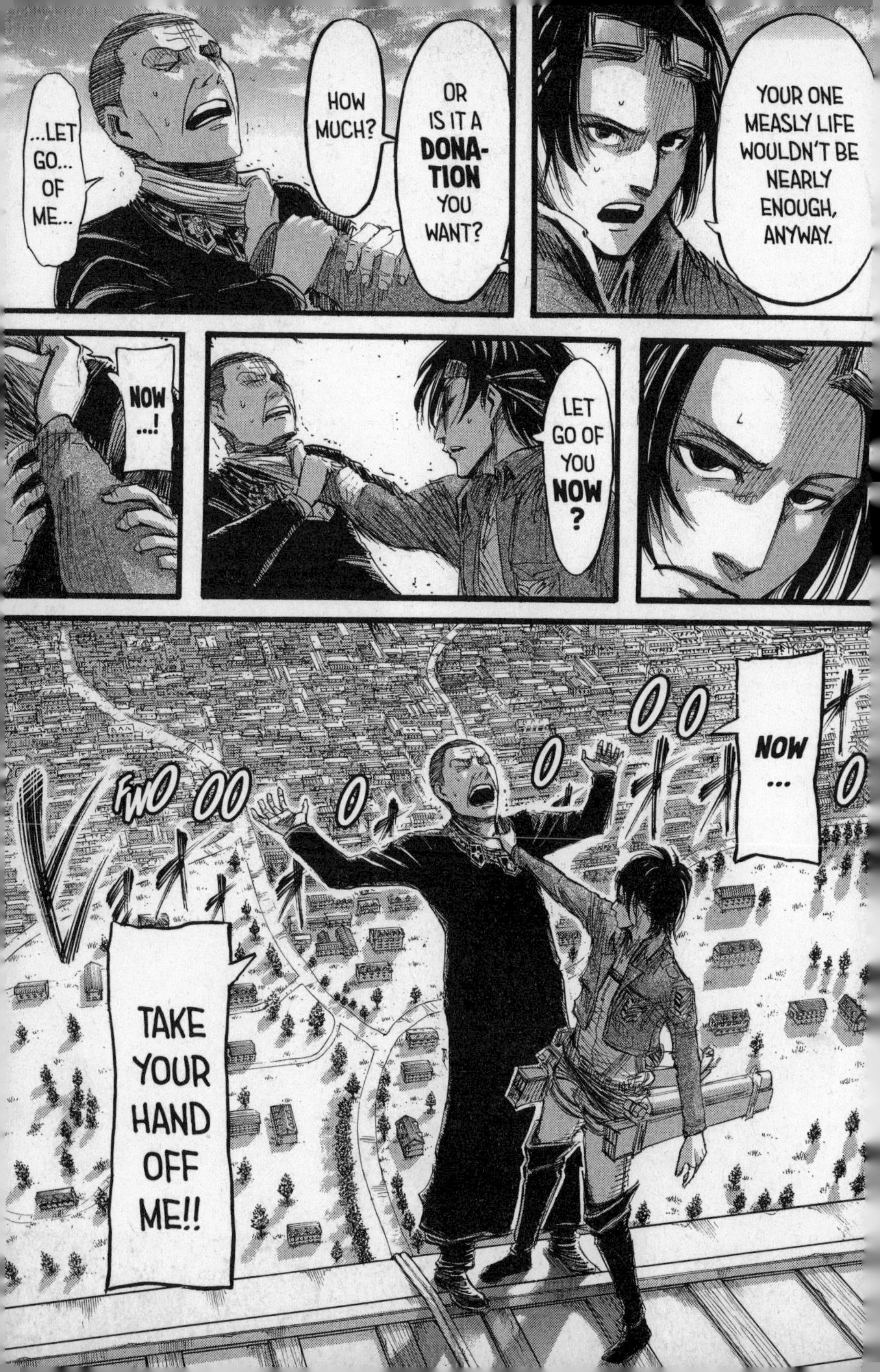
YOUR ONE MEASLY LIFE WOULDN'T BE NEARLY ENOUGH, ANYWAY.
OR IS IT A **DONATION** YOU WANT?
HOW MUCH?
...LET GO... OF ME...
LET GO OF YOU **NOW?**
NOW ...!
NOW ...
FWOOOOOOOOO
TAKE YOUR HAND OFF ME!!

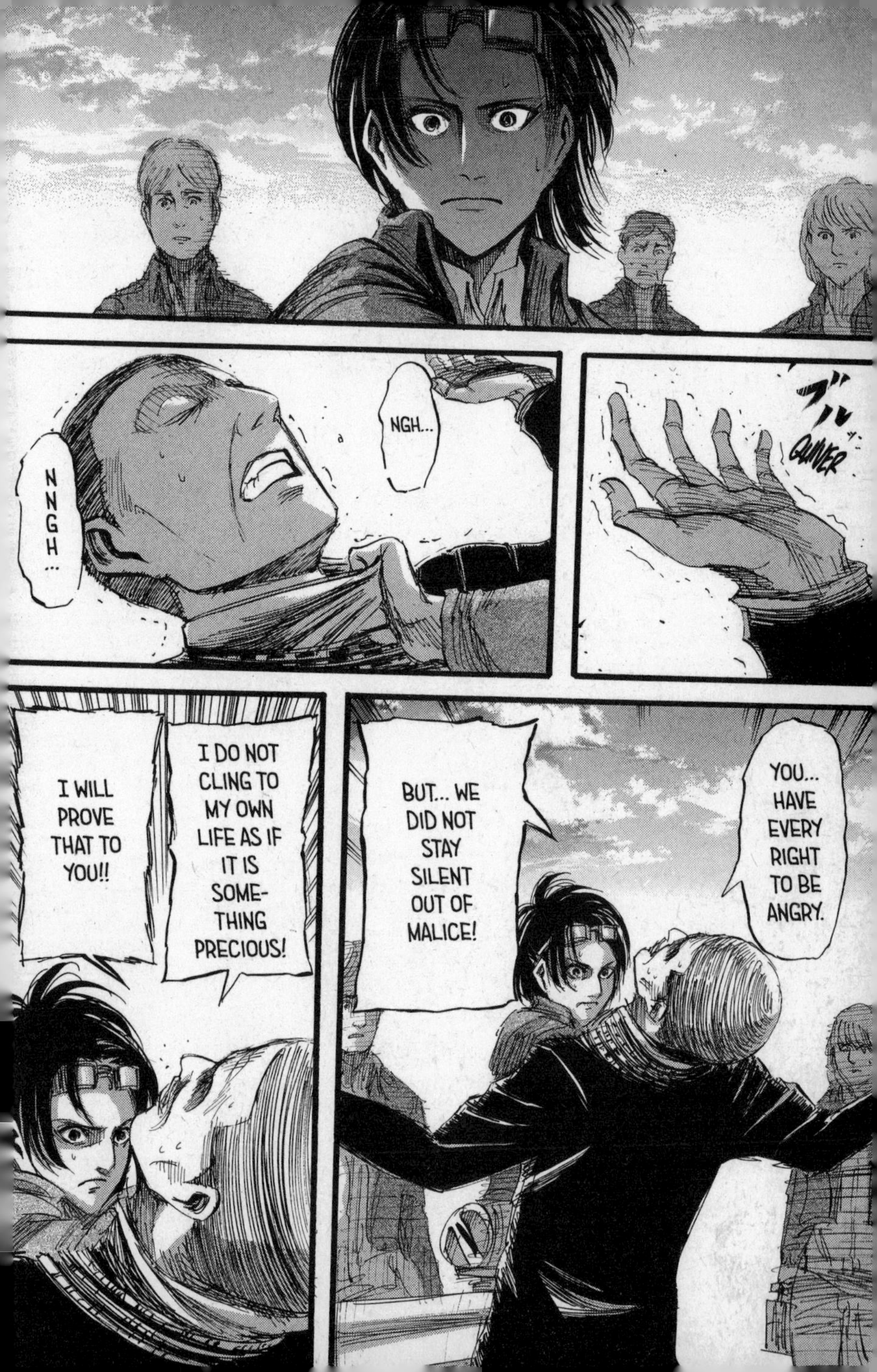
QUIVER
NGH...
NNGH...
YOU... HAVE EVERY RIGHT TO BE ANGRY.
BUT... WE DID NOT STAY SILENT OUT OF MALICE!
I DO NOT CLING TO MY OWN LIFE AS IF IT IS SOME-THING PRECIOUS!
I WILL PROVE THAT TO YOU!!

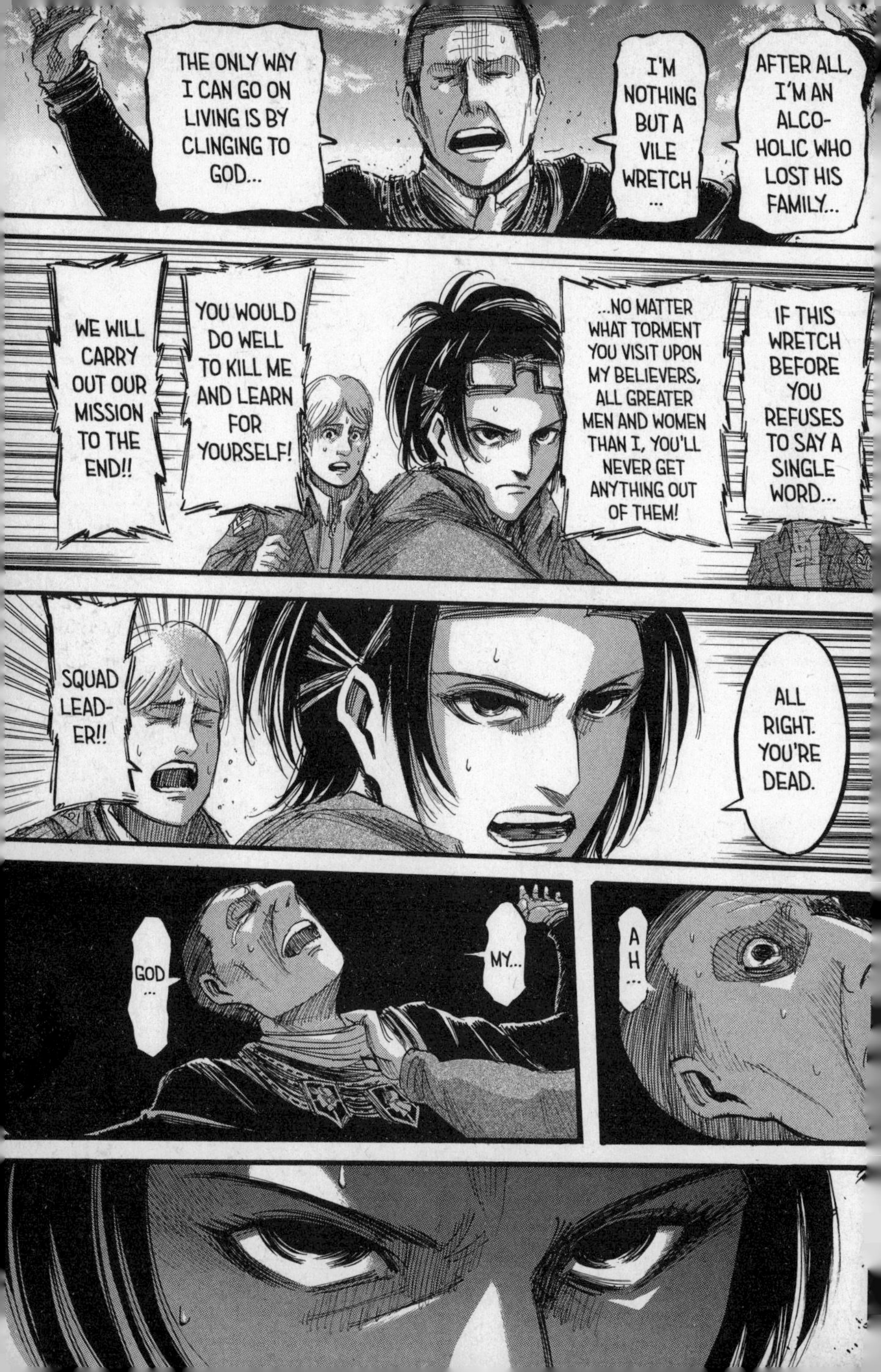
AFTER ALL, I'M AN ALCOHOLIC WHO LOST HIS FAMILY...
I'M NOTHING BUT A VILE WRETCH...
THE ONLY WAY I CAN GO ON LIVING IS BY CLINGING TO GOD...
IF THIS WRETCH BEFORE YOU REFUSES TO SAY A SINGLE WORD...
...NO MATTER WHAT TORMENT YOU VISIT UPON MY BELIEVERS, ALL GREATER MEN AND WOMEN THAN I, YOU'LL NEVER GET ANYTHING OUT OF THEM!
YOU WOULD DO WELL TO KILL ME AND LEARN FOR YOURSELF!
WE WILL CARRY OUT OUR MISSION TO THE END!!
ALL RIGHT. YOU'RE DEAD.
SQUAD LEADER!!
AH...
MY...
GOD...

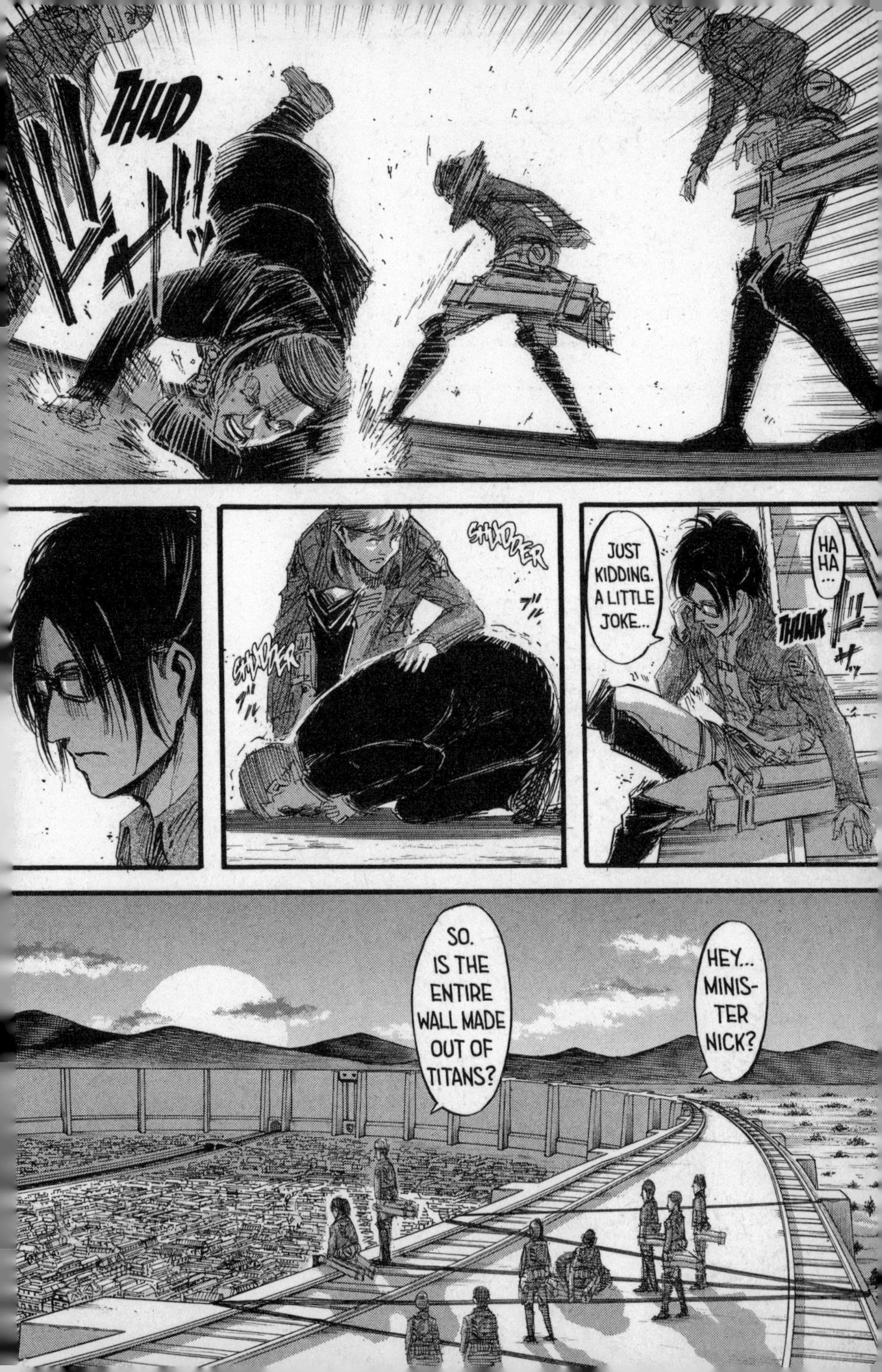
THUD
HA HA...
JUST KIDDING. A LITTLE JOKE...
THUNK
SHUDDER
SHUDDER
HEY... MINISTER NICK?
SO. IS THE ENTIRE WALL MADE OUT OF TITANS?

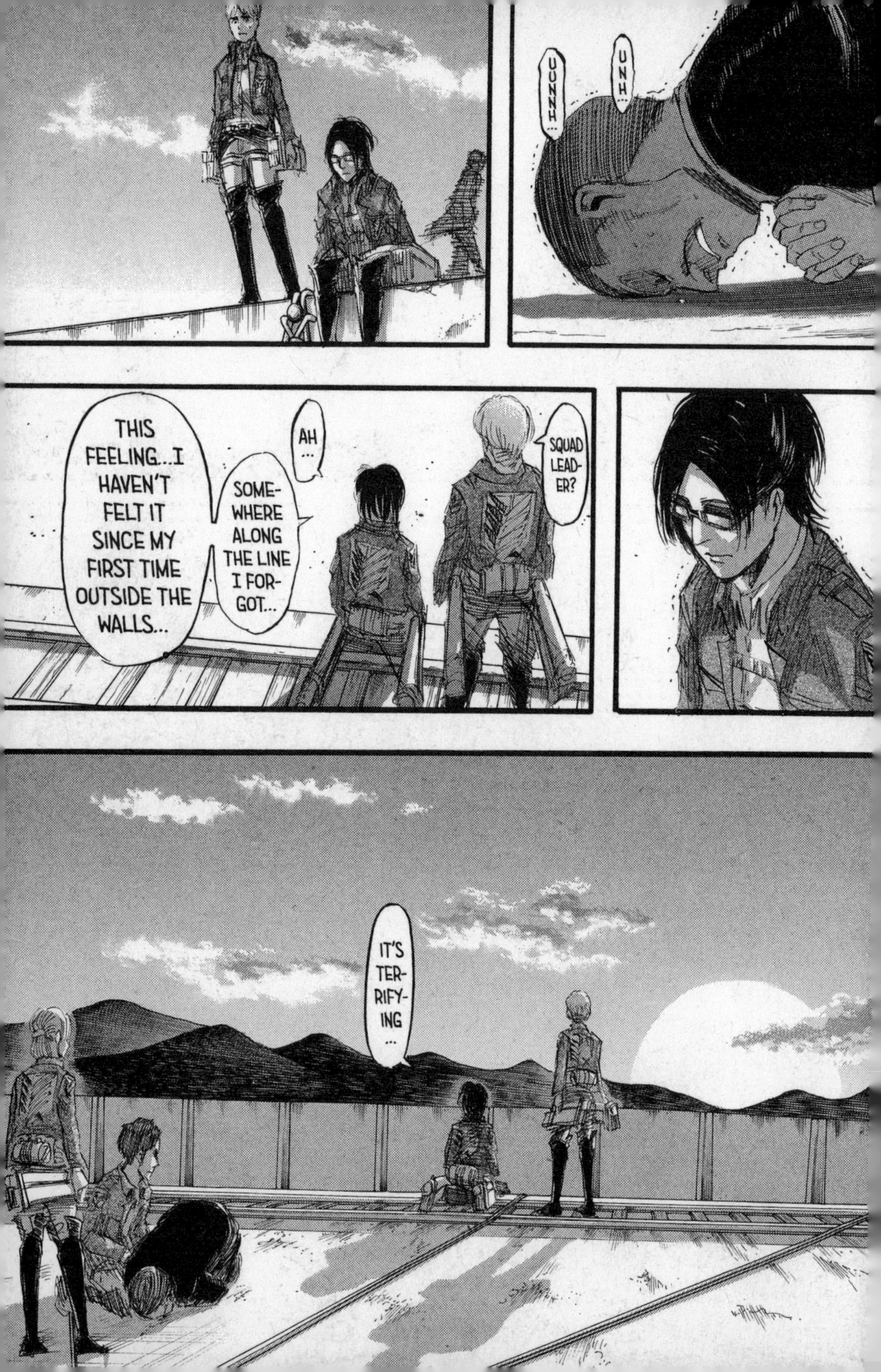
UNH...
UUNNH...
SQUAD LEADER?
AH...
SOMEWHERE ALONG THE LINE I FORGOT...
THIS FEELING...I HAVEN'T FELT IT SINCE MY FIRST TIME OUTSIDE THE WALLS...
IT'S TERRIFYING...

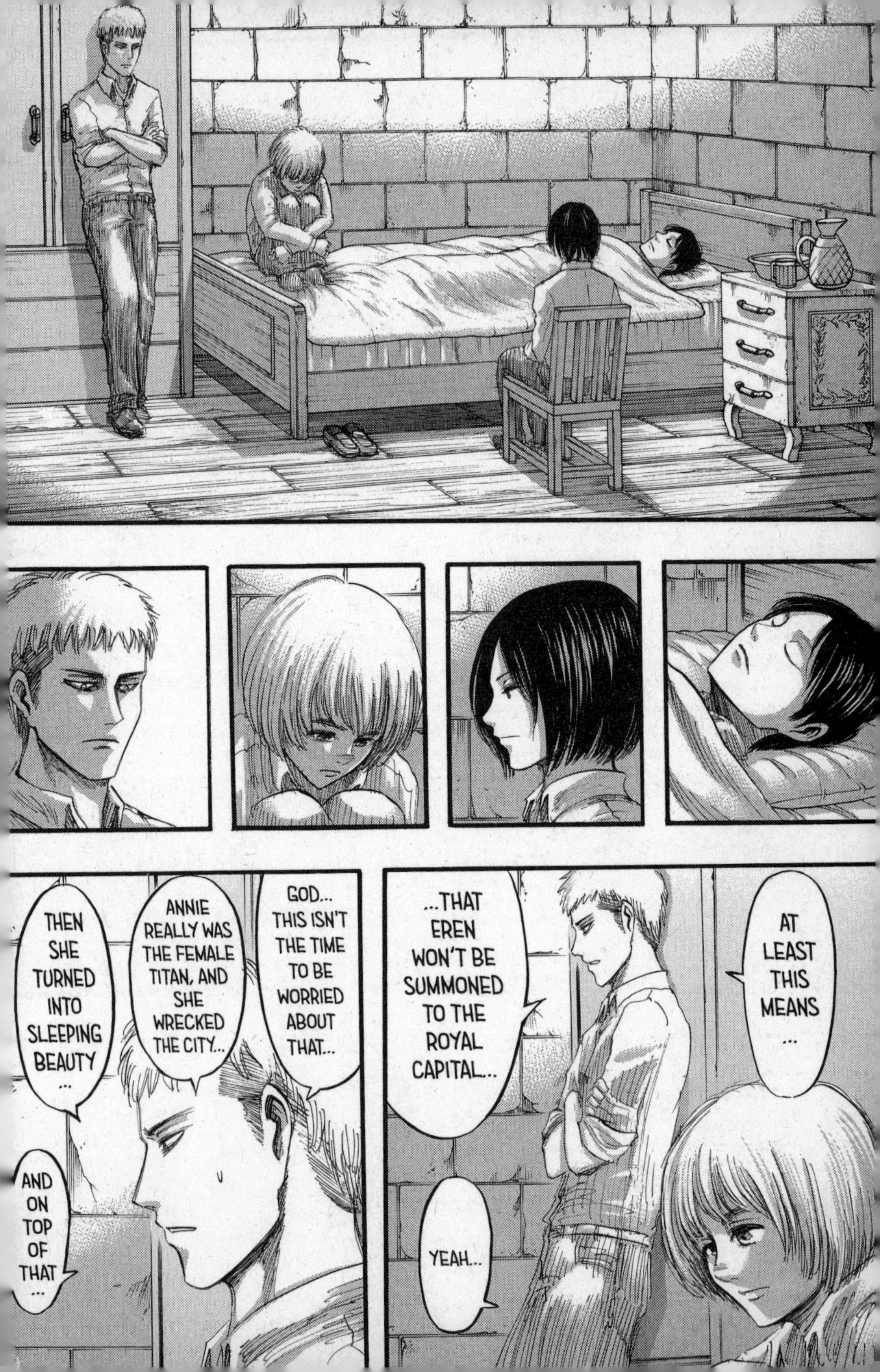
AT LEAST THIS MEANS ...
...THAT EREN WON'T BE SUMMONED TO THE ROYAL CAPITAL...
YEAH...
GOD... THIS ISN'T THE TIME TO BE WORRIED ABOUT THAT...
ANNIE REALLY WAS THE FEMALE TITAN, AND SHE WRECKED THE CITY...
THEN SHE TURNED INTO SLEEPING BEAUTY ...
AND ON TOP OF THAT ...

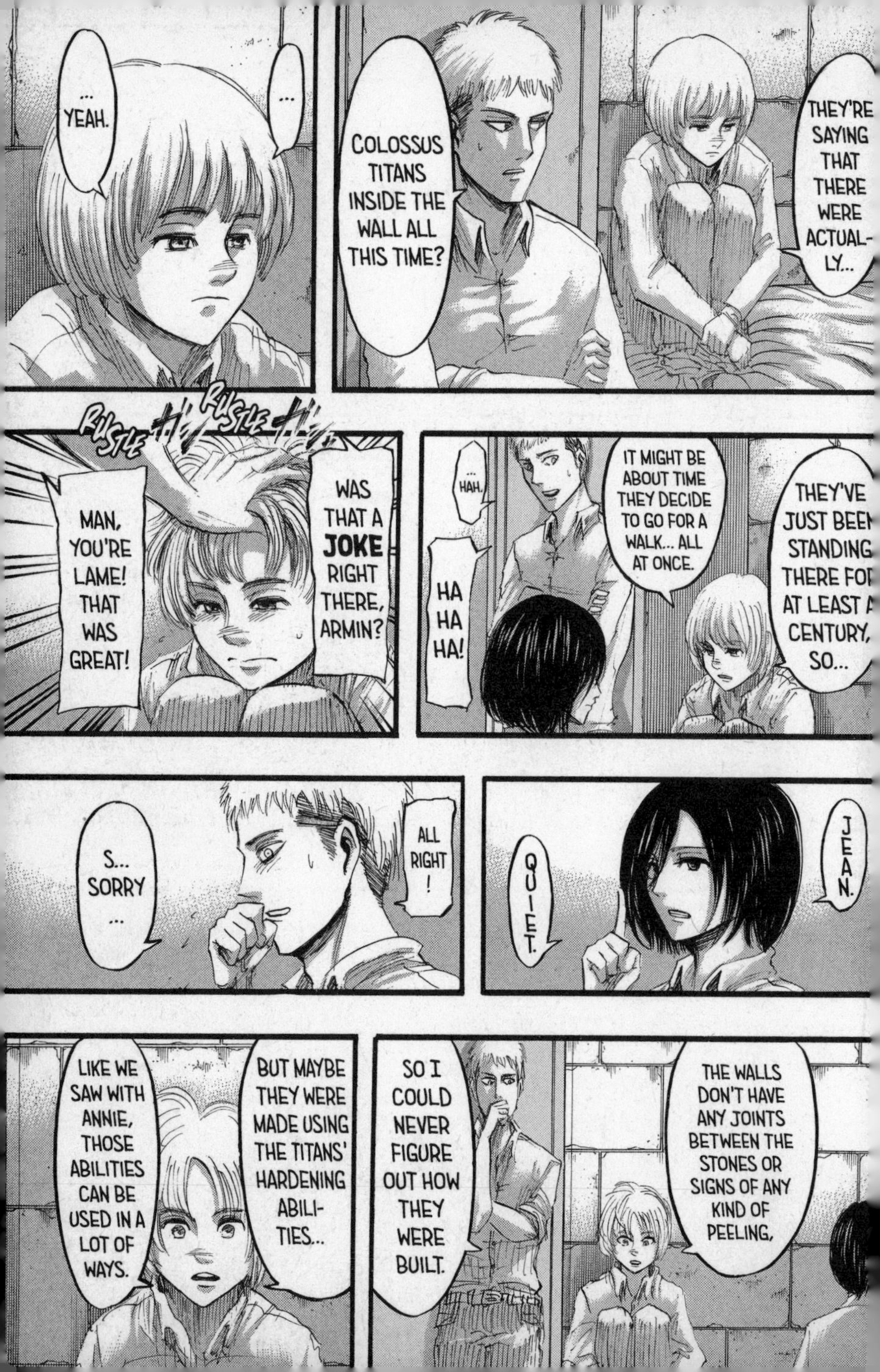
THEY'RE SAYING THAT THERE WERE ACTUALLY...
COLOSSUS TITANS INSIDE THE WALL ALL THIS TIME?
...
... YEAH.
THEY'VE JUST BEEN STANDING THERE FOR AT LEAST A CENTURY, SO...
IT MIGHT BE ABOUT TIME THEY DECIDE TO GO FOR A WALK... ALL AT ONCE.
... HAH.
HA HA HA!
RUSTLE RUSTLE
RUSTLE RUSTLE
WAS THAT A JOKE RIGHT THERE, ARMIN?
MAN, YOU'RE LAME! THAT WAS GREAT!
JEAN.
QUIET.
ALL RIGHT!
S... SORRY...
THE WALLS DON'T HAVE ANY JOINTS BETWEEN THE STONES OR SIGNS OF ANY KIND OF PEELING,
SO I COULD NEVER FIGURE OUT HOW THEY WERE BUILT.
BUT MAYBE THEY WERE MADE USING THE TITANS' HARDENING ABILITIES...
LIKE WE SAW WITH ANNIE, THOSE ABILITIES CAN BE USED IN A LOT OF WAYS.

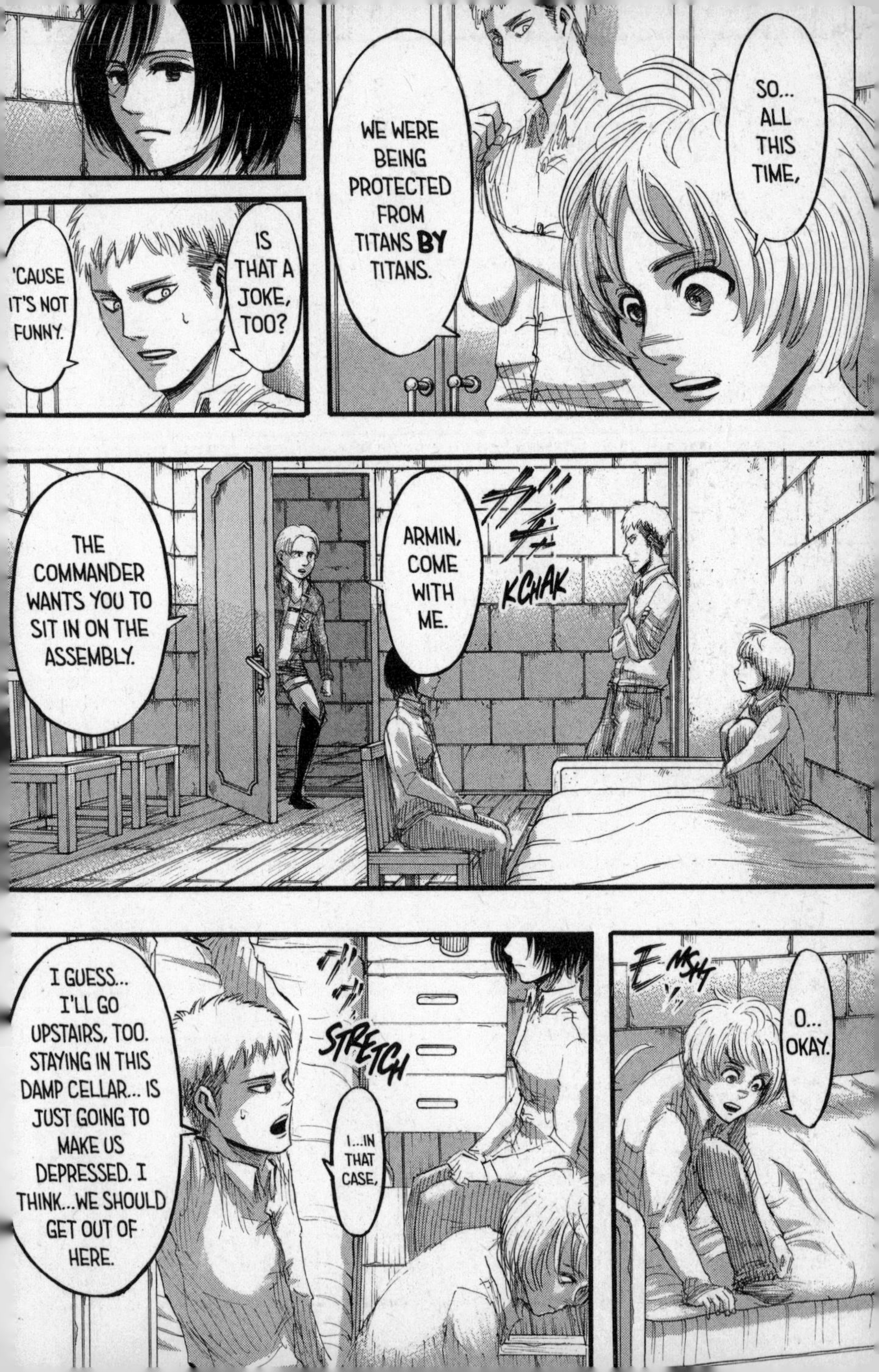
SO... ALL THIS TIME,
WE WERE BEING PROTECTED FROM TITANS **BY** TITANS.
IS THAT A JOKE, TOO?
'CAUSE IT'S NOT FUNNY.
KCHAK
ARMIN, COME WITH ME.
THE COMMANDER WANTS YOU TO SIT IN ON THE ASSEMBLY.
MSHH
O... OKAY.
STRETCH
I...IN THAT CASE,
I GUESS... I'LL GO UPSTAIRS, TOO. STAYING IN THIS DAMP CELLAR... IS JUST GOING TO MAKE US DEPRESSED. I THINK...WE SHOULD GET OUT OF HERE.

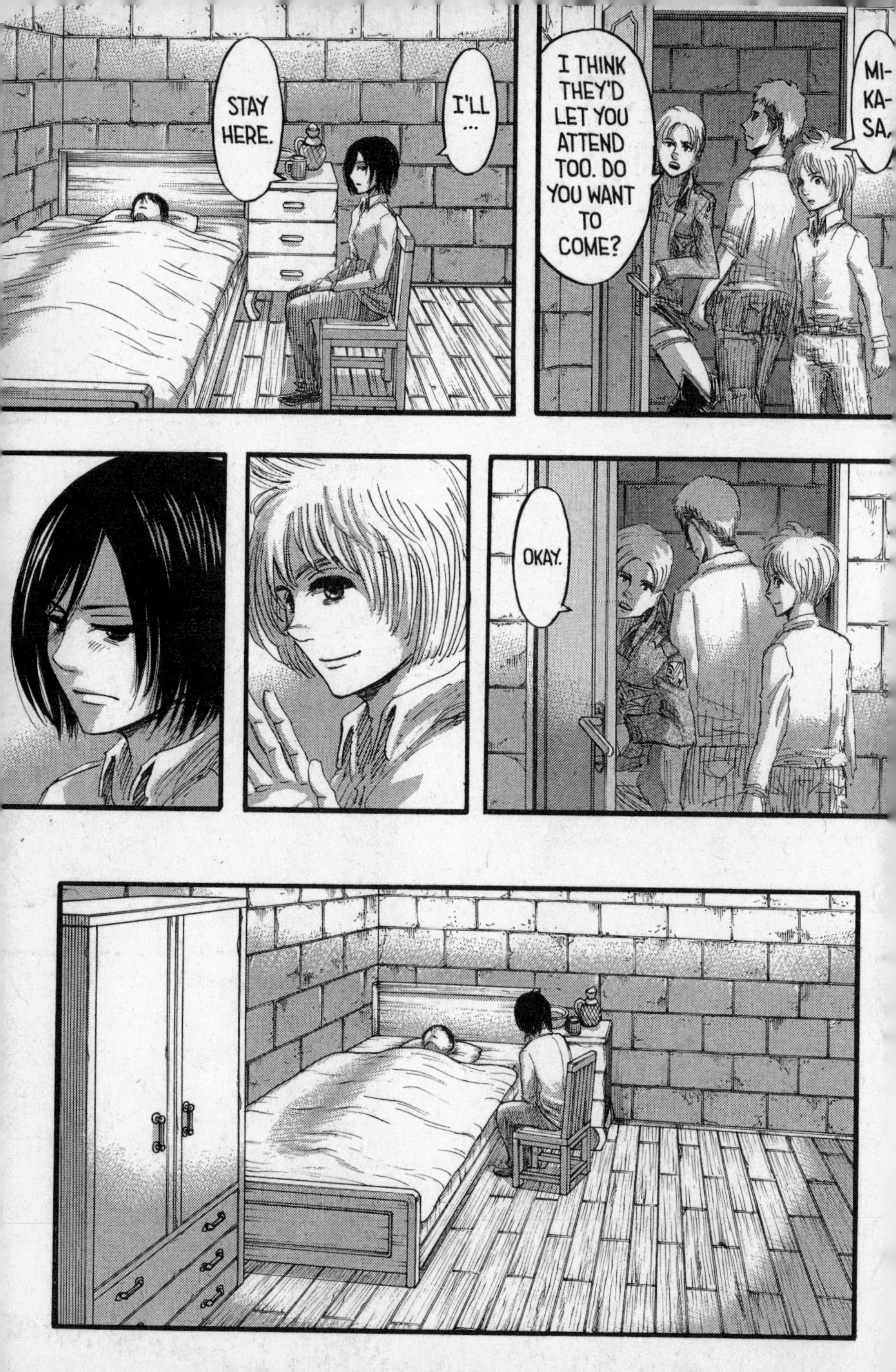
MI-KA-SA,
I THINK THEY'D LET YOU ATTEND TOO. DO YOU WANT TO COME?
I'LL ...
STAY HERE.
OKAY.

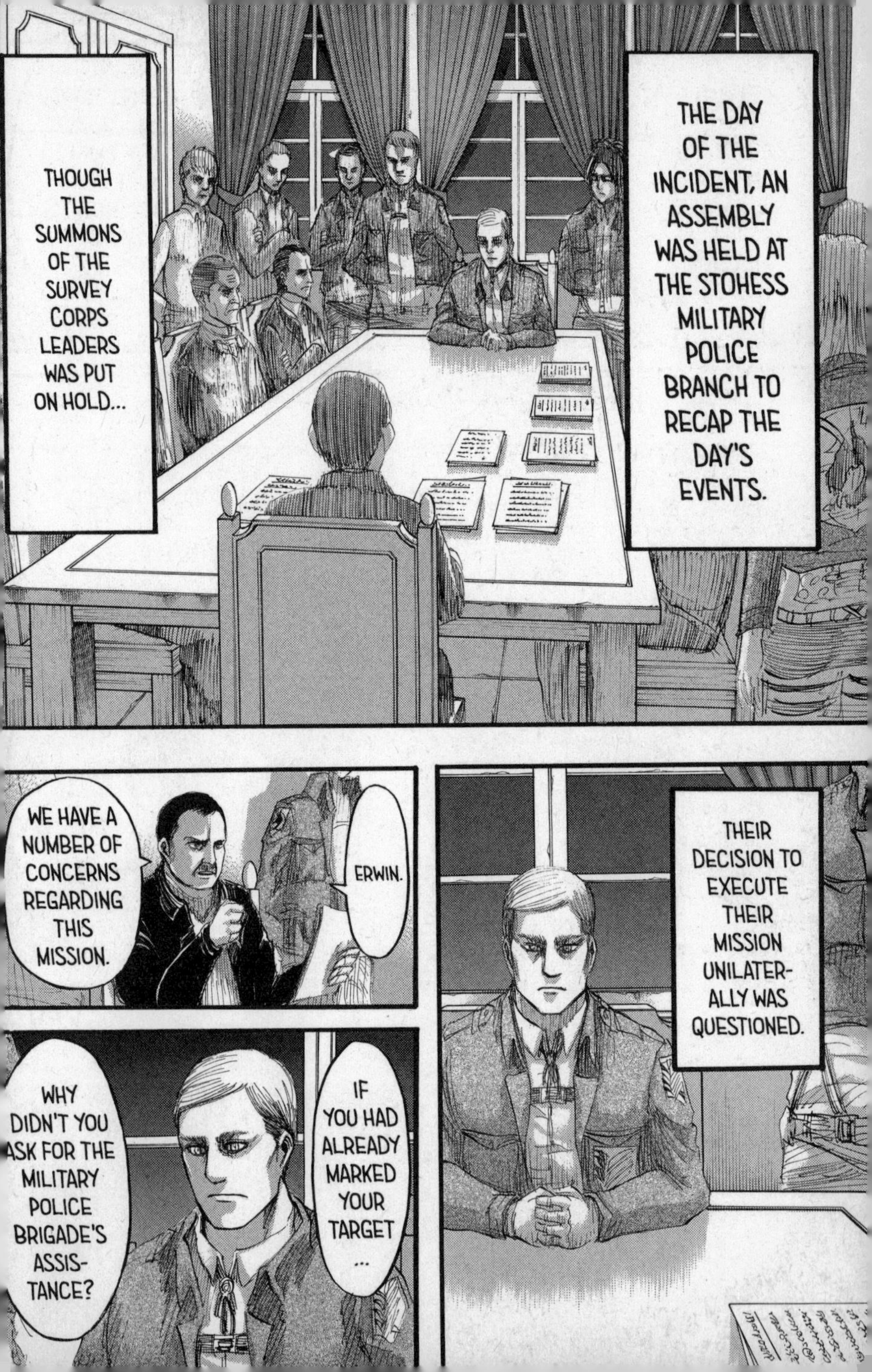
THE DAY OF THE INCIDENT, AN ASSEMBLY WAS HELD AT THE STOHESS MILITARY POLICE BRANCH TO RECAP THE DAY'S EVENTS.
THOUGH THE SUMMONS OF THE SURVEY CORPS LEADERS WAS PUT ON HOLD...
THEIR DECISION TO EXECUTE THEIR MISSION UNILATER-ALLY WAS QUESTIONED.
ERWIN.
WE HAVE A NUMBER OF CONCERNS REGARDING THIS MISSION.
IF YOU HAD ALREADY MARKED YOUR TARGET ...
WHY DIDN'T YOU ASK FOR THE MILITARY POLICE BRIGADE'S ASSIS-TANCE?

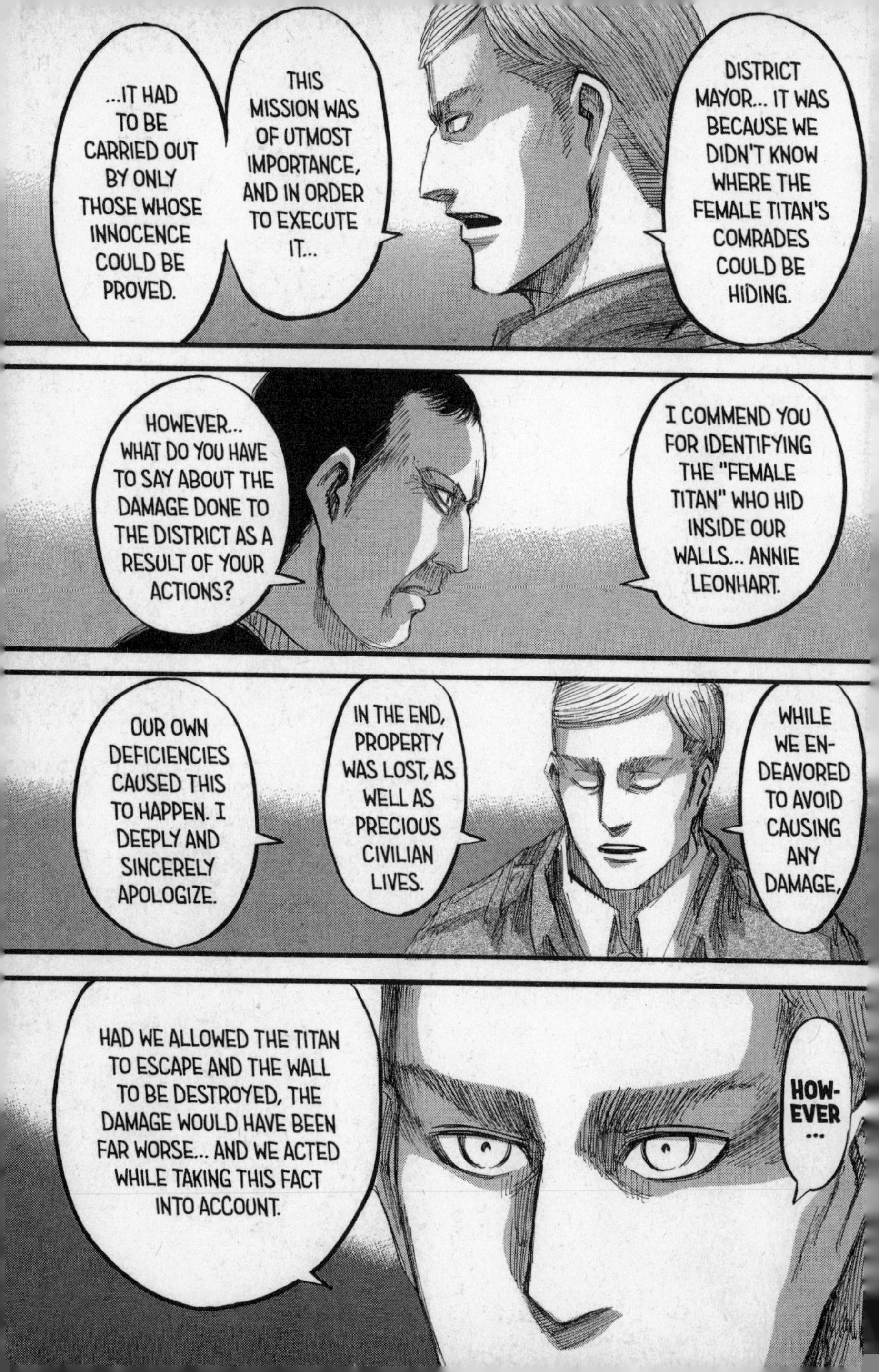
DISTRICT MAYOR... IT WAS BECAUSE WE DIDN'T KNOW WHERE THE FEMALE TITAN'S COMRADES COULD BE HIDING.
THIS MISSION WAS OF UTMOST IMPORTANCE, AND IN ORDER TO EXECUTE IT...
...IT HAD TO BE CARRIED OUT BY ONLY THOSE WHOSE INNOCENCE COULD BE PROVED.
I COMMEND YOU FOR IDENTIFYING THE "FEMALE TITAN" WHO HID INSIDE OUR WALLS... ANNIE LEONHART.
HOWEVER... WHAT DO YOU HAVE TO SAY ABOUT THE DAMAGE DONE TO THE DISTRICT AS A RESULT OF YOUR ACTIONS?
WHILE WE EN-DEAVORED TO AVOID CAUSING ANY DAMAGE,
IN THE END, PROPERTY WAS LOST, AS WELL AS PRECIOUS CIVILIAN LIVES.
OUR OWN DEFICIENCIES CAUSED THIS TO HAPPEN. I DEEPLY AND SINCERELY APOLOGIZE.
HOW-EVER...
HAD WE ALLOWED THE TITAN TO ESCAPE AND THE WALL TO BE DESTROYED, THE DAMAGE WOULD HAVE BEEN FAR WORSE... AND WE ACTED WHILE TAKING THIS FACT INTO ACCOUNT.

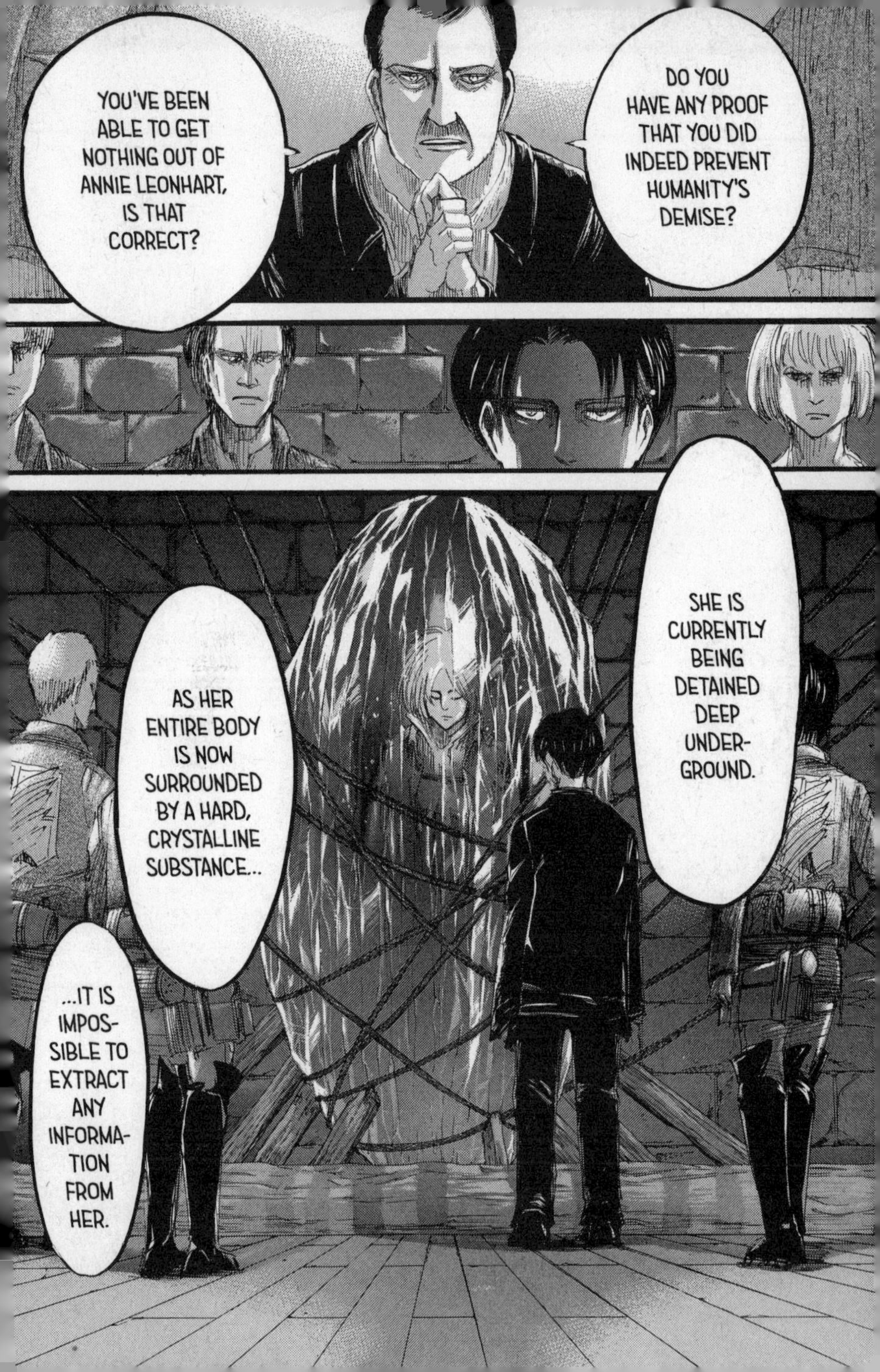

DO YOU HAVE ANY PROOF THAT YOU DID INDEED PREVENT HUMANITY'S DEMISE?
YOU'VE BEEN ABLE TO GET NOTHING OUT OF ANNIE LEONHART, IS THAT CORRECT?
SHE IS CURRENTLY BEING DETAINED DEEP UNDER-GROUND.
AS HER ENTIRE BODY IS NOW SURROUNDED BY A HARD, CRYSTALLINE SUBSTANCE...
...IT IS IMPOS-SIBLE TO EXTRACT ANY INFORMA-TION FROM HER.

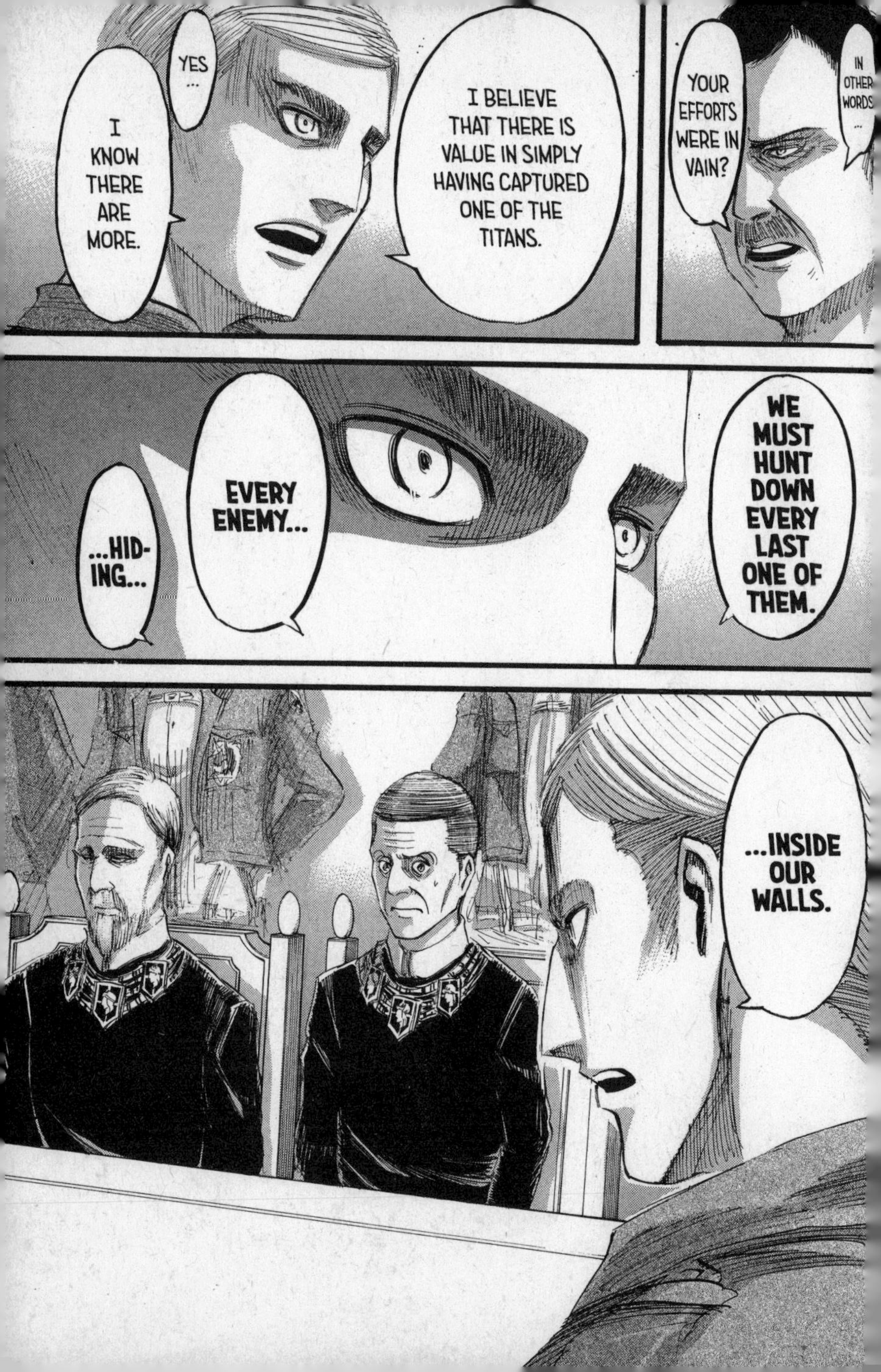
IN OTHER WORDS...
YOUR EFFORTS WERE IN VAIN?
I BELIEVE THAT THERE IS VALUE IN SIMPLY HAVING CAPTURED ONE OF THE TITANS.
YES...
I KNOW THERE ARE MORE.
WE MUST HUNT DOWN EVERY LAST ONE OF THEM.
EVERY ENEMY...
...HID-ING...
...INSIDE OUR WALLS.

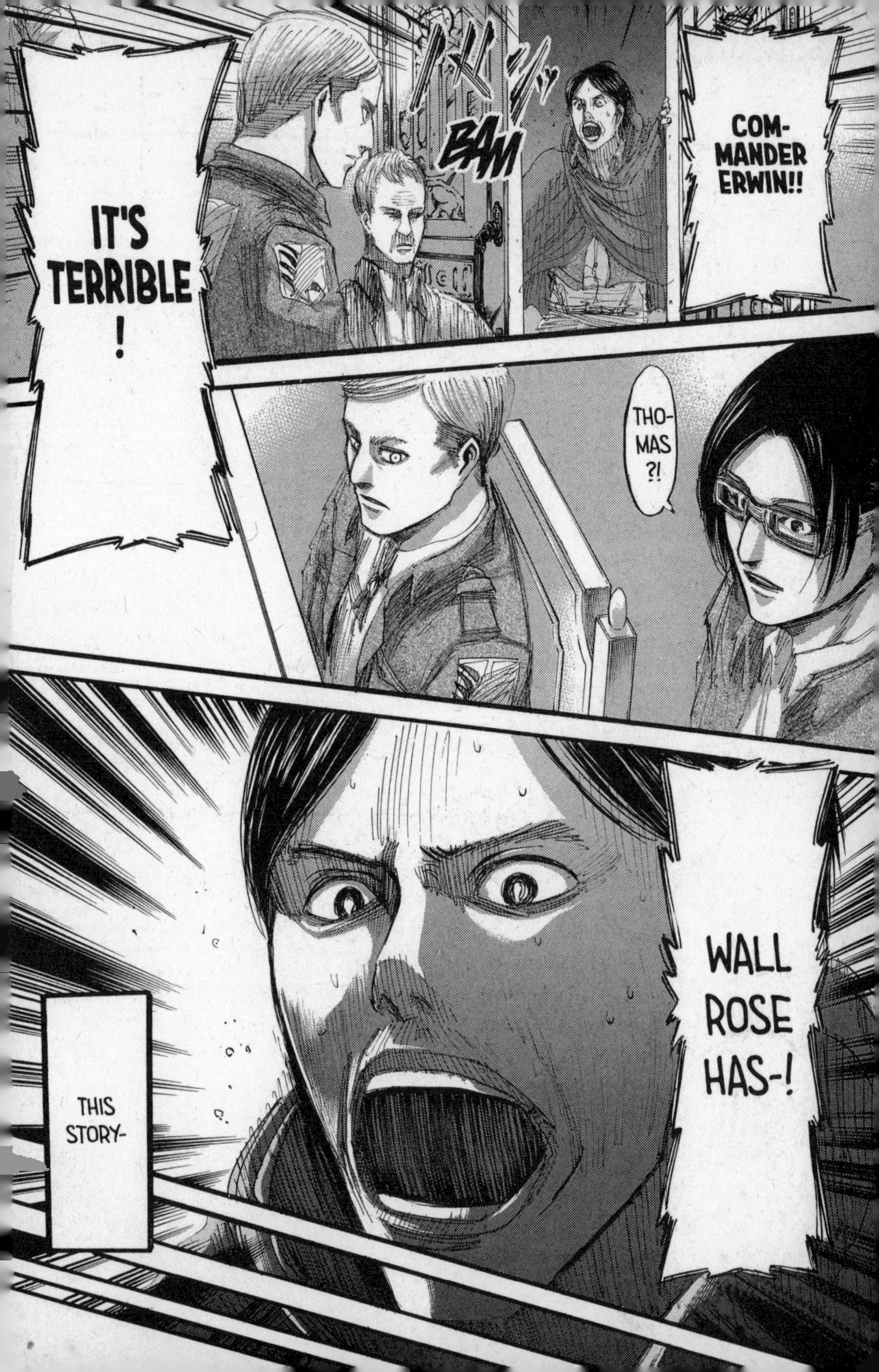
COM-MANDER ERWIN!!
BAM
IT'S TERRIBLE!
THO-MAS?!
WALL ROSE HAS-!
THIS STORY-

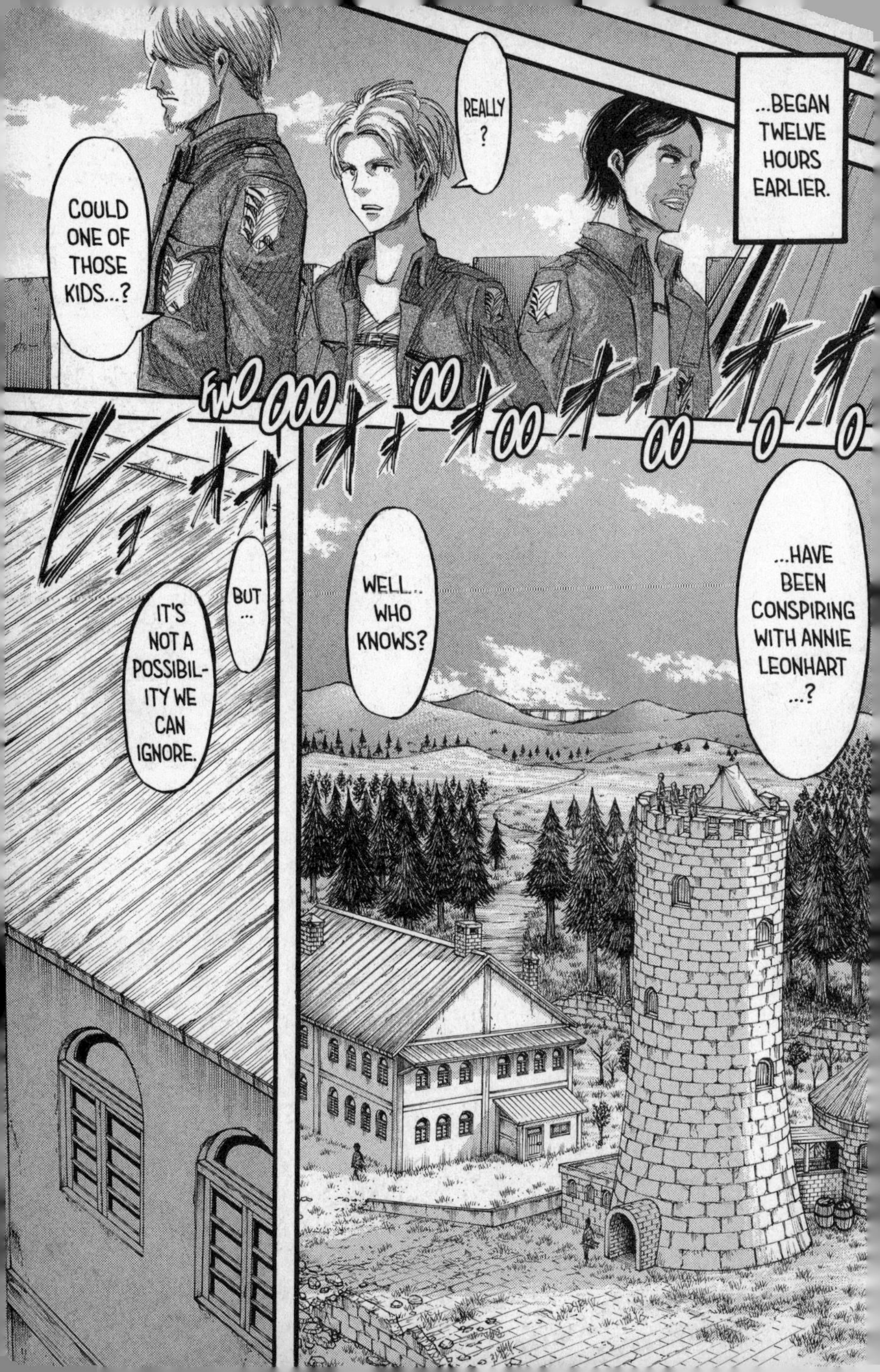

...BEGAN TWELVE HOURS EARLIER.
REALLY?
COULD ONE OF THOSE KIDS...?
FWOOOOOOOOOOO
...HAVE BEEN CONSPIRING WITH ANNIE LEONHART...?
WELL... WHO KNOWS?
BUT...
IT'S NOT A POSSIBIL-ITY WE CAN IGNORE.

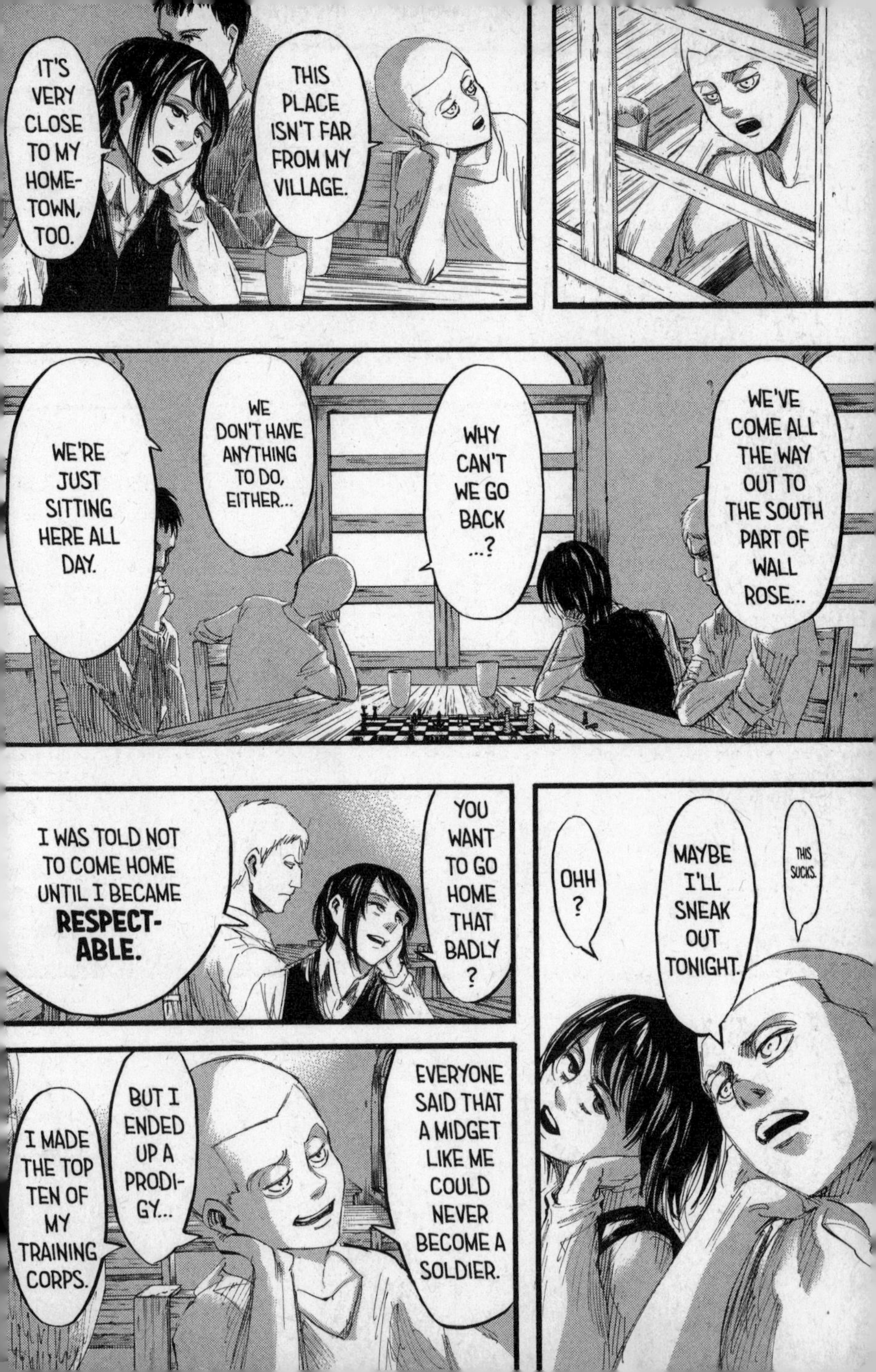
THIS PLACE ISN'T FAR FROM MY VILLAGE.
IT'S VERY CLOSE TO MY HOME-TOWN, TOO.
WE'VE COME ALL THE WAY OUT TO THE SOUTH PART OF WALL ROSE...
WHY CAN'T WE GO BACK ...?
WE DON'T HAVE ANYTHING TO DO, EITHER...
WE'RE JUST SITTING HERE ALL DAY.
THIS SUCKS.
MAYBE I'LL SNEAK OUT TONIGHT.
OHH ?
YOU WANT TO GO HOME THAT BADLY ?
I WAS TOLD NOT TO COME HOME UNTIL I BECAME **RESPECT-ABLE.**
EVERYONE SAID THAT A MIDGET LIKE ME COULD NEVER BECOME A SOLDIER.
BUT I ENDED UP A PRODI-GY...
I MADE THE TOP TEN OF MY TRAINING CORPS.

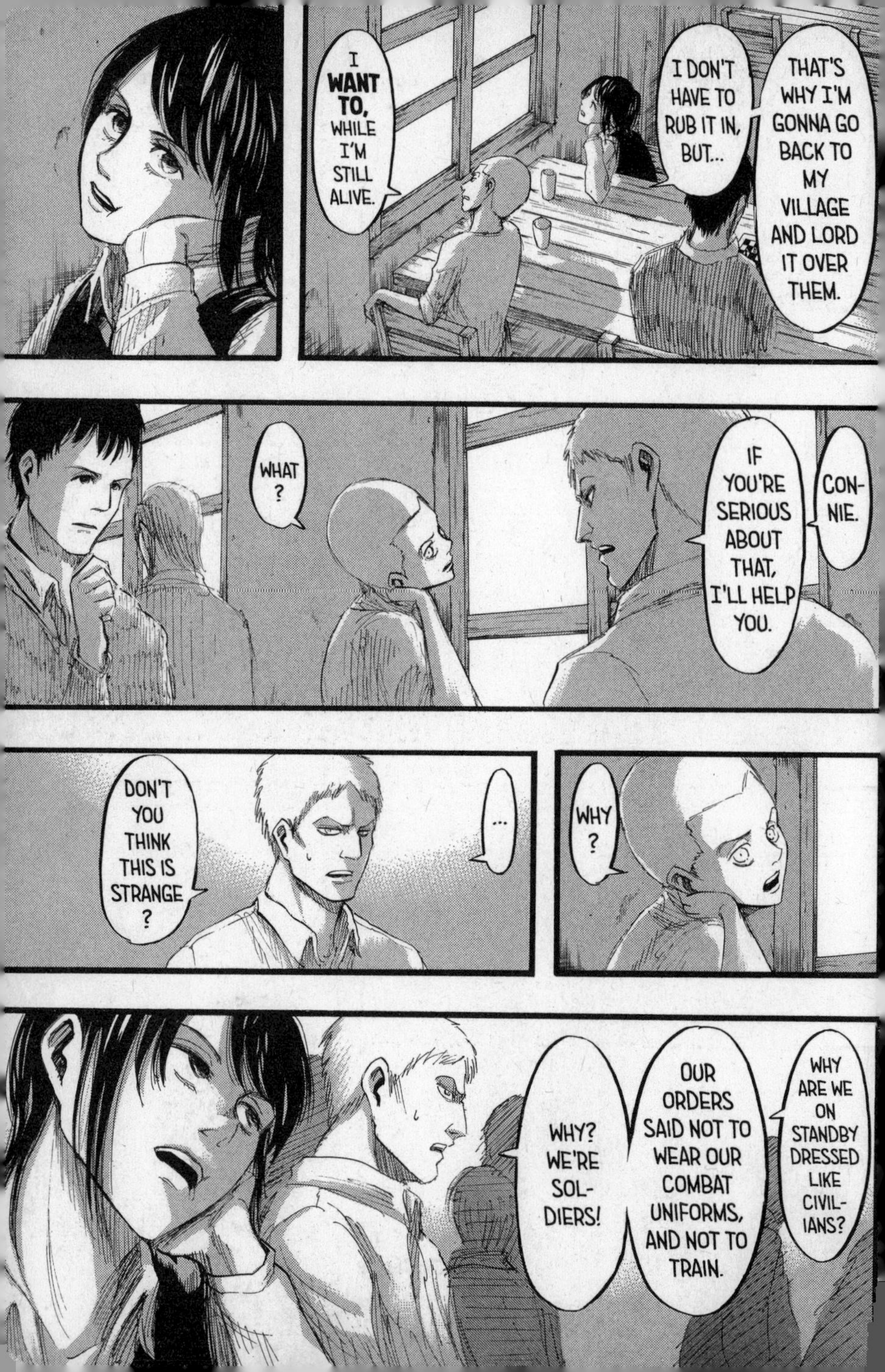
THAT'S WHY I'M GONNA GO BACK TO MY VILLAGE AND LORD IT OVER THEM.
I DON'T HAVE TO RUB IT IN, BUT...
I **WANT TO,** WHILE I'M STILL ALIVE.
CON-NIE.
IF YOU'RE SERIOUS ABOUT THAT, I'LL HELP YOU.
WHAT?
WHY?
...
DON'T YOU THINK THIS IS STRANGE?
WHY ARE WE ON STANDBY DRESSED LIKE CIVILIANS?
OUR ORDERS SAID NOT TO WEAR OUR COMBAT UNIFORMS, AND NOT TO TRAIN.
WHY? WE'RE SOL-DIERS!

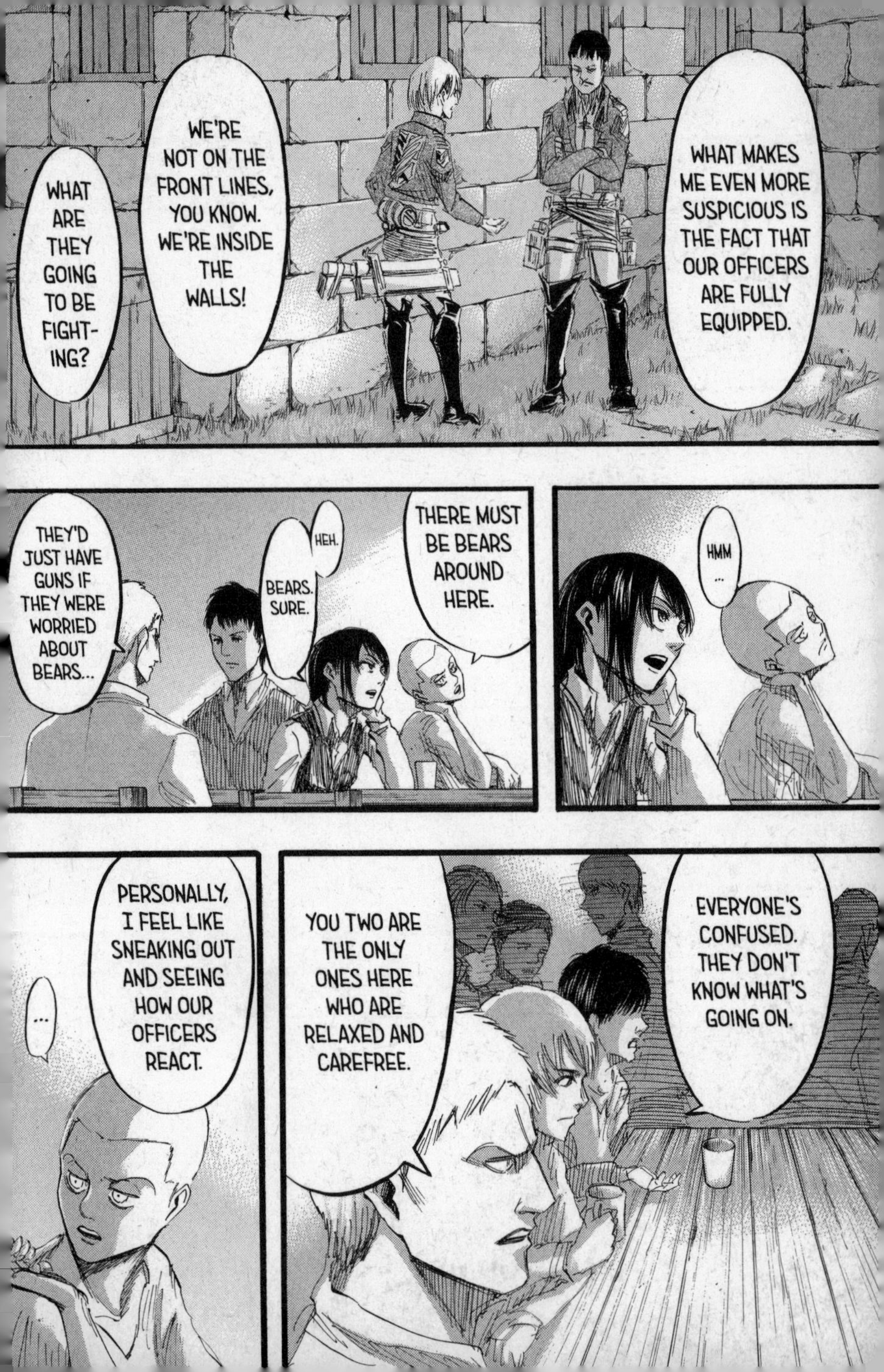
WHAT MAKES ME EVEN MORE SUSPICIOUS IS THE FACT THAT OUR OFFICERS ARE FULLY EQUIPPED.
WE'RE NOT ON THE FRONT LINES, YOU KNOW. WE'RE INSIDE THE WALLS!
WHAT ARE THEY GOING TO BE FIGHT-ING?
HMM ...
THERE MUST BE BEARS AROUND HERE.
HEH.
BEARS. SURE.
THEY'D JUST HAVE GUNS IF THEY WERE WORRIED ABOUT BEARS...
EVERYONE'S CONFUSED. THEY DON'T KNOW WHAT'S GOING ON.
YOU TWO ARE THE ONLY ONES HERE WHO ARE RELAXED AND CAREFREE.
PERSONALLY, I FEEL LIKE SNEAKING OUT AND SEEING HOW OUR OFFICERS REACT.
...

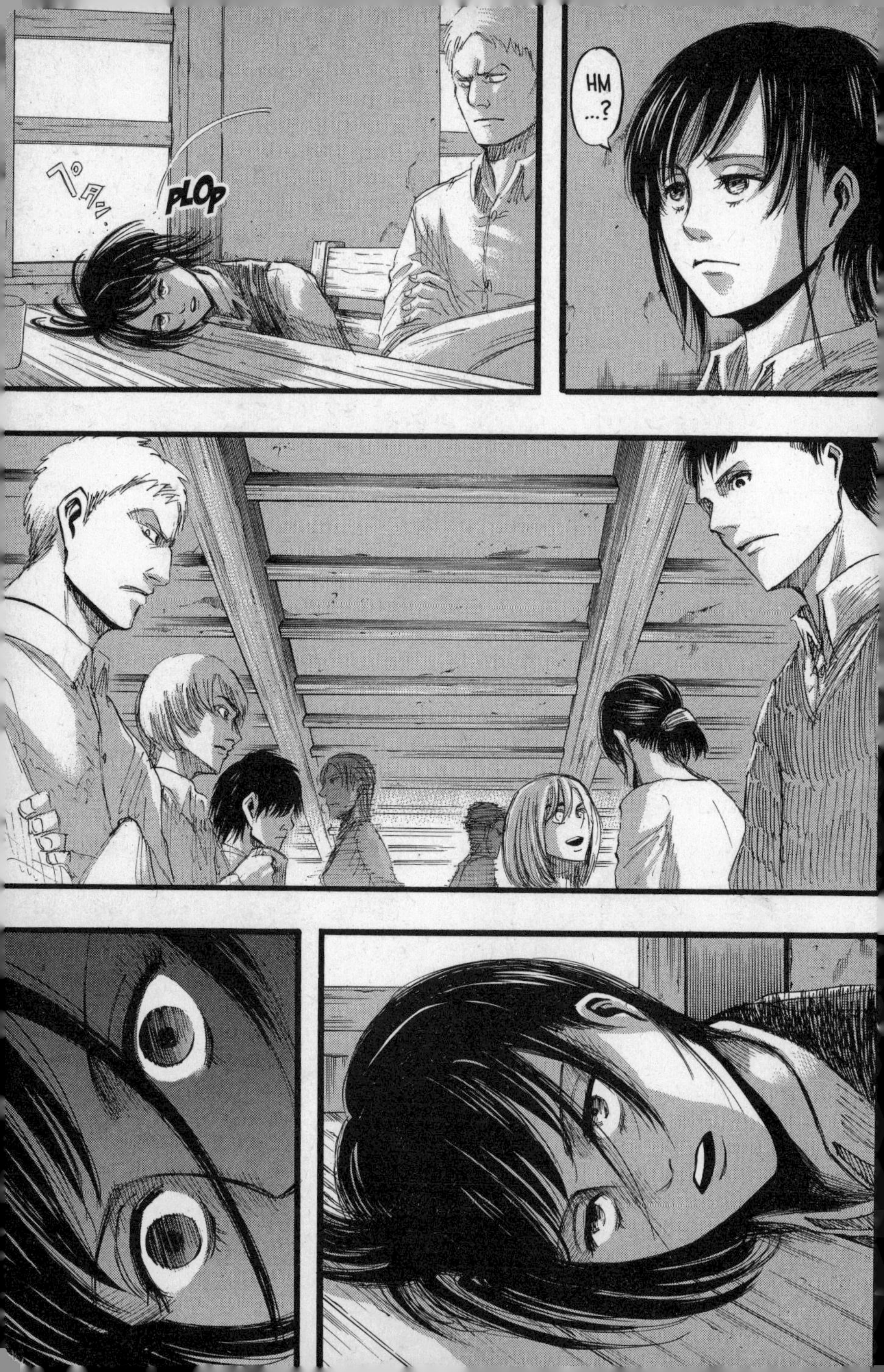
HM ...?
PLOP

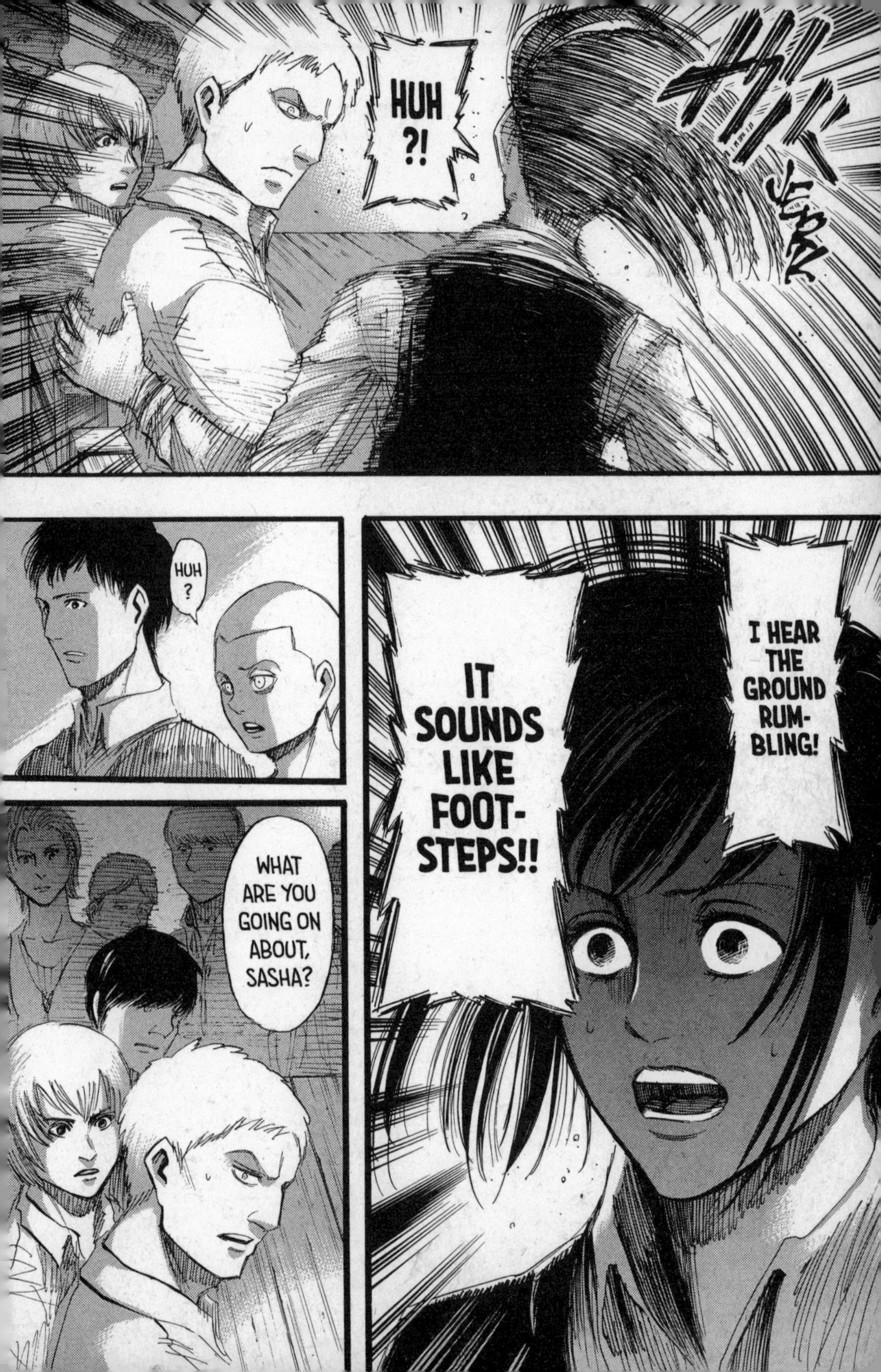

JERK
HUH ?!
I HEAR THE GROUND RUM-BLING!
IT SOUNDS LIKE FOOT-STEPS!!
HUH ?
WHAT ARE YOU GOING ON ABOUT, SASHA?

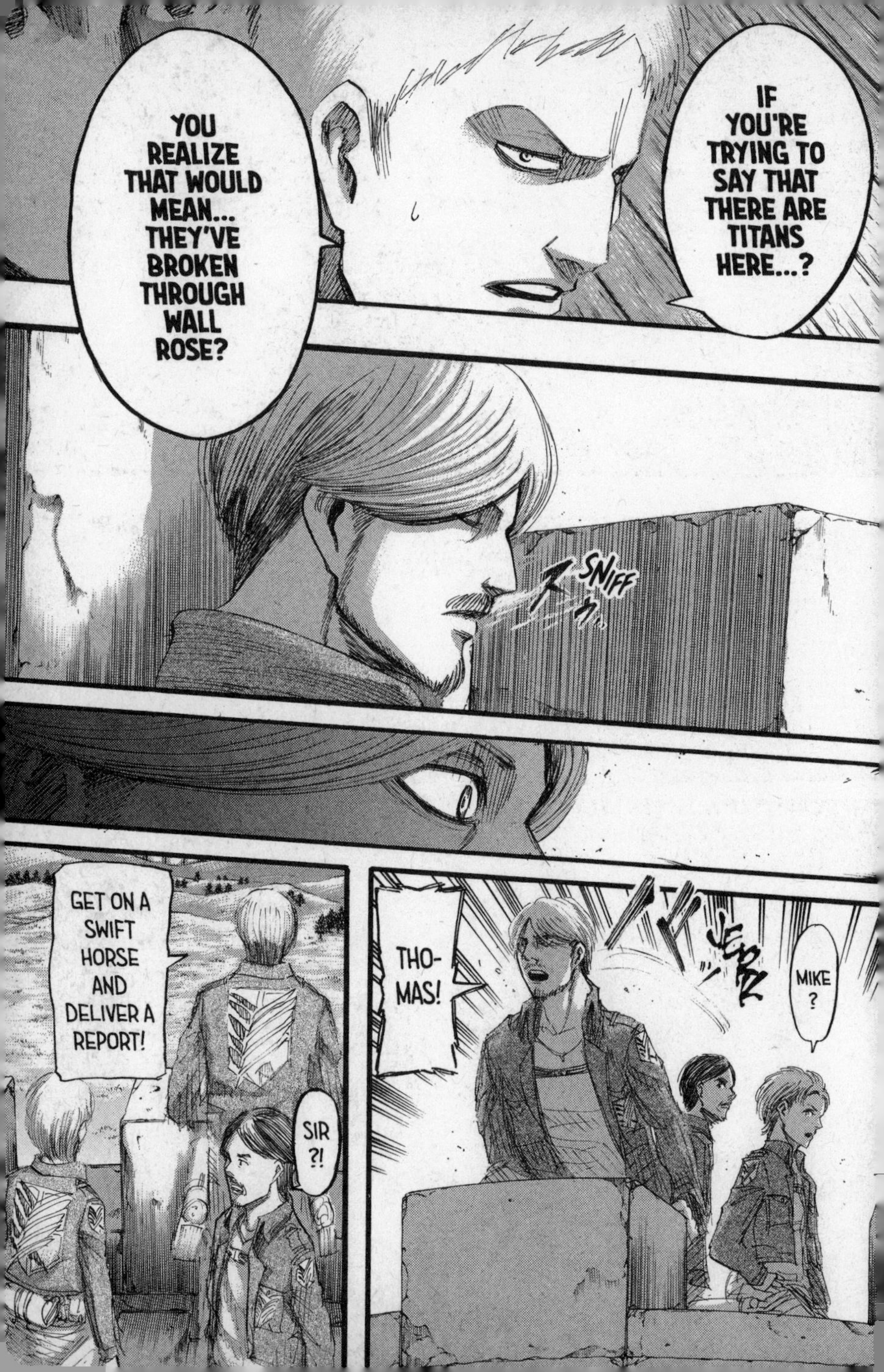
IF YOU'RE TRYING TO SAY THAT THERE ARE TITANS HERE...?
YOU REALIZE THAT WOULD MEAN... THEY'VE BROKEN THROUGH WALL ROSE?
SNIFF
MIKE?
JERK
THO-MAS!
GET ON A SWIFT HORSE AND DELIVER A REPORT!
SIR?!

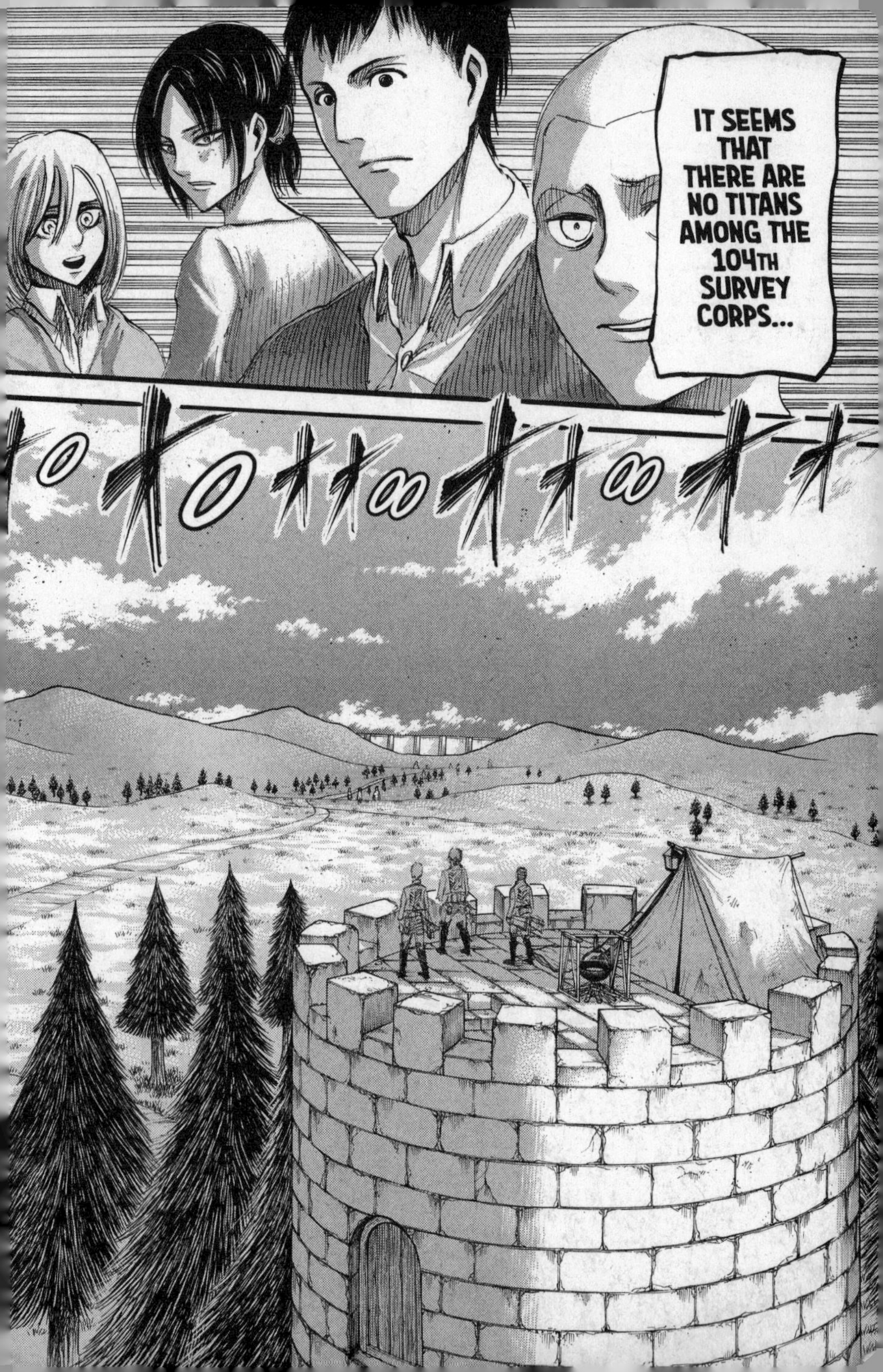
IT SEEMS THAT THERE ARE NO TITANS AMONG THE 104TH SURVEY CORPS...

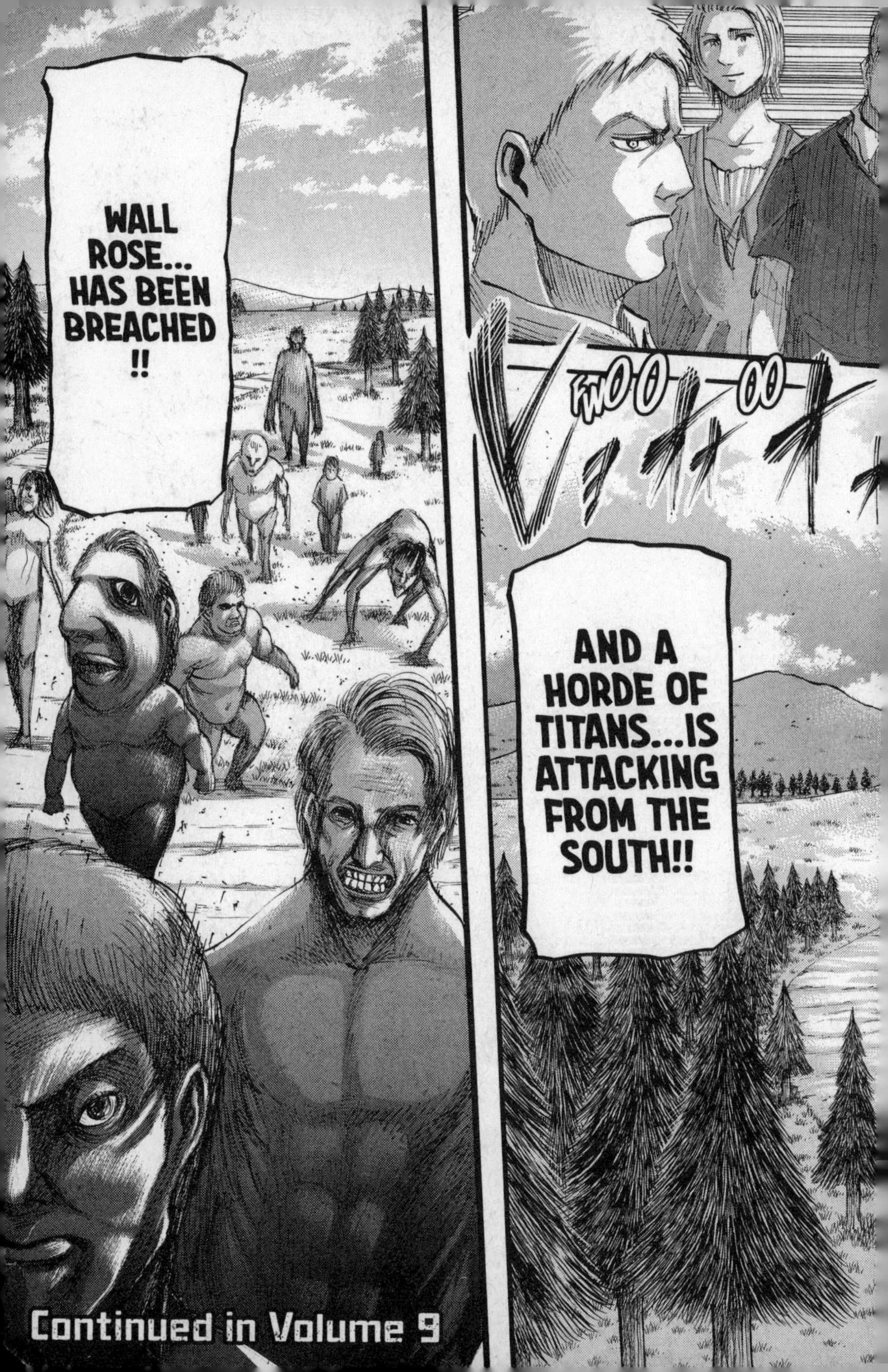
WALL ROSE... HAS BEEN BREACHED !!
FWOOO—OO
AND A HORDE OF TITANS...IS ATTACKING FROM THE SOUTH!!
Continued in Volume 9

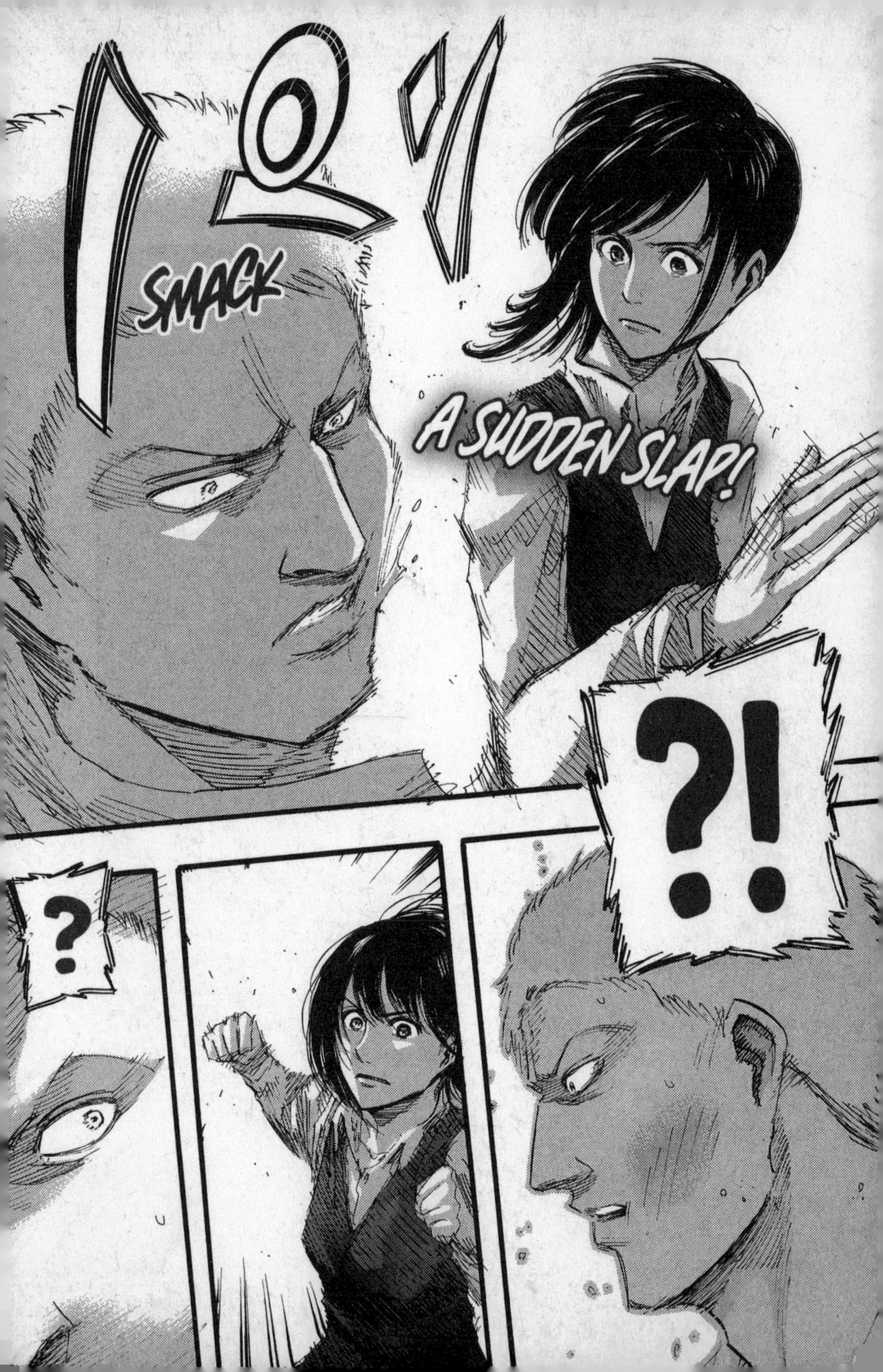
A SUDDEN SLAP!
SMACK
?!
?

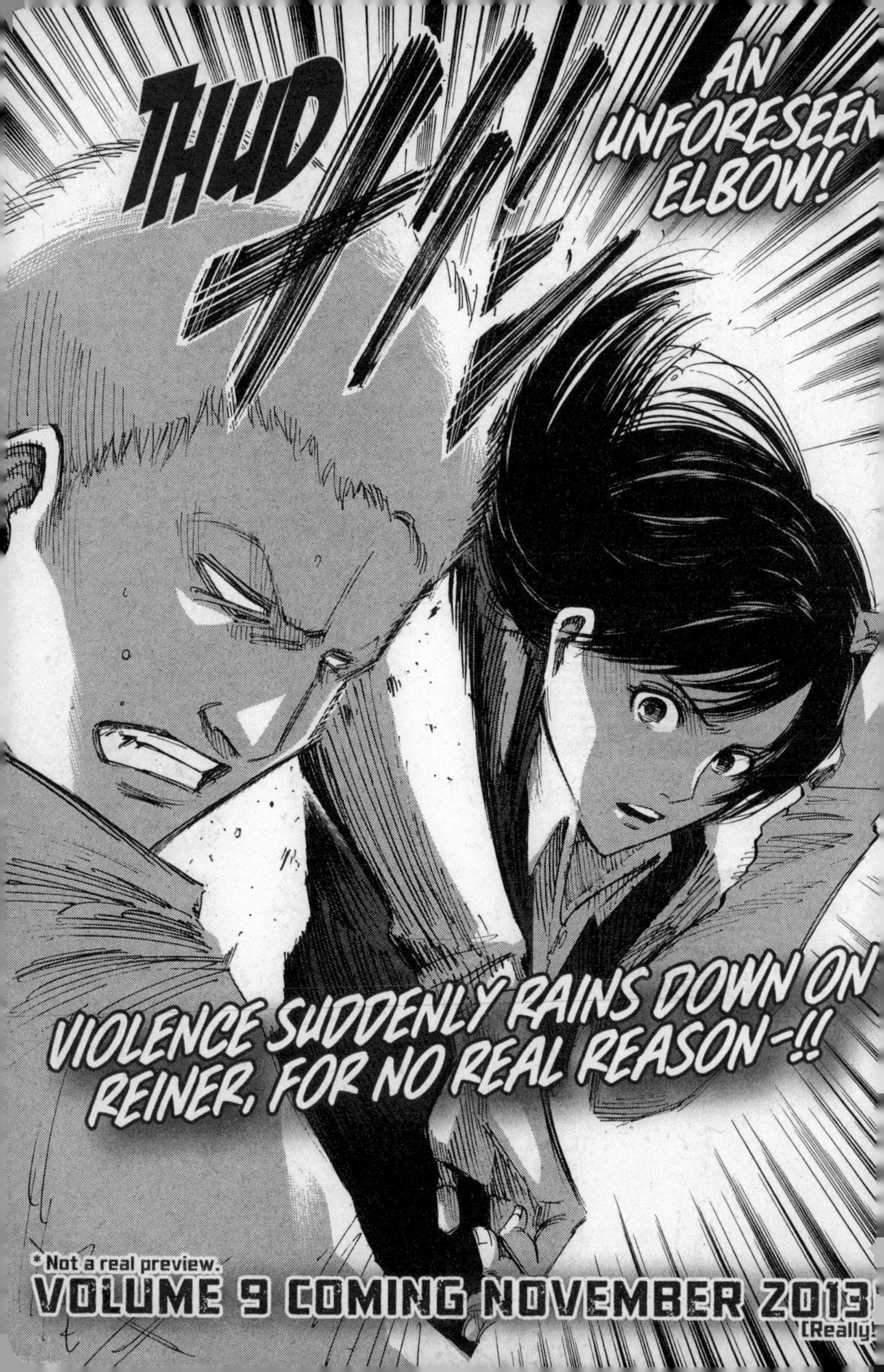
THUD
AN UNFORESEEN ELBOW!
VIOLENCE SUDDENLY RAINS DOWN ON REINER, FOR NO REAL REASON-!!
* Not a real preview.
VOLUME 9 COMING NOVEMBER 2013!
[Really!]

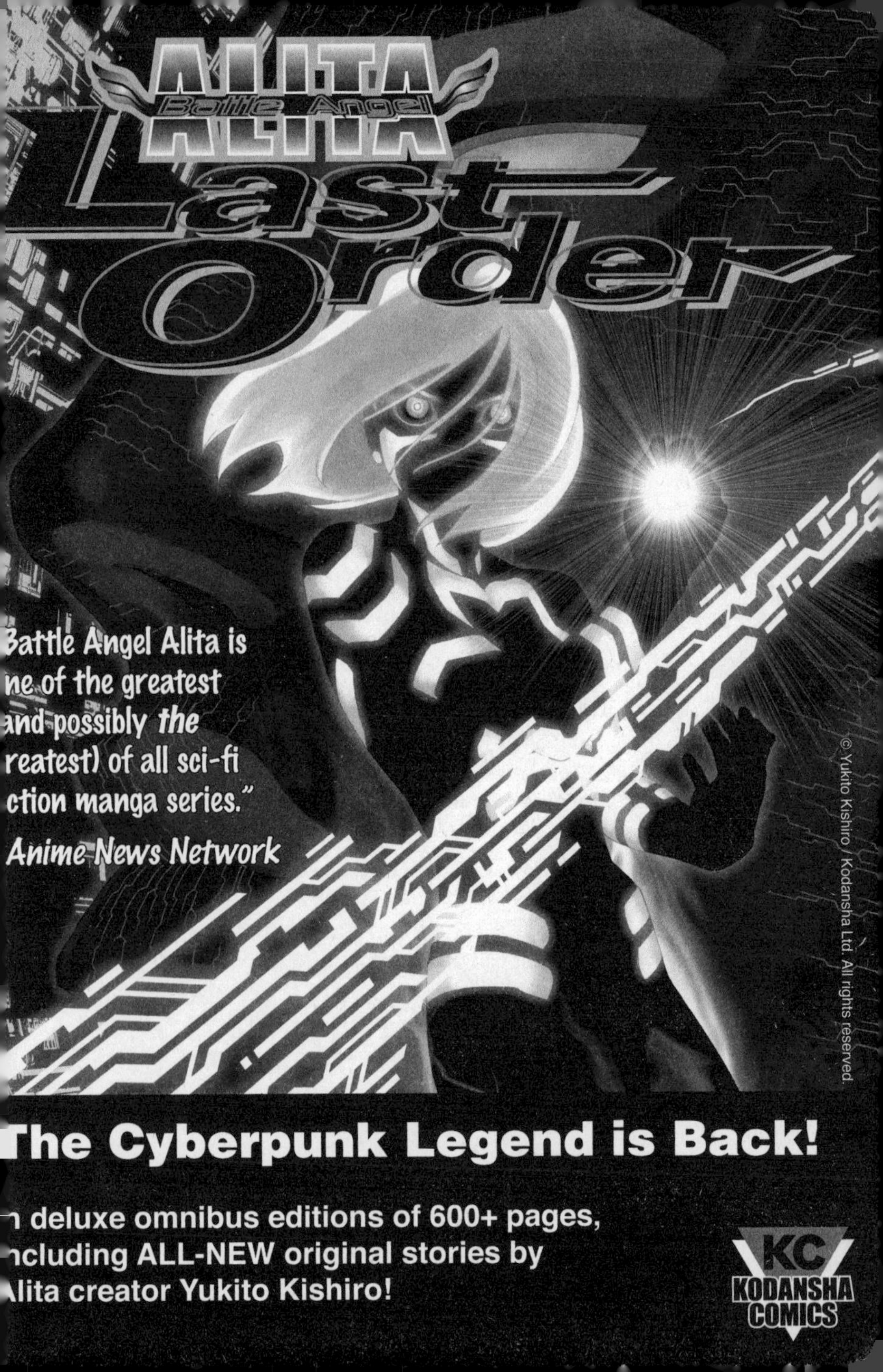
ALITA
Battle Angel
ALITA
Last Order
Battle Angel Alita is
ne of the greatest
and possibly *the*
reatest) of all sci-fi
ction manga series.”
Anime News Network
© Yukito Kishiro / Kodansha Ltd. All rights reserved.